Introduction to Securing Virtual Environments

For a listing of recent titles in the
Artech House Information Security and Privacy Library,
turn to the back of this book.

Introduction to Securing Virtual Environments

Rajkumar Singh Rathore
Liqaa Nawaf
Shiv Prakash

ARTECH
HOUSE
BOSTON | LONDON
artechhouse.com

Library of Congress Cataloging-in-Publication Data
A catalog record for this book is available from the US Library of Congress.

British Library Cataloguing in Publication Data
A catalog record for this book is available from the British Library.

ISBN-13: 978-1-68569-055-7

Cover design by Iain Hill

685 Canton Street
Norwood, MA 02062

10 9 8 7 6 5 4 3 2 1

Contents

Preface *xiii*

Introduction *xv*

Summary of Key Points *xv*

CHAPTER 1

Introduction to Virtualization Security 1

1.1 Overview of Virtualization Technology 2

1.1.1 Definition of Virtualization 2

1.1.2 Brief History and Development of the Technology 2

1.1.3 Roles and Significance of Virtualization in Modern Information Technology Infrastructure 5

1.2 Types of Virtualizations 7

1.2.1 Server Virtualization 7

1.2.2 Desktop Virtualization 9

1.2.3 OS Virtualization 11

1.2.4 Application Virtualization 12

1.2.5 Storage Virtualization 12

1.2.6 Data Virtualization 12

1.2.7 Network Virtualization 12

1.3 Security Risks Associated with Virtualization 13

1.3.1 Hypervisor Attacks 13

1.3.2 Guest OS Attacks 14

1.3.3 Inter-VM Attacks 15

1.3.4 Network Security Vulnerabilities 16

1.3.5 Vulnerabilities Due to Misconfiguration 17

1.4 Role of Virtualization for Enhancing Cybersecurity 18

1.5 Importance of Maintaining Security in Virtualized Environments 19

1.5.1 Impact of Security Breaches on Businesses 19

1.5.2 Role of Virtualization Security in Maintaining Integrity and Reliability of IT Infrastructure 19

1.5.3 Benefits of Strong Security Measures in a Virtual Environment 20

1.5.4 Legal and Regulatory Obligations 20

1.6 Virtualization Security and Specific Issues 20

1.6.1 Intricacy of Virtual Networks 20

1.6.2 Potential Risks in Virtual Local Area Networks 21
1.6.3 The Phenomenon of VM Sprawl 21
1.6.4 The Threat of Distributed Denial-of-Service Attacks 21
1.6.5 Risks Related to Hypervisor Attacks 21
1.6.6 Dilemmas Pulled in by Cloud Infrastructure 21
1.7 Which Type of Virtualization Should You Use? 21
1.8 Summary 22
References 23

CHAPTER 2

Network Security in Virtualized Environments 25

2.1 Introduction 25
2.1.1 A Brief Overview of Network Security in Virtual Environments 26
2.1.2 Importance of Network Security in Virtual Environments 27
2.2 Virtual Network Architecture 28
2.2.1 Definition of and Understanding Virtual Network Architecture 28
2.2.2 Components of Virtual Network Architecture 28
2.2.3 Relationship of Virtual Network Architecture with Network Security 30
2.2.4 Case Study of a Virtual Network Architecture 31
2.3 Securing Virtual Switches 32
2.3.1 Understanding Virtual Switches and Their Role in Network Security 32
2.3.2 Potential Vulnerabilities in Virtual Switches 33
2.3.3 Techniques for Securing Virtual Switches 34
2.3.4 Case Study of Securing a Virtual Switch 34
2.4 Securing Virtual Firewalls 35
2.4.1 The Role of Virtual Firewalls in Network Security 35
2.4.2 Potential Vulnerabilities and Risks Associated with Virtual Firewalls 35
2.4.3 Techniques for Securing Virtual Firewalls 36
2.4.4 Case Study of a Virtual Firewall Implementation 36
2.5 Securing Virtual Routers 37
2.5.1 Function and Significance of Virtual Routers in Network Security 37
2.5.2 Potential Security Risks Associated with Virtual Routers 37
2.5.3 Techniques for Securing Virtual Routers 38
2.5.4 A Case Study of Virtual Router Security 38
2.6 Securing Virtual Networks 39
2.6.1 Overarching Techniques to Secure Virtual Networks 39
2.6.2 Significance of Regular Software Updates 39
2.6.3 The Role of Spam Filters in Ensuring Network Security 40
2.6.4 Understanding Identity and Access Control in Securing Virtual Networks 40
2.6.5 Importance of Robust and Updated Firewall Rules 40
2.6.6 Encryption Measures for Data in Virtual Networks 41
2.6.7 Regular Audits to Assess Vulnerabilities 41
2.7 Best Practices for Network Security in Virtualized Environments 41
2.7.1 Regular Patching and Updating of Software 41
2.7.2 Implementing a Solid Data Encryption Strategy 42

2.7.3 Ensuring Robust Identity and Access Control 42
2.7.4 Vulnerability Audits 43
2.7.5 Network Segmentation Approach 44
2.7.6 Proper Configuration of Virtual Network Components 44
2.7.7 Implementing Failover Measures 45
2.8 Summary 46
References 47

CHAPTER 3

Virtual Machine Security 51
3.1 Introduction 51
3.2 VM Architecture 52
3.3 Components of VM Architecture 53
3.3.1 Hypervisor 53
3.3.2 Types of Hypervisors 54
3.3.3 Guest OSs 56
3.3.4 Virtual Hardware 57
3.3.5 Management Interfaces 57
3.3.6 Virtualization Technology 58
3.3.7 Network Interface Virtualization 58
3.4 Securing Guest OSs 59
3.4.1 OS Hardening 59
3.4.2 IDPS 60
3.4.3 Access Control Mechanisms 61
3.4.4 Security Policies and Awareness Training 62
3.5 Securing Hypervisors 62
3.5.1 Hypervisor Security Vulnerabilities 62
3.5.2 Secure Configuration of Hypervisors 63
3.5.3 Hypervisor Monitoring and Audit 64
3.5.4 Incident Response 65
3.6 Securing Virtualization Management Servers 66
3.6.1 Understanding Risks and Vulnerabilities 66
3.6.2 Security Controls for Management Servers 67
3.6.3 Monitoring and Auditing 67
3.6.4 Incident Response in Management Server Security 68
3.7 Best Practices for VM Security 69
3.7.1 Conduct a Thorough Risk Assessment 69
3.7.2 Secure the Virtual Environment During Deployment 69
3.7.3 Hardening Guest OSs 70
3.7.4 Secure Hypervisor and Management Servers 70
3.7.5 Continuous Monitoring and Incident Response 71
3.7.6 User Education and Security Awareness 71
3.7.7 Regular Security Audits and Compliance Checks 72
3.8 Future Trends in VM Security 72
3.8.1 AI and ML for Threat Detection and Response 72
3.9 Zero Trust Architecture 73

3.10 Summary 73
References 76

CHAPTER 4
Storage Security in Virtualized Environments 79
4.1 Virtual Storage Architecture 79
4.1.1 Introduction to Virtual Storage and Case Studies 80
4.1.2 Challenges of the VSA 83
4.1.3 Benefits and Efficiency of Using VSA 87
4.2 Securing Virtual Disks 89
4.2.1 Introduction to Virtual Disks 89
4.2.2 Advantages of Securing Virtual Disks 90
4.2.3 Implementing Secure Virtual Disk Techniques 92
4.3 Securing Storage Networks 93
4.3.1 Introduction to Storage Networks 93
4.3.2 Techniques of Securing Storage Networks 94
4.4 Securing Storage Arrays 94
4.4.1 Introduction to Storage Arrays 94
4.4.2 Benefits of Storage Arrays 95
4.5 Best Practices for Storage Security in Virtualized Environments 96
4.5.1 Introduction of Storage Security 96
4.5.2 Storage Limitation 99
4.5.3 Securing VSA 99
4.6 Summary 100
References 101

CHAPTER 5
Virtualization Security in Cloud Computing 103
5.1 Introduction 103
5.1.1 Types of Virtualizations in Cloud Computing 105
5.1.2 Server Virtualization 105
5.2 Network Virtualization 106
5.3 Storage Virtualization 107
5.4 Desktop Virtualization 107
5.5 Benefits 108
5.6 Challenges 109
5.6.1 Security Risks 109
5.6.2 Resource Contention 110
5.6.3 Complex Management 111
5.6.4 Compliance and Data Privacy 112
5.6.5 Performance Overhead 112
5.6.6 Licensing Costs and Constraints 112
5.6.7 Backup and Recovery 112
5.6.8 Vendor Lock-In 113
5.7 Summary 113

5.7.1 Virtualization Management Tools in Cloud Computing 113
5.7.2 Cloud Service Providers Offering Virtualization 115
5.7.3 Virtualization Security in Cloud Computing 118
5.7.4 Confidential Computing 122
5.7.5 Encryption in Virtualized Environments 125
5.8 Conclusion 129
References 130

CHAPTER 6
Application Security in Virtualized Environments 135
6.1 Overview of Virtualized Applications 135
6.2 Securing Web Servers 136
6.3 Securing Database Servers 145
6.4 Securing Other Critical Applications 147
6.5 Best Practices for Application Security in Virtualized Environments 147
6.5.1 Microsoft Application Virtualization 4.5 148
6.6 Summary 149
References 150

CHAPTER 7
Compliance and Audit in Virtualized Environments 155
7.1 Introduction 155
7.1.1 Impact of Shared Responsibility Models in Cloud Compliance 158
7.1.2 Compliance Challenges in Containerization and Orchestration Platforms 160
7.1.3 Cross-Border Data Transfers and Virtual Infrastructure Compliance 161
7.2 Guidelines for Compliance and Audit 163
7.2.1 Structural Versus Operational Properties in Cloud Compliance 163
7.2.2 Automated Compliance Tools and Solutions for Virtual Environments 163
7.2.3 Auditing APIs and Management Consoles in Virtual Infrastructures 165
7.2.4 Handling and Reporting Security Incidents in a Compliance Context 165
7.2.5 Data Life-Cycle Management, Archiving, and Right to Erasure 166
7.2.6 Third-Party Vendor and Supply Chain Compliance in Virtualized Ecosystems 167
7.2.7 Privacy Impact Assessments and Compliance by Design 168
7.3 Importance of Compliance and Audit in Virtualized Environments 171
7.3.1 Human Factors and Compliance Culture in Virtualized Operations 171
7.3.2 Auditor's Perspective: Preparing for and Managing Virtualization Audits 172
7.4 Best Practices for Compliance and Audit in Virtualized Environments 175
7.4.1 The Move to Zero Trust Architectures 176
7.4.2 Confidential Computing and Trusted Execution Environments 176
7.4.3 The Shift to Privacy-First Standards: ISO/IEC 27701 and Beyond 177
7.4.4 Towards Integrated, Automated Compliance Platforms 177

7.4.5 The Influence of Evolving Regulatory Ecosystems: NIS2, DORA, and Others 178
7.4.6 Preparing for the Future: Best Practice Takeaways 180
7.5 Case Studies 181
7.5.1 Case Study 1: Capital One Cloud Data Breach and Compliance Gaps (2019) 181
7.5.2 Case Study 2: British Airways GDPR Fine and Virtualized Infrastructure Gaps (2018–2020) 181
7.5.3 Case Study 3: Equifax Data Breach—Patch Management Failures in a Virtualized Context (2017) 182
7.5.4 Case Study 4: VMware ESXiArgs Ransomware—Patch Audit Gaps Exposed (2023) 182
7.5.5 Case Study 5: Tesla Insider Data Leak—Virtual Desktop Audit Weakness (2023) 182
7.6 Summary 183
References 184

CHAPTER 8
Disaster Recovery and Business Continuity in Virtualized Environments 187
8.1 Overview of Disaster Recovery and Business Continuity Planning 187
8.1.1 Disaster Recovery 187
8.1.2 Planning for Business Continuity 189
8.1.3 Case Study: For Disaster Recovery 191
8.2 Importance of Disaster Recovery and Business Continuity 193
8.2.1 The Connection Between Disaster Recovery and Business Continuity 195
8.3 Guidelines for Implementing Disaster Recovery and Business Continuity 195
8.3.1 Implementing Disaster Recovery and Business Continuity 198
8.3.2 Advantages 199
8.4 Best Practices for Disaster Recovery and Business Continuity 200
8.4.1 Overview of Best Practices 200
8.4.2 Best Practices for Disaster Recovery and Business Continuity 202
8.5 Summary 203
References 204

CHAPTER 9
Best Practices for Virtualization Security 207
9.1 Overview of Best Practices 207
9.2 Guidelines for Implementing Best Practices 210
9.2.1 Security Framework Guidance 213
9.3 Importance of Best Practices 213
9.4 Best Practices for Monitoring and Reporting 215
9.4.1 Technical Case Studies 222
9.5 Summary 222
References 223

CHAPTER 10

Emerging Trends in Virtualization Security 227

10.1 Overview of Emerging Trends (Containers and Micro-Services) 227
10.1.1 Container and Kubernetes Security 228
10.1.2 Micro-Services 229
10.1.3 Micro-Service Security 229
10.1.4 Securing North-South Traffic (External Consumers) 230
10.1.5 Securing Traffic Going East-West 231
10.2 Guidelines for Preparing for the Future 233
10.2.1 Evaluating the Risks 233
10.2.2 Protecting VMs 234
10.2.3 The Future of Virtualization Security 234
10.2.4 Container Scanning Tools 234
10.3 Importance of Staying Ahead of Emerging Trends 235
10.3.1 Virtual Memory Manager Implementation Issues 235
10.3.2 CPU Virtualization 235
10.3.3 Challenges 237
10.3.4 I/O Virtualization 237
10.3.5 Challenges 237
10.3.6 Future Support 238
10.4 Best Practices for Addressing Emerging Trends in Virtualization Security 239
10.4.1 Protect VMs by Using Authentication and Access Control in Windows-Azure 239
10.4.2 Manage VM Updates 240
10.4.3 Manage VM Security Posture 241
10.4.4 Monitor VM Performance 241
10.4.5 Encrypt Virtual Complex Disk Files 241
10.4.6 Manipulation Attack 243
10.4.7 Security Requirements and Challenges to 6G 244
10.4.8 Post-Quantum Resilience 245
10.4.9 Differentiated and Customized Security 245
10.4.10 Context-Aware-Based Intelligent Security 246
10.5 Summary 246
References 247

CHAPTER 11

Conclusion 251

11.1 Final Thoughts and Recommendations 251
11.2 Future Outlook for Virtualization Security 251

About the Authors 253

Index 255

Preface

The last decade has witnessed a profound transformation in the way that organizations conceive and deliver digital services. At the heart of this revolution lies the rapid growth of virtualization, a technology that has unlocked unprecedented flexibility, scalability, and efficiency across data centers, corporate information technology (IT), and the cloud. Yet with progress comes new complexity, and with possibility comes fresh risk. As enterprises increasingly entrust their critical assets to virtual platforms, the question of how best to secure and govern these environments has assumed paramount importance. This book has been written with a singular aim: to chart a clear and practical course through the challenges of safeguarding virtual environments, from the fundamental concepts of architecture and threat to the finer points of compliance, audit, and resilience. Drawing upon industry best practice, real-world case studies, and emerging trends, it offers practitioners, students, and strategists alike a comprehensive guide to mastering security in this new era.

We open with a careful introduction to virtualization security itself, demystifying the technology and setting out the unique challenges it presents compared to traditional computing. With the proliferation of servers, desktops, applications, and now containers, virtualization is no longer the sole preserve of enterprise IT departments. Instead, it is the foundation upon which much of the modern digital economy is built. Understanding both the opportunities and the inherent vulnerabilities is a prerequisite for anyone charged with protecting organizational assets. Subsequent chapters examine in detail the various domains in which virtualization intersects with security. From the intricacies of virtual network architecture and securing software-defined networking to the defense of virtual machines, storage infrastructure, and cloud workloads, this book delves into both the strategic and the technical. Notably, special attention is given to the distinct characteristics and risks of cloud-based virtualization, recognizing that many businesses now inhabit a hybrid world where on-premises and cloud environments intermingle.

Compliance and audit, too, are given their due. It is not enough merely to construct secure systems; one must also demonstrate due care and regulatory alignment, especially in industries governed by the likes of Payment Card Industry Data Security Standard (PCI DSS), Health Insurance Portability and Accountability Act (HIPAA), Sarbanes-Oxley Act (SOX), and General Data Protection Regulation (GDPR). With regulators ever more alert to the risks arising from virtualized and cloud-based services, robust governance has become a business necessity rather than an afterthought. This book provides actionable guidance for meeting the demands of various standards, automating compliance monitoring, and preparing for the scrutiny of auditors. Vital, too, is resilience. Disruption, whether from cyber-attack, human error, or natural event, remains a constant threat. Hence, disaster recovery, business continuity, and the maintenance of operations in the face of adversity are central themes. Readers will find practical advice on planning, implementing, and testing recovery strategies appropriate for the dynamic, distributed nature of modern virtual environments. Importantly, this book looks forward. A dedicated chapter addresses emerging trends like containers, micro-services, confidential computing, and Zero Trust architectures equipping organizations to adapt security and compliance postures in step with technological evolution and regulatory change. The final chapter gathers these threads, offering a succinct synthesis, practical recommendations, and a future outlook designed to empower both seasoned professionals and newcomers to this discipline. Throughout, the content is enriched with illustrative case studies, drawn from genuine events and scenarios, which anchor theory to practice and provide valuable lessons for readers at all levels.

In essence, this volume serves both as a textbook for structured learning and a practical reference for busy professionals: clear, thorough, and designed to remain relevant as the field continues to evolve. It is hoped that, by navigating these pages, the reader will find themselves better equipped to secure, govern, and future-proof their virtualized environments in a complex and ever-changing world.

Introduction

This book provides the fundamental aspects of ensuring security in virtualized environments and discusses the basic concepts of virtualized environments and best practices in this area. Also, this book helps undergraduate and postgraduate students, research scholars, and industry professionals to understand the practical aspects of why securing the environments is important and how they can be secured through different strategies, along with their implementation.

A thorough, in-depth comprehension of the real-world applications of virtualized environment security is provided. Emerging technologies such as serverless computing and edge virtualization require different approaches, future risks, and quantum-safe encryption techniques.

Summary of Key Points

Chapter 1 introduces security in virtualization, including an overview of technological growth in virtualization, including server, desktop, and application development. Some of the most prominent and vital security risks, such as hypervisor attacks and guest operating service (OS) attacks, related to virtualization are presented in this book. This chapter also discusses the importance of security maintenance in virtualized environments along with a summary of the chapter.

Chapter 2 discusses network security in virtualized environments through virtual networks architecture, virtual switches, virtual firewalls, and virtual routers. It also discusses the best practices for network security in virtualized environments along with a summary of the chapter.

Chapter 3 provides an overview of virtual machine security and its architecture. It also discusses the virtual machines protecting OS for visitors protecting hypervisors and servers for virtualization management. Best practices for virtual machine security are also discussed, along with the chapter summary.

Chapter 4 provides aspects of storage security in virtualized environments that comprise architecture for virtual storage. It also highlights the protection of virtual disks, network storage, and storage arrays and discusses best practices for storage security in virtualized environments and provides a chapter summary.

Chapter 5 provides an introduction to virtualization in cloud computing. Different types of virtualization, such as servers, networks, storage, and desktops, are also discussed and broadly used in cloud computing. Also discussed in this chapter are the benefits of cloud computing and the challenges of cloud computing virtualization. In addition, we also review several management tools (Citrix XenServer, Microsoft Hyper-V, VMware vSphere, and OpenStack), cloud service providers that provide virtualization (Google Cloud Platform, Microsoft Azure, IBM Cloud, and Amazon Web Services), virtualization security in cloud computing (network security, virtual machine security, and hypervisor security), manufacturers of confidential computing, and encryption of virtual machines (randomness generation and key management). Finally, there is also a summary overview of the chapter.

Chapter 6 provides the security of applications in virtualized environments with an overview of virtualized applications. It also discusses the protection of web servers, database servers, and other additional vital applications. The best methods for protecting applications in virtualized settings are also discussed, and an overview of the chapter is provided.

Chapter 7 overviews industry regulations and standards, such as SOX, HIPAA, and PCI DSS Rules for Audit and Compliance. Top techniques used for audit and compliance in a virtualized environment and relevant best practices are also discussed, along with a summary of the chapter.

Chapter 8 describes disaster recovery and business continuity planning in virtualized environments. Also, guidelines and best practices used for implementing disaster recovery and business continuity in virtualized environments and their significance are stated. A brief overview of the chapter is also included.

Chapter 9 discusses best practices and recommendations for virtualization security. Additionally, methods used for tracking and reporting in virtualized settings are discussed, along with an overview of the chapter.

Chapter 10 elaborates on new developments in security for virtualization, such as micro-services and containers. We discuss best practices, future-readiness, the value of keeping up with new trends, and the top techniques for handling emerging trends in virtualization. A summary of this chapter is also given.

Chapter 11 discusses the generalized effects of virtualization technologies on IT infrastructures, emphasizing improvements in scalability, efficiency, and innovation while acknowledging the associated security challenges. It advocates for proactive strategies, including threat analysis and real-time monitoring, to balance security and performance. The future of virtualization security is likely to see advancements such as enhanced isolation, micro-segmentation, Zero-Trust architecture, and stricter regulatory compliance measures. Additionally, the emergence of serverless computing and edge virtualization underscores the need for advanced security tactics to protect lightweight systems and ensure data security. Organizations are encouraged to adopt quantum-safe security measures to bolster their defenses in evolving virtualized environments.

CHAPTER 1

Introduction to Virtualization Security

In the arena of the modern digital landscape, virtualization has emerged as a significant innovation. It marks the transition from physical and on-premises infrastructure to virtual machines (VMs) and cloud-based systems. Virtualization has emerged as a monumental paradigm shift, responsible for the transformation of the way that we manage, secure, and optimize technical resources across various domains, thereby streamlining operations, reducing costs, and enhancing scalability. However, with every modern solution comes an array of challenges, among which security figures prominently. Hence, the term "virtualization security" is coined. Virtualization security, at its core, seeks to protect virtual environments. These environments can encompass anything from virtual desktops, VMs, or other software-based applications, all residing on a physical host machine. Just like traditional physical servers require a robust security protocol to prevent breaches, virtual environments also need a dedicated security strategy.

The emphasis on virtualization security reflects its compelling need to protect virtual environments, which function as integral backbone systems in various industries, from banking through academia to space exploration. It exists to counteract the vulnerabilities exploited by malicious entities, as virtual environments can be susceptible to cyberattacks just as much as, if not more than, physical ones. The divergence in maintaining security in strategic physical servers and virtual servers emanates from the fundamental shift in their structure. Because VMs can be created, cloned, moved, and deleted at a moment's notice, there is a requirement for a novel security approach. The infrastructure is more dynamic and fluid, involving dramatically different interfaces within its space. In an era where cyber threats are widespread, understanding virtualization security is crucial to maintain the sanctity and operational effectiveness of an organization's information technology (IT) ecosystem. This topic aims to impart knowledge about the fundamentals of virtualization security, the threats and vulnerabilities pertaining to it, measures to mitigate them, and best practices in securing a virtual environment.

This chapter aims to paint a comprehensive picture of virtualization security by elucidating its core concepts, principles, and mechanisms. Beginning with a broad understanding of virtualization and its remarkable merits, we will delve into the darker side of this technology: the emergence of threats and vulnerabilities that exploit the virtual world and the spectrum of possibilities they open up for cybercriminals. With a deep dive into various types of virtualizations, such as hardware virtualization, operating system (OS) level virtualization, and application virtualization, we will carve a path into understanding the intricacies of each and their unique security requirements. We will explore the foundations of secure virtualization, encompassing critical aspects such as hypervisor security, access control, network virtualization security, and VM intrusion detection.

On the journey to demystify virtualization security, we will also learn about the cutting-edge technologies and strategies employed to protect virtual systems and data, all of which provide indispensable insights for putative security specialists, IT professionals, students, researchers, and anyone interested in the field of cybersecurity. Therefore, the purpose is not just to recognize the existence of threats to virtual systems, but also to understand them, analyze their impacts, and explore solutions to build robust defenses against these threats. The labyrinth of virtualization security is complex, yet incredibly intriguing. Embarking on this path might challenge your current understanding, but it ultimately has the potential to redefine your perspective on the virtual world. Let's begin this exploration into the intricate and captivating world of virtualization security.

1.1 Overview of Virtualization Technology

1.1.1 Definition of Virtualization

Virtualization defines the process in which multiple instances of computing resources, including hardware platforms, OSs, and storage devices, or network resources, are emulated within a system. This technology allows systems to create a virtual version of an actual, physical entity. The main idea is to achieve a level of abstraction between the hardware and the software that runs on it, enabling improved efficiency and flexibility in the use of underlying resources.

1.1.2 Brief History and Development of the Technology

Virtualization technology, which enables multiple computing environments to exist within a single physical environment, boasts a remarkable evolution. Virtualization is not a new concept and can be traced back to the 1960s when IBM introduced the concept to boost the utilization rate of their mainframe computers. They were seeking to split system resources effectively between different applications, and hence, virtualization was born as a solution to this challenge. Over time, this technology advanced significantly and made virtualization more accessible and attractive to businesses. It was not until the late 1990s and early 2000s that virtualization gained popularity with the advent of VMware. This company popularized the x86 architecture, bringing virtualization to commercial servers and desktops, thus revolutionizing computational efficiency and flexibility. Since then, virtualization technology has taken many forms, including network, storage, and server virtualization, underpinned by advancements in cloud computing. Today, virtualization is an integral part of IT infrastructure, driving scalability, reducing hardware dependency, and forging the path for emergent technologies such as containers and microservices. Meanwhile, the surge in edge computing and the continuing expansion of the Internet of Things (IoT) present promising avenues for virtualization's future growth and development.

With the growing demand for more efficient computing systems and the innovation of hardware-assisted virtualization technologies, a new era of virtualization was ushered in during the early twenty-first century. Companies such as VMware, Microsoft, and Citrix propelled the industry forward with powerful new platforms that enabled organizations to run various operating systems and applications on a single server.

Figure 1.1 illustrates the virtualization technology framework with multiple layers; the lower layer in this framework is known as the physical hardware layer or the hardware infrastructure layer. The physical hardware layer, also known as the hardware infrastructure layer, in a virtualization technology framework is the foundation layer upon which all virtual services are built. It consists of the hard physical elements such as servers, storage systems, networks, central processing units (CPUs), memory, and other peripherals. This hardware infrastructure serves as the support system for host OSs and hypervisors, which are essential for creating, managing, and maintaining VMs. The physical layer's performance, resilience, and scalability directly impact the efficiency and effectiveness of the virtualization processes.

In other words, virtualization allows multiple virtual machines to run on these physical components, sharing resources intelligently. Also, certain hardware-enabled virtualization technologies (such as Intel-VT and AMD-V) embedded in

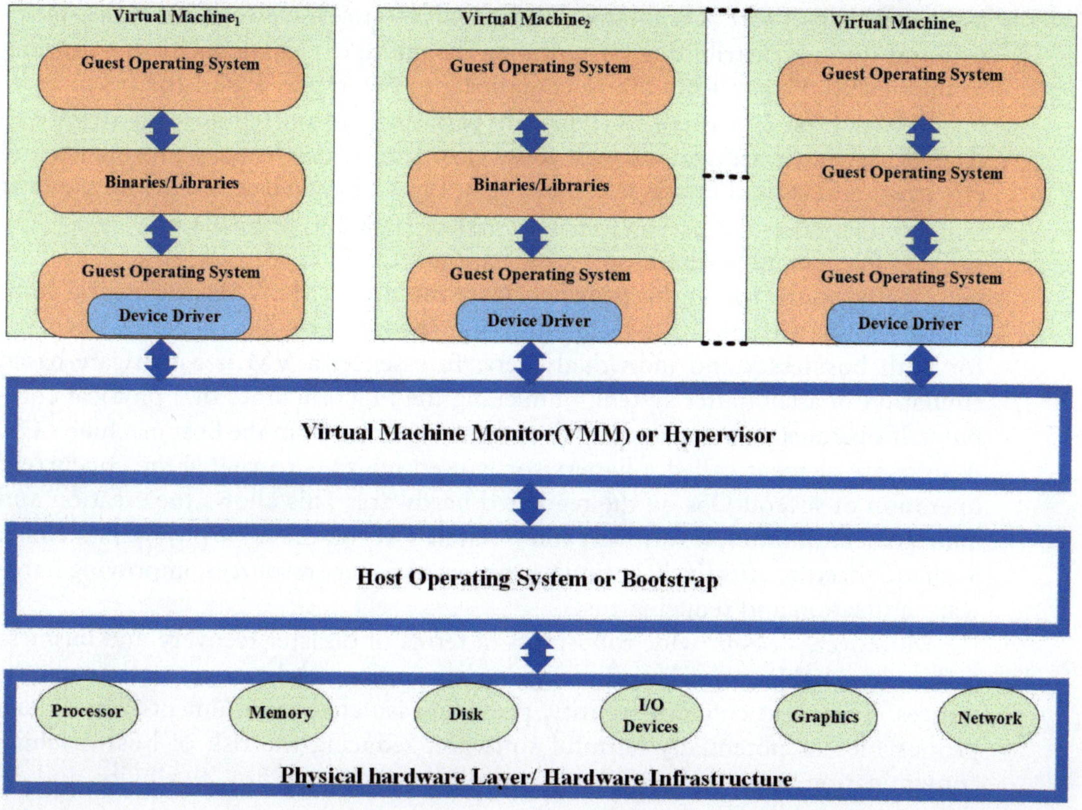

Figure 1.1 Virtualization technology framework.

modern processors increase the efficiency of the hypervisor, ultimately boosting the overall performance of the virtualized environment. Hence, it is crucial to ensure this underlying infrastructure is robust, reliable, and properly managed to provide an optimized environment for the workloads processed in the virtual layer above.

The next layer is for the host OS or bootstrap loader. The host OS in virtualization technology is the software that directly manages the physical resources of a machine such as the CPU, memory, disks, and network interface. This OS runs on a physical server, known as the host machine, and creates and manages VMs. Control over physical resources allows the host OS to allocate resources to virtual environments, also known as VMs or guest OS. Bootstrap in virtualization technology is crucial in initializing a VM. The bootstrap process begins with the host OS running a software called a hypervisor. This software is responsible for starting each VM and allocating the necessary resources. Once a virtual machine launches, the "bootstrap" sequence kicks off the guest OS and any necessary system configurations. The bootstrap process thus plays a significant role in efficiently maintaining the balance between the host and virtual systems in a virtualization technology framework.

The third layer from the bottom is a virtualization machine monitor or hypervisor. A hypervisor is also known as a VM monitor (VMM) and is a core part of virtualization technology architecture. A hypervisor's role as software or firmware is to create, execute, and manage multiple VMs on a single physical host machine. The hypervisor sits between the hardware and the virtual environments, and it acts as a traffic cop of sort. It regulates the physical resources, such as CPU cycles, memory, and storage, distributing them among the multiple virtual machines according to their needs. Hypervisors can be classified into two types: Type 1 (native or bare-metal) and Type 2 (hosted). A Type-1 hypervisor runs on the host's hardware to control the hardware and manage guest OSs. It provides better performance and efficiency and is used in server scenarios. A Type-2 hypervisor installs on the host OS and then hosts the guest VMs. This makes Type-2 hypervisors easy to use and suitable for personal or desktop virtualization.

Finally, on the top of this framework are multiple VMs. VMs are integral components of the virtualization technology framework, providing numerous benefits for both businesses and individual users. In essence, a VM is a software-based emulation of a computer system, mimicking the functionalities of a physical computer. It operates on an isolated environment, separate from the host machine's OS. A software element called a hypervisor is used by VMs to enable the concurrent operation of several OSs on the regulated hardware. This allows the creation and management of multiple, distinct, and isolated VMs on the same physical machine. Such architecture effectively optimizes the use of system resources, improving hardware utilization and reducing costs.

Moreover, VMs provide robustness in terms of disaster recovery and business continuity, enabling quick replication, redistribution, and recovery of virtual instances. They also enhance security, providing isolated environments to test suspicious files or potentially harmful software, reducing the risk of host machine contamination. VMs are significant contributors to the agility, flexibility, and efficiency of modern IT infrastructures.

1.1.3 Roles and Significance of Virtualization in Modern Information Technology Infrastructure

Virtualization plays several significant roles in modern IT infrastructure. Here are some key roles and benefits:

- *Increase in efficiency and cost reduction:* Virtualization helps to increase hardware utilization and decrease hardware needs, which, in turn, results in significant cost savings. Often, many physical machines operate at a fraction of their capacity. By using virtualization, multiple systems can be consolidated onto fewer physical servers, significantly increasing utilization and reducing wasted capacity.
- *Simplified management:* With fewer physical machines to manage and maintain, virtualization simplifies IT operations. In addition, features such as live migration, disaster recovery, and automated backups give professionals more control over their operations and can drastically reduce downtime.
- *Environment friendly:* By reducing the need for physical hardware, virtualization also reduces the power and cooling demands of an IT department, making operations more eco-friendly.
- *Rapid deployment of applications:* Virtualization provides a scalable model that allows businesses to swiftly respond to changes in their computing needs, enabling the quick deployment of additional or updated systems, applications, or resources.

Properly understanding virtualization and its functions is the foundation of optimizing IT resources and building highly effective and efficient modern IT infrastructures. As the rate of virtualization adoption continues to rise, its role in IT will continue to evolve, thus demonstrating the fundamental importance of understanding this technology and using it to its fullest potential. Figure 1.2 is the continuation of Figure 1.1, with two new planes, namely, security monitoring and virtualization technology management planes, respectively, in the existing framework constituting a virtualization technology framework with modern IT infrastructure. In the context of a virtualization technology framework with modern IT infrastructure, the roles of the security monitoring plane and virtualization technology management plane are crucial.

1.1.3.1 Security Monitoring Plane

The security monitoring plane refers to the systems and tools used to continuously monitor and safeguard the virtual environment against potential threats and cyberattacks. Here are some of its key responsibilities:

- *Inspecting:* The plane identifies and examines virtual machines and their activities to spot potential vulnerabilities or threats.
- *Reporting:* The plane generates reports highlighting potential security risks, digital attacks, and breaches, providing insights into the security status of the virtual environment.

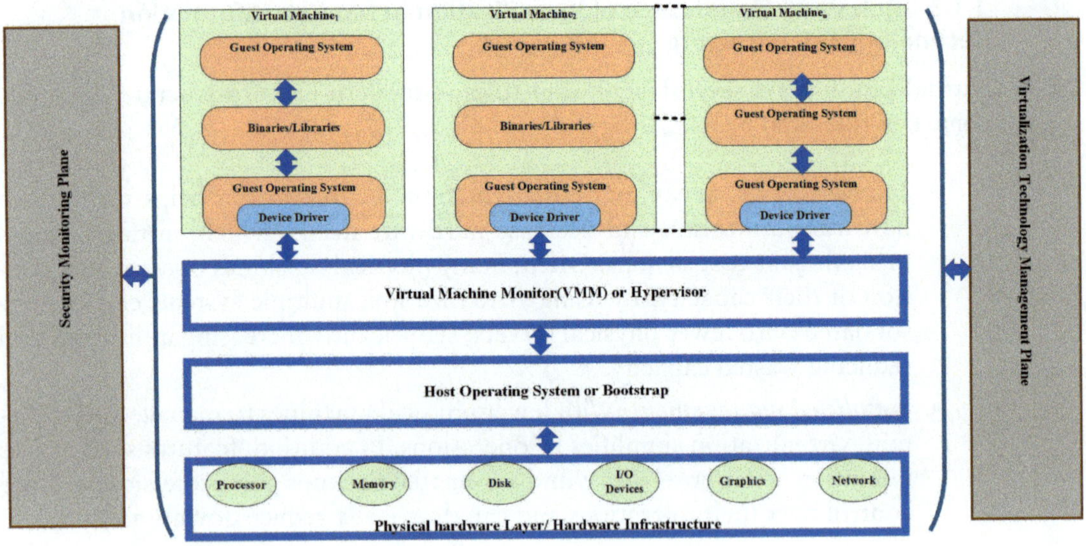

Figure 1.2 Virtualization technology framework with modern IT infrastructure.

- *Alerting:* In case of any unplanned or unauthorized actions, the plane sends alert notifications to the IT team promptly. This allows for quick action to mitigate the damage.
- *Compliance:* The plane also ensures the virtual environment adheres to security compliance and regulatory standards set by the organization or national or international authorities.

1.1.3.2 Virtualization Technology Management Plane

The virtualization technology management plane is responsible for the overall management and orchestration of the virtualized resources and services. Here are some of its main responsibilities:

- *Provisioning and deployment:* This plane manages resource allocation and distribution for virtual environments, maintaining an appropriate balance of resources among all the VMs.
- *Performance monitoring:* This plane includes overseeing the dynamic and statistical performance of virtual resources. It adjusts and optimizes resources based on actual demand and usage metrics.
- *Configuration management:* The plane manages configurations or changes that need to be implemented across the virtual environment. This ensures stability and integrity.
- *Disaster recovery:* The plane takes care of backup, restoration, and recovery processes, ensuring business continuity in case of any unforeseen disaster or data loss situation.

Both the planes interact with each other to provide a comprehensive and secure virtualization environment and be able to adapt and respond to the modern demands of an IT infrastructure.

1.2 Types of Virtualizations

There are various types of virtualizations in the modern era of IT such as server, desktop, OS, application, storage, data, and network virtualization. Figure 1.3 shows the virtualization reservoir.

1.2.1 Server Virtualization

Server virtualization is a method by which a physical server contains multiple separate virtual servers, which is achieved through a software application called hypervisor. Each server has its own OS and operates independently. This way, powerful server resources are shared among multiple tasks while maintaining separation between operations.

1.2.1.1 Importance and Uses in the Business World

Server virtualization is of high importance in a business setting due to several reasons:

- *Resource optimization:* It allows the full utilization of server resources, thereby reducing the need for more physical servers.
- *Cost-effective:* It helps to cut down on costs associated with hardware, maintenance, energy, and space.

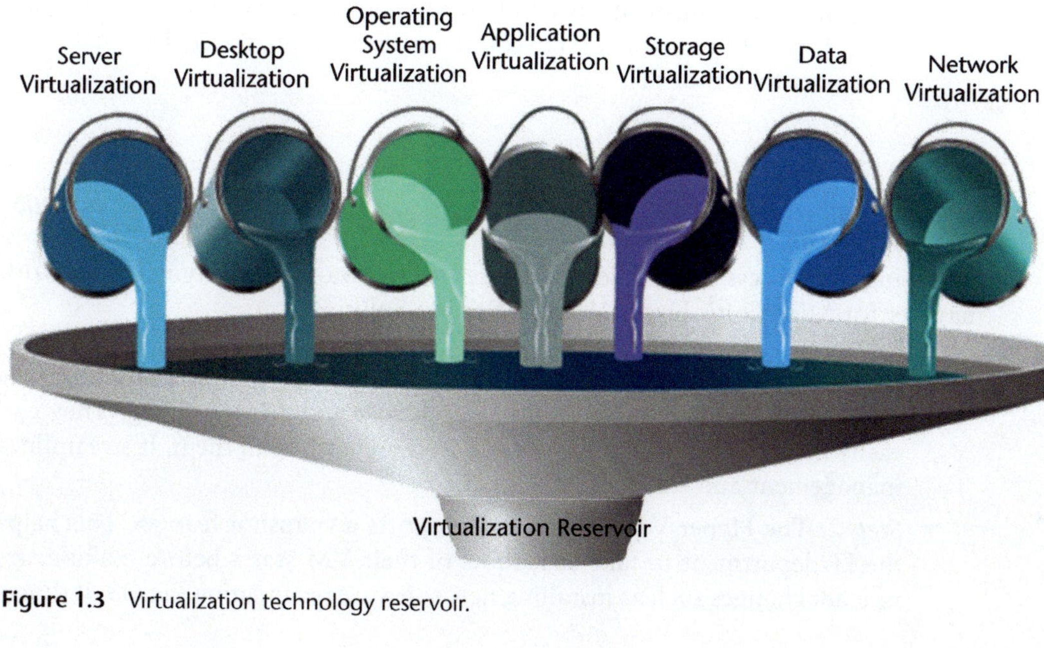

Figure 1.3 Virtualization technology reservoir.

- *Business continuity:* Through features such as live migration, disaster recovery, and high availability, it ensures that business operations continue without interruption.
- *Scalability:* It enables easier and quicker adaptations to changes in business needs and growth.

Some common examples of server virtualization platforms include VMware's vSphere, Microsoft's Hyper-V, and Citrix's XenServer.

1.2.1.2 Use Cases

There are several use case scenarios as follows.

Case 1: Healthcare Facility Virtualization

In a healthcare facility, managing data and applications for various departments, namely, medical records, billing, and prescription management systems, involves multiple servers. Possessing a physical server for each application and department can quickly become inefficient and expensive in terms of management, energy consumption, and space usage. Therefore, adopting server virtualization can solve these issues.

Let's consider that a healthcare facility opts for VMware's vSphere for their infrastructure.

- *Step 1:* The IT department may implement VMware's vSphere to consolidate physical servers into VMs. Instead of having 10 separate physical servers for different applications, they now may have 10 virtual servers all housed within one or a few physical servers. The healthcare facility thus may drastically reduce its hardware footprint [1].
- *Step 2:* This consolidation allows for failover protection. In case one VM fails, the load is automatically shifted to another VM with no effect on end-users. It simplifies disaster recovery processes, making the critical healthcare data safer than ever [1].

Case 2: Another Facility in the Network Choosing Microsoft's Hyper-V Virtualization Solution

Following the success within the healthcare facility, another facility in the network may opt for Microsoft's Hyper-V Virtualization Solution.

- *Step 1:* By using Hyper-V, the IT department may be able to run multiple OSs as VMs on a single physical server with cost and energy saving. They can easily assign different OSs to the departments that need them. It streamlines management and slashes IT costs [2].
- *Step 2:* The Hyper-V platform also supports a snapshot feature. This helps the IT department to take snapshots of their VM states before making significant changes such as installing new software or updating the OS. If things

go wrong, they can quickly revert to the snapshot, saving the IT department a lot of time and stress [2].

Case 3: A University Scenario Adopting Citrix XenServer for Their Labs
Lastly, consider a university scenario, in which a university network may adopt Citrix XenServer for their labs to provide students with the distinct environments that they need for their studies.

- *Step 1:* The university IT department implements XenServer to create VMs that can be accessed by students anytime, anywhere, helping to create a flexible learning environment without requiring physical presence in a lab [3].
- *Step 2:* XenServer's virtualization capability allows the IT department to rapidly create distinct learning environments for an array of courses, respond to new lab requirements dynamically, and manage them with ease [3].

These use case scenarios illustrate how server virtualization platforms such as VMware's vSphere, Microsoft's Hyper-V, and Citrix's XenServer can generate significant efficiency and cost benefits across a variety of environments.

1.2.2 Desktop Virtualization

Desktop virtualization is one type of virtualization technology that separates a desktop environment from the computer itself. The virtual desktop is kept on a centralized server rather than locally on a user's computer.

1.2.2.1 Advantages and Differences from Traditional Personal Computers

Compared to traditional personal computers (PCs), desktop virtualization has several advantages as follows:

- *Centralized management:* All virtual desktops can be managed and updated from a single location.
- *Cost savings:* There can be significant savings on hardware costs because high-powered PCs are not required at the user end.
- *Improved security:* As all data resides on the central server, risks of data theft are minimized.

1.2.2.2 Use Cases

Desktop virtualization is effective where security, data integrity, and accessibility are important. This includes sectors such as education, healthcare, call centers, and remote work scenarios. The technology known as desktop virtualization isolates a computer's desktop environment from the actual computer. A VM located on a central or distant server powers desktop images. This tool proves to be exceptionally effective for businesses and institutions by providing numerous benefits such as reduced costs, better security, and increased manageability and scalability.

Usage Scenario: School Management Solution

Let's consider a large school with thousands of students, teachers, and administrative personnel using computers for studying, teaching, testing, grading, and managing the school. The routine tasks of managing and maintaining such a colossal number of computers exhibits several challenges:

- *Hardware and software management:* With each computer having different hardware, maintaining uniformity across all software installations becomes difficult. Additionally, hardware upgrades and replacements are often frequent and costly.
- *Security and data vulnerability:* Computers may store some sensitive data that, if it gets into unwanted hands, can have serious repercussions. Traditional desktop computing may not offer the required security layers to prevent this, further enhancing the risk.
- *Energy costs:* Powering such a large number of computers adds a significant cost to the school's budget.

The school management may decide to adopt desktop virtualization technology to address these issues. They may partner with a tech company that specializes in setting up and maintaining virtual desktop infrastructures.

- *Central management:* With desktop virtualization, the entire software stack from the operating system to applications is managed centrally. Regardless of the hardware of each individual PC, students and staff access a standard, uniform desktop environment.
- *Enhanced security:* Since all data is stored on centralized servers, it is easier to manage security, perform necessary updates, and carry out routine backups. In case of breach at any point, there is no data leakage as all information resides on the server and not the local device.
- *Reduced cost:* As the heavy lifting takes place on the server rather than individual machines, the need for high-end PCs is eliminated. This results in reduced capital expenditure. Energy costs are also considerably reduced since the power consumption is significantly lower.
- *Simplified tech support:* If a user encounters a technical problem, the IT staff can troubleshoot the issue centrally, reducing the time to resolve technical difficulties.

This example depicts how a large school could improve efficiency, security, and cost-savings through the use of desktop virtualization. It is important to note that, while desktop virtualization can be beneficial, the individual requirement of an organization will dictate the technologies and approach used.

1.2.3 OS Virtualization

Also known as software virtualization, this type allows different OSs to run on the hardware of a single physical server. Hypervisors such as VMware ESX and Microsoft Hyper-V allow for this functionality where each OS acts as if it is running on its own dedicated server.

The benefits are as follows:

- *Increased efficiency and usage of resources:* OS virtualization allows one physical server to act as multiple separate servers, thus maximizing the utilization of hardware resources. It significantly decreases the number of physical servers required, reducing hardware and maintenance costs.
- *Improved system scalability:* With virtualization, new systems can be deployed more quickly and easily. Scaling resources up or down to meet changing business needs becomes a faster process, often achievable without the need for any additional physical hardware.
- *Faster recovery:* In the event of a crash or failure, virtual environments are quicker to restore as you can create full backups of the virtual OS. These backups or snapshots allow you to restore your system to a previous state quickly.
- *Enhanced security:* Virtualization provides sandboxed environments where potential threats can be isolated and analyzed without risking the entire infrastructure. In addition, the ability to restore a previous state of the system helps in mitigating the effects of a potential security incident.
- *Increased uptime:* Several virtualization platforms provide advanced capabilities not found in physical environments, such as live migration, storage migration, fault tolerance, high availability, and distributed resource scheduling. These technologies keep virtual machines online or restore them in the quickest timeframe, thereby increasing uptime.
- *Testing and development:* Virtualization provides a safe and isolated environment to test new software, OSs, or patches before deploying them into the production environment.
- *Lower energy costs:* By reducing the number of physical servers, companies can gain significant savings on energy consumption and cooling costs, contributing to greener IT operations.
- *Legacy system support:* OS virtualization can also keep legacy applications running on outdated OSs operational while planning for the software migration to a more current platform.
- *Example of OS virtualization:* The use of Oracle VM VirtualBox or VMware Workstation that allows for running a Linux OS and Windows OS simultaneously on the same hardware (like a Mac).

1.2.4 Application Virtualization

Application virtualization refers to a method that encapsulates an application from the underlying OS on which it is running. A fully virtualized application is not installed in the traditional sense; nonetheless, it is still executed as if it is.

Application virtualization offers several benefits as follows:

- *Compatibility:* It solves the problem of application conflicts, allowing incompatible applications to coexist on the same system.
- *Portability:* Applications can be run on any system without needing installation.
- *Simplified management:* Centralized administration allows easier management and updates.

An example of application virtualization is that application virtualization has uses in scenarios where multiple conflicting applications need to be run on the same systems, or when applications need to be easily transported and run on multiple systems. Microsoft App-V and VMware ThinApp are two popular application virtualization solutions. Microsoft App-V provides application virtualization for enterprise Windows environments. It allows users to run applications that could otherwise be incompatible with their system or create conflicts with other applications.

1.2.5 Storage Virtualization

This type of virtualization treats all storage devices in the network as a single storage entity. It can improve the efficiency and speed of storage backup and recovery.

An example of storage virtualization is that companies such as IBM or Dell EMC offer software and hardware solutions that enable storage virtualization, treating multiple storage devices across a network as one consolidated and flexible storage pool.

1.2.6 Data Virtualization

This involves gathering data from multiple sources, which can be accessed from a single interface. It helps in data management and reporting.

An example of data virtualization is that Denodo is a data virtualization tool that provides real-time access to disparate data sources, such as databases, application programming interfaces (APIs), and more, in a unified view, without needing to replicate the data.

1.2.7 Network Virtualization

This splits the available network bandwidth into independent channels. Each can be separately assigned to servers or devices in real time, increasing the efficiency and security of the network.

An example of network virtualization is the VMware's NSX solution. It allows the creation of entire networks in software, provisioning virtual network functions in minutes as opposed to the traditional hardware approach.

1.3 Security Risks Associated with Virtualization

1.3.1 Hypervisor Attacks

A hypervisor, sometimes referred to as a VM monitor (VMM), is a software, firmware, or hardware layer that creates, runs, and manages VMs. A hypervisor is a platform for operating systems, allowing direct access to system hardware and resources.

One of the main types of hypervisor attacks is an escape attack, in which the malicious code within a VM interacts directly with the hypervisor, aiming to either corrupt it or escape entirely to the host environment. Another common type is a hyperjacking attack, where a hacker installs a rogue hypervisor to take control of the entire system.

The mitigation strategies include regular patching and updating of hypervisor software to avoid known vulnerabilities, implementing secure boot mechanisms to ensure the integrity of hypervisor code, and using intrusion detection and prevention systems at the hypervisor level.

1.3.1.1 Case Studies

Hypervisors, the software systems responsible for managing VMs, have become critical components in modern computing infrastructure. However, like all software, they can be susceptible to various attacks. Two such attack categories are hyperjacking and escape attacks.

Case 1: Hyperjacking Attack

A hyperjacking attack, colloquially known as Virtual Machine Based Rootkits (VMBRs) or Hypervisor Rootkits, is an intrusion attempt where the attacker compromises the hypervisor to gain control over the hosted VMs and potentially the host system.

Security firm Mandiant, under Google's ownership, and virtualization company VMware have issued joint alerts suggesting that an advanced group of hackers has been deploying backdoors on several victims' networks via VMware's virtualization software, seemingly embarking on an espionage operation. The intruders inserted their own nefarious code into the victims' hypervisors, which is a subset of VMware software installed on a physical server to oversee all its hosted VMs. This stealth infiltration enabled the attackers to inconspicuously monitor and execute commands on the overseen computers. Importantly, since the malicious code primarily focuses on the physical machine's hypervisor rather than the victim's VMs, the intrusion expands their range of influence and successfully eludes the majority of traditional security tools implemented to track any suspicious activities on those target machines [4].

Case 2: Escape Attack

Escape attacks represent a specific form of hypervisor attack where a program running inside a VM is able to access the host system's resources, breaking the isolation that the hypervisor is supposed to maintain.

A VM escape attack is a sophisticated form of assault in which the malicious actor successfully breaks free from a constrained virtual environment that separates individual VMs from their managing hypervisor. Taking the example of a Type-1 hypervisor such as Xen, the guest operating systems are operated within a safeguarded, sandbox-like environment with strict boundaries. They are purposefully isolated from the hypervisor, which cannot be altered or affected by these OSs for security reasons. Moreover, these OS instances are kept distinct from one another to avoid interference. However, a VM escape attack disrupts this intentional isolation, enabling the attacker to breach the hypervisor by bypassing these safety measures. Upon gaining unauthorized access, the attacker can then exploit the hypervisor as a launch pad to infiltrate other areas of the network or potentially take control of other VMs residing on the very same system [5].

Both hyperjacking and escape attacks can have serious repercussions, as demonstrated in these cases. The key to reducing such attacks lies in regular and stringent system updates, careful security reviews, revising peripheral device emulators, and maintaining general security best practices.

1.3.2 Guest OS Attacks

In a virtual environment, a guest OS runs on the hypervisor or a host OS. These guest OSs can act as an entry point for attackers aiming to compromise the whole virtualized environment.

Guest OS attacks mainly involve vulnerabilities that naturally occur in the operating system itself, such as unpatched software, insecure settings, and common bugs. An attacker might insert malicious code into the guest OS, essentially exploiting it as a stepping stone to infiltrate the host system or other guest OSs.

Mitigations include regular patching and updating of guest OSs, hardening the guest OS by turning off unnecessary services, implementing strong access control mechanisms, and using antivirus software.

1.3.2.1 Case Study

In 2018, Ticketmaster UK, the renowned online ticket sales company, experienced a major security breach that affected approximately 40,000 customers. The attack, initiated through the third-party chat service Inbenta, exploited a malicious JavaScript code that was deployed on the Ticketmaster website [6].

Incident

The attack vector was initially misinterpreted as a singular host compromise. However, with evidence from the cybersecurity firm RiskIQ, it was revealed that the breach was part of a larger infrastructure attack called "Magecart attack." RiskIQ concluded that the threat actor had corrupted a JavaScript library from Inbenta deployed on Ticketmaster's websites. The third-party chat application was running as a guest OS on Ticketmaster's micro-services-based infrastructure [7].

Investigation

Upon deeper investigation by cybersecurity communities, it was discovered that this attack was not just limited to Ticketmaster. The attackers "Magecart" had targeted numerous e-commerce platforms with similar digital skimming attacks, with the aim of stealing payment information from digital transactions [7].

Impact

The unauthorized access resulted in a significant number of customers' personal and payment details being compromised. This led to serious implications for the company's reputation and a substantial financial impact. It also enforced regulatory repercussions under the newly enacted General Data Protection Regulations (GDPR) due to the leakage of sensitive customer data [8].

Resolution and Measures Taken

Ticketmaster UK, after the attack, implemented extensive security measures to mitigate the breach, including disabling the Inbenta product across their websites and reaching out to all potentially affected customers. The incident conveyed the importance of maintaining robust security measures for third-party applications running on guest OSs.

Lessons Learned

Security in a virtualized environment, including third-party services, plays a crucial role in the overall cybersecurity of an organization. Continuous monitoring and security assessment of these applications can prevent potential cyber threats. This also emphasized the need for companies to ensure that third-party software is subject to the same rigorous security protocols as their internal systems are.

1.3.3 Inter-VM Attacks

Inter-VM attacks involve an attacker using a compromised VM to launch attacks on other VMs within the same environment. This happens when VMs residing on the same physical host share resources with one another, creating a potential attack surface.

These types of attacks manifest in different forms, such as side-channel attacks where an attacker infers data from another VM by analyzing shared resources, or VM hopping, where an attacker directly accesses another VM.

Precautions include strictly managing VM-to-VM communications and interactions, isolating VM resources as much as possible, and regularly monitoring and auditing VM activity for any signs of compromise.

1.3.3.1 Case Study

An older case study of an inter-VM attack is the Xen Hypervisor Exploit discovered and presented by Rafal Wojtczuk and Joanna Rutkowska of Invisible Things Lab in 2008 [9]. They found a way to exploit Intel's SYSRET implementation, enabling different types of escalating privilege attacks. This was one of the first cases of an inter-VM attack on a widely used service.

In a summary of this attack, it was specifically targeted against paravirtualized machine (PVM) guests. PVM guests are VMs that explicitly share their kernel with the hypervisor for performance purposes.

The attackers, using a malicious kernel running in a PVM, managed to manipulate the returns from system calls in such a way that they were misinterpreted by the XEN hypervisor.

Once the XEN hypervisor was tricked into executing attacker-controlled domain kernel code with escalated privileges, the attacker was able to take over all other VMs controlled by the same hypervisor.

This situation was an example of a return-into-libc (ret2libc) attack, which is part of a class of cyberattacks that exploit components in computer memory to circumvent normal system security control.

The result of this hack resulted in the XEN project making various changes to their code to mitigate the exposed security vulnerability. Again, the implication was that data security in virtualized and cloud data centers needed to be a higher priority.

1.3.4 Network Security Vulnerabilities

Virtual networks, just like physical ones, are susceptible to various security threats. These include eavesdropping on virtual system network traffic, denial-of-service (DoS) attacks on a virtual network device, and unauthorized access to the management interface of a virtual network device.

Mitigation tactics encompass implementing network security measures such as firewalls, intrusion prevention systems, and secure network architecture design. Additionally, encryption of data in transit and rigorous authentication and access controls also fortify defenses.

1.3.4.1 Case Study

Virtualization technologies have revolutionized IT, providing enhanced scalability, cost savings, and flexible management. However, these benefits come with a real risk: network security vulnerabilities. The virtual network may highlight significant susceptibilities in security model, including eavesdropping, DoS attacks, and unauthorized access.

Use Case Scenario: Consider the Case of an Online Retail Company

Despite the various benefits, the retail company may realize that virtualization also introduces potential network security vulnerabilities as per the following:

- *Eavesdropping:* For instance, a malicious user, maybe even an employee, might find a way to gain access to the hypervisor, the software that enables virtualization. They could potentially eavesdrop on digital data (credit card details, personal information) flowing between different VMs.
- *DoS attacks:* This type of attack can affect a retail company significantly. A hacker may target retail company servers, overloading them with fake traffic, which can potentially crash the server. This risk is magnified in a

virtualized environment as multiple VMs share the same physical resources. If one virtual machine crashes due to a DoS attack, it may affect the performance of others.

- *Unauthorized access:* There might be cases where defaulting on continuous patching and updates or weak security configurations can allow unauthorized users to gain access, manipulate the system, or steal sensitive data.

To deal with these vulnerabilities, the retail company might implement security measures such as robust hypervisor security, regular patch management, intrusion prediction systems, encrypted data transfers, and implement strict access control and user privilege rules. Although virtualization brings its own set of challenges, an appropriate security model can significantly mitigate these risks, allowing companies to fully leverage the extensive benefits of virtualization technologies.

1.3.5 Vulnerabilities Due to Misconfiguration

Misconfigurations in a virtual environment represent another major security risk. A common scenario involves incorrectly configured security settings or access control policies, potentially offering unlimited access to a malicious actor.

These vulnerabilities can occur at various levels, from the hypervisor to the VM, and even within applications running on the VM. Misconfigurations may also lead to resource overconsumption by certain VMs, providing an avenue for DoS attacks.

Mitigation includes conducting regular security audits of configurations, setting up robust change management processes, and employing automated tools that continuously check for and report configuration issues. Training staff to understand the complexities of virtual environments is also crucial.

1.3.5.1 Case Study: The CapitalOne Data Breach

Misconfigurations in virtual environments represent significant security risks for business systems. One real-world representation of this risk is the significant data breach suffered by CapitalOne in 2019. Implementing effective security measures in virtual environments is critical, but one crucial aspect that gets overlooked is proper configuration management, a loophole that cybercriminals can exploit with devastating repercussions.

In 2019, CapitalOne Financial Corporation experienced a critical data breach that exposed the data of about 100 million individuals in the United States and 6 million in Canada. The cause of the breach was traced back to a misconfigured Web Application Firewall (WAF), exploited using a Server-Side Request Forgery (SSRF) attack. The hacker was able to execute commands that they should ordinarily have been barred from performing. A misconfiguration in CapitalOne's WAF enabled the hacker to trick the firewall into relaying requests to the metadata service of the Amazon's Elastic Compute Cloud (EC2) instance. The hacker extracted security credentials for the instances that had excess permissions due to internal mismanagement of identity and access management roles. This unusual configuration made it possible for the hacker to access and extract data from any storage bucket [10–13].

Impact and Consequences

The CapitalOne Data breach has had far-reaching consequences. It has cost the company approximately $150 million, including customer notifications, credit monitoring, technology costs, and legal support [11].

1.4 Role of Virtualization for Enhancing Cybersecurity

Virtualization effectively addresses security risks in several ways, underlining its crucial role in enhancing security. For instance, virtualization facilitates the centralization of data, thereby eliminating the need to store information on potentially insecure devices used by end-users.

The following points explain how virtualization aids in mitigating security risks:

- *Refined access control:* Virtualization provides IT teams with enhanced control over network access as compared to traditional hardware-based infrastructure. They can implement micro-segmentation techniques, assigning user access to specific resources or applications at a workload level.
- *Isolation of applications:* One of the prominent security advantages of virtualization is its ability to segregate applications within the network. This isolation safeguards data by preventing inadvertent sharing across applications or blocking the spread of malware that has infected other components of the system. Such isolation is commonly achieved through methods such as sandboxing and containerization.
- *Streamlined updates on desktops and applications:* The process of updating OSs and applications is constant due to regular security patches. However, it is challenging to ensure that each device used by employees is updated. Through desktop virtualization, the IT department gains total control to maintain up-to-date systems and applications.
- *Isolation of VMs:* The practice of operating numerous VMs on a single server enhances security through isolation. If one VM is compromised, the others remain secure due to this separation.
- *Network segmentation and isolation:* With virtualization, standalone workloads or applications can be divided and assigned to separate virtual networks, each isolated from the others. As a result, access permissions and information flow are not shared across the entire network, further bolstering security.
- *Efficient hypervisor maintenance:* Hypervisors that generate and manage VMs normally require fewer resources compared to hardware-based alternatives, reducing their vulnerability to attacks. In addition, hypervisors typically update autonomously, ticking off a crucial security maintenance task.

- *Disaster recovery and business continuity:* Virtualization plays a vital role in disaster recovery strategies and maintaining business continuity. In case of a network failure or attack, virtualized systems can quickly be restored to their previous states, minimizing downtime and potential data loss. This resilience is thanks to the ability to migrate VMs and applications between different physical hosts with ease.
- *Enhanced incident response:* During a security breach, virtualization can allow for quick isolation and analysis of affected systems while still maintaining general operations. It can aid in gathering information about the incident, avoiding additional damage, and expediting the restoration process.
- *Scalable security solutions:* Virtualization can help to scale security along with network expansion. Virtual firewalls or intrusion detection systems can be amplified and retracted based on the network's needs, providing a tailored and scalable security solution.
- *Secure workloads in hybrid clouds:* With increasing migration towards hybrid cloud structures, virtualization ensures optimal workload protection. It enables enterprises to share resources securely among both private and public cloud platforms.
- *Effective resource allocation:* Virtualization allows for the optimal use of hardware resources by appropriately allocating them to various functions as needed. This helps to reduce the risk of overloading individual systems that can be potentially exploited by cyberattackers.
- *Proactive threat monitoring:* Virtualization allows for the implementation of advanced monitoring and alerting systems. By actively overseeing the virtual environment for any potential threats or unusual activities, security teams can proactively respond to issues as they arise.

1.5 Importance of Maintaining Security in Virtualized Environments

1.5.1 Impact of Security Breaches on Businesses

Security breaches in a virtualized environment can lead to devastating outcomes for businesses. The unauthorized access of sensitive data can lead to financial losses due to theft of intellectual property, financial information, or customer data. Moreover, it could also damage the company's reputation and erode client trust, elements that are difficult to measure yet crucial to a company's success. Breaches can also interrupt business operations, causing significant downtime and loss of productivity.

1.5.2 Role of Virtualization Security in Maintaining Integrity and Reliability of IT Infrastructure

When a virtual environment is secure, the underlying IT infrastructure is reliable and robust. With the high interdependence of VMs, the compromising of a single VM can pose a risk to the entire infrastructure. By maintaining a strong security posture, operational continuity is preserved, and the risk of disruptions is minimized.

Secure virtual environments also contribute to data integrity, ensuring the accuracy, consistency, and trustworthiness of data over its entire life cycle.

1.5.3 Benefits of Strong Security Measures in a Virtual Environment

Proactively securing a virtual environment reduces the risk of security breaches, thereby preserving client trust. Clients gain confidence knowing their data is well-protected. On a strategic level, this could translate into customer retention and new business acquisition.

Another key benefit is the protection of sensitive data, which includes customer records, financial data, and intellectual property. When such data is secure, the risk of financial and reputational damage is significantly minimized.

Additionally, a secure environment ensures business continuity, as the risk of operational interruptions due to security incidents is significantly reduced. This translates into consistent performance, productivity, and ultimately, profitability.

1.5.4 Legal and Regulatory Obligations

Businesses are subject to a variety of legal and regulatory obligations regarding cybersecurity. Depending on the jurisdiction and the nature of the business, these regulations could involve specific methods of data protection, regular auditing, or timely incident reporting.

The GDPR in the EU, the California Consumer Privacy Act (CCPA) in the United States, and the Personal Data Protection Act (PDPA) in Singapore are all examples of regulatory frameworks that have provisions concerning data security, and they apply to data in virtual environments.

Failures in securing virtual environments could lead to violations of these regulations, which, in turn, could result in hefty fines and legal penalties, further underscoring the importance of maintaining strong security in virtualized environments.

1.6 Virtualization Security and Specific Issues

Virtualization security indeed offers multiple advantages, including infrastructure flexibility, cost-effectiveness, improved disaster recovery processes, and optimized resource consumption. However, it does not come without its share of specific issues. Some specific issues are highlighted below.

1.6.1 Intricacy of Virtual Networks

Virtualization dramatically alters the landscape of network operations, accompanying its numerous benefits with a fair share of concerns surrounding its complexity. As several applications and workloads are transitioned over to various servers, the ensuing complexity makes it a daunting task for IT teams to comply with security best practices, ensuring smooth implementation of standard configurations and policies across the wider network.

1.6.2 Potential Risks in Virtual Local Area Networks

Integrating virtual local area networks (VLANs) into a virtualized environment poses specific security vulnerabilities as network traffic is rerouted from the host system to a firewall. As a result, latency may spike within the network. Furthermore, communication exchanges between multiple VMs within a VLAN may not provide room for inspection, undermining network security.

1.6.3 The Phenomenon of VM Sprawl

VM sprawl is a virtualization specific issue, occurring as a result of unchecked multiplication of unused and obsolete VMs in the system. Due to the easy deployment of VMs, IT teams sometimes create these elements extravagantly, often for testing, and frequently forget to delete them after usage. These ignored VMs usually miss out on crucial security updates, thus remaining unhardened and vulnerable to cyber threats and cyberattacks.

1.6.4 The Threat of Distributed Denial-of-Service Attacks

Despite being distinct entities within the virtualized environment, VMs share server resources like CPU, random access memory (RAM), and memory. When a distributed denial-of-service (DDoS) attack targets a VM with heavy, damaging traffic, other VMs sharing the server also suffer. This collective degradation in performance highlights one of the potential security risks of virtualization.

1.6.5 Risks Related to Hypervisor Attacks

Hypervisors, while having relatively smaller attack surfaces, still can pose a threat. If a hypervisor comes under a successful assault, all the VMs functioning on the same server are put at risk. This allows for a centralized point of access for cyberattackers. Moreover, the security credentials of these hypervisors are handled by the admins, posing an additional risk if a malicious insider gains access to these credentials.

1.6.6 Dilemmas Pulled in by Cloud Infrastructure

In addition to the considerations brought about with virtualization, your organization's cloud infrastructure introduces its own network security risks. Its integration with virtualization systems can augment the initial risk factor, necessitating a holistic view of IT security that takes into account both virtualization and cloud components.

1.7 Which Type of Virtualization Should You Use?

Virtualization is undoubtedly a potent technology that has the potential to revolutionize your operational efficiencies, considerably reduce costs, and enhance your cybersecurity infrastructure. However, before adopting any form of virtualization, it is crucial to understand your unique needs and challenges.

When selecting a type of virtualization, it is crucial that your choice aligns with your organization's specific requirements. Striking an effective balance between existing security measures and bridging current gaps is the key.

Working with a reputable service provider can help to guide this selection process, providing expertise and invaluable insights into choosing the best virtualization methods suited for your needs. An experienced provider is not just key for addressing present challenges but also anticipates potential future issues, thus putting you in a more robust standing in the challenging digital landscape.

1.8 Summary

In this chapter, we delved into the concept and inner workings of virtualization technology, beginning with a detailed definition and its historical development. We highlighted the integral role that virtualization plays in modern IT infrastructure and discussed its various types: server, desktop, and application virtualization.

Server virtualization was discussed in detail, exploring its concept, importance, and utilization in the business world. We illustrated common examples of server virtualization platforms that aid businesses in managing resources efficiently.

Thereafter, desktop virtualization was defined, delving into its advantages and how it varies from traditional PC usage. We explored its use cases and how it enhances user accessibility and control.

In the context of application virtualization, we discussed its definition and benefits, along with examples of scenarios where it proves useful, such as remote working and software testing environments.

An in-depth discourse was provided on security risks associated with virtualization, discussing threats such as hypervisor attacks, guest OS attacks, and inter-VM attacks. We emphasized the potential vulnerabilities that can be exploited in virtual networks, along with the risks created due to the misconfiguration in the virtual environment.

The significance of maintaining security in virtualized environments was discussed extensively. We elaborated on the harm security breaches can inflict on businesses, both on a practical and reputational level. We underlined the role of virtualization security in maintaining the integrity and reliability of IT infrastructure and the legal and regulatory obligations that businesses carry with respect to securing their virtual environments.

In conclusion, understanding virtualization and its associated security risks are of utmost importance in our digitized world. Companies, large and small, must invest in maintaining robust security measures in their virtual environments to guarantee business continuity, protect sensitive data, and uphold client trust. This chapter serves as a comprehensive guide to navigate the complexities and intricacies of virtualization and its inherent security aspects.

References

[1] https://www.vmware.com/uk/products/vsphere.html.

[2] https://learn.microsoft.com/en-us/windows-server/virtualization/hyper-v/hyper-v-technology-overview.

[3] https://www.citrix.com/blogs/2013/06/25/xenserver-6-2-is-now-fully-open-source/.

[4] https://www.wired.com/story/hyperjacking-vmware-mandiant/.

[5] https://www.techtarget.com/searchsecurity/tip/Breaking-down-the-risks-of-VM-escapes.

[6] https://www.bbc.co.uk/news/technology-44628874.

[7] https://www.brighttalk.com/webcast/14683/339117.

[8] SC Media UK, "GDPR Implications in the Spotlight Following Ticketmaster Data Breach," October 30, 2018, https://www.scmagazine.com/news/ticketmaster-uk-customers-hit-in-third-party-breach.

[9] Rutkowska, J., and R. Wojtczuk, "Preventing and Detecting Xen Hypervisor Subversions," Blackhat Briefings USA, 2008.

[10] CapitalOne, "CapitalOne Announces Data Security Incident," 2019, https://www.capital-one.com/facts2019/.

[11] https://www.latimes.com/business/la-xpm-2012-jul-18-la-fi-mo-capital-one-refunds-fine-consumer-financial-protection-bureau-20120718-story.

[12] https://krebsonsecurity.com/2019/08/what-we-can-learn-from-the-capital-one-hack/.

[13] https://ejj.io/blog/capital-one.

CHAPTER 2

Network Security in Virtualized Environments

2.1 Introduction

In an era of digital advancement, a technology revolution profoundly changes how businesses operate the industry's function. It has several tools, such as collaborative software and communication tools [1]. One of the essential tools powering these transformations is the implementation of virtualized environments. They have significant benefits such as cost savings, increased flexibility, and optimized resource usage, but they still face some challenges [2]. The most critical and complex challenges lie in safeguarding such environments from a burgeoning array of security threats; this is where the crucial concept of network security in virtualized environments comes into play.

The core purpose of this chapter is to delve into the complexities and nuances of network security within these cyber territories, demystifying and illuminating this increasingly critical domain. In a virtualized environment, network resources, services, and applications are abstracted from their underlying hardware, thus creating a need for unique security strategies that go beyond the traditional approaches used in physical environments [3]. Henceforth, network security must be recalibrated to account for these virtualized landscapes. This chapter will address the essential elements of promoting network security in virtualized environments, analyzing how security threats emerge, evolve, and can be effectively mitigated in such settings.

The reader will be introduced to various aspects, such as designing and implementing robust security protocols, limiting attack surfaces, data protection, and risk mitigation strategies within virtualized environments. In essence, we will dissect how traditional security models must be reconsidered and revamped to meet the unique demands posed by virtualization [4].

This chapter will walk you through the intersection of cybersecurity and virtualized environments, exploring the enhanced importance of network security within such contexts, the unique challenges that it presents, and potential solutions to these emerging issues. It will address the science behind balancing virtual efficiency, integrity, availability, and confidentiality, including a comprehensive overview of best practices to maintain a secure virtualized network. This chapter is structured to benefit both beginner-level readers, who will appreciate the clarity and fundamental explanations, and advanced professionals, who will find value in the complex analysis, latest research, and forward-looking perspectives discussed. Regardless of your professional standing, comprehending these emerging dynamics is vital in an increasingly virtual world. By unearthing and understanding the new challenges and opportunities of network security in a virtualized environment, the reader shall be better equipped to design, implement, and manage secure infrastructures in tune with modern demands.

The objective is to increase your awareness and empower you with actionable tactics that can contribute significantly to securing and managing secure virtualized networks. As we advance into the digital age, network security in virtualization offers timely insight that is a must-read for IT professionals, security analysts, and anyone operating within a virtual environment.

2.1.1 A Brief Overview of Network Security in Virtual Environments

Virtualization in network environments is an evolving technology that allows multiple computing environments to run on a single physical host. This enables more efficient resource utilization and provides users with the desired level of isolation [5].

Network security in virtualized environments refers to the measures taken to protect the integrity, confidentiality, and availability of data running through virtual networks. It involves practices, procedures, technologies, and systems that secure virtual networks and the resources running on them from any security threat.

The virtualized environment is different from traditional physical environments. Here, physical servers are replaced with VMs on a single physical server. Multiple VMs can run on a single machine, each with its OS and applications as if on separate physical servers. The virtual environment can be complex, with different VMs sharing resources, networks, and security domains [6].

This complexity can lead to vulnerabilities that cyberattackers can exploit, making network security critically important in a virtual environment. Virtualization is a widely used concept in computing that permits the creation of several virtualized platform within a single physical structure, enabling heterogeneous architectures to run on the similar hardware system. It also optimizes the usage of physical resources by dynamically instantiating and removing virtual nodes to fulfill changeable demands at every level. Researchers have begun investigating the use of virtualization in network infrastructures due to the growing demand for web services and adaptive networks with progressively different requirements. A virtualized network enables several separate virtualized network instances across a specific hardware system, creating topologies that are not constrained by the hardware network's architecture. Individual virtual network infrastructures that are specifically suited to various network applications are made possible by the fact that virtualized networks are not constrained by other aspects of the hardware network, such as its protocol stack [7]. Network virtualization has attracted interest from researchers from all over the world, mainly in future internet research. Key players from industries offer devices that support virtualization, allowing infrastructure providers to offer new services. However, security issues are raised by the shared use of communication channels and routing devices. Users from a virtual network may be able to access or disrupt traffic from other crowded networks without the proper protection, which would violate security properties such as confidentiality and integrity. Furthermore, a variety of attacks could target the system, resulting in problems with availability for virtualized networks that are instantiated over it. The need for a thorough examination of recent advancements in the field of virtual network security has been brought to light by the recent revelation of widespread electronic surveillance worldwide.

2.1.2 Importance of Network Security in Virtual Environments

It is impossible to exaggerate the significance of network security in virtual environments. Organizations are now more vulnerable to possible cyber threats as a result of their growing adoption of virtualization technologies to reduce expenses and boost operational effectiveness. These weaknesses can include more serious risks such as intellectual property theft as well as more serious ones such as illegal data access and breaches.

Network security in virtual environments protects sensitive data, prevents unauthorized access, and provides secure communication channels within and between the virtual infrastructures [7]. It also helps maintain the organization's reputation by preventing any potential breach that could lead to legal issues and loss of customer trust.

Moreover, with organizations having to comply with numerous data protection and privacy regulations, network security in virtual environments is paramount in ensuring regulatory compliance. Failure to comply can result in heavy fines and legal penalties.

The different complexities inherent in virtual environment mean that traditional physical security measures are often insufficient to secure the entire network. Therefore, specialized security measures tailored to the virtual environment are essential. It includes special security software for virtualization, careful management and monitoring of VM activity, and procedures to maintain network security.

In essence, network security in virtualized environments is vital for data protection and business continuity. It helps to mitigate the risks associated with cyber threats, ensuring that business operations remain functional and secure in an increasingly digitally reliant world [8].

Virtual infrastructure is a popular choice for businesses due to its flexible, straightforward, and reasonable pricing. Still, it needs a complete methodology for security, as there is a greater risk of data loss. Businesses should concentrate on three common issues: viruses, file sharing and copy-pasting, and external attacks in order to improve the security of their virtualization infrastructure. Hackers can easily access other important components of the system by breaking into host-level or server management software through external attacks. Usually, file sharing and copy-pasting are turned off, but if a hacker manages to access the management console, they can install malware on the VM or copy data outside of it. Another frequent danger to virtualized infrastructure is viruses, especially ransomware. It is essential to regularly back up website data and store it off-site in a location that prevents hackers from encrypting it [9]. Businesses should work to control their virtualized infrastructure security by managing virtual sprawl, following virtual golden template configuration setup, securing all layers of the infrastructure (including physical and virtual guest systems and cloud systems), and having a proper backup plan. To manage virtual sprawl, businesses should inventory every machine in the environment, establish lookouts with multilocation monitoring, review all VMs' access regarding their composing hardware, monitor VMs for locked tables, avoid granting privileges using database grant statements to other database users, maintain a central log of systems, and establish a patch maintenance schedule around every machine [10]. Employing security measures for all layers of your infrastructure includes your physical components, your virtual components, guest systems, and cloud systems. Having a proper backup plan is paramount to business continuity after an attack. Businesses should back up both their VMs and physical servers, preferably to ensure that there are at least three copies of data, two stored in different locations locally and at least one stored in an off-site source. One more suggestion would be to even replicate VMs to a different data center that would be of value for emergencies.

2.2 Virtual Network Architecture

2.2.1 Definition of and Understanding Virtual Network Architecture

Virtual network architecture is a technology that enables software-based network functionalities to be deployed on a virtual platform. It essentially outlines how network resources and services, such as routers, firewalls, and load balancers, are deployed and associated within a virtual environment. It is integral to any virtualized environment and forms the backbone for establishing a secure, reliable, and efficient networking solution.

In virtual network architecture, the traditional physical network topology is abstracted into a virtual one. This architecture relies on a hypervisor, a layer of software that creates and manages VMs. It is responsible for developing, managing, and securing multiple instances of virtual networks on physical hardware [11]. Figure 2.1 illustrates the architecture of a virtual network, which is a software-defined network that emulates the functions of a physical network in a virtualized environment, enabling secure and scalable communication between VMs and applications.

2.2.2 Components of Virtual Network Architecture

Virtual switches, bridges, Ethernet adapters, network address translation (NAT), dynamic host configuration protocol (DHCP) servers, and host-only adapters are examples of virtual networks. After a VMware ESX Server is installed, a virtual switch that links the network components becomes available automatically [13]. Virtual bridges connect a VM to the host computer's local area network (LAN), and additional virtual bridges can be configured for special purposes. When a host computer, using a single Internet Protocol (IP) network address, communicates with the VMs, the host-only adapter is a virtual Ethernet adapter that appears to the host

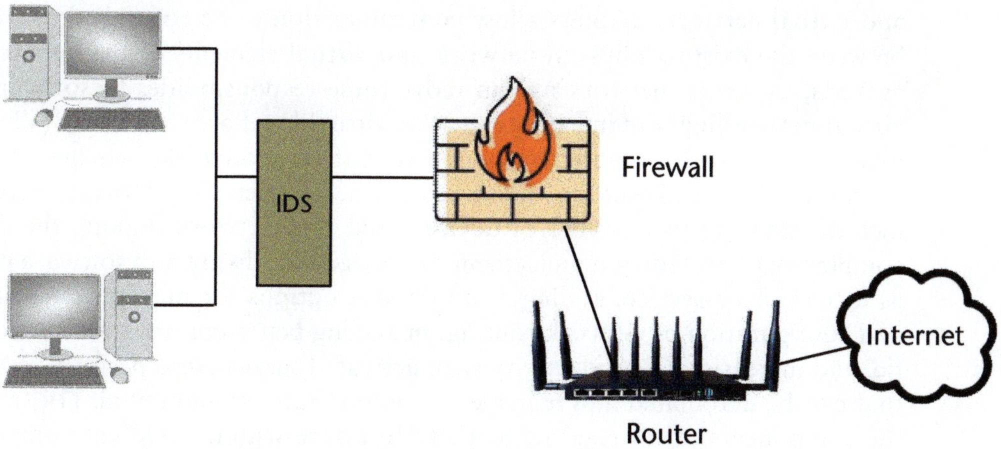

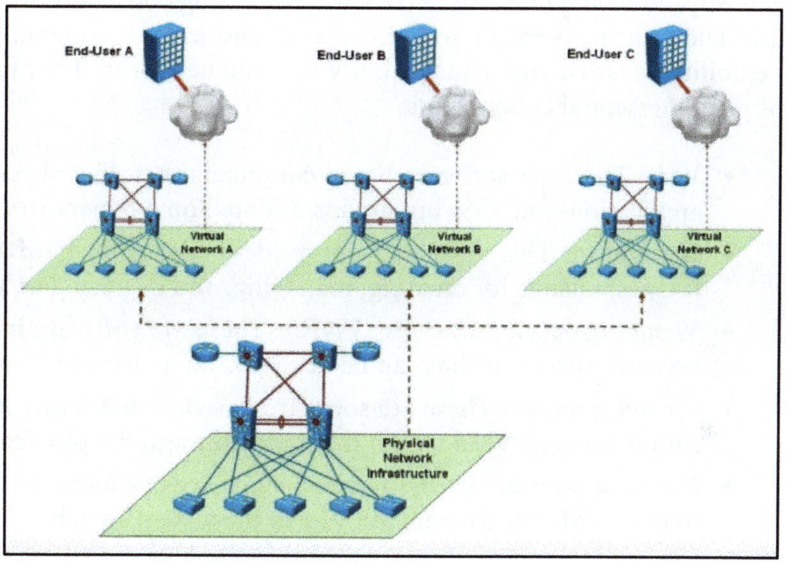

Figure 2.1 Virtual network architecture [12].

OS as a host-only interface. A NAT device is the connection between the VMs and a superconnected external network. Using separate DHCP servers, the DHCP server assigns IP network addresses to the VMs for any host-only and NAT configuration. The Configuration Wizard will configure an Ethernet adapter for a VM using any number of networking devices that show as an AMD PCNET PCI adapter on the virtual network guest OS.

Virtual networking technology allows many PCs, virtual servers, VMs, and other devices in different offices and data centers to communicate with each other. It uses software management to connect PCs and servers across the internet, thus allowing open-ended possibilities for physical networking. Traditional networks can be virtualized such as switches and network adapters, which will increase routing efficiency and simplify changes made to network configure.

In contrast, computers and servers are connected to the network through physical network interface cards (NIC) and network adapters. Virtual network switches and virtual network adapters allow communication to be controlled and directed between the existing physical network and virtual elements of the network, such as VMs, as virtual networking can move these responsibilities to software. With virtual networking, organizations can use virtual local area networks (VLANs) to make it possible for computers bound to different network switches to operate as though they are bound to the same switch. The benefits of virtual networking include reducing the number of devices used in a network making the cost and complexity of providing management of network hardware and software provided as a centralized service, adding more flexible options for managing the structure and configuration of network routing, providing better control over network traffic, and increasing IT productivity with activated services and performance testing that can be automated and managed remotely. Subramanian et al. [14] presented the components of a virtual network architecture within cloud environments, including subnets, network security groups, VPN gateway, load balancer, application gateway, domain name system (DNS), and peering connections, as shown in Figure 2.2. These elements ensure secure, isolated, and scalable communication, providing flexibility, security, and manageability in cloud networks. The architecture consists of several essential components:

- *VMs:* These are software-based computers that, like physical machines, run applications and OSs but are instantiated on a hypervisor.
- *Hypervisor:* This software layer resides between the hardware and the VMs. It is responsible for creating, managing, and disposing of VMs.
- *Virtual network functions (VNFs):* These are software implementations of network functions that can be deployed on a virtualized infrastructure.
- *Virtual switches:* These are software-based switches that manage communication between VMs within the same host and the physical network.
- *Network interface cards:* These virtual network interface cards are assigned to each VM that connect the VM to the virtual switch.

2.2.3 Relationship of Virtual Network Architecture with Network Security

The virtual network architecture plays a vital role in network security in a virtualized environment. By intelligently arranging virtual network devices, firewalls, intrusion detection systems, and segregating network services, administrators can minimize the attack surface of the virtual infrastructure [15]. Security policies are enforced at every network interface, providing granular control over network access. Network traffic is often isolated using VLANs or other tunneling methods to segregate different types of traffic and services. Furthermore, virtual network architecture also plays a crucial role in implementing advanced security technologies such as micro-segmentation. This concept allows for further division of a network into isolated security zones to restrict the lateral movement of threats within networks, providing more robust security across the virtual network. Figure 2.3 illustrates the relationship between virtual network architecture and network security, incorporating features such as network security groups (NSGs), VPN gateways,

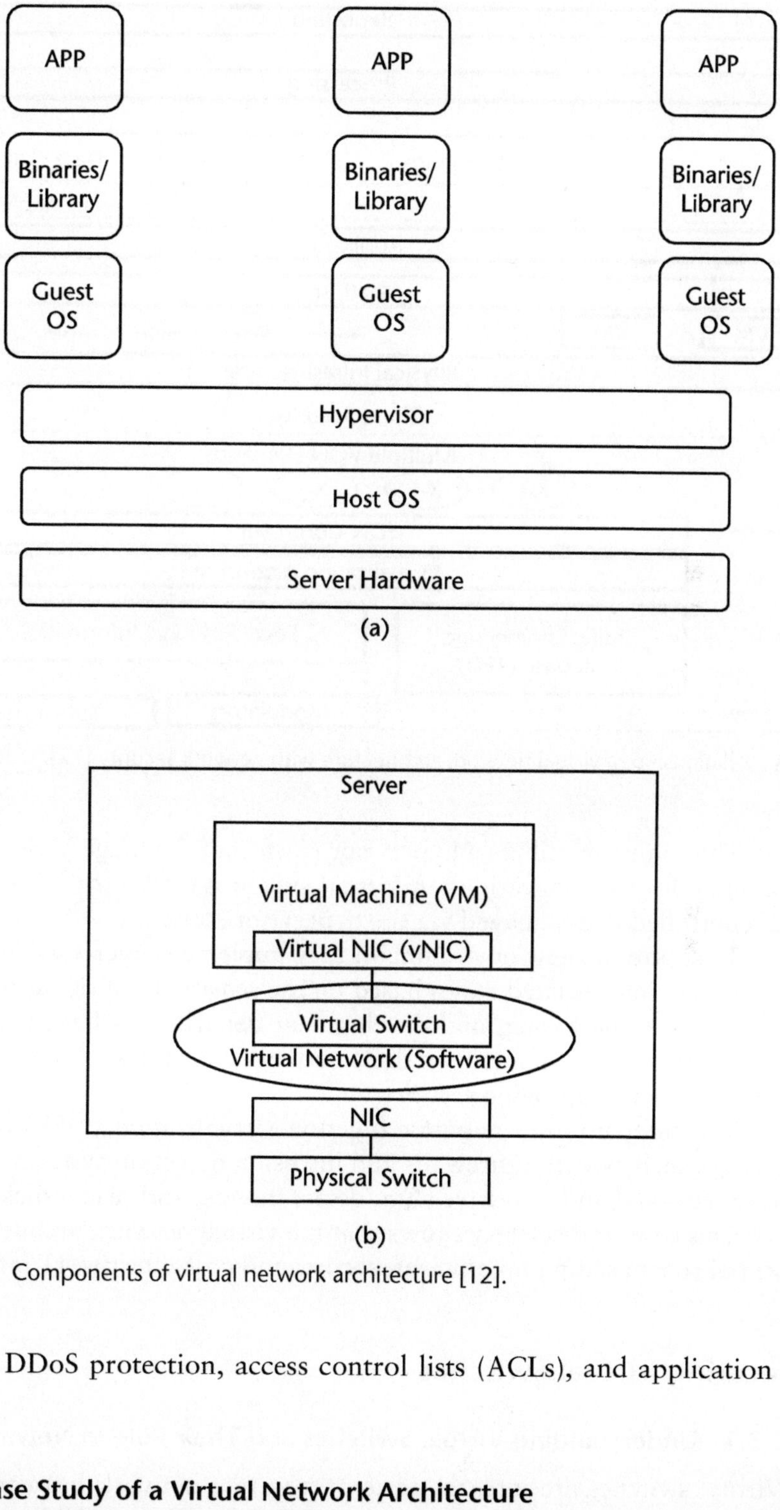

Figure 2.2 Components of virtual network architecture [12].

firewalls, DDoS protection, access control lists (ACLs), and application security groups.

2.2.4 Case Study of a Virtual Network Architecture

This case study illustrates the implementation of virtual network architecture in a medium-sized IT enterprise. The organization migrated its traditional data center to a virtualized one, aiming to reduce cost, increase efficiency, and enhance security.

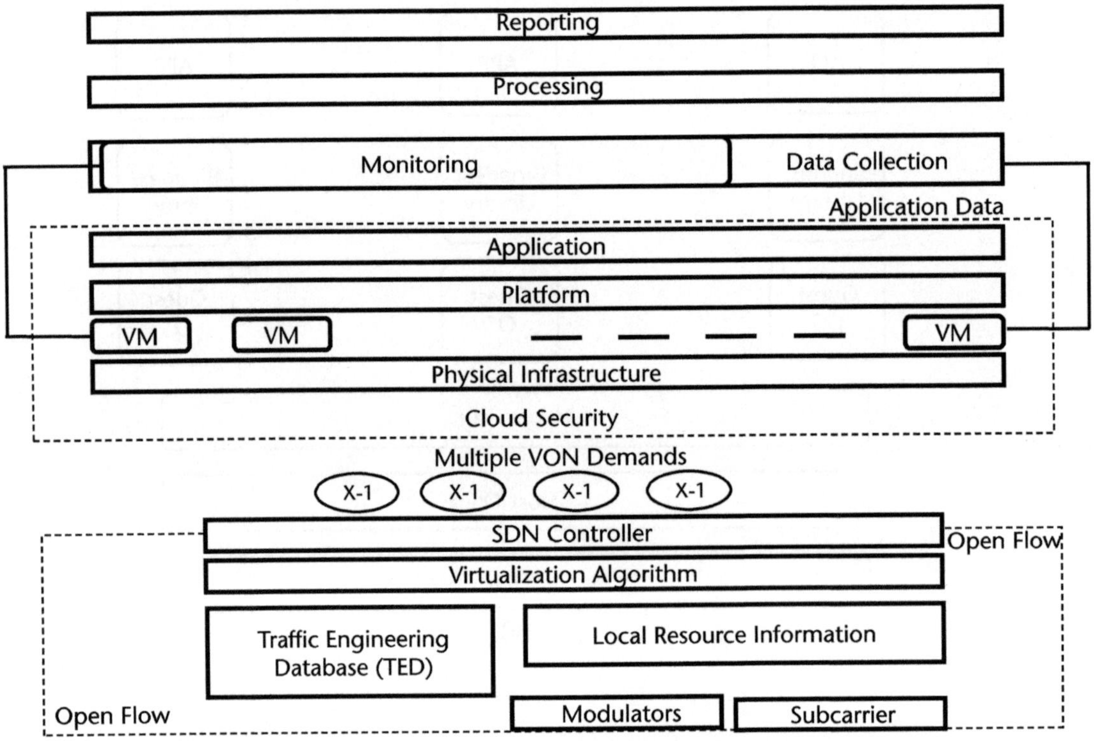

Figure 2.3 Relationship of virtual network architecture with network security [17].

The company utilizes a hypervisor platform to manage VMs, with various OSs running diverse applications. A virtual switch is set up for VMs to communicate, all controlled and managed via the hypervisor software.

To secure the new environment, they implement micro-segmentation, dividing the system into isolated zones based on the sensitivity of the information handled. The finance, marketing, and development departments have isolated virtual networks [16]. All traffic between these networks must pass through a virtual firewall for inspection, improving security.

The company uses network function virtualization (NFV) to deploy security services such as virtual firewalls and intrusion detection systems. This allows them to process and audit massive data, detect threats, and react quickly.

This case study clearly shows that the virtual network architecture plays an essential role in setting up efficient, secure, and cost-effective IT infrastructure.

2.3 Securing Virtual Switches

2.3.1 Understanding Virtual Switches and Their Role in Network Security

Virtual switches are integral parts of a virtual network infrastructure. They are software applications that allow communication between VMs and external physical machines on the same physical host [18]. They function similarly to physical switches, forwarding data packets based on media access control (MAC) addresses within a network but packaged within a virtual system.

Regarding network security, virtual switches offer protection at the virtual network's edge. They control and monitor the traffic between VMs and between a VM and the external network, allowing the enforcement of security policies. They can be used to implement features like firewalling, quality of service, and network segmentation between VMs, thus playing a vital role in maintaining network security [19]. Figure 2.4 depicts virtual switches and network security, which play a crucial role in network virtualization by providing data routing and connectivity for VMs. They enhance security by isolating network traffic, controlling traffic flow with ACLs or port-level filtering, segmenting networks using VLANs, monitoring traffic through port mirroring, and protecting against threats such as MAC address spoofing and DHCP snooping. These switches are crucial for network performance and security in virtualized infrastructures.

2.3.2 Potential Vulnerabilities in Virtual Switches

Despite their significant role, virtual switches are not immune to threats and vulnerabilities. These might include:

- *Unauthorized access:* Since virtual switches are often overlooked in security planning, they may be vulnerable to unauthorized access, leading to potential exploitation.

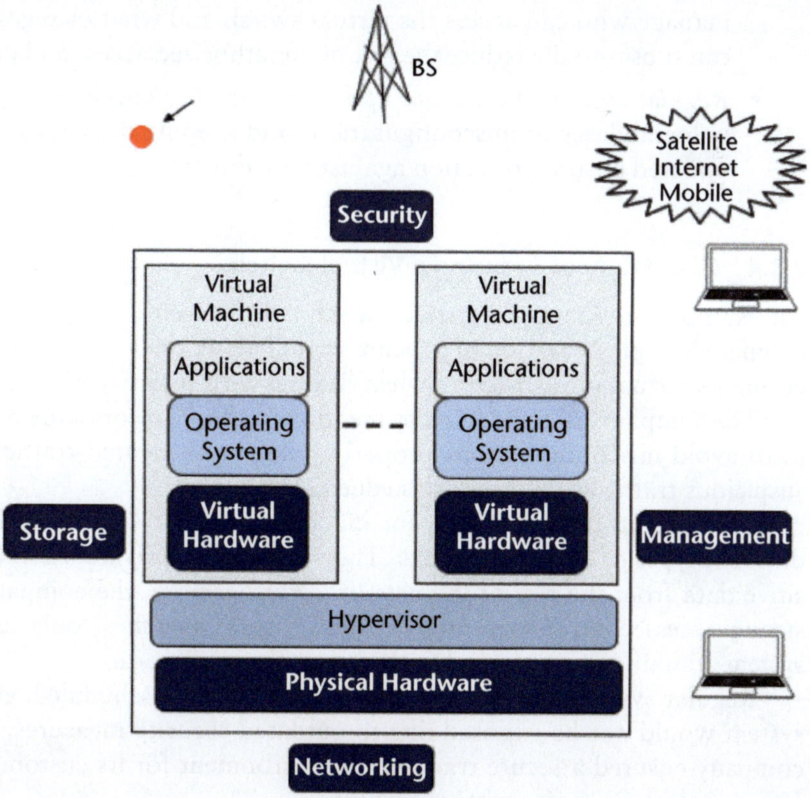

Figure 2.4 Virtual switches and network security [20].

- *Inter-VM attacks:* A compromised VM could exploit vulnerabilities in the virtual switch, spreading the attack to other connected VMs.
- *Misconfiguration:* Incorrect configurations can create vulnerabilities, exposing the virtual switch to potential attacks.
- *DoS attacks:* A flood of fabricated requests can overload the virtual switch, disrupting the network communication.

2.3.3 Techniques for Securing Virtual Switches

Securing virtual switches involves several best practices:

- *Traffic limitation and filtering:* By implementing security policies that limit incoming and outgoing traffic based on predefined rules, illegal or harmful data can be effectively filtered out.
- *Network segmentation:* By segregating the network into separate segments, each with its virtual switch, the risk of lateral spread of threats within the network can be mitigated.
- *Use of private VLANs:* By creating private VLANs, the data traffic can be isolated, ensuring sensitive data is transmitted securely.
- *Access control measures:* Implementing strong access control measures to manage who can access the virtual switch and what changes they can make can substantially reduce the risk of unauthorized access and potential attacks.
- *Regular system checks and updates:* Regularly checking the system for any vulnerabilities or misconfigurations and keeping the virtual switch software updated ensure protection against new threats.

2.3.4 Case Study of Securing a Virtual Switch

An example of securing a virtual switch can be seen in a mid-sized e-commerce company's implementation of a secure virtual network. The company prioritized securing its virtual infrastructure when dealing with sensitive customer information.

The company used the security mentioned above to configure all virtual switches to avoid misconfigurations properly. They implemented traffic filters to block suspicious traffic at the network's edge [21].

They set up traffic limiters for incoming traffic to protect their system from different types of flooding attacks. They established private VLANs to isolate sensitive data from the rest of the network. Furthermore, the company implemented strong access control measures on their virtual switches, only allowing specific system administrators to modify the network configuration.

Regular system checks and security updates were scheduled, ensuring that the system would not be exposed due to outdated security measures. As a result, the company ensured a secure transaction environment for its customers, proving the effectiveness of securing virtual switches.

2.4 Securing Virtual Firewalls

2.4.1 The Role of Virtual Firewalls in Network Security

Virtual firewalls are software-based security systems that are designed to protect virtual environments in the same manner as physical firewalls protect hardware systems [22]. Their principal role is to control and monitor the traffic between various network layers, VMs, or specific network segments within a virtual environment.

They are an essential instrument in the maintenance of securing the network. They safeguard the integrity, confidentiality, and availability of data by blocking unauthorized access, denying harmful traffic, and shielding virtual networks from various types of cyberattacks, such as DDoS attacks. User requests and how virtual firewalls protect user requests are shown in Figure 2.5. Virtual firewalls are vital in virtual network architectures, ensuring secure handling of user requests and regulating access to resources. They filter traffic, block unauthorized access, and monitor network communications in line with security policies, acting as gatekeepers to protect against potential cyber threats.

2.4.2 Potential Vulnerabilities and Risks Associated with Virtual Firewalls

While virtual firewalls play a crucial role in overall network security, they also come with their potential risks and vulnerabilities:

- *Misconfiguration:* Mishandled configuration could potentially jeopardize the security, creating loopholes that cybercriminals might exploit.
- *Software vulnerabilities:* Any flaw or vulnerability in the firewall's software could open the network to attack.

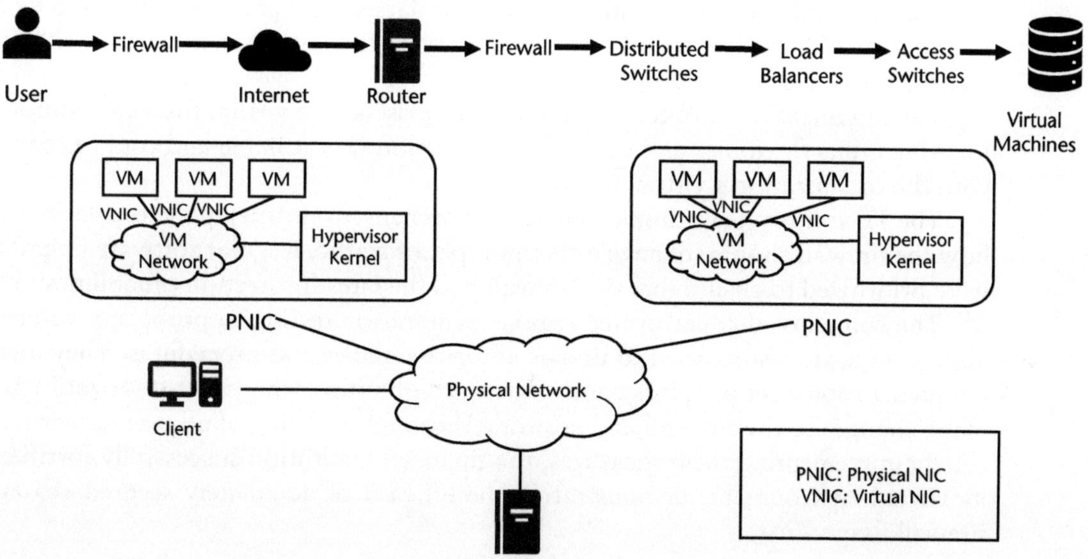

Figure 2.5 User request and securing virtual firewalls [23].

- *Unauthorized access:* Without proper access control, unauthorized users could bypass the firewall or manipulate its settings.
- *Lack of visibility and control:* In complex virtual environments, firewalls may lack complete visibility, potentially allowing traffic to pass without inspection.

2.4.3 Techniques for Securing Virtual Firewalls

Securing virtual firewalls requires a continued commitment to various practices:

- *Regular software updates:* Keeping the firewall software up-to-date ensures that the newest patches for vulnerabilities are in place, reducing the chances of exploitation.
- *Creating comprehensive security policies:* A thorough policy detailing how the firewall should handle incoming and outgoing traffic can drastically decrease the chance of security breaches. This includes defining specific rules for traffic filtering.
- *Regular vulnerability testing:* Scanning and testing the virtual firewall for known vulnerabilities can help to prevent potential attacks. Penetration testing is one effective method to ensure that the defense mechanism is robust.
- *Prioritizing scalability:* As the virtual environment grows, so too should the capabilities of the virtual firewall. Scalability ensures that the firewall can handle increasing traffic without compromising network security.

2.4.4 Case Study of a Virtual Firewall Implementation

A large financial institution with a virtualized data center provides an example of a virtual firewall strategy. Given the sensitivity of the data that it handles, robust security measures were paramount.

The organization adopted a popular, enterprise-grade virtual firewall solution, focusing on its flexibility and control. The solution was scalable and could expand with the organization's virtual environment.

The IT security team implemented comprehensive security policies specifying how the firewall should manage different types of traffic. Regular software updates were prioritized to ensure that the firewall had the latest protection capabilities [5].

The company also performed regular penetration testing to probe any vulnerability, with the results used to update security policies and procedures. They also adopted a robust set of access control measures, limiting who had authorization to make changes to the firewall and ensuring thorough tracking of all user activities.

By implementing these measures, the financial institution successfully fortified its virtual environment, demonstrating the efficacy of adequately secured virtual firewall usage.

2.5 Securing Virtual Routers

2.5.1 Function and Significance of Virtual Routers in Network Security

A virtual router is a software-based routing framework that forwards traffic between different virtual networks or the external network within a virtual environment [24]. Like their physical counterparts, virtual routers use routing tables and protocols to determine the most efficient path for data packet transmission.

In terms of network security, virtual routers play a significant role. They can isolate network traffic, serving a function similar to physical routers in creating boundaries between virtual network segments. They also can enforce security policies and provide a point of security control within a virtual network that can better protect it from intrusion and attacks. Figure 2.6 depicts the role of securing virtual routers, essential for maintaining a secure and efficient network. Key elements include ACLs, authentication, authorization, routing protocol security, traffic filtering, inspection, logging, monitoring, and data encryption. These components manage incoming and outgoing traffic, restrict administrative access, and support rapid detection and response to security incidents.

2.5.2 Potential Security Risks Associated with Virtual Routers

Albeit crucial, virtual routers also come with potential security risks:

- *Misconfiguration:* Incorrect settings may inadvertently create vulnerabilities that can be exploited.
- *Unauthorized access:* Weak access control may lead to unauthorized changes in the network configuration that can compromise system security.

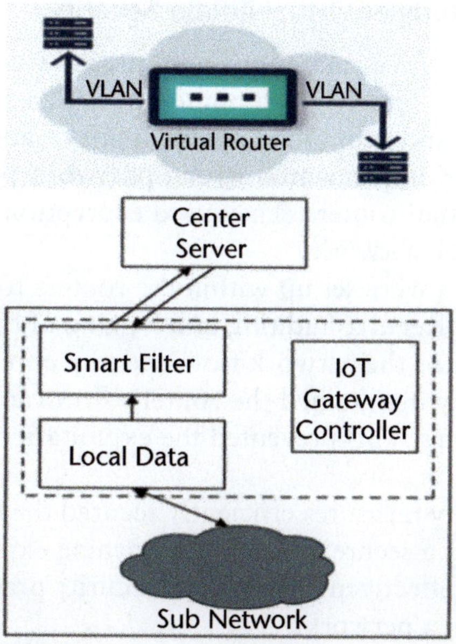

Figure 2.6 Securing virtual routers [25].

- *Software vulnerabilities:* Bugs or flaws in the router's software can expose the system to cyber threats.
- *Routing attacks:* These attacks could manipulate routing information to redirect, block, or modify traffic, leading to potential data loss or network compromise.

2.5.3 Techniques for Securing Virtual Routers

The following procedures can help to secure virtual routers:

- *Strong password policies:* Implement robust password policies for router access. This includes using long, complex passwords and regularly changing them.
- *Usage of encryption protocols:* Utilize secure routing protocols with encryption to protect sensitive routing information.
- *Router firewall rules implementation:* Use embedded or standalone firewalls with specific rules to control incoming and outgoing traffic through the router.
- *Regular auditing and logging:* Regularly audit and log router configuration, security policies, and all user activity to identify potential threats or unauthorized changes.
- *Software updates:* Keep the router's software updated to reduce the risk of known vulnerability exploitation.

2.5.4 A Case Study of Virtual Router Security

A global e-learning company provides a case study of securing a virtual router. Security was a top priority with numerous daily users accessing wide-ranging educational content and submitting personal information.

The company implemented strong password policies to prevent unauthorized access to the virtual routers. They used encryption protocols to secure data transmission across the network.

Firewall rules were set up within the routers to filter out any malicious or undesirable traffic. Regular auditing and logging of the router's activities enabled the IT team to monitor the network flow and any potential unauthorized access [26].

The company maintained the router's firmware through proactive monitoring and timely updates. This prevented the exploitation of any known firmware-based vulnerabilities.

These security measures efficiently secured the company's virtual environment, ensuring its users a secure and smooth learning experience. This case highlights the importance and effectiveness of proper security practices in managing and securing virtual routers in a network.

2.6 Securing Virtual Networks

2.6.1 Overarching Techniques to Secure Virtual Networks

Security can be improved by virtualization because it abstracts the underlying hardware. All network traffic is routed through a central gateway, enabling enterprises to manage secure networks, isolate sensitive data, and segment their networks. Making monitoring and control easier stops harmful activity such as malware and DoS attacks. Because desktop virtualization stores all data and apps on a single server, it also aids in desktop system management and security. This prevents data leaks and illegal access, and only authorized users can access particular data and applications. Virtualization can be a useful tool for companies of all sizes, even though it is not a panacea for all security issues. Thanks to virtual networks' higher security level, sensitive data is more difficult for hackers to access than traditional physical networks.

Securing virtual networks involves a multifaceted approach, which includes:

- Implementing network segmentation to isolate network traffic, thus preventing lateral movement of threats;
- Creating and enforcing stringent access and identity controls to limit who can access the network;
- Leveraging encryption protocols to secure sensitive data during transmission;
- Routinely updating all security software to patch known vulnerabilities;
- Regularly auditing the network to identify potential weaknesses;
- Designing robust firewall configurations to control and monitor all incoming and outgoing network traffic;
- Implementing spam filters to block potentially harmful emails.

Figure 2.7 illustrates the security of virtual networks, designed to safeguard resources and data within cloud environments. Key components include network security groups (NSGs), virtual firewalls, encryption, network segmentation, access control, intrusion detection and prevention systems, and ongoing auditing and monitoring. Together, these measures create a layered security strategy, ensuring authorized access, secure communication, enhanced visibility, and reduced impact from potential threats.

2.6.2 Significance of Regular Software Updates

Software updates in regular intervals are essential in securing virtual networks. They frequently contain patches for known security vulnerabilities and helping the nature of the system stay ahead of the evolving threat landscape. Outdated software has vulnerabilities that exploit the hackers regularly. Therefore, continuous updates facilitate optimal network security.

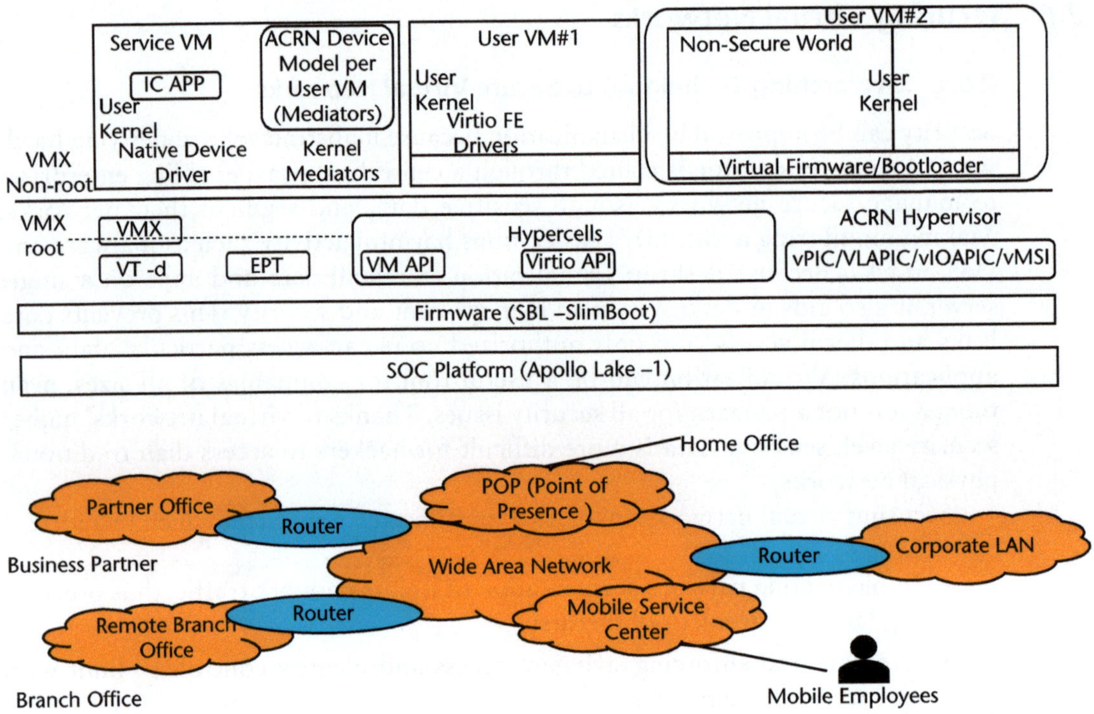

Figure 2.7 Securing virtual networks [28].

2.6.3 The Role of Spam Filters in Ensuring Network Security

Spam filters are significant for network security as they help to block incoming and outgoing malicious emails carrying threats such as malware, phishing attempts, or ransomware attacks. Spam filters play a proactive role in protecting the network by preventing these emails from reaching the users or being sent out.

2.6.4 Understanding Identity and Access Control in Securing Virtual Networks

The identity and access control tool is sophisticated to manage so that we can have data regarding who gets access to the network and what they can do within it. Such control measures mitigate the risk of unauthorized access and potential network compromises. Techniques such as multifactor authentication, most minor privilege policies, and role-based access control are common strategies for solidifying network security.

2.6.5 Importance of Robust and Updated Firewall Rules

Firewall rules serve as a first line of defense in a network by regulating network traffic. Regularly updating these rules allows for adaptation to new risks and threats. Moreover, well-defined firewall rules facilitate the effective filtering of suspicious connections and the prevention of attacks.

2.6.6 Encryption Measures for Data in Virtual Networks

Data encryption translates data into another form or code so only users with access to a secret key or password can read it. Encryption is a powerful tool for protecting sensitive data during transmission across a virtual network. It reduces the potential risk of data breaches or leaks, even if unwarranted interception occurs.

2.6.7 Regular Audits to Assess Vulnerabilities

A regular audit of a network's security helps to identify potential vulnerabilities that could expose the network to threats. These audits can include penetration testing, security reviews, and checks for adherence to security policies [28]. Regular audits allow prompt mitigation of mitigable vulnerabilities and reinforce the network's security.

Adhering to these principles will help to safeguard any virtual network against a wide range of threats, ensuring the confidentiality, integrity, and availability of network data and services.

2.7 Best Practices for Network Security in Virtualized Environments

Securing VMs is essential to protect the integrity, confidentiality, and availability of data and applications in virtualized environments. As VMs host multiple OSs on shared hardware, they bring increased flexibility but also unique security challenges [29]. To ensure robust security, organizations must implement best practices across general security, establish strong security policies and procedures, and stay aware of emerging trends. This chapter covers these core areas, emphasizing proactive strategies and forward-thinking solutions for VM security.

2.7.1 Regular Patching and Updating of Software

Patching and updating virtual network components, including firewalls, routers, and switches, must be done regularly. This process ensures that these components have the latest security patches and bug fixes, reducing known vulnerabilities. It shields the network against attacks that exploit these known security gaps. Patch management and routine updates are essential for VM security. Cyber criminals take advantage of flaws in operating systems, apps, and hypervisors [31]. Automated patch management reduces security flaws and guarantees uniformity across virtual environments. Before being deployed, patches should be tested in a controlled setting to guarantee compatibility and prevent interruptions. Frequent software updates are also necessary because out-of-date software may not be compatible with new security standards and can expose systems to vulnerabilities. For systems with complex configurations or critical applications, regular software updates are especially crucial.

2.7.2 Implementing a Solid Data Encryption Strategy

Securely transmitting data across a virtual network is crucial. Implementing a solid data encryption strategy helps to protect data from interceptors. Data encryption converts plaintext into unreadable ciphertext, rendering the stolen data useless without the decryption key [31]. Secure transmission protocols such as Secure Sockets Layer (SSL) or Transport Layer Security (TLS) can be used for additional data security in virtual networks.

2.7.3 Ensuring Robust Identity and Access Control

Implementing effective identity and access management (IAM) policies is necessary. IAM policies ensure that only authorized users have access to sensitive network areas or data, through a variety of implementation methods such as multifactor authentication, role-based access control, or the least privilege policy. Azure Identity Management and Access Control security best practices are based on consensus opinions and Azure platform capabilities and feature sets. This section aims to be a generalized map, in any existing state, to a more robust security posture after deployment and is based on the "5 steps to securing your identity infrastructure" checklist. Azure Identity Management and Access Control security best practices are: (1) treat identity as a primary security perimeter; (2) centralize identity management; (3) manage connected tenants; (4) enable single sign on (SSO); (5) turn on conditional access plan as a regular security improvement; (6) enable password management; (7a) an enforce multifactor verification for users; (7b) a use role-based access control; (8) lower exposure of privileged accounts; (9) control where resources are located; and (10) use Microsoft Entra ID for storage authentication. To make security controls and detections focusing on user and service identities, use Microsoft Entra ID to collocate your controls with user and service identities [32]. You can bring identity management into a centralized way of managing and protecting identities in a hybrid identity scenario by collocating on-premises and cloud directories to manage and bridge identities using a single Microsoft Entra instance, and using Microsoft Entra Connect to synchronize your on-premises and cloud directories. You want to not synchronize accounts that have high privileges in your existing Active Directory instances and enable password hash synchronization to stop attackers from being able to replay leaked credentials from previous attacks. When developing new applications, use Microsoft Entra ID as an authentication service and leverage the capabilities that are available to you to support authentication, which include using Microsoft Entra ID for employees, Microsoft Entra B2B for guest users and external partners, and Azure AD B2C, which controls the manner how customers sign up, sign in, and manage their profiles as they use your applications [33]. These organizations that do not connect their on-premises identity to their cloud identity will have greater management burdens and more opportunity for error and potential security exposure. You can manage connected tenants by essentially having a way to see all subscriptions connected to your production environment or network using either Azure ExpressRoute or via site-to-site VPN. A global administrator in Microsoft Entra ID can elevate permissions to the user access administrator role and see all subscriptions and managed groups connected to your environment [34]. Once you assess the risks, you can remove this elevated access. Then enable SSO for devices, apps, and services from anywhere to increase user productivity when and where required. Using the same identity solution for all apps and resources means you will achieve SSO and your users will be able to sign in and access resources (on premises or in the cloud) using the same set of credentials. Microsoft Entra ID continues to extend the Active Directory to the cloud. Users can now use their primary work or school account on domain-joined devices, for company resources, as well as for all web and software as a service (SaaS) applications. Users do not have to remember multiple usernames and passwords, and their application access can be automatically provisioned (or redirected) to the cloud. In conclusion, Azure identity management and access control security best practices emphasize treating identity as the primary security perimeter, centralizing identity management, managing connected tenants, allowing SSO, and enabling SSO [35]. By utilizing the best practices of Azure identity management and access control, organizations can improve not only their security posture, but also their productivity by establishing a more secure user environment.

2.7.4 Vulnerability Audits

Periodic vulnerability audits assess potential weaknesses in the network. These audits may include penetration testing (simulating cybersecurity attacks) and regular scans for unpatched software or configuration errors. These practices highlight vulnerabilities, allowing network administrators to fortify the network accordingly [36]. Vulnerability assessment is a process for identifying security weaknesses in an information system. Vulnerability assessments help to determine whether an information system is susceptible to known vulnerabilities, categorize the severity of the identified vulnerabilities, and recommend a course of action based on the risks and vulnerabilities found. This layer of security can identify and prevent threats, such as SQL injection attacks, cross-site scripting (XSS) attacks, privilege escalation from inadequate authentication methods, and poorly secured defaults. Vulnerability assessments may include host assessments, network and wireless assessments, database assessments, and application scans. The vulnerability scan process has four distinct parts: the testing, analysis, assessment, and remediation stages. Identifying vulnerabilities takes the form of a compiled list of vulnerabilities for a specific application or information system. Vulnerabilities can be identified through manual testing and analysis or modern automated tools. Analyzing vulnerabilities includes identifying the source of the vulnerability and the root cause of the vulnerability. Simultaneously, risk assessment assigns a rank or severity score to each vulnerability based on factors such as system impact, data at risk, business functions at risk, effort to exploit, and potential impact. Remediation represents the closing of security gaps usually completed in a joint effort involving security, development, and operation team members. Vulnerability assessment tools, such as web applications, protocols, and network scanners, should be set to automatically scan for both new and previously identified vulnerabilities. New and regular automated scanning of critical IT systems should be part of the ongoing vulnerability assessment process [37].

2.7.5 Network Segmentation Approach

Network segmentation involves dividing a network into smaller, isolated networks or subnetworks. This reduces the attack surface and limits the potential spread of threats within the network, thus enhancing security. Techniques such as setting up private VLANs or implementing micro-segmentation can help significantly. Network segmentation is a process that divides a computer network into smaller parts to improve performance and security [38]. It is about managing how traffic flows across the parts, whether by blocking any traffic in one part from reaching another or by limiting the flow by traffic type, source, and destination. Your segmentation policies outline how your network is segmented. For example, a large bank that has multiple branch offices can enforce its security policy by blocking any branch traffic from reaching its financial system. This will reduce overall traffic on the network, allowing the financial system to perform better for the financial analysts. Historically, using things such as internal firewalls, ACLs and VLAN configurations were possible strategies of segmentation [39]. However with software-defined access technology, segmentation became easier, simply by tagging or grouping types of networks that enable more detailed and flexible policies that meet their specific business use or organizational needs. Micro-segmentation uses more information within the segmentation policies such as application layer information in order to meet their specific business use or organization needs.

2.7.6 Proper Configuration of Virtual Network Components

The proper configuration of all elements in a virtual network, including virtual switches, routers, and firewalls, is extremely important. Misconfiguration can lead to weaknesses in security. Therefore, it is very important to practice sound configurations with verification on a regular basis in order to maintain the highest level of network security. Hyper-V Virtual Networking configuration and best practices are important to those who are new to virtualization and are used to another hypervisor [40]. The Hyper-V Virtual Switch is the most important element of networking in Hyper-V, since it works at layer 2 as the middleman to the virtual switch ports directing packets to MAC addresses, tagging VLANs, performing quality-of-service tasks, and isolating traffic to the virtual adapter that has received it. There are three types of Hyper-V network switches: private, internal, and external. Private switches only allow communications between VMs on its host, but do not use any physical adapter. Internal switches will allow the management OS to have a virtual adapter and will allow direct communications between VMs and virtual adapters using the same internal switch. External switches must connect to a physical adapter in order to be able to communicate between the physical network, the management OS, and the virtual adapters on the VMs [41]. After recognizing the different types of virtual switches, the various elements connected to virtual switches, how to use best practices, and the differences between Hyper-V and other hypervisors or virtualization technologies, a user should feel confident in being able to set up and manage their virtual networks in Hyper-V. The Hyper-V Manager GUI and PowerShell with New-VMSwitch cmdlet provide vagaries in the description of settings, and it may not be readily apparent what the underlying technology is designed to accomplish. Network adapter teaming is natively supported in the Windows Server Operating

System, allowing a user to bond two or more adapters into a single logical communications channel (link) and share or transit network traffic. The Hyper-V server can team the physical adapters and create a new adapter called "virtual" that can no longer be bound to anything other than the teaming protocol. The dynamic load balancing method is usually preferred, as it provides the best of the Hyper-V Port and Transport Ports [42].

2.7.7 Implementing Failover Measures

Having failover measures in place enhances network resilience by automatically rerouting network traffic in case of a system failure or disruption. This ensures the virtual network's availability, a vital aspect of network security. Leveraging virtualization's inherent redundancy and scalability capabilities allows for the quick spin-up of replacement VMs or entire networks, thereby minimizing downtime. Downtime is inevitable for most enterprise services, whether for maintenance, patching, malicious attacks, mistakes, or natural disasters. To minimize data loss and recover services as quickly as possible, the following best practices for configuring your data center and applications to failover and restart as soon as possible are essential. Automated monitoring and restarting before VM failover are critical in modern data centers. Management tools should recognize when a service is down, log the failure, alert the administrator, and automatically attempt to restart the service, or the VM, on the same host. From a timing perspective, resumption on a VM on the original host will be the fastest, as the resources will already be assigned. A remote failover would need to remount the disk and assign memory as well as CPU. There are several local VM failover options, but, first, you must deploy a highly available host cluster for VMs. If the application cannot be started on the original host, it could fail over and restart on a different server, in the same local cluster, and domain if applicable. Failover clusters usually have configurable options that allow for how quickly a failure will be detected through the intra-cluster health check between the nodes. These settings consist of the frequency of a health check (same subnet delay and cross subnet delay) and how many health checks that it can miss before failover takes place (same subnet threshold and cross subnet threshold). When a failure has been detected, the VM will move to a different node and it will start again with its last valid configuration that was saved to shared storage. The replicating to a disaster recovery site to enable VM failover process is another layer of disaster recovery and failover, which many organizations do take for granted. When the overall data center is down, you must recover your business services at a secondary site using a disaster recovery methodology. Even in the case where the business does not have an additional location, many disaster recovery technologies, such as Microsoft Azure public cloud, can leverage best practices. When a VM fails over to a different host, keeping the same IP address is recommended so that end-users can connect to it right away, without having to reconfigure their endpoints. This means that the app or VM should use the same subnet across all host environments to allow for the same IP address to be used. The most common methods for maintaining a static IP address on the same subnet following the failover are to use a stretched VLAN across the sites or using network virtualization to abstract the physical networks of both sites. Speeding up clients' reconnection times during a VM failover with different IPs is important [43]. If you need to alter the IP address following the failover, there are several approaches to hasten the process by which the client receives the new IP address and reconnects to the VM. For example, if you are using known static IP addresses at both sites, you can configure the application or VM to try using either IP address in the cluster property that says Register All Providers IP, set to TRUE. While replication is critical, it is also necessary to do backups and test your recovery processes routinely. Backup providers typically offer more functionality than replication and are more fault-tolerant to various failures. Most backups are completed offline and prevent "bad" data from being replicated from your primary VM to your replica [44].

2.8 Summary

This chapter gave an introduction to network security within virtualized environments. It shared a definition of security in virtualized environments, components of virtual network architecture, and the relationships between network security and virtual network architecture. This chapter talked about the use of virtual switches and how they can fit into network security, and what their vulnerabilities are and how to secure them. It also considered what a virtual firewall does, its vulnerabilities, and the risk associated with protecting a virtual environment. Techniques for securing virtual firewalls include regular software updates, creating comprehensive security policies, vulnerability testing, and prioritizing scalability. The chapter also discussed the function and significance of virtual routers in network security, including potential security risks and methods for securing them. Techniques include strong password policies, encryption protocols, router firewall rules implementation, regular auditing and logging, and software updates. This chapter concluded with a case study of virtual router security. Further, this chapter delved into the multifaceted and essential subject of network security in virtual environments. We started by understanding the basic tenets of network security and elucidating the significance of honing a secure network within a virtual infrastructure to mitigate potential threats and secure data and systems in virtual environments.

A comprehensive review of the virtual network architecture was conducted, explicating its constituents and impact on network security. By analyzing a case study, we could tangibly perceive the practical implications of this architecture and its significance in terms of security.

Diving deeper into individual components, we explored the security dynamics related to virtual switches. From comprehending their role in network security to identifying vulnerabilities, we examined various measures such as traffic filtering, network segmentation, usage of private VLANs, regularly conducting system checks and updates, and implementing access control measures to secure these switches. Our understanding was further enriched through the examination of a case study.

Virtual firewalls, another crucial asset in network security, expose potential vulnerabilities that can be mitigated through regular software updates, stringent security policies, regular vulnerability testing, and prioritizing scalability. An insightful case study further helped to consolidate the learned concepts.

We broached the concept of virtual routers, their relevance in network security, and the prevalent security risks that they can pose. Approaches like solid password policies, encryption protocol adherence, firewall rules, and routine audits were highlighted as techniques to secure virtual routers. A case study on virtual router security provided practical insights.

This chapter also offered an overview of measures to secure virtual networks, emphasizing regular software updates, spam filters, identity control, robust firewall rules, encryption procedures, and routine audits to identify vulnerabilities.

Concerning best practices in network security for virtualized settings, we emphasized the need for regular updates and patching of software, data encryption strategies, sturdy identity, and access controls, regular vulnerability audits, the adoption of the network segmentation approach, the correct configuration of virtual network components, and the incorporation of failover measures.

Wrapping up, this chapter affirmed the critical role of continuous monitoring and updates in ensuring network security. It is crucial to keep guards up-to-date against evolving threats and to ensure the effectiveness of applied measures. Reflecting on it, it is evident that network security in virtual environments is not a set-it-and-forget-it job but a relentless endeavor where constant vigilance, knowledge updating, and adaptability make a robust defense.

References

[1] Schwab, K., *The Fourth Industrial Revolution*, New York: Crown Currency, 2017.

[2] Schulz, G., *The Green and Virtual Data Center*, Boca Raton, FL: CRC Press, 2016.

[3] Mitcham, Z. S., *Key Security Concepts That All CISOs Should Know-Cyber Guardians: A CISO's Guide to Protecting the Digital World*, eBookIt.com, 2024.

[4] Belapurkar, A., et al., *Distributed Systems Security: Issues, Processes and Solutions*, New York: John Wiley & Sons, 2009.

[5] Mukherjee, A., *Network Security Strategies: Protect Your Network and Enterprise Against Advanced Cybersecurity Attacks and Threats*, Birmingham, UK: Packt Publishing Ltd., 2020.

[6] Kadu, N. B., and P. P. Jadhav, "High Performance Computing with Inter-Virtual-Machine Communication," *Journal of Cyber Security Technology*, Vol. 8, No. 3, July 2, 2024, pp. 191–203.

[7] Knapp, E. D., *Industrial Network Security: Securing Critical Infrastructure Networks for Smart Grid, SCADA, and Other Industrial Control Systems*, New York: Elsevier, 2024.

[8] Jariwala, M., *The Cyber Security Roadmap A Comprehensive Guide to Cyber Threats, Cyber Laws, and Cyber Security Training for a Safer Digital World*, Mayur Jariwala, 2023.

[9] Harmening, J. T., and R. DeVitto, "Cloud Security Access Control," *Cloud Computing Security: Foundations and Challenges*, September 19, 2016, p. 141.

[10] Ibrahim, A. S., J. Hamlyn-Harris, and J. Grundy, "Emerging Security Challenges of Cloud Virtual Infrastructure," arXiv preprint arXiv:1612.09059, December 29, 2016.

[11] Chandramouli, R., *Security Recommendations for Hypervisor Deployment*, National Institute of Standards and Technology, 2014.

[12] Jain, R., S. Paul, and J. Kim, "Network Virtualization and Software Defined Networking for Cloud Computing: A Survey," *IEEE Communications Magazine*, Vol. 51, No. 11, November 2013, pp. 24–31.

[13] Provos, N., and T. Holz, *Virtual Honeypots: From Botnet Tracking to Intrusion Detection*, Boston, MA: Pearson Education, 2007.

[14] Subramanian, M., T. A. Gonsalves, and N. U. Rani, *Network Management: Principles and Practice*, Delhi, India: Pearson Education India, 2010.

[15] Nayyar, A., B. Singla, and P. Nagrath, (eds.), *Software Defined Networks: Architecture and Applications*, New York: John Wiley & Sons, 2022.

[16] Jebbar, W. A., and M. Al-Zubaidie, "Transaction-Based Blockchain Systems Security Improvement Employing Micro-Segmentation Controlled by Smart Contracts and Detection of Saddle Goatfish," *SN Computer Science*, Vol. 5, No. 7, October 2024, pp. 1–23.

[17] Patel, H. L., D. L. DeMenthon, and A. R. Al-Khaddar, "A Survey of Security for Cloud Computing Virtual Networks," *IEEE Access*, Vol. 5, 2017, pp. 13115–13131.

[18] Pujolle, G., *Software Networks: Virtualization, SDN, 5G, and Security*, New York: John Wiley & Sons, 2020.

[19] Bringhenti, D., et al., "Automatic, Verifiable and Optimized Policy-Based Security Enforcement for SDN-Aware IoT Networks," *Computer Networks*, Vol. 213, August 4, 2022, p. 109123.

[20] Gupta, S., A. Kumar, and S. N. Singh, "Virtual Switches for Efficient Virtual Network Management," *IEEE Communications Magazine*, Vol. 53, No. 5, May 2015, pp. 72–79.

[21] Desalegn, W., J. Shaikh, and B. Taye, *Methodology to Improve Control Plane Security in SDN Environments*, Boca Raton, FL: CRC Press, 2024.

[22] Kurek, T., M. Niemiec, and A. Lason, "Performance Evaluation of a Firewall Service Based on Virtualized IncludeOS Unikernels," *Scientific Reports*, Vol. 14, No. 1, January 4, 2024, p. 557.

[23] Mishra, S. R., N. P. Singh, and S. K. Jena, "A Survey of Virtual Firewalls for Cloud Computing Security," *IEEE Transactions on Cloud Computing*, Vol. 5, No. 2, 2017, pp. 99–107.

[24] Mohamed, A., et al., "Software-Defined Networks for Resource Allocation in Cloud Computing: A Survey," *Computer Networks*, Vol. 195, August 4, 2021, p. 108151.

[25] Chan, A. T., A. S. K. Chai, and D. Z. Adzic, "Virtual Router Architectures for Secure Cloud Computing," *IEEE Transactions on Network and Service Management*, Vol. 12, No. 4, 2015, pp. 456–467.

[26] Rajasoundaran, S., et al., "A Deep Experimental Analysis of Energy-Proficient Firewall Policies and Security Practices for Resource Limited Wireless Networks," *Security and Privacy*, 2024, p. e450.

[27] Zhang, X., et al., "Virtual Network Security in Cloud Computing," *IEEE Transactions on Cloud Computing*, Vol. 4, No. 4, October-December 2016, pp. 395–408.

[28] Anirudh, U. N., and S. S. Darshan, "Role-Based Virtuosity in Virtual Environments: A Technical Exploration of Access Control and Authentication Mechanisms," in *Cloud Security*, London, UK: Chapman and Hall/CRC, 2024, pp. 183–196.

[29] Singh, S., *The Cybercrime Spectrum: Understanding Digital Threats and Security*, Laxmi Book Publication, 2024.

[30] Bhatia, D., *Cryptography: The Hidden Message*, Blue Rose Publishers, 2022.

[31] Maxwell, R., *Azure Arc Systems Management: Governance and Administration of Multi-Cloud and Hybrid IT Estates*, New York: Springer Nature, 2024.

[32] Rising, P., *Microsoft 365 Security, Compliance, and Identity Administration: Plan and Implement Security and Compliance Strategies for Microsoft 365 and Hybrid Environments*, Birmingham, UK: Packt Publishing Ltd., 2023.

[33] Pluta, C., *Exam Ref AZ-104 Microsoft Azure Administrator*, Seattle, WA: Microsoft Press, 2024.

[34] Tlili, F., et al., "Investigation on Vulnerabilities, Threats and Attacks Prohibiting UAVs Charging and Depleting UAVs Batteries: Assessments & Countermeasures," *Ad Hoc Networks*, Vol. 129, April 15, 2022, p. 102805.

[35] Magnusson, A., *Practical Vulnerability Management: A Strategic Approach to Managing Cyber Risk*, No Starch Press, 2020.

[36] Kumar, A., "Study and Analysis of Different Segmentation Methods for Brain Tumor MRI Application," *Multimedia Tools and Applications*, Vol. 82, No. 5, February 2023, pp. 7117–7139.

[37] Vemula, S., J. Gooley, and R. Hasan, *Cisco Software-Defined Access*, Cisco Press, 2020.

[38] Dakic, V., et al., *Mastering KVM Virtualization: Design Expert Data Center Virtualization Solutions with the Power of Linux KVM*, Birmingham, UK: Packt Publishing Ltd., 2020.

[39] Patrão, L., *VMware VSphere Essentials: A Practical Approach to VSphere Deployment and Management*, New York: Springer Nature, 2024.

[40] Krause, J., *Mastering Windows Server 2022: Comprehensive Administration of Your Windows Server Environment*, Birmingham, UK: Packt Publishing Ltd., 2023.

[41] Davis, J., *Modern System Administration*, New York: O'Reilly Media, 2022.

[42] Sun, K., J. Lee, and Y. Kim, "LISP-Based Control Plane for Service Connectivity in Multi-Cluster Cloud Systems," *IEEE Access*, Vol. 10, February 28, 2022, pp. 24786–24796.

[43] Hao, F., Q. Xiao, and K. Chon, "COVID-19 and China's Hotel Industry: Impacts, a Disaster Management Framework, and Post-Pandemic Agenda," *International Journal of Hospitality Management*, Vol. 90, September 1, 2020, p. 102636.

[44] Kvet, M., *Developing Robust Date and Time Oriented Applications in Oracle Cloud: A Comprehensive Guide to Efficient Date and Time Management in Oracle Cloud*, Birmingham, UK: Packt Publishing Ltd., 2023.

CHAPTER 3

Virtual Machine Security

3.1 Introduction

With organizations continuing to embrace cloud computing and virtualization technologies to increase efficiency and scalability, the need for VM security becomes more urgent. VMs provide abstraction of hardware resources, which allows for multiple operating systems to run as a single physical host simultaneously [1]. This paradigm shift maximizes resource utilization and facilitates flexibility in deploying applications across diverse environments. However, the convenience of VMs comes with inherent security challenges, demanding a rigorous and multilayered approach to protect both the underlying infrastructure and the virtual workloads.

In essence, VM security is a critical aspect of modern IT governance, encompassing the protection of various components—from the hypervisor that manages the VMs to the guest OSs that directly support applications [2]. Each layer presents unique vulnerabilities that, if left unaddressed, may lead to catastrophic breaches or data loss. For instance, a vulnerability in a guest operating system can potentially be exploited to gain unauthorized access to other VMs or, in extreme cases, compromise the host itself. This interconnectedness necessitates an integrated security strategy that addresses the specific risks associated with each component of a virtualization environment [3].

This chapter unfolds by first examining the VM architecture, which lays the foundation for understanding how virtual machines operate and interact with each other and the host hardware. This section will describe the critical components of a VM, covering the hypervisor, the virtual hardware layer, and the guest OSs. The distinctions between Type-1 and Type-2 hypervisors help to illustrate how the selection of a hypervisor will affect the overall security posture. Furthermore, the underlying technologies enabling virtualization, such as paravirtualization and full virtualization, will be explored to illustrate their significance in resource management and performance [4].

Following the architecture overview, the focus will shift to securing guest OSs. The security of a VM is often only as strong as the OS that it runs. This section will delve into practices for hardening guest OSs, such as timely application of security patches, turning off unnecessary services, and implementing stringent configurations [5]. We will also review the integration of intrusion detection and prevention systems (IDPS), which are important in monitoring activities happening within the guest OS, and the significance of solid access control systems designed to prevent unauthorized access.

Next, we will discuss securing hypervisors, the critical software that abstracts and allocates resources among VMs. Hypervisors serve as the first line of defense against inter-VM threats, making their security paramount [6]. In this segment, we will identify common vulnerabilities and attack vectors targeting hypervisors and highlight best practices for secure configuration. Measures such as segregation of management interfaces, enforcement of robust authentication protocols, and consistent monitoring will be examined to safeguard this pivotal component of the virtual infrastructure.

The chapter will then address the security of virtualization management servers, which orchestrate virtual resources' deployment, management, and scaling. These servers are desirable targets for attackers, as gaining control can lead to the manipulation of multiple VMs [7]. We will uncover security controls for protecting management servers, including regular software updates, network segmentation, and incident response strategies to ensure rapid recovery from security incidents.

Following these in-depth analyses, we will present a compilation of best practices for VM security. This section will synthesize the knowledge acquired throughout the chapter, providing actionable strategies organizations can implement to create a resilient security posture. Emphasizing the importance of regular security audits, automation of security measures, and user training, we will underscore that adequate security is not a one-time effort but an ongoing commitment requiring vigilance and adaptability [8].

Finally, the summary will encapsulate the critical discussions, reinforcing the necessity of a thorough understanding of VM security principles and practices. As organizations continue to embrace virtualization, IT security professionals must have the knowledge and tactics to secure these environments against the evolving landscape of cyber threats [9].

Therefore, this chapter aims to deliver a holistic understanding of VM security, guiding readers through the complexities of securing virtual environments. We strive to empower IT professionals to protect their organizations in an increasingly virtualized world by addressing architectural fundamentals and practical security measures.

3.2 VM Architecture

The architecture of the VM is one of the major foundations of virtualization technology that allows several OSs to operate independently on the same physical hardware [10]. The architecture uses a hypervisor, which manages hardware, to provide a service to create, operate, and manage isolated environments in the same machine. This capability has revolutionized resource utilization, management, and optimization, particularly in data centers and cloud computing environments, where flexibility, scalability, and cost savings are essential [10].

Each VM operates independently with its own operating system, applications, and virtualized hardware, offering a highly efficient way to deploy heterogeneous workloads on common resources. Figure 3.1 illustrates the VM architecture and encompasses three key components: the host hardware, the hypervisor, and the VM. The host hardware provides CPU, memory, storage, and network resources, while the hypervisor manages the resources [11]. VMs are isolated instances with their operating systems and applications, enabling efficient resource usage, isolation, and scalability on the same physical machine. In this section, we will explore the components of VM architecture, examine different types of hypervisors, and discuss the technologies that support virtualization.

3.3 Components of VM Architecture

At the core of VM architecture are essential components that work together to create an isolated, secure, and efficient virtualized environment [4]. These components include the hypervisor, guest OS, and virtualization management servers, each playing a crucial role in delivering a seamless virtualization experience.

3.3.1 Hypervisor

A hypervisor, or VMM, is an essential component of the VM architecture. The hypervisor is the virtualization layer that allows multiple OSs to operate simultaneously on the same physical machine by managing the hardware resources and isolating VMs [12]. Its core functions include resource allocation, isolation, hardware virtualization, and performance monitoring:

- *Resource allocation:* The hypervisor controls and allocates CPU, memory, disk, and network resources to each VM based on its requirements.
- *Isolation:* Each VM runs in its isolated environment, preventing interference between VMs and enhancing security and stability.

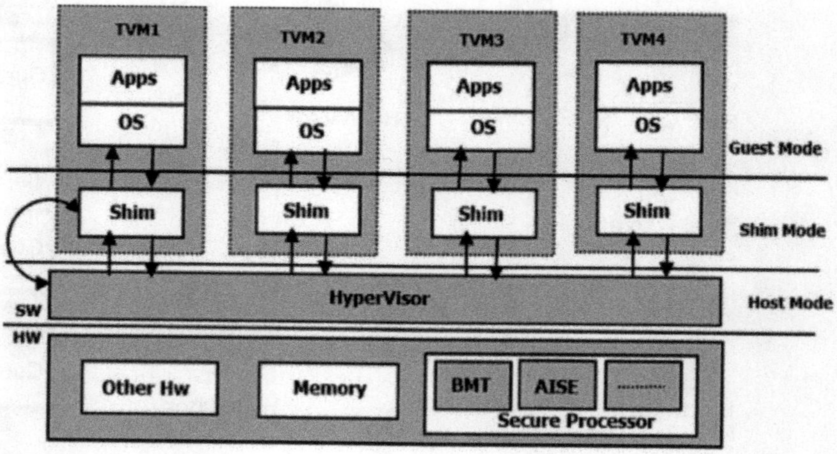

Figure 3.1 VM architecture [10].

- *Hardware virtualization:* The hypervisor abstracts physical hardware, presenting virtualized CPU, memory, storage, and network resources to each VM.
- *Performance monitoring:* It monitors VM performance and resource usage, ensuring efficient allocation and identifying potential bottlenecks.

3.3.2 Types of Hypervisors

Hypervisors, which are the basic technology that enables virtualization, are separated into two types. These types of hypervisors have different characteristics, and uses, and some advantages and disadvantages. Figure 3.2 shows types of hypervisors and explains two main types: type-1 hypervisor (bare-metal), which runs directly on hardware for better performance and efficiency, and type-2 hypervisor (hosted), which runs on a host OS, making it less efficient while easier to set up.

3.3.2.1 Type-1 (Bare-Metal) Hypervisors

Type-1 hypervisors, or bare-metal hypervisors, run directly on physical hardware without needing a host OS. This direct connection to hardware maximizes efficiency, performance, and security.

Their characteristics are:

- *Direct hardware access:* They interact directly with hardware components such as CPU and memory, reducing latency.

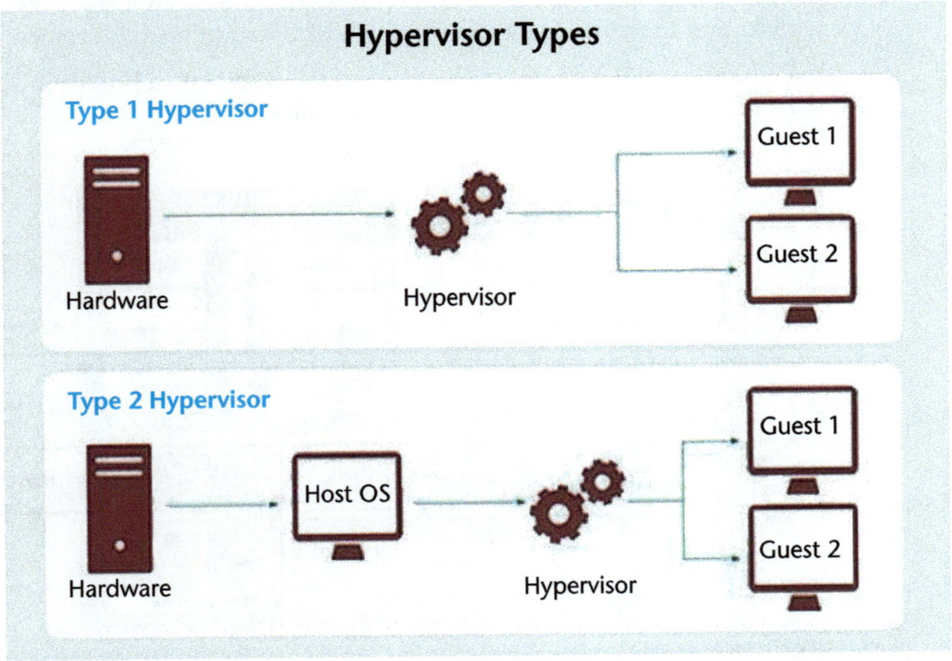

Figure 3.2 Types of hypervisors.

- *Enhanced security and isolation:* These hypervisors reduce security vulnerabilities by operating independently from a host OS.
- *Efficient resource management:* They dynamically allocate resources based on VM needs, lowering the risk of resource contention.

Examples of type-1 hypervisors are:

- *VMware ESXi:* Known for reliability and compatibility, it is widely used in enterprise environments.
- *Microsoft Hyper-V:* Popular for Windows infrastructures, particularly in data centers and the cloud.
- *Xen:* Open-source, commonly used in cloud platforms such as AWS.

Their benefits are:

- *Performance:* Near-native performance suited for demanding applications such as databases.
- *Scalability:* Ideal for large deployments such as data centers and cloud services.
- *Security:* Lack of a host OS reduces vulnerabilities to external threats.

3.3.2.2 Type-2 (Hosted) Hypervisors

Type-2 hypervisors, or hosted hypervisors, operate on top of an existing host OS, leveraging it for resource and device management. These hypervisors are often used in testing and development environments, where setup simplicity and flexibility are priorities.

Their characteristics are:

- *Runs on a host OS:* Requires a fully installed OS (e.g., Windows, macOS, Linux) and runs as an application.
- *Ease of use:* Simple to install and configure, making them ideal for personal use and small environments.
- *Lower performance:* Relies on the host OS, which introduces latency and may not support high-performance needs.

Examples of type-2 hypervisors are:

- *VMware workstation:* A flexible hypervisor for running multiple OSs on desktops and laptops, popular with developers.
- *Oracle VirtualBox:* Open-source and compatible with various OSs, widely used for personal and development work.
- *Parallels desktop:* Often used on macOS to run Windows applications.

Their benefits are:

- *Flexibility and accessibility:* Works across different OSs, supporting cross-platform development.
- *Cost-effective:* Many type-2 hypervisors are accessible or affordable without specialized hardware.
- *Personal use suitability:* Convenient for users needing different OSs on a single machine.

Their limitations are:

- *Performance overhead:* Relies on a host OS, adding layers that reduce performance.
- *Security dependence:* Inherits vulnerabilities from the host OS, exposing VMs if the host is compromised.

3.3.2.3 Summary of Type-1 and Type-2 Hypervisors

Type-1 hypervisor (bare-metal) is directly installed on hardware. Type 1 provides the best performance and security and is recommended for enterprise and large scale implementations.

Type-2 hypervisor (hosted) is installed on top of a host operating system, Type 2 is more user-friendly, has a higher overhead, and is typically only recommended for testing, development, and personal use. Table 3.1 shows the differences.

3.3.3 Guest OSs

Guest OSs are the systems installed on VMs within a virtualized environment [13]. Each VM runs independently with its own OS kernel, applications, and settings, treating the virtualized hardware provided by the hypervisor as though it were physical hardware. This design allows multiple OS types, such as Windows, Linux, and macOS, to run simultaneously on a single host system.

The benefits of guest OSs in VM architecture are:

- *Flexibility:* VMs can host diverse OS types, enabling various applications to coexist within the same physical infrastructure.

Table 3.1 Type-1 Versus Type-2 Hypervisors

Feature	*Type 1 (Bare-Metal)*	*Type 2 (Hosted)*
Deployment	Directly on hardware	On top of a host OS
Performance	Near-native	Lower, due to host OS overhead
Security	High, due to reduced attack surface	Dependent on host OS security
Use case	Data centers, cloud, enterprise	Testing, development, personal use
Examples	VMware ESXi, Microsoft Hyper-V, Xen	VMware Workstation, VirtualBox

- *Isolation:* Each guest OS operates independently, so issues such as crashes or malware in one VM do not affect others.
- *Efficient resource utilization:* Guest OSs leverage shared physical resources while providing a user experience similar to a standalone machine.

The critical functions of guest OSs are:

- *Application hosting:* Each guest OS manages applications, processes, and system resources within its VM as on physical hardware.
- *Network management:* Configures virtual network interfaces and enables communication between VMs and external networks.
- *Security and user management:* Enforces authentication, access controls, and firewall configurations specific to each VM.

3.3.4 Virtual Hardware

VMs are equipped with virtual hardware components that emulate the functions of physical hardware. This virtual hardware typically includes:

- *Virtual CPUs:* The hypervisor allocates abstracted versions of physical CPUs to each VM, allowing the OS to execute tasks.
- *Virtual memory:* Memory allocated to the VM managed by the hypervisor ensures that each VM operates within its designated memory limits.
- *Virtual disk drives:* Emulated storage devices that use image files (such as VMDK VDI) to represent physical storage. The hypervisor translates read/write requests from the guest OS into operations on the storage hardware.
- *Virtual network interfaces:* Network adapters that provide network connectivity to VMs. These interfaces can be bridged to the physical network or configured to remain isolated within internal networks.

3.3.5 Management Interfaces

Hypervisors often come with tools or interfaces that allow system administrators to configure, monitor, and manage the VMs [4]. Standard management functionalities include:

- *Provisioning and deployment:* Creating new VMs from predefined templates or images.
- *Resource allocation:* Dynamically adjusting allocated resources such as CPU, memory, and storage as per demand.
- *Monitoring and reporting:* Tools to observe VM performance metrics, resource consumption, and operational logs.

3.3.6 Virtualization Technology

The technological backbone of VM architecture rests on several key concepts and methodologies that enhance its efficiency and effectiveness:

- *Full virtualization:* Full virtualization allows the guest OS to run unmodified. The hypervisor emulates all necessary hardware, making it appear to the guest OS as if running on a complete physical machine [14]. This technique makes running multiple OS types on the same platform easy, as each VM believes it has direct access to the hardware.
- *Paravirtualization:* In paravirtualization, the guest OS is aware that it is in a virtualized environment and issues certain commands directly to the hypervisor. This method requires modification to the guest OS, but can provide a considerable performance improvement due to the reduction in overhead associated with hardware emulation.
- *Hardware-assisted virtualization:* Modern CPUs come equipped with built-in support for virtualization through technology such as Intel VT-x and AMD-V. This hardware-assisted virtualization allows hypervisors to more efficiently manage VMs by providing hardware-level support for tasks such as memory management and CPU scheduling [15]. It enhances performance and increases the isolation between VMs, reducing the chances of cross-VM tampering.

3.3.7 Network Interface Virtualization

Networking capabilities in a virtualized environment are as critical as performance in other areas. Network interface virtualization allows VMs to communicate with each other, with the host, and with external networks.

- *Virtual switches:* Virtual switches operate similarly to physical network switches but exist in software. They facilitate communication between VMs on the same host and between VMs and external networks [16]. Virtual switches can implement security policies, traffic shaping, and network segmentation within virtual environments.
- *Virtual local area networks (VLANs):* VLANs in a virtual context allow for the segregation of network traffic, much like traditional networking. VMs can be grouped into logical networks, ensuring that sensitive information remains private and secure. The hypervisor manages the implementation of VLANs to maintain segregation and protect data integrity.
- *Network address translation (NAT):* NAT can be used to manage how VMs access external networks while maintaining security by hiding internal IP addresses. This enables VMs to connect to the internet without exposing their actual network configuration, thus reinforcing network security.

Understanding the architecture of VMs is pivotal for comprehending the security risks and implementation strategies that permeate the virtualization landscape.

We gain insights into the complexities of VM operations by examining the integral components, such as hypervisors, guest OSs, and the virtual hardware that they utilize [4]. Additionally, exploring virtualization technologies and network interface virtualization highlights these elements' profound impact on virtualized environments' performance, security, and overall efficiency. As we progress through this chapter, the knowledge of VM architecture will serve as a critical foundation for our exploration of securing guest OSs hand hypervisors and preparing effective management strategies.

3.4 Securing Guest OSs

Securing guest OSs is a crucial aspect of VM security, as vulnerabilities in guest OS can be exploited to compromise the VM itself, the underlying host, and other VMs [17]. A robust security posture for guest OSs involves applying layers of protection, implementing best practices for hardening, and continuously monitoring potential threats.

This section will explore the essential components of securing guest OSs, including hardening practices, access control mechanisms, and the role of IDPS.

3.4.1 OS Hardening

OS hardening is configuring a guest OS to reduce its surface vulnerabilities and improve its security posture [18]. Critical practices for hardening guest OSs include:

- *Regular software updates and patching:* Keeping the guest OS and all installed applications up to date is essential in addressing known vulnerabilities. This involves:
    - Applying security patches immediately upon release, particularly for critical, risky vulnerabilities;
    - Implementing an automated patch management solution ensures consistency and timely updates without human error;
    - Regularly reviewing vendor announcements and security bulletins to remain abreast of necessary updates.
- *Minimizing installed services and applications:* Reducing the number of installed applications and services decreases potential attack vectors [19]. This entails:
    - Conducting an inventory of installed software and disabling or uninstalling any nonessential services or applications;
    - Ensuring that default services are disabled, especially those not actively used.
- *Configuration management:* Configuration management involves setting system settings to secure defaults. This includes:
    - Customizing security configurations for file permissions, network settings, and system logging to enforce least privilege principles;

    - Employing tools such as the Security Content Automation Protocol (SCAP) to assess security configurations against established benchmarks.
- *Firewall and intrusion prevention systems:* Configuring a host-based firewall can significantly enhance security by controlling incoming and outgoing traffic. Features should include:
    - Defining rules to allow traffic only from trusted sources and denying all other access by default;
    - Implementing an intrusion prevention system to monitor inputs for suspicious activities and automatically mitigate any found threats.
- *User and group management:* Establishing strict user and group policies is essential for reducing insider threats and maintaining accountability. This involves:
    - Enforcing strict password regulations, such as those pertaining to complexity and frequent changes;
    - Implementing two-factor authentication for administrative accounts to strengthen access controls;
    - By giving users only the permissions necessary to carry out their duties, the principle of least privilege is being applied. When required, accounts with the proper privileges should be used for all administrative tasks.
- *Data encryption:* Protect sensitive data stored on guest OSs by implementing encryption solutions. This includes:
    - Encrypting disks utilizing technologies such as BitLocker or LUKS for data-at-rest protection.
    - Using Transport Layer Security (TLS) to secure data in transit, particularly when interacting with external networks or services.

3.4.2 IDPS

IDPS are vital in monitoring the security of guest OAs [20]. These systems are designed to identify hostile activity and automatically mitigate threats. Essential aspects of IDPS for guest OS security include:

- Monitoring and analytics:
    - Continuous monitoring of system logs and network traffic for anomalies and signs of intrusion;
    - Utilizing anomaly detection techniques to identify unusual patterns that may signal security breaches.
- *Signature-based detection:* IDPS may use signature-based detection mechanisms akin to antivirus systems [21]:
    - This method compares real-time data against known attack signatures to swiftly identify and respond to potential threats.
    - Regular updates to signature databases are imperative to ensure the IDPS can accurately detect the latest threats.

- Prevention mechanisms:
    - Active prevention mechanisms can be employed that can automatically isolate compromised guest OSs by severing their network connections or shutting them down.
    - Configurable rules that allow for automatic responses to detected intrusions, such as blocking malicious IP addresses or terminating harmful processes.
- Alerts and reporting:
    - Establishing automated alerts for suspicious activities so security teams can respond promptly to incidents.
    - Generating detailed reports that provide insights into detected threats, which can guide further security policy enhancements.

3.4.3 Access Control Mechanisms

Access control is fundamental to securing guest OSs, preventing unauthorized access, and maintaining the system's integrity [22]. The key components of access control include:

- *User authentication:* Strong authentication mechanisms are crucial in validating the identity of users accessing the guest OS. Best practices include:
    - Utilizing complex passwords combined with multifactor authentication to enhance security;
    - Implementing account lockout policies to prevent brute-force attacks.
- *Role-based access control (RBAC):* RBAC assigns permissions based on users' roles within an organization, allowing for better user rights management. This can include:
    - Grouping users based on job functions and assigning permissions accordingly, reducing the risk of privilege escalation;
    - Periodic reviews of roles and access rights to continuously align with current business needs.
- *Audit trails:* Maintaining detailed logs of user activities is crucial for accountability and traceability:
    - Regularly reviewing logs to identify unauthorized access attempts and other suspicious actions;
    - Implementing logging of security-related events, such as changes to system configurations, access to sensitive data, and failed authentication attempts.
- *Use of virtual private networks (VPNs):* When remote access is necessary, using a VPN can enhance security by encrypting communications over untrusted networks [23]. This step ensures that sensitive data remains protected while being transmitted.

3.4.4 Security Policies and Awareness Training

In addition to technical measures, implementing comprehensive security policies and ongoing awareness training for users can significantly enhance the security of guest OSs.

- Establishing security policies:
  - Developing clear security policies tailored to the use and management of guest OS, specifying acceptable usage, incident response protocols, and data management practices;
  - Ensuring that policies are consistently enforced through organizational guidelines and conducting follow-up audits.
- *User education:* Regular training programs are essential in fostering a culture of security within an organization:
  - Training users on recognizing phishing attempts, social engineering tactics, and other common attack vectors;
  - Encouraging the reporting of suspicious activities or potential vulnerabilities, ensuring prompt responses to emerging threats.

Securing guest OSs is a multifaceted endeavor encompassing various practices and controls. Organizations can significantly reduce the risks associated with VMs by focusing on operating system hardening, employing intrusion detection and prevention mechanisms, enforcing robust access controls, and fostering user awareness [24]. As the landscape of cyber threats evolves, continuous improvement and adaptation of security strategies will be necessary to maintain a strong security posture that protects both the guest OS and the broader virtual environment. Implementing these measures safeguards sensitive data and supports organizational integrity and trust in virtualization technology.

3.5 Securing Hypervisors

Hypervisors play a pivotal role within virtualization environments, managing and coordinating the operation of VMs [25]. Hypervisors are the link connecting the physical hardware and virtualized workloads. Thus, it is important that hypervisors are secured to maintain the confidentiality of the VMs and infrastructure. Successful exploitation of hypervisor vulnerabilities can lead to critical security issues, whether it allows an attacker to access sensitive data or take control of several VMs. This section outlines the crucial aspects of securing hypervisors, including understanding hypervisor vulnerabilities, secure configuration practices, monitoring and auditing, and incident response strategies.

3.5.1 Hypervisor Security Vulnerabilities

Understanding the vulnerabilities inherent in hypervisors is the first step in establishing effective security measures [26]. Common threats and vulnerabilities include:

- *Resource-sharing vulnerabilities:* Hypervisors allocate physical resources to VMs, which can lead to contention and potential information leakage between VMs. Attackers could exploit this through side-channel attacks (e.g., Spectre, Meltdown), where one VM inappropriately accesses memory or CPU caches allocated to another.
- *Misconfiguration:* Poorly configured hypervisors can expose security weaknesses, including improper network segmentation or inadequate access controls, which malicious actors can exploit.
- *Privilege escalation:* Vulnerabilities in the hypervisor software can allow attackers to escalate their privileges from a guest OS to the hypervisor layer, potentially compromising the entire physical host and all hosted VMs.
- *Insecure management interfaces:* Interfaces used to manage hypervisors, such as web-based dashboards or command-line interfaces, can be vulnerable to attacks if not appropriately secured, enabling unauthorized access to sensitive management features.
- *Denial-of-service (DoS) attacks:* Hypervisors themselves can be targets of DoS attacks that aim to consume resources, making VMs unresponsive or causing crashes.

3.5.2 Secure Configuration of Hypervisors

Configuring hypervisors securely is vital for reducing vulnerability risks. Some essential practices include:

- Minimal installation and patch management:
  - *Install only necessary components:* When deploying a hypervisor, installing only the components required to operate is imperative, reducing the potential attack surface.
  - *Regular updates and patching:* Timely application of patches and updates is critical. Hypervisor vendors frequently release updates addressing security vulnerabilities. Automated patch management solutions can help maintain compliance.
- Network configuration:
  - Segment networks to isolate management traffic from regular VM traffic. VLANs can be employed to segregate sensitive management interfaces.
  - Ensure management interfaces are not directly exposed to public networks. Use VPNs or dedicated management networks to restrict access and enhance security.
- Secure remote access:
  - Implement robust authentication mechanisms on hypervisor management interfaces, such as multifactor authentication.
  - Limit remote management access to trusted IP addresses and employ strong passwords and account lockout policies to deter brute-force login attempts.

- Principle of least privilege:
  - Enforce strict user access controls, granting minimum privileges for users to perform their functions, for example, separate responsibility for management tasks from those that require direct interaction with VMs.
- Disable unused features:
  - Disable unnecessary services or functionalities that could serve as entry points for attackers, thereby simplifying the security of the hypervisor.

3.5.3 Hypervisor Monitoring and Audit

Continuous monitoring of hypervisors is essential for early threat detection and response. Figure 3.3 illustrates the hypervisor monitoring and audit system. This system tracks CPU, memory, and storage usage to identify bottlenecks and optimize resource allocation. It detects unauthorized access and vulnerabilities, enforces security policy compliance, and provides real-time alerts to support proactive management of the virtual environment.

This includes:

- Logging and auditing:
  - Implement comprehensive logging mechanisms to capture management actions and access attempts. Maintain logs for a predetermined period to facilitate forensic investigations if necessary.

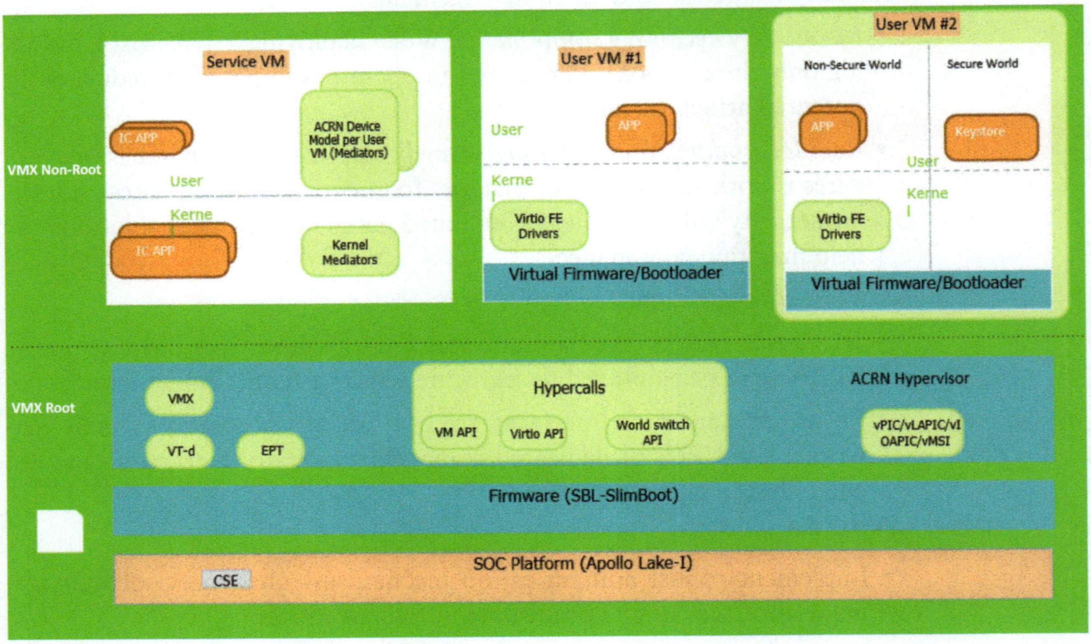

Figure 3.3 Hypervisor monitoring and audit.

- Use log aggregation tools to centralize monitoring and analysis, enabling quicker detection of abnormal patterns or potential security incidents.
- Real-time monitoring:
  - Establish real-time monitoring mechanisms to alert administrators to suspicious activities, such as multiple failed login attempts, unexpected VM configurations, or resource changes.
  - Implement an intrusion detection system (IDS) specifically designed to monitor hypervisor activities, looking for indicators of compromise or violation of security policies.
- Performance and resource monitoring:
  - Continuously monitor the performance of the hypervisor and its VMs. Sudden spikes in resource usage could indicate exploitation attempts, potentially alerting administrators to a breach.
- Compliance auditing:
  - Conduct regular audits to verify compliance with security standards. Automated tools scan configurations against security benchmarks such as the Center for Internet Security (CIS) benchmarks for hypervisors.

3.5.4 Incident Response

A robust incident response strategy tailored for hypervisors can significantly mitigate damage in a security breach. This involves:

- Preparation:
  - Create thorough incident response plans that specify roles, duties, and protocols for handling incidents involving a particular hypervisor. Regularly train staff on these protocols.
- Detection and analysis:
  - Rapidly detect incidents through monitoring and utilize forensic tools to analyze the extent and impact of the breach. This will help to assess whether the hypervisor has been compromised and determine the necessary response.
- Containment, eradication, and recovery:
  - Implement containment procedures to prevent further damage. This may include isolating affected VMs or temporarily turning off the hypervisor.
  - Eradicate the cause of the breach and apply patches or configuration changes to prevent reoccurrence.
  - Plan for recovery by restoring affected systems from backups and validating the integrity of those systems before bringing them back online.
- Post-incident review:
  - To assess the response and pinpoint areas that require improvement, carry out a comprehensive post-event review. Security policy changes

and increased awareness of potential threats can be influenced by lessons learned.

Securing hypervisors is essential to maintaining virtualization environments' overall integrity and security. By understanding the vulnerabilities that can affect hypervisors, implementing secure configuration practices, active monitoring, and having a solid incident response plan, organizations can significantly enhance their resilience against threats [27]. As hypervisors are the foundation for virtualization, an organization using VMs must secure the hypervisor to protect the confidentiality, integrity, and availability of their data and resources. The security review and improvement process for hypervisors will never stop. As security threats are constantly changing, it is imperative that hypervisor security measures are kept current and modernized.

3.6 Securing Virtualization Management Servers

Virtualization management servers are critical components in any virtual infrastructure and are responsible for orchestrating and managing the entire virtualization environment. These servers often provide administrative capabilities to deploy, monitor, and maintain VMs and allocate resources among them [28]. Given their access to sensitive configurations and controls, securing these servers is paramount to maintaining the integrity and confidentiality of the entire virtualization stack. This section explores the critical aspects of obtaining virtualization management servers, including understanding the risks, implementing security controls, access management, monitoring, and incident response.

3.6.1 Understanding Risks and Vulnerabilities

Before implementing security measures, it is essential to understand the potential risks associated with virtualization management servers:

- *Privilege escalation:* Management servers often host administrative interfaces that attackers can exploit to escalate privileges, potentially allowing them to take control of the hypervisor and all associated VMs.
- *Data breaches:* Because management servers hold configurations, user credentials, and sensitive information about VMs, they are attractive targets for attackers looking to steal data or capture sensitive information.
- *Service disruption:* Attackers may attempt to launch DoS attacks against management servers to disrupt the availability of the virtualization infrastructure.
- *Insecure interfaces:* Web-based management consoles and APIs can be vulnerable to attacks, such as cross-site scripting (XSS) and SQL injection, necessitating stringent protections.
- *Insider threats:* Users with legitimate access to management servers could intentionally or unintentionally compromise the environment, leading to data loss or configuration issues.

3.6.2 Security Controls for Management Servers

To mitigate the risks outlined above, organizations should implement a robust set of security controls:

- Harden the OS:
    - *Minimal installation:* Install only the necessary components on the OS of the management server to reduce the attack surface.
    - *Regular patching:* Continuously apply security patches and updates to the OS and management software to protect against known vulnerabilities.
    - *Configuration hardening:* Use configuration benchmarks (CIS benchmarks) to secure the server according to best practices.
- Network security:
    - *Segmentation:* Isolate management servers from general network traffic using firewalls and VLANs. This segmentation prevents unauthorized access to management interfaces.
    - *Restrict management access:* Limit access to management servers to specific, trusted IP addresses and use VPNs for remote access to add a layer of security.
- Implement strong authentication mechanisms:
    - *Multifactor authentication:* To improve security against credential theft, multifactor authentication is necessary for all administrative accounts that access the management server.
    - *Strong password policies:* Implement stringent password regulations, such as those pertaining to complexity, password expiration, and account lockout procedures following a predefined number of unsuccessful login attempts.
- Access control:
    - *RBAC:* Assign permissions based on user roles to enforce the principle of least privilege. Ensure users are granted only the permissions necessary to fulfill their job responsibilities.
    - *Audit access:* Review access permissions and logs regularly to identify and rectify unnecessary privileges.
- Encryption:
    - Use encryption to secure data at rest and in transit. Communication between management servers and other components (such as hypervisors or storage systems) is encrypted.
    - Secure sensitive configuration files and credentials stored on the management server using encryption.

3.6.3 Monitoring and Auditing

Continuous monitoring and auditing are vital for detecting potential threats and maintaining compliance:

- Real-time monitoring:
  - Implement monitoring solutions capable of tracking access and activity on management servers. This allows for immediate detection of unauthorized access attempts or suspicious activities.
  - Utilize security information and event management (SIEM) systems to correlate logs generated from management servers and detect anomalies.
- Logging and audit trails:
  - Maintain detailed logs of all activities on the management server, including login attempts, configuration changes, and administrative actions.
  - Regularly review logs to detect potential security incidents, misuse of privileges, or compliance violations.
- IDS:
  - Deploy IDS to monitor network traffic and system events for signs of malicious activity or policy violations. IDS can provide alerts for suspicious behavior, enabling a prompt response.

3.6.4 Incident Response in Management Server Security

Developing and implementing an incident response plan specific to management servers can significantly reduce the impact of security incidents:

- Preparation:
  - Establish clear incident response procedures, including roles and responsibilities of team members involved in incident handling.
  - Regularly test and update the incident response plan through tabletop exercises or simulations.
- Detection and analysis:
  - Utilize incident detection mechanisms to monitor for irregularities that may indicate a security breach.
  - Upon detecting an incident, analyze the scope, potential impact, and root cause through forensic investigation methods.
- Containment, eradication, and recovery:
  - Contain the incident by isolating affected systems and preventing further damage (e.g., deactivating compromised accounts or isolating affected VMs).
  - Eradicate the incident's root cause, which may involve applying patches, changing credentials, or reconfiguring access controls.
  - Recovery plan, ensuring that affected services are restored from clean backups and verifying their integrity.
- Post-incident review:
  - Conduct a post-incident analysis to assess the response's effectiveness and identify areas for improvement.

- Document lessons learned and update security policies, training, and the incident response plan accordingly.

Securing virtualization management servers is essential to safeguarding the overall virtualization infrastructure. These servers are critical access points that require a comprehensive strategy involving risk assessment, robust security controls, continuous monitoring and auditing, and a well-defined incident response plan [29]. By adopting these measures, organizations can considerably reduce their vulnerability to attacks targeting management servers, thereby protecting the integrity of their virtual environments and the sensitive data that they manage. A proactive approach to security is essential to navigate the evolving threat landscape and foster a resilient virtualization ecosystem [30].

3.7 Best Practices for VM Security

Securing VMs is critical for maintaining data integrity, confidentiality, availability, and operations within virtualized environments. As organizations increasingly rely on virtualization technologies for their IT strategies, implementing best practices for VM security is essential [25]. This section outlines comprehensive best practices organizations should adopt to bolster their VM security frameworks, encompassing deployment, configuration, monitoring, and response strategies.

3.7.1 Conduct a Thorough Risk Assessment

A robust security strategy begins with understanding the specific risks associated with your virtual environment. Conducting a risk assessment involves:

- *Identifying assets:* Determine all virtual machines, hypervisors, management servers, and related software and data assets within the virtual environment.
- *Assessing vulnerabilities:* Evaluate vulnerabilities in the architecture, configurations, and operational processes affecting these assets. Tools such as vulnerability scanners can assist in this phase.
- *Mapping threats:* Identify potential threats to VMs, including insider threats, malware, DoS attacks, and configuration errors.
- *Prioritizing risks:* Based on potential impact and likelihood, prioritize risks and address the most critical first. This prioritization helps to guide subsequent security measures and resource allocations.

3.7.2 Secure the Virtual Environment During Deployment

The deployment phase is critical in establishing a secure virtualization environment. Best practices include:

- *Use secure configurations:* Adhere to security benchmarks and best practices for configuring hypervisors, guest OSs, and any associated management servers. Frameworks such as the CIS provide guidelines on secure configurations.

- *Minimize image footprint:* Create minimal base images for VMs, installing only necessary components to reduce the attack surface. This principle extends to the software, services, and applications that run on each VM.
- *Implement network segmentation:* Use network segmentation to isolate different workloads and environments. Establishing demilitarized zones (DMZs) for critical applications can contain potential security breaches.
- *Consider resource allocation:* Avoid overprovisioning resources to lessen the risk of resource contention attacks. Ensure that resource allocation policies take security into account.

3.7.3 Hardening Guest OSs

Guest OSs encapsulate VMs and must be hardened effectively:

- *Regular patch management:* Implement automated patch management for guest OS to ensure timely application of security updates and fixes.
- *Disable unused services:* Identify and turn off any unnecessary services or applications on the guest OS. The fewer processes that a machine runs, the lower the risk of exploitation.
- *Implement strong password policies:* Enforce strong password policies and require multifactor authentication to access guest OSs.
- *Firewall configuration:* Use host-based and virtual layer firewalls to control traffic between VMs, limiting unnecessary communication that could be exploited.

3.7.4 Secure Hypervisor and Management Servers

The hypervisor and its management components serve as the backbone of the virtual environment and must be robustly secured:

- *Access control mechanisms:* To restrict user privileges to the bare minimum required for their roles, implement RBAC. Review access rights frequently and adjust them as necessary.
- *Secure management interfaces:* Ensure management interfaces are secured with robust authentication methods, such as multifactor authentication. Access should be restricted based on IP addresses, and management tools must be kept off public networks.
- *Implement logging and monitoring:* Enable logging on hypervisors and management servers to audit activities and configure alerts for suspicious activities that may indicate a security incident.

- *Network security protocols:* Use VPNs and encryption for management communications, ensuring that data exchanged with management servers is protected from interception.

3.7.5 Continuous Monitoring and Incident Response

Establishing continuous monitoring practices ensures prompt detection of potential issues and threats:

- *Real-time monitoring:* Track user activity, security events, and VM performance with real-time monitoring tools to enable prompt responses to questionable activity.
- *IDS:* Use IDS to monitor system activity and network traffic in order to identify possible intrusions. For thorough analysis, IDS and SIEM systems ought to be connected.
- *Incident response planning:* Create and update an incident response strategy specific to the online setting. Roles, duties, and protocols for handling security incidents should all be part of this plan.
- *Regular testing:* Regularly test incident response plans using tabletop exercises and simulations to make sure staff members are equipped to handle situations.

3.7.6 User Education and Security Awareness

Human factors are critical in maintaining security within virtualized environments. Comprehensive user education and awareness programs should be instituted:

- *Training programs:* Regularly conduct security training sessions for all personnel, focusing on security best practices, threat recognition, and the importance of following protocols.
- *Phishing awareness:* Educate employees about phishing tactics and social engineering techniques, guiding, recognizing, and reporting suspicious activities.
- *Establish a security culture:* Promote a security culture across the organization, encouraging collaboration and communication about security issues and the importance of safeguarding data and systems.

A lack of security awareness can cause organizations to ignore many explicit security threats in their day-to-day operations, which include viruses, phishing, Trojan horses, and misappropriation of intellectual property. While contributing to serious risk for the organization this ignorance can leave advanced internet security tools rendered irrelevant. As a case study, this study examines the security awareness needs of an online insurance company using the systems development research method. This involved a security awareness system pilot to frame the study. The study included participation from several of the organization's managers. The pilot security awareness system was refined based on feedback, comments, and usage experiences from the participating managers.

3.7.7 Regular Security Audits and Compliance Checks

Ongoing evaluations of the security posture will identify gaps and areas for improvement:

- *Conduct regular audits:* Schedule regular security audits to assess compliance with established security policies and frameworks. These audits should include both technical and procedural reviews.
- *Utilize third-party assessments:* Consider engaging third-party security firms for external audits and penetration testing to identify vulnerabilities from an outsider's perspective.
- *Adapt to changing threats:* Continuously update security policies and practices based on evolving threats, vulnerabilities, and regulatory compliance requirements.

Implementing best practices for VM security is essential for protecting the integrity and confidentiality of data in virtualization environments. Organizations can significantly enhance their security posture by conducting thorough risk assessments, securing deployment processes, hardening guest OSs, ensuring the security of hypervisors and management servers, maintaining continuous monitoring, educating users, and conducting regular audits [31]. An ongoing commitment to security best practices will help organizations safeguard their virtual resources and maintain operational resilience in a landscape where cyber threats are evolving rapidly.

3.8 Future Trends in VM Security

As cyber threats become more sophisticated, emerging technologies and strategies are being developed to protect VM environments [31]. These include using AI and machine learning (ML) for advanced threat detection and adopting Zero Trust architecture (ZTA) to enhance access control.

3.8.1 AI and ML for Threat Detection and Response

AI and ML can provide sophisticated means of detecting and acting on a security threat in VM environments. These technologies can recognize patterns in large amounts of data, detect abnormal behavior, and learn new ways of behaving or adapting to changing threat patterns.

- *Anomaly detection:* AI-driven systems can identify unusual real-time behavior, such as unexpected access patterns or irregular resource usage. By flagging these anomalies, AI helps administrators to respond quickly to potential threats.

- *Predictive analytics:* ML models can identify trends in historical data to predict potential security incidents before they occur. This enables organizations to implement preemptive measures, reducing the likelihood of breaches.
- *Automated response:* AI-driven security platforms can automate responses to specific threats, such as isolating compromised VMs or blocking suspicious IP addresses. Organizations can reduce response time and improve security effectiveness by automating these processes.

3.9 Zero Trust Architecture

Figure 3.4 presents ZTA, a security model and framework designed to reduce the risk of cyberattacks and data breaches. ZTA is based on the principle of least privilege, granting devices and users only the permissions needed to perform their tasks. To enforce this principle, ZTA utilizes a variety of security technologies. ZTA is an increasingly popular security framework that emphasizes verifying every access request, regardless of origin [33]. Zero trust policies can strengthen VM security in a virtualized environment by ensuring that every user, device, or application must be authenticated and authorized before gaining access.

The goal of the zero trust security model, sometimes called perimeter less security or ZTA, is to "never trust, always verify" when it comes to IT systems. This model ensures that, even if a user or device has been previously verified or connected to a permissioned network, they are not trusted by default. Robust identity verification, confirming device compliance, and guaranteeing least privilege access to only explicitly authorized resources are how ZTA is put into practice. The conventional strategy of relying on users and devices within a corporate perimeter or VPN connections must be revised in contemporary corporate networks, including interconnected zones, cloud services, infrastructure, remote and mobile environments, and nonconventional IT. The zero trust approach promotes mutual authentication, location-independent user, and device identity and integrity checks, and access to apps and services based on device health and user and device identity. ZTA can be used for data management and access, guaranteeing the least privileged access to resources and dynamic authentication. Attribute-Based Access Control (ABAC) allows policies to be applied according to environment type, user identity, and data attributes. Data access is safeguarded by this zero trust data security method. The market for remote access products built with zero trust principles, known as zero trust network access (ZTNA), is primarily based on the software-defined perimeter specification created by the Cloud Security Alliance (CSA).

3.10 Summary

We examined the complex topic of VM security in this chapter, describing the essential elements and procedures required to protect virtualized environments.

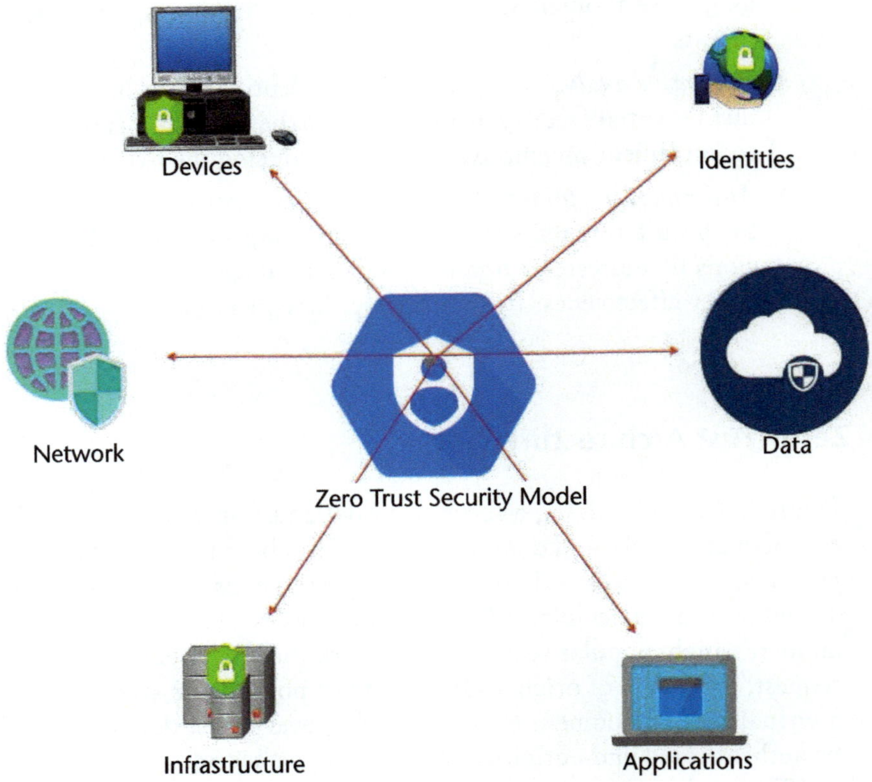

Figure 3.4 ZTA.

Understanding and putting into practice efficient security measures are crucial as more businesses use virtualization technologies to safeguard confidential information, preserve operational integrity, and lessen possible risks.

This chapter began with an in-depth examination of VM architecture, detailing the components of a VM ecosystem. We discussed how type-1 and type-2 hypervisors, which are the foundation of virtualization technology, allow several OSs to run simultaneously on a single physical host. This chapter highlighted the distinction between virtual hardware and the guest OSs, all interacting within this architectural framework. Understanding this structure is essential for recognizing VMs' unique security implications and vulnerabilities.

Following the architectural overview, we delved into the intricacies of securing guest OSs. We discussed how it is important to harden guest OS to protect against exploits that could impact the VM itself and potentially the hypervisor, guest OS, and infrastructure as a whole. Suggestions for OS hardening included adopting a strategy for update and patch management, limiting installed services, and establishing access control, use of firewalls, and IDS. By utilizing hardening principles, an organization can minimize its attack surface and better secure its VMs.

Next, this chapter focused on securing hypervisors, the fundamental layer of managing the interaction between VMs and physical resources. We identified common vulnerabilities, such as misconfiguration and privilege escalation risks, and outlined best practices for securing hypervisors. This included configuring secure management interfaces, employing rigorous access control mechanisms, and monitoring hypervisor activities to detect irregularities. These measures are crucial for ensuring that the hypervisor remains a safe and secure anchor point for virtual operations.

The discussion continued with securing virtualization management servers responsible for administering the virtual environment. Since these components play a crucial role in the virtualization security stack, we have stressed the points of strong access control, secure of management interfaces, and regular logging and auditing. By incorporating strong virtualization security practices, organizations can counter possible insider threats and attacks from outside attackers targeting these often overlooked aspects of the virtualization security stack.

We then summarized key practices for VM security, providing a comprehensive toolkit for organizations to enhance their virtual security posture. This included conducting thorough risk assessments, securing deployment processes, hardening guest OS, ensuring vigilant monitoring, and promoting user education and awareness. Regular security audits and adherence to compliance standards were highlighted as essential components of an ongoing security strategy, allowing organizations to adapt to evolving threats.

In summary, this chapter has examined the personification of practical strategies necessary for utilizing effective VM security processes. The connectivity of virtualized environments calls for a thoughtful and strategic approach to security, involving every aspect from the architecture of the infrastructure to the users and incident response. By following these principles and making the commitment for alertness, organizations can greatly reduce their risk landscape, assuring security for virtualized environments within today's threat landscape. As technology continues to develop, organizations must plan and anticipate a level of scrutiny to protect precious assets. Consequently, developing and maintaining effective security measures will be a business as usual vision for the effective evolution of virtual assets.

- *Micro-segmentation:* In ZTA, micro-segmentation restricts access at the individual VM level, ensuring that VMs only interact with authorized resources. This granular control minimizes the impact of potential breaches.
- *Continuous verification:* Zero trust requires continuous user and device behavior monitoring, enabling organizations to detect any changes that might indicate a compromise. This approach verifies that access remains secure throughout each session.
- *Identity and access management (IAM):* IAM solution is foundational to zero trust in its management of user identity, roles, and permissions. IAM solutions control access to VM resources for trusted users and devices by enforcing strict access policies and evaluating every access request.
- *Policy enforcement points (PEPs):* Zero trust employs PEPs to enforce access policies at multiple points within the network. These points monitor and verify all requests, providing an added layer of security for VM environments.

References

[1] Thyagaturu, A. S., et al., "Operating Systems and Hypervisors for Network Functions: A Survey of Enabling Technologies and Research Studies," *IEEE Access*, Vol. 10, July 29, 2022, pp. 79825–79873.

[2] Haletky, E., *VmWare vSphere and Virtual Infrastructure Security: Securing the Virtual Environment*, Boston, MA: Pearson Education, 2009.

[3] James, E., and F. Rabbi, "Fortifying the IoT Landscape: Strategies to Counter Security Risks in Connected Systems," *Tensorgate Journal of Sustainable Technology and Infrastructure for Developing Countries*, Vol. 6, No. 1, January 9, 2023, pp. 32–46.

[4] Portnoy, M., *Virtualization Essentials*, New York: John Wiley & Sons, 2012.

[5] Brotherston, L., A. Berlin, and W. F. Reyor III, *Defensive Security Handbook: Best Practices for Securing Infrastructure*, Sebastopol, CA: O'Reilly Media, 2024.

[6] Aburukba, R., Y. Kaddoura, and M. Hiba, "Cloud Computing Infrastructure Security: Challenges and Solutions," *2022 International Symposium on Networks, Computers and Communications (ISNCC)*, July 19, 2022, pp. 1–7.

[7] Albanese, M., E. Battista, and S. Jajodia, "Deceiving Attackers by Creating a Virtual Attack Surface," *Cyber Deception: Building the Scientific Foundation*, 2016, pp. 167–199.

[8] Mitcham, Z. S., *Key Security Concepts That All CISOs Should Know-Cyber Guardians: A CISO's Guide to Protecting the Digital World*, eBookIt.com, 2024.

[9] Reveron, D. S., (ed.), *Cyberspace and National Security: Threats, Opportunities, and Power in a Virtual World*, Washington, DC: Georgetown University Press, 2012.

[10] Josyula, V., M. Orr, and G. Page, *Cloud Computing: Automating the Virtualized Data Center*, Indianapolis, IN: Cisco Press, 2011.

[11] Bugnion, E., J. Nieh, and D. Tsafrir, *Hardware and Software Support for Virtualization*, Morgan & Claypool Publishers, 2017.

[12] Graniszewski, W., and A. Arciszewski, "Performance Analysis of Selected Hypervisors (Virtual Machine Monitors-VMMs)," *International Journal of Electronics and Telecommunications*, Vol. 62, 2016.

[13] Kamaludin, H., et al., "Implementing Virtual Machine: A Performance Evaluation. Recent Advances on Soft Computing and Data Mining," *Proceedings of the Fourth International Conference on Soft Computing and Data Mining (SCDM 2020)*, Melaka, Malaysia, January 22–23, 2020, pp. 373–381.

[14] Li, S. W., J. S. Koh, and J. Nieh, "Protecting Cloud Virtual Machines from Hypervisor and Host Operating System Exploits," *28th USENIX Security Symposium (USENIX Security 19)*, 2019, pp. 1357–1374.

[15] Thyagaturu, A. S., et al., "Operating Systems and Hypervisors for Network Functions: A Survey of Enabling Technologies and Research Studies," *IEEE Access*, Vol. 10, July 29, 2022, pp. 79825–79873.

[16] Firestone, D., "{VFP}: A Virtual Switch Platform for Host {SDN} in the Public Cloud," *14th USENIX Symposium on Networked Systems Design and Implementation (NSDI 17)*, 2017, pp. 315–328.

[17] Gurrala, R. R., T. S. Kumar, and K. Anuradha, "Virtual Machine Security Issues and Solutions When in Host," *2024 10th International Conference on Advanced Computing and Communication Systems (ICACCS)*, Vol. 1, March 14, 2024, pp. 441–449.

[18] Laverdière-Papineau, M. A., *Towards Systematic Software Security Hardening*, Master's thesis, Concordia University, 2008.

[19] Iqbal, S., et al., "On Cloud Security Attacks: A Taxonomy and Intrusion Detection and Prevention as a Service," *Journal of Network and Computer Applications*, Vol. 74, October 10, 2016, pp. 98–120.

[20] Ribeiro, J., et al., "Hidroid: Prototyping a Behavioral Host-Based Intrusion Detection and Prevention System for Android," *IEEE Access*, Vol. 8, January 28, 2020, pp. 23154–23168.

[21] Rao, U. H., et al., "Intrusion Detection and Prevention Systems," in *The InfoSec Handbook: An Introduction to Information Security*, New York: Apress, 2014, pp. 225–243.

[22] Borky, J. M., et al., "Protecting Information with Cybersecurity," in *Effective Model-Based Systems Engineering*, New York: Springer Nature, 2019, pp. 345–404.

[23] Lekkala, S., and P. Gurijala, "Secure Connectivity with Virtual Private Networks," in *Security and Privacy for Modern Networks: Strategies and Insights for Safeguarding Digital Infrastructures*, Berkeley, CA: Apress, 2024, pp. 109–120.

[24] Weiss, J., *Protecting Industrial Control Systems from Electronic Threats*, New York: Momentum Press, 2010.

[25] Shackleford, D., *Virtualization Security: Protecting Virtualized Environments*, New York: John Wiley & Sons, 2012.

[26] Lefray, A., et al., "Microarchitecture-Aware Virtual Machine Placement Under Information Leakage Constraints," *2015 IEEE 8th International Conference on Cloud Computing*, June 27, 2015, pp. 588–595.

[27] Diogenes, Y., and E. Ozkaya, *Cybersecurity–Attack and Defense Strategies: Counter Modern Threats and Employ State-of-the-Art Tools and Techniques to Protect Your Organization Against Cybercriminals*, Birmingham, UK: Packt Publishing Ltd., 2019.

[28] Kaur, K., V. Mangat, and K. Kumar, "A Review on Virtualized Infrastructure Managers with Management and Orchestration Features in NFV Architecture," *Computer Networks*, Vol. 217, November 9, 2022, p. 109281.

[29] Pompon, R., *IT Security Risk Control Management: An Audit Preparation Plan*, New York: Apress, 2016.

[30] Safitra, M. F., M. Lubis, and H. Fakhrurroja, "Counterattacking Cyber Threats: A Framework for the Future of Cybersecurity," *Sustainability*, Vol. 15, No. 18, September 6, 2023, p. 13369.

[31] Xu, X., G. Liu, and J. Zhu, "Cloud Data Security and Integrity Protection Model Based on Distributed Virtual Machine Agents," *2016 International Conference on Cyber-Enabled Distributed Computing and Knowledge Discovery (CyberC)*, October 13, 2016, pp. 6–13.

[32] El Kafhali, S., I. El Mir, and M. Hanini, "Security Threats, Defense Mechanisms, Challenges, and Future Directions in Cloud Computing," *Archives of Computational Methods in Engineering*, Vol. 29, No. 1, January 29, 2022, pp. 223–246.

[33] Moresi, G., *Zero Trust Network & Zero Internet: Defense Strategies Against the Zero Day Kill Chain*, 2023.

CHAPTER 4

Storage Security in Virtualized Environments

4.1 Virtual Storage Architecture

The virtual storage architecture (VSA) is a type of storage architecture that extracts storage resources and poses them to applications as virtualized storage devices. The VSA can be executed in software and hardware or by blending them both. Virtual memory streamlines programming by enabling developers to adjust to changes in local memory or network configurations without the need to recompile their code [1]. Storage virtualization can streamline storage system usage, lower management costs, enhance performance, and boost efficiency across local, wide, and cloud storage networks [2].

The optimal definition of storage virtualization involves consolidating physical storage from multiple storage devices into what appears as a single storage device or a collective of available storage capacity. A central repository oversees this storage amalgamation. Meanwhile, network storage architecture pertains to the physical and conceptual arrangement of a network facilitating data transfer between storage devices and servers. It serves as the backbone for most operational endeavors, allowing users to fulfill their needs. In their article, "Cloud Storage Virtualization Technology and Its Architecture," Hu et al. examined three types of storage virtualization technology in cloud computing, discussed their application value, and introduced a platform architecture model for cloud storage [3]. Figure 4.1 provides a general overview of the VSA, highlighting both its hardware and software components.

The primary, archive, and backup applications are the cloud principal functions of virtual storage.

- Primary storage retains all ongoing work for sharing among multiple users or devices.
- Archive storage preserves data that is no longer current but still necessitates retention in case of future need.
- As for backup purposes, virtual storage serves as a foundational component of backup infrastructure, enabling organizations to protect their data,

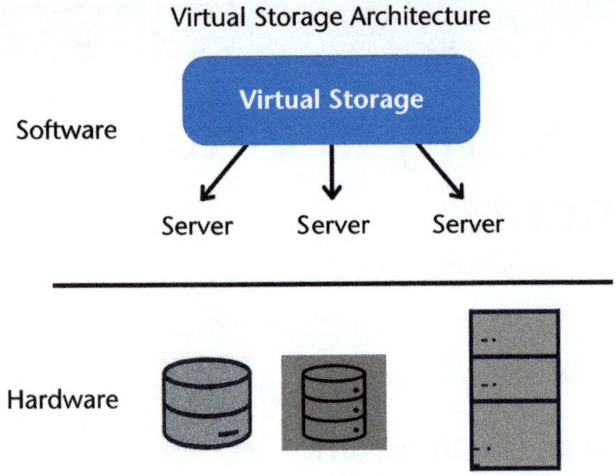

Figure 4.1 Overview of the VSA.

manage backup storage resources efficiently, perform backup and restore operations smoothly, perform data deduplication and compression, manage backup policies effectively, and prepare for disaster recovery scenarios.

In essence, virtual storage encompasses the fusion of actual storage with supplementary or backup storage. In the case of z/OS, a sequence of tables and indexes is utilized to establish connections between locations on auxiliary storage and those in central storage. Special settings, or bit settings, are employed to monitor the identity and authorization of each user or program [4].

4.1.1 Introduction to Virtual Storage and Case Studies

Storage virtualization, also known as software-defined storage (SDS) or a virtual storage area network (SAN), involves consolidating multiple physical storage arrays from SANs to create a single virtual storage device. This pooling process integrates disparate storage hardware from various networks, retailers, or data centers into a unified logical view, which can be managed from a single interface [5].

SDS is a technology utilized in data storage management that deliberately separates functions responsible for saving capacity, data protection, and data placement from the underlying physical hardware. This separation enables storage hardware to be easily replaced, upgraded, or extended without disrupting established operational procedures or removal of significant software investments.

By virtualizing storage, the storage management software is decoupled from the underlying hardware infrastructure, offering enhanced resilience, and creating accessible pools of storage resources. Additionally, virtualization abstracts storage hardware such as arrays and disks into virtual storage pools, similar to how compute virtualization (e.g., VMWare ESX or Hyper-V) abstracts physical servers into virtual machine (VM) instances. A storage virtualization node serves as a virtualized controller responsible for abstracting and overseeing physical storage resources. All disk arrays are enclosed within a "virtual pool" and thinly provisioned to maximize capacity utilization. Following the creation of the virtual pool, "virtual disks" are generated within the pool and subsequently presented to host servers as raw logical unit numbers (LUNs) for data storage purposes [6].

Virtual storage enables each active program to operate under the assumption that it possesses access to all storage designated by the architecture's addressing framework. The sole restriction is the number of bits allocated to a storage address. This capability to utilize a vast array of storage locations holds significance as programs can be extensive and intricate, necessitating both program code and requisite data to reside in central storage for processor accessibility.

Over time, this technology has been instrumental in addressing numerous challenges associated with storage expansion and management of large data volumes. Particularly in the present era, with data volumes experiencing exponential growth annually, the importance of virtualized storage has escalated significantly.

In the field of VSA, recent case studies have highlighted innovation solutions and approaches. One particular study examined the integrated architecture for in-memory and in-storage computing, assessing energy consumption and processing speed based on workload distribution and system conditions [7]. The results demonstrated that in-memory computing increased performance by 4.4 times and decreased total energy consumption by 4.6 times compared to the baseline host CPU. Additionally, in-storage computing was confirmed to significantly contribute to energy savings.

Another case study discussed a comparative analysis of object-based big data storage was performed, emphasizing the flexibility of object storage systems, where data is stored as individual objects [8]. This approach is well-suited for big data in cloud environments. These studies offer valuable insights into advancements and applications in VSA, aiding engineers who specialize in this field. They address the challenges posed by recent technologies and the increase in data volumes.

An example of a case study for VMware, Inc., is briefly demonstrated.

4.1.1.1 Case Study for VMware, Inc.

VMware, Inc., is a legitimate business that specializes in cloud computing and virtualization software and services. With technologies such as VMware vSAN (virtual storage area network), and VMware vSphere, which are frequently used for virtualizing storage infrastructure, VMware is a global leader in virtual storage solutions. Since its founding in 1998, VMware, Inc., has grown to be a significant participant in the IT sector by providing a variety of cloud computing and virtualization solutions. The company's main goal is to make it possible for businesses to virtualize their computing, storage, and networking infrastructure in order to increase productivity, flexibility, and scalability.

Security Measures in VSA

VMware hopes to give clients a safe and dependable platform for virtualizing their storage infrastructure and operating their business-critical workloads by putting these security measures in place and remaining watchful against emerging threats.

- *Step 1: Data held.* VMware may store a variety of data on its clients' IT infrastructure as a provider of virtualization and cloud computing solutions.

Information such as customer accounts, names, contact information, and billing details, may be included in this data, as well as performance indicators and configuration data pertaining to the virtualized environments of clients and system logs and audit trails produced for security and troubleshooting needs by VMware products, and information produced by VMware's cloud services, including invoicing and consumption information.

- *Step 2: Security of virtual storage.* VMware understands how crucial it is to secure virtual storage infrastructure in order to safeguard the availability, confidentiality, and integrity of client data. The business uses a variety of methods and best practices to protect its virtual storage solutions, such as data encryption to guard against unauthorized access both in transit and at rest, multifactor authentication and role-based access restrictions to limit access to critical information and administrative tasks, integration with compliance frameworks and industry-standard security solutions to guarantee adherence to legal standards and security best practices, constantly keeping an eye on and auditing virtual storage infrastructures to quickly identify and address security risks and vulnerabilities, and working together with industry partners and security experts to recognize and resolve new security threats and weaknesses in cloud computing and virtualization systems.

4.1.1.2 Techniques of Securing Virtual Storage

Two techniques for securing virtual storage are:

1. Traditional strategy:
    - *Traditional access controls:* In the early stages of VMware's virtual storage solutions, security relied on conventional access control methods such as username/password authentication and access control lists (ACLs). These controls were typically managed at the hypervisor or storage array level to limit access to authorized users and administrators.
    - *Perimeter security:* Many organizations using VMware's virtual storage solutions implemented perimeter security measures such as firewalls and network segmentation. By isolating virtual storage systems from external networks and regulating inbound/outbound traffic, organizations aimed to minimize the risk of unauthorized access and data breaches.
    - *Encryption:* Encryption of data at rest was a common practice to bolster the security of VMware's virtual storage environments. Techniques such as full disk encryption (FDE) and encryption of virtual disk files provided an additional layer of protection against unauthorized access to stored data.
    - *Patch management:* Regular patch management was crucial to addressing security vulnerabilities in VMware's hypervisor and storage software. By staying current with the latest security patches and updates, organizations sought to mitigate the risk of exploitation by malicious actors targeting known vulnerabilities.

2. Current strategy:
   - *Micro-segmentation:* With the increasing complexity of virtualized environments, micro-segmentation has emerged as a potent approach to securing VMware's virtual storage solutions. Micro-segmentation involves dividing the network into smaller, isolated segments and applying granular access controls based on workload characteristics. This approach helps to prevent lateral movement by attackers within VMware's virtualized environments and limits the impact of security breaches.
   - *Software-defined security:* Software-defined security solutions are gaining momentum for securing VMware's virtual storage environments. Leveraging software-defined networking (SDN) and software-defined security (SDSec) technologies, these solutions dynamically adapt security policies based on changing workload requirements. By decoupling security policies from physical infrastructure, software-defined security enhances agility and scalability in securing VMware's virtual storage solutions.
   - *Zero Trust security model:* The zero trust security model has become increasingly relevant for VMware's virtual storage environments. Unlike traditional perimeter-based models, zero trust assumes that threats can originate from both internal and external sources. As such, zero trust advocates for strict access controls, continuous authentication, and real-time monitoring to verify the identity and trustworthiness of users and devices accessing VMware's virtual storage resources.
   - *Behavioral analytics:* Behavioral analytics solutions are gaining traction in VMware environments for detecting anomalous behavior and potential security threats. By analyzing user and entity behavior patterns, these solutions can identify suspicious activities indicative of unauthorized access or data exfiltration. Behavioral analytics complements traditional security measures by providing insights into emerging threats and enabling proactive threat detection and response in VMware's virtual storage environments.
   - *Cloud-native security controls:* As organizations adopt VMware's cloud-native architectures and services, cloud-native security controls are essential for securing virtual storage in cloud environments. These controls include native encryption, identity, and access management (IAM), network security groups (NSGs), and cloud security posture management (CSPM) tools. Leveraging these controls, organizations can ensure consistent security policies and enforcement across hybrid and multicloud environments in VMware's virtual storage solutions.

4.1.2 Challenges of the VSA

Virtualization presents distinct challenges that prove challenging to address using conventional solutions not designed specifically for virtualized environments. Effectively managing an expanding and progressively intricate virtual infrastructure, along with its underlying physical framework and associated applications, places considerable demand on personnel resources typically constrained and specialized.

Furthermore, organizations are tasked with fulfilling the promises of virtualization, namely, cost reduction and increased efficiency, among these complexities. Additionally, they seek to realize the maximum returns from their investments in virtualization.

Figure 4.2 presents the challenges of VSA in a practical manner, highlighting real-world issues encountered during implementation and management in virtualized environments.

The next section will provide guidance on overcoming five common challenges encountered in achieving successful virtualization. It will explore into the requisite management practices, tools, and techniques essential for addressing these five challenges effectively.

4.1.2.1 Identifying Performance Constraints

Sustaining consistent availability and performance stands as a vital concern within virtualized setups. The advantages of virtualization, including cost savings stemming from enhanced efficiency, reduced overhead, and improved agility, are clear. However, a notable drawback often arises in the form of unidentified performance risks, particularly when lacking the requisite staff expertise, tools, or processes for effective management. According to Gartner, an IT research and advisory company [9], "[Virtualization] changes how you manage, how and what you buy, how you deploy, how you plan, and how you charge." Therefore, obtaining the appropriate tools for detecting, diagnosing, and rectifying performance constraints emerges as crucial for ensuring the sustained success of your virtual environment. The process flow encompassing detect, diagnose, and resolve outlines a systematic approach for performance assessment in virtual environments, enabling precise identification, root cause analysis, and remediation of operational issues.

- *Detect:* A crucial role of an effective monitoring tool is its capability to accurately identify issues that pose a threat to the availability and performance of the virtual environment. There four categories of detection issues such as predictive issues, best practice issues, indicating behavioral issues, and performance risk to system condition issues.
- *Diagnose:* Upon successful detection and classification of a performance issue as predictive, best practice, behavioral, or conditional, an optimal solution should promptly and precisely diagnose the problem. This is especially

Figure 4.2 Challenges of the VSA.

critical in virtual environments where complexities stemming from shared resources can lead to operational challenges. Appropriate diagnosis is essential to prevent slow and cumbersome resolution, which can delay organizational productivity. It offers a deep understanding of the underlying problems, providing visual indicators and relevant insights.

- *Resolve:* Prompt resolution of issues is vital. An ideal tool should not only resolve issues promptly but also offer guidance, recommendations, or automation capabilities for resolution. Expedited time to resolution is desired, and problem-resolution guidance can take various forms. After diagnosing the root cause, rectifying the issue using customized best practices tailored to the specific environment is essential. Additionally, employing a tool that suggests workflow adjustments and automates execution based on the problem framework (also known as alert remediation) is beneficial.

Typical issues encountered with VMs include VM sprawl, limitations in data and memory capacity, bottlenecks in data transmission, and suboptimal CPU performance. VM sprawl refers to the situation where it becomes challenging to adequately oversee and manage all VMs linked to a network. This scenario frequently arises when various departments within an organization independently establish virtualized instances, leading to a network that exceeds manageable proportions [9].

4.1.2.2 Confidently Virtualizing More and Visibility into Application Layer

Enhancing insight into the application layer, numerous organizations are effectively virtualizing and consolidating straightforward components such as file/print servers and less critical applications. As the trend toward virtualized workloads continues, organizations seek methods to bolster stakeholder confidence and minimize risk further within the application stack. With the evolution of virtualization technology, there is a corresponding advancement in processes and solutions to maintain a virtual system efficiently. One such solution involves enhancing visibility into the application stack and its supporting infrastructure. This visibility must be comprehensive, enabling a clear understanding of component resources and their interrelationships within the virtual environment. Several organizations lack the necessary tools or processes to manage availability and run time deep within the layers of critical application infrastructure. Challenges exacerbate when managing the complexity of mixed physical and virtual implementations, where some components are virtualized, while others remain in fully physical environments.

Accurate and meaningful key metrics from both the virtualization and application layers are crucial to identify performance issues and potential risks effectively. Understanding the performance of individual components within business-critical applications, such as Microsoft Exchange and Active Directory, within the context of the underlying virtual or physical infrastructure, is essential to fully harness the capabilities of any virtual infrastructure. Successful server virtualization relies on comprehensive performance management technologies and practices. Organizations virtualizing Tier-1 applications and their supporting infrastructure require solutions capable of managing and monitoring performance across diverse components within physical and virtual environments.

Storage challenges in virtualized environments apart from virtualizing higher layers of the stack, organizations encounter difficulties managing down the stack and into the supporting physical storage infrastructure. Storage often bears the responsibility and blames for poor application performance. Issues such as inadequate bandwidth, disk hot spots, and input/output (I/O) bottlenecks make storage monitoring and optimization a complex undertaking.

Therefore, to effectively optimize virtualized applications, it is essential to grasp their connections to the physical storage infrastructure beneath their designated data stores. Regrettably, existing hypervisor management tools lack inclusion of physical storage in their performance monitoring reports and architectural diagrams. Consequently, it is challenging to determine whether underperforming VMs stem from underlying network connectivity or storage issues. Instead, one must depend on storage administrators to investigate the I/O challenges impacting VMs, virtual hosts, and the overall virtual infrastructures.

4.1.2.3 Infrastructure Management and Reporting

Once the organization secures buy-in and commences the virtualization process, it is crucial to sustain the environment effectively. To achieve this, it is imperative to acquire tools that furnish dependable data regarding performance, inventory, and configuration, presenting this information in a format easily comprehensible to all stakeholders. The organization requires performing and running a reporting and dashboards successfully to mitigate the risks of overall exploitation; striving for real-time insights in real-time dashboards is the optimal solution. Additionally, an automated reporting and streamlined data compilation address the unique characteristics of the virtual infrastructure in reporting.

4.1.2.4 Understanding Capacity Needs and Strategizing for Scalability

The inherent flexibility and mobility of virtualization offer significant benefits to IT infrastructure, but they also present challenges in effectively balancing system capacity with user demands. The dynamic nature of virtual infrastructure adds complexity to maintaining the optimal level of capacity consistently.

Capacity fluctuations can be predicted or unpredicted. For instance, a planned application release may introduce new features, increasing resource demands. This predicted change necessitates proactive resource allocation.

Unpredictable changes pose greater difficulties. Unexpectedly, the business might onboard a new user group or launch a marketing campaign that strains system resources. In such cases, inadequate understanding and planning for capacity can lead to either overspending on underutilized resources or revenue loss due to insufficient resources failing to meet service-level requirements. Effective management of capacity demands within a dynamic virtual infrastructure is crucial for successful virtualization implementation.

Preparing for predicted changes involves assessing how these changes will impact the resources within your virtual infrastructure. Subsequently, once the changes are implemented, it is crucial to determine when additional resources will be necessary to uphold optimal performance of the virtual infrastructure. In the long run, the organization will require a mechanism to monitor the virtual infrastructure for unpredicted events that could potentially disrupt performance and availability.

Understanding the impact of changes on current infrastructure, when planning for change, it is essential to have insight into whether the existing virtual infrastructure can accommodate the new requirements. If not, it is important to ascertain the extent of additional capacity needed. A lack of visibility into proposed changes may lead to unnecessary overspending.

4.1.2.5 Ensuring Service-Level Agreement Compliance in Virtualized Environments

Virtualization holds the promise of delivering IT services to businesses more efficiently, faster, and at lower costs compared to traditional methods. However, as virtualization becomes increasingly prevalent in traditional data centers, fulfilling this promise becomes more challenging. The complexity introduced by virtualization and its disruption of established IT processes and procedures contribute to this difficulty.

In recent years, there has been significant pressure on IT departments to become more strategic and align better with business objectives, focusing on proactive cost avoidance rather than merely functioning as a cost center. IT has made notable progress in process improvement, aimed at better supporting business needs with established service-level agreements and increased agility to facilitate progressive business initiatives.

Upon the integration of virtualization into the data center, it is essential to institute service management practices. Effective virtualization deployments will define service-level agreements that integrate appropriate and precise virtualization management solutions to handle the intricacies of both the underlying virtual and supporting physical infrastructures.

In conclusion, as virtualization technology and its applications evolve, the demands for efficient management also grow. The above five challenges tackle the typical barriers organizations encounter during virtualization, whether advancing higher into the application stack or delving deeper into the supporting infrastructure. To keep under control the full benefits of virtualization, organizations need to adopt a comprehensive solution encompassing supporting processes to address performance problems and ensure availability effectively. The optimal solution should include a streamlined performance management framework comprising detection, diagnosis, and resolution, empowered by intelligent automation for swift problem-solving. Moreover, it should incorporate robust reporting, capacity planning, and chargeback capabilities compatible with diverse vendor-hypervisor platforms. Additionally, it should be backed by a scalable and adaptable common repository platform. By adhering to these principles, a well-managed, virtualized infrastructure can serve as a catalyst for enhanced success in agile and dynamic private cloud initiatives.

4.1.3 Benefits and Efficiency of Using VSA

The main benefits of storage virtualization include improving space utilization and providing storage options for disorganized data and resources, simplifying the management of large datasets by enabling proper location and integration, and enhancing data backup capabilities through storage resource snapshots. The storage virtualization provides cost-effective, high-availability storage management across three levels: storage device, host, and SAN fabric, each with its own advantages and limitations depending on their capabilities [10].

In terms of modernization, traditional siloed applications and data storage methodologies are outdated. Moving toward storage virtualization creates significant opportunities for organizations to leverage the latest advancements in virtualization, software-defined technologies, and hyperconvergence. As a result, transitioning from traditional data storage infrastructure to a VSA offers numerous advantages to organizations. These advantages include:

- *Simplicity.* One of the primary benefits of moving from conventional data storage infrastructure to a virtualized storage model is the potential to significantly simplify your IT environment. Transitioning to storage virtualization reduces complexities within the data center by minimizing the hardware required to support applications. Unlike traditional data storage models, which demand separate servers for each application, storage virtualization allows these applications to operate from a single server or a considerably reduced number of servers. Consequently, simplified management is a hallmark of virtual storage solutions, typically providing centralized management interfaces and automation features that streamline tasks such as storage provisioning, monitoring, and maintenance.
- *Affordable and cost-effective.* Cost represents another significant advantage of storage virtualization. In traditional data centers, the necessity for numerous servers' results in a considerably more intricate infrastructure and network, leading to higher initial expenses and ongoing maintenance costs. By optimizing storage utilization and minimizing the reliance on physical storage hardware, VSAs can generate cost savings in terms of hardware acquisition, upkeep, and energy usage. It is lightweight and fundamentally demands fewer resources overall, rendering it notably more economical.
- *Flexibility.* The VSA facilitates and permits the dynamic allocation and reallocation of storage resources, empowering organizations to swiftly respond to shifting storage requirements without the necessity for physical reconfiguration.
- *Scalability.* Virtual storage possesses the capability to effortlessly adjust to growing or fluctuating storage demands, affording organizations the opportunity to enhance and expand their storage capacity without requiring substantial investments in hardware.
- *Optimize performance.* Virtual storage architectures frequently integrate sophisticated functionalities like automated tiering and caching, which enhance data access speeds and overall system performance.
- *Increase data protection.* Virtual storage solutions commonly come equipped with inherent data protection features such as snapshots, replication, and data deduplication, which aid organizations in protecting their data from loss or corruption. For example, a financial services company migrates from

a traditional SAN to a VMware vSAN-based VSA [11]. The traditional architecture required costly, dedicated hardware and manual saving for capacity scaling. In contrast, vSAN aggregates local storage resources from ESXi cluster nodes into a unified, supplied datastore, offering:

- Automated saving of storage as new VMs are installed;
- Policy-driven control of performance and availability through storage polices (e.g., redundant array of independent disks (RAID) levels, input/output operations per second (IOPS) limits);
- Flexible scalability, enabling the company to add storage by simply adding new host nodes or physical disks;
- Optimize performance through solid-state drive (SSD) caching and data locality;
- Reduce assets and operational expenditure by eliminating the requirement for proprietary SAN hardware and minimize system downtime.

This architecture improves storage flexibility, simplifies management, and aligns with modern data center requirements. In summary, VSA provides organizations with enhanced simplicity, flexibility, scalability, performance, and cost-effectiveness when compared to traditional storage infrastructure.

4.2 Securing Virtual Disks

4.2.1 Introduction to Virtual Disks

A virtual disk, also known as a virtual hard disk (VHD) or a virtual disk image, is a file that represents a physical disk drive in a virtualized computing environment and including all data and structural elements. It mimics the functionality of a physical disk drive, allowing data to be stored, retrieved, and manipulated as if it was on a physical disk. Virtual disks are commonly used in virtualization technologies such as VMs and virtual desktop infrastructure (VDI). They can be dynamically allocated or preallocated and can vary in size based on the requirements of the virtualized environment. Virtual disks provide a convenient and efficient way to manage storage in virtual environments, providing flexibility, scalability, and user friendly. Securing virtual disks involves implementing measures to protect the data stored on virtual disk drives from unauthorized access, data breaches, and other security threats. This typically includes encryption techniques to safeguard data confidentiality, access controls to manage who can read, write, or modify data on the virtual disks, and authentication mechanisms to verify the identities of users or systems accessing the virtual disks. Additionally, securing virtual disks may involve implementing intrusion detection and prevention systems, monitoring tools, and regular security audits to identify and mitigate any potential vulnerabilities or security risks. Overall, securing virtual disks is essential for maintaining the CIA triad (confidentiality, integrity, and availability (CIA)) of data stored in virtual environments.

The concept of running multiple OSs concurrently on a single machine is not a recent development, originating as early as the 1960s. However, with the decreasing cost of computing systems and advancements in performance, virtualization has regained interest and is now a rapidly growing field in both commercial and academic spheres. It is no surprise then that virtualization is increasingly popular in the context of grid computing due to its benefits in management, utilization, and flexibility. Additionally, it allows heterogeneous OSs and applications to cooperate on the same machine while maintaining strong isolation between them. Despite the numerous advantages virtualization offers, it also brings forth new security concerns and challenges.

Addressing these security issues will necessitate the implementation of a sophisticated architecture founded on robust security principles and the creation of secure modules.

4.2.2 Advantages of Securing Virtual Disks

Security measures applied to virtual disks may include encryption techniques to protect data confidentiality, access controls to regulate user permissions, authentication mechanisms to verify user identities, and integrity checks to ensure data consistency and reliability.

In this section, securing virtual disks constitutes a specific aspect, presenting one potential threat is the unauthorized modification of virtual disk content without the user's knowledge, which could compromise sensitive data and security credentials.

Virtual disk files can contain entire operating systems, data, and applications, and their location and access method may vary. For the guest system, this presents new security challenges, as it cannot assume the integrity or confidentiality of its own hard drive content.

Data alterations could occur deliberately or inadvertently during storage or transmission without the guest's knowledge. While cryptographic protection of individual files within the guest OS may partially mitigate this threat, not all applications utilize cryptographic technology and may presume the execution environment's inherent security.

Other applications may rely on nonkeyed hash functions or checksums for integrity protection, assuming that attackers lack access to the integrity metric itself. While these assumptions may be reasonable for nonvirtualized systems operating in controlled environments, once virtualized, virtual disks may exit the controlled environment, be copied, and be accessible to attackers for offline manipulation. Traditional security concepts typically assume static hard drives with limited physical access. However, virtual disks necessitate a more dynamic and flexible security approach akin to the security requirements of mobile devices such as laptops. Consequently, many noncryptographic integrity protection mechanisms employed within the guest system may be insufficient.

Similar threats extend to confidentiality protection mechanisms, which, although effective in nonvirtualized systems, may falter once the virtual disk becomes available offline. In this section, we propose our vision for a secure virtual disk to address these security concerns. To address these concerns, our security objectives include providing data integrity, data confidentiality, and ensuring the use of a specific hypervisor for a particular image [12].

Physical data integrity is guaranteed by the underlying storage system, but it lacks protection against unauthorized access. Our goal is to offer integrity and confidentiality assurance to the image owner while preserving flexibility and backward compatibility. These security mechanisms must be transparent to the guest system to ensure seamless operation. While security is paramount, we also aim to minimize any impact on overhead and performance.

A virtual disk consists of two main elements: the virtual disk itself, which is visible within a guest domain, and the virtual disk backend, where data is stored, and virtual I/O operations are directed. The virtual disk backend is exported from a service domain by the virtual disk server (VSD) driver. Communication between the VDS driver and the virtual disk client (VDC) driver within the guest domain is facilitated by the hypervisor through a logical domain channel (LDC), enabling low-latency, high-throughput data exchange, as illustrated in Figure 4.3 and demonstrated through an accompanying technical example.

4.2.2.1 Technical Example

Virtual Disk I/O in Oracle VM Server for SPARC (LDoms)

In an Oracle VM Server for SPARC (Logical Domains) environment, a guest domain (e.g., ldom1) needs to operate disk I/O. The actual physical storage is located in the service domain, where a VDS maps and presents virtual disk devices to the guest domain.

1. *Guest domain request:* The VDC driver in ldom1 admits a read/write operation to a virtual disk.
2. *LDC transmission:* This request is transmitted via an LDC, a high-throughput, memory-mapped communication interface managed by the hypervisor for efficient interdomain data exchange.
3. *Service domain processing:* The VDS within the service domain receives the I/O request via LDC, accesses the designed physical storage (e.g., a Z file system (ZFS) volume), and sends the data back through the same LCD channel.
4. *Guest domain receives data:* The VDC driver receives the data response via LCD and passes it to the OS running within the quest domain (e.g., ldom1) for further processing.

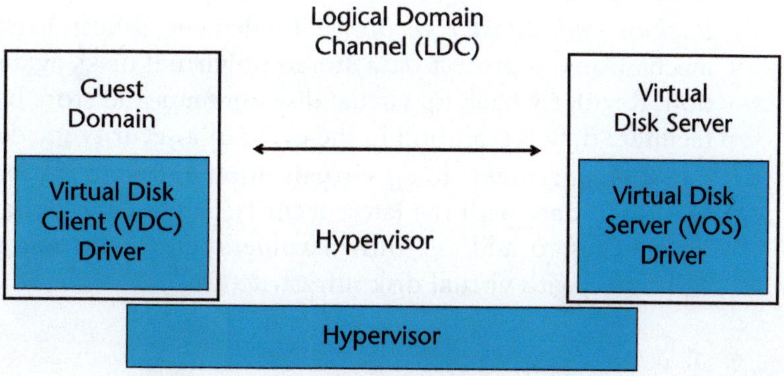

Figure 4.3 Virtual disks with logical domain channel progress.

This architecture allows a high-bandwidth and low-latency communication by bypassing traditional network and physical bus bottlenecks. Additionally, optimized storage virtualization, supporting dynamic resources provisioning, live VM migration, and efficient fault isolation. This mechanism is essential in high-performance virtualized data centers where efficient I/O operations are necessary to support scalable and effective storage infrastructure.

4.2.3 Implementing Secure Virtual Disk Techniques

Securing virtual disks involves implementing various measures to safeguard the data stored on them from unauthorized access, data breaches, and other security threats. Here are some essential actions to ensure the security of virtual disks [13].

1. *Encryption:* Implement encryption techniques to encrypt the data stored on virtual disks, ensuring that it remains protected even if the disk file is compromised. Use strong encryption algorithms and manage encryption keys securely to prevent unauthorized access to encrypted data.
2. *Access controls:* Implement access controls to regulate who can read, write, or modify data on the virtual disks. This includes setting up user permissions and role-based access controls (RBACs) to restrict access to authorized users only.
3. *Authentication:* Deploy strong authentication mechanisms to verify the identities of users or systems accessing virtual disks. Implement multifactor authentication and digital certificates to ensure secure access to virtual disk resources.
4. *Integrity checks:* Perform regular integrity checks to verify the consistency and reliability of data stored on virtual disks. Implement checksums, hash functions, or digital signatures to detect unauthorized modifications or tampering of disk contents.
5. *Auditing and logging:* Enable auditing and logging mechanisms to track access to virtual disks, monitor user activities, and detect security incidents. Maintain comprehensive audit trails to facilitate forensic analysis and investigation of security breaches.
6. *Intrusion detection and prevention:* Deploy IDPS to monitor virtual disk activity, detect suspicious behavior, and prevent unauthorized access or data breaches. Configure IDPS rules and alerts to respond to security threats proactively.
7. *Backup and disaster recovery:* Implement robust backup and recovery mechanisms to protect data stored on virtual disks against loss or corruption. Regularly back up virtual disk contents and store backups securely to facilitate data restoration in the event of a security incident.
8. *Patch management:* Keep virtualization software, hypervisors, and guest OSs up to date with the latest security patches and updates. Regularly apply patches to address known vulnerabilities and mitigate security risks associated with virtual disk infrastructure.

9. *Network segmentation:* Segregate virtual disks and their associated VMs into separate network segments or VLANs to minimize the risk of unauthorized access or lateral movement within the network.
10. *VM isolation:* Isolate VMs and virtual disks from each other to prevent cross-VM attacks and unauthorized access to sensitive data.
11. *Security policies and procedures:* Establish best practices and security policies and procedures governing the use and management of virtual disks. Define security guidelines, best practices, and incident response protocols to ensure consistent enforcement of security measures across the virtualized environment.

By implementing these security measures, organizations can enhance the protection of data stored on virtual disks and mitigate the risks associated with virtualization environments.

Securing virtual disks is crucial not only within the realm of grid computing but also across various contexts for the ongoing advancement of virtualization. While security measures within data centers, whether hardware-based or software-based, may safeguard virtual disks, it becomes imperative to ensure their protection when they are transported beyond the secure confines of the data center. This entails safeguarding all data contained on virtual disks, encompassing log files, applications, and any other components of the OS.

4.3 Securing Storage Networks

This section details different techniques for securing storage and storage networks, highlighting the need to implement multiple layers of protection and comprehend potential threats to ensure data security.

4.3.1 Introduction to Storage Networks

A storage network is a specialized type of computer network designed to facilitate the storage, retrieval, and management of data across multiple storage devices. It enables storage resources such as disks, tape drives, and storage arrays to be connected to servers and other computing devices, allowing them to access and share data efficiently.

Storage networks generally utilize specialized hardware and protocols designed specifically for data storage purposes, including fiber channel, Internet Small Computer System Interface (iSCSI), and network attached storage (NAS) protocols such as network file system (NFS) or server message block (SMB). These networks frequently adopt SAN or NAS architectures to centralize storage management, optimize performance, improve scalability, and safeguard the availability of data storage resources.

Storage networks play a crucial role in modern IT infrastructures by providing a flexible and scalable framework for storing, accessing, and managing large volumes of data, while also enabling data sharing and collaboration among multiple users and applications. However, ensuring the security of storage networks is paramount to protect sensitive information, prevent data breaches, and maintain regulatory compliance. This introduction provides an overview of the key considerations and best practices for securing storage networks.

4.3.2 Techniques of Securing Storage Networks

Securing storage networks involves implementing a combination of technical controls, policies, and procedures to safeguard data at rest and in transit. This includes protecting the integrity and confidentiality of data stored on storage devices, as well as controlling access to storage resources to prevent unauthorized disclosure or modification [14].

The major elements of securing storage networks are mostly like the techniques used in securing virtual disks, which we discussed in Section 4.2.3. Also, the physical security included secure physical access to storage devices and infrastructure to prevent unauthorized tampering or theft. Use locks, access controls, and surveillance cameras to protect storage facilities and data centers.

4.4 Securing Storage Arrays

This section introduces the storage arrays, and the advantages of storage arrays include scalability, reliability, high performance, cost efficiency, and advanced capabilities as follows.

4.4.1 Introduction to Storage Arrays

The advancement of digital information technology has had a profound impact on both economies and societies. As a result, the storage of information across various sectors such as education, entertainment, health, and business has become an integral part of human activities in the information age. Consequently, we are witnessing an era of information explosion, with the volume of data generated across major sectors nearly doubling each year. However, there exists a growing disparity between the increasing amount of digital data being produced and the available storage capacities to accommodate it.

To address this challenge, big data centers with petabyte and even exabyte capacities have emerged as vital enabling technologies and core platforms for cloud computing and storage. These have been hailed as the primary technical solution for the next generation of big data storage. Nonetheless, the infrastructure of current information technology faces mounting challenges due to the limited storage capacity of existing digital media and associated drawbacks such as high energy consumption and short lifespans. The sustainability of evolving technology is thus provoked several critical storage-related issues [15].

Storage arrays are essentially robust computing systems equipped with substantial storage capacities. They are configured to provide storage to multiple servers, typically through a dedicated network. A disk array, also referred to as a storage array, serves as a data storage system capable of handling block-based storage, file-based storage, or object storage. Comprising multiple disk drives, a disk array, or aggregate, such as RAID, implements redundancy and other data management features. This array offers storage volumes to meet the storage needs of physical machines.

Storage arrays find utility across a spectrum of applications, spanning from small-scale businesses to expansive enterprises. They commonly feature in data centers for the storage of substantial data volumes, offering dependable data storage and safeguarding capabilities. Moreover, they play a fundamental role in virtualized environments, furnishing storage for VMs and enhancing VM performance through the dispersion of data across multiple disks. Storage arrays serve various purposes, including data backup and recovery, data archiving, and acting as a shared storage resource for virtualized environments. They present several advantages over traditional direct-attached storage (DAS) systems, such as enhanced reliability, scalability, and performance [16].

4.4.2 Benefits of Storage Arrays

The benefits of storage arrays encompass scalability, reliability, performance, cost-effectiveness, and advanced features such as data protection and data tiering:

- *Scalability:* Storage arrays offer the flexibility to expand easily by incorporating extra disks or without the necessity of replacing the entire storage system. Hence, storage arrays represent a cost-effective storage solution suitable for businesses of any size.
- *Reliability:* Storage arrays are engineered with redundancy and data protection functionalities, guaranteeing data safety in the event of hardware failures. Such features mitigate the likelihood of data loss and ensure that businesses have access to their data whenever necessary.
- *Improve performance:* Storage arrays have the potential to enhance performance in contrast to conventional single-disk storage setups by dispersing data across numerous disks. This facilitates swifter read and write speeds, thereby enhancing the performance of applications demanding rapid data access, particularly in environments with high data processing demands.
- *Cost-effectiveness:* Through the reinforcement of storage resources and the optimization of storage utilization, storage arrays can aid organizations in decreasing expenses associated with storage.
- *Advanced features:* Storage arrays frequently encompass sophisticated functionalities such as data protection, data tiering, and data deduplication. Data protection mechanisms such as RAID guarantee data integrity in case of hardware failures, while data tiering automatically transfers frequently accessed data to faster storage devices such as SSDs. Additionally, data deduplication minimizes storage demands by eliminating redundant data.

The storage arrays provide a wide range of benefits such as expanded storage capacity, enhanced data security, improved performance, scalability, centralized management, cost-effectiveness, compatibility with virtualization, and improved data accessibility. These benefits position storage arrays as integral elements of contemporary IT infrastructures, empowering organizations to effectively fulfill their data storage requirements.

In conclusion, storage arrays represent a robust storage solution capable of securely and effectively storing substantial data volumes. Their scalability, redundancy, and advanced functionalities render them an optimal option for both businesses and individuals seeking dependable, high-performance data storage. Whether you operate a data center, oversee a virtualized environment, or work within the media and entertainment sector, a storage array can deliver the necessary storage capacity and performance to ensure seamless operations.

The advantages of storage arrays position them as an optimal storage solution for businesses seeking high-performance, dependable, and scalable storage. They serve as a vital element of contemporary data center infrastructure and find application across various sectors, ranging from small businesses to large enterprises. Storage arrays offer versatility and reliability, catering to diverse storage needs across a broad spectrum of applications. Whether overseeing a data center, administering a virtualized environment, or operating within the media and entertainment domain, a storage array can furnish the requisite storage capacity and performance to ensure seamless operations.

In conclusion, storage arrays offer a highly scalable, reliable, and performance-optimized solution that meets the complex demands of modern IT infrastructures. Their modular architecture enables organizations to efficiently manage large volumes of structured and unstructured data, making them ideal for use in data centers, virtualized environments, high-performance computing, and industries with intensive data throughput such as media and entertainment. Advanced features such as tiered storage, automated data management, deduplication, and redundancy mechanisms significantly enhance data protection and operational resilience. Furthermore, storage arrays support continuous integration with cloud services and virtualization platforms, providing flexibility and agility for hybrid and multicloud strategies [17]. Their ability to deliver high IOPS and low latency ensures consistent performance for mission-critical applications. As data growth continues to accelerate, storage arrays serve as a foundational component for organizations seeking to maintain service continuity, data integrity, and strategic scalability across their digital ecosystems.

4.5 Best Practices for Storage Security in Virtualized Environments

Virtual security appliances run inside a virtual environment with a prepackaged, hardened OS running on virtualized hardware.

4.5.1 Introduction of Storage Security

The store data refers to data at rest and there are various types of storage devices that retain the data when no user or process is using it. A storage device can be local (on a computing device) or centralized (on the network). Several options exist for storing data.

The storage security in virtualized environments refers to the measures and practices put in place to protect data stored within virtualized systems and storage resources such as virtual disks, SANs, storage virtualization (virtual layer), and NAS in virtualized environments.

Storage security refers to the comprehensive set of technical measures and policies designed to defense data across all phases at rest, in transit, and during processing within various storage environments such as SAN, NAS, cloud, or virtualized infrastructures [18]. It is governed by three core principles: *confidentiality*, ensuring that sensitive data is accessed only by authorized users through mechanisms such as encryption and RBAC; *integrity*, protecting data from unauthorized modifications using checksums, hashing, and version control systems; and *availability*, which guarantees timely and reliable access to storage resources through redundancy, failover systems, and robust backup strategies. Successful storage security demands continual monitoring, threat detection, and compliance with standards such as ISO/IEC 27040 [19]. The storage resources in the virtual environment are shown in Figure 4.4.

SAN virtualization has multiple physical storage devices into a single virtualized storage. It provides features such as simplified management, data migration, and load balancing.

NAS virtualization is a multiple NAS device aggregated into a single virtualized file system, providing flexible, scalable, and effective file storage.

Virtualization allows multiple VMs to run on a single physical server, sharing its resources. Storage virtualization enables administrators to manage storage resources more efficiently by pooling and allocating them as needed to different VMs. However, this also creates new security challenges, as multiple VMs share the same physical storage resources, making it easier for an attacker to access and compromise sensitive data. Therefore, the VMs and virtualized storage are susceptible to several security risks, and ensuring the confidentiality, integrity, and availability of data is very crucial.

Storage security in virtual environments is a continuing process that requires a blend of technology, policies, and user attention to protect sensitive data from numerous threats and risks.

The following essential key characteristics of storage security in virtual environments are illustrated:

- *Access control:* Implement the RBAC to restrict access to virtual storage resources based on user roles and responsibilities. Employ robust authentication methods and grant access only to authorized users and applications.

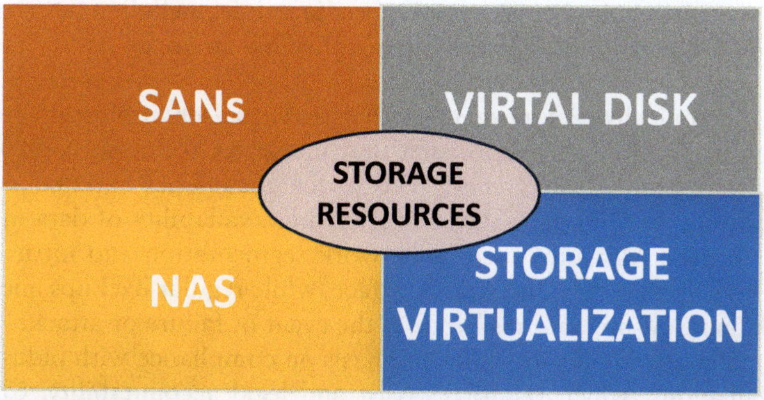

Figure 4.4 Storage resources.

- *Data encryption:* Encrypt data stored in virtual disks and storage repositories to protect against unauthorized access in case of data breaches or theft. Similarly, encrypt data transmitted between VMs, storage devices, and other components to prevent interception.
- *Patch management:* Frequently update and patch virtualization software, OS, and application to report any recognize vulnerabilities and improve security.
- *Hypervisor security:* Secure the hypervisor layer to prevent unauthorized access and protect against vulnerabilities that could compromise virtual storage resources. Keep the hypervisor software up to date with regular patching to address security vulnerabilities.
- *Network segmentation:* Use network segmentation (separate virtual networks) to isolate VMs and storage resources, reducing the attack surface and restrictive lateral movement of threats.
- *Data backup and recovery:* Implement automated and secure backup solutions to ensure data availability in case of data corruption, hardware failures, or cyberattacks. Develop a comprehensive disaster recovery plan that includes virtualized storage resources to minimize downtime and data loss.
- *Monitoring and logging:* Employ IDPS to detect and block suspicious activities within virtual storage environments. Maintain detailed logs of storage activities and regularly review them for signs of unauthorized access or data breaches.
- *VM isolation:* Ensure that VMs are properly isolated and have appropriate resource allocations to prevent resource contention and unauthorized access. Use the Virtual Trusted Platform Module (vTPM) to enhance the security of VMs by providing hardware-based encryption and integrity verification.
- *Vendor and compliance considerations:* Select reputable virtualization vendors and virtualization solutions from trusted vendors with a strong track record in security. Also ensure that your virtual storage environment complies with relevant industry standards and regulations, such as GDPR, Health Insurance Portability and Accountability Act (HIPAA), or Payment Card Industry Data Security Standard (PCI DSS)
- *End-user training and awareness:* Train and educate users and administrators about storage security best practices, including data handling, password management, and identifying phishing attempts.

Technically, the storage security in virtual environments requires a comprehensive, multilayered approach that integrates technical controls, administrative policies, and user awareness. The key characteristics outlined are foundational to ensuring the confidentiality, integrity, and availability of data in virtualized infrastructures. Measures such as network segmentation and intrusion detection systems help to reduce the attack surface, while regular backups and disaster recovery planning ensure data resilience in the event of failure or attack.

Equally important is the emphasis on compliance with industry standards and regulations, which reinforces trust and legal accountability. Choosing reputable vendors and maintaining up-to-date systems are essential for staying ahead of evolving threats. Finally, ongoing user training ensures that all stakeholders understand their role in protecting data.

In conclusion, by implementing these best practices, organizations can significantly strengthen the security posture of their virtual storage environments, mitigate risks, and ensure operational continuity in an increasingly complex digital landscape [20].

4.5.2 Storage Limitation

When dealing with large quantities of data daily, making sure excess data is not kept for longer than required is a significant fact. For example, the National Health Service (NHS) receives a large amount of data per day, meaning that they would be required to remove any data or information they do not need after completing the reviewing carefully to upsurge the storage capacity availability. Holding excess data can overload storage and be a potential risk if the information is not required and still accessible. The NHS can also choose to make any data or information anonymous if it is regarding a patient's personal information. Lastly, if the company needs to keep any information for a specific reason and purpose, then the company should archive the data rather than keeping it on the main storage servers; certainly this will minimize excess storage load, while keeping the data that they may need in the future if required.

Overall, storage security in virtualized environments requires a multilayered approach that involves a combination of technical controls, policies, and procedures to protect against both internal and external threats.

4.5.3 Securing VSA

This section focuses on implementing security measures to protect the storage architecture in a virtualized environment. Securing the VSA involves safeguarding storage devices, managing access controls, encrypting data at rest, ensuring data integrity, and mitigating storage-related vulnerabilities and threats. The purpose is to protect the virtualized storage infrastructure from unauthorized access, data breaches, and other security risks.

4.5.3.1 A Case Study for Securing VSA at AB Corporation

AB Corporation, a multinational technology company, delivers cloud computing services to diverse clientele worldwide. Throughout its evolution, the company has evolved its virtual storage infrastructure to fulfill the expanding needs of its clients for scalable and protected storage solutions. This case study investigates the historical and contemporary methods employed by AB Corporation to secure its VSA.

Techniques for Securing VSA

The following clearly demonstrates two techniques for securing VSA.

1. *Traditional strategy:* AB Corporation relied on traditional storage solutions that lacked the scalability and adaptability needed to satisfy its clients' requirements. Physical storage devices were susceptible to performance

constraints and posed difficulties in efficient management. Consequently, the company shifted towards VSA, utilizing technologies such as SANs and NAS to enhance scalability and performance. However, securing VSA at AB Corporation in the past has experienced various challenges. Data security emerged as a significant concern, with virtualized environments being vulnerable to cyber threats such as malware and data breaches. Furthermore, ensuring compliance with industry regulations and standards proved intricate due to the dynamic nature of virtualized storage environments.

2. *Current strategy:* Addressing these obstacles, AB Corporation has embraced a multilayered strategy for securing VSA. The company now enforces stringent security protocols at every layer of the storage infrastructure, encompassing:
   - *Data encryption:* AB Corporation employs encryption for all data stored in virtual environments, whether at rest or in transit, to safeguard against unauthorized access and data breaches.
   - *Access control:* RBAC mechanisms are utilized to limit access to sensitive data and resources, ensuring that only authorized personnel can access critical storage infrastructure.
   - *Intrusion detection and prevention:* Sophisticated IDPS are implemented to continuously monitor network traffic, swiftly detecting potential security threats in real time.
   - *Regular security audits:* AB Corporation performs routine security audits and vulnerability assessments to identify and rectify potential security vulnerabilities in its VSA.
   - *Disaster recovery and business continuity:* The company upholds resilient disaster recovery and business continuity plans to expedite recovery and mitigate data loss in case of system failures or disasters.

In conclusion, through the implementation of this comprehensive strategy for securing VSA, AB Corporation has notably bolstered the security and reliability of its storage infrastructure. The company has effectively managed security risks and compliance complexities, instilling trust, and assurance with clients regarding the safety of their data. Furthermore, the enhanced scalability and performance of the virtual storage architecture have empowered AB Corporation to effectively address clients' changing requirements, consolidating its status as a frontrunner in the cloud computing sector. Keep in mind that successful implementation hinges on meticulous planning, selecting the appropriate technology, and ensuring that your team is adequately prepared to handle the new virtualized environment.

4.6 Summary

In this chapter, we delved into the concept and inner workings of storage security in virtualized environment, originating with a detailed definition of case study and its historical development. We emphasized the security storage and the challenges of storage architecture in modern IT infrastructure and discussion of its storage limitation.

Securing virtual disks was discussed in detail, exploring its concept, importance, and utilization in the organization. We demonstrated everyday examples of securing virtual disks that service businesses in managing storage effectively.

Following that, we defined desk virtualization and explored its benefits compared to traditional security measures. We examined its practical applications and how it improves user accessibility and control. Moving on to application virtualization, we outlined its advantages and provided examples of its usefulness in scenarios such as remote work and software testing environments.

We also delved into the security risks associated with virtualization, discussing threats such as hypervisor attacks, guest OS attacks, and inter-VM attacks. We highlighted potential vulnerabilities in virtual disk and storage security and the risks posed by misconfigurations. Our secure storage area network solution facilitates effective key management and data sharing, ensuring data integrity and confidentiality without the need for centralized servers.

The importance of maintaining security in virtualized environments was thoroughly discussed, emphasizing the detrimental effects of security breaches on businesses, both operationally and reputationally. We emphasized the role of virtualization security in preserving the integrity and reliability of IT infrastructure, as well as the legal and regulatory obligations that businesses have regarding securing their virtual environments.

Understanding virtualization and its security risks is crucial in today's digital landscape. Businesses of all sizes must invest in robust security measures for their virtual environments to ensure business continuity, protect sensitive data, and maintain client trust.

In conclusion, securing virtualized environments is not merely a technical necessity but a strategic imperative in today's digital infrastructure. As organizations increasingly adopt virtualization to enhance scalability, efficiency, and resource utilization, the corresponding security risks also grow in complexity. This chapter highlighted how a breach in a virtual environment can have far-reaching impacts, affecting service availability, data confidentiality, and overall trust in an organization's IT ecosystem.

Virtualization security [21] plays a vital role in ensuring the integrity of VMs, hypervisors, and storage systems, while simultaneously helping businesses to meet compliance standards such as GDPR, HIPAA, or PCI DSS. From RBAC to encryption, patch management, and hypervisor hardening, each security layer forms part of a defense-in-depth strategy critical for maintaining secure operations.

Therefore, understanding the unique vulnerabilities of virtualization and proactively implementing robust, layered security controls is essential. By doing so, businesses can better safeguard their digital assets, reduce downtime, and foster long-term resilience in an ever-evolving threat landscape.

References

[1] Denning, P. J., "Virtual Memory," *ACM Computing Surveys,* 1996.

[2] Hai, J., "A Survey of Storage Virtualization," *Mini-Micro Systems*, 2003.

[3] Hu, Y., L. Wang, and X. Zhang, "Cloud Storage Virtualization Technology and Its Architecture," *Applied Mechanics and Materials*, Vol. 713-715, 2015, pp. 2435–2439.

[4] https://www.ibm.com/docs/en/zos-basic-skills?topic=1960s-what-is-virtual-storage.

[5] https://www.datacore.com/software-defined-storage/.

[6] https://www.datacore.com/solutions/storage-for-vmware/.

[7] Kim, M., et al., "Case Study on Integrated Architecture for In-Memory and In-Storage Computing," *Electronics*, Vol. 10, No. 15, 2021, p. 1750.

[8] Mondal, A. S., et al., "Comparative Analysis of Object-Based Big Data Storage Systems on Architectures and Services: A Recent Survey," *Journal of the Institue of Engineers India Series B*, 2024.

[9] https://www.gartner.com/en/information-technology.

[10] Bhore, P., "A Survey on Storage Virtualization and Its Levels Along with the Benefits and Limitations," *International Journal of Computer Sciences and Engineering*, Vol. 4, No. 7, July 31, 2016, https://doi.org/10.5281/ZENODO.59985.

[11] VMware, *VMware Security Hardening Guide*, 2023, https://core.vmware.com/security.

[12] National Institute of Standards and Technology (NIST), *Security Recommendations for Hypervisor Deployment (SP 800-125A)*, 2020, https://nvlpubs.nist.gov/nistpubs/SpecialPublications/NIST.SP.800-125A.pdf.

[13] Gebhardt, C., and A. Tomlinson, "Secure Virtual Disk Images for Grid Computing," *2008 Third Asia-Pacific Trusted Infrastructure Technologies Conference*, October 2008, pp. 19–29.

[14] http://www.cybok.org/media/downloads/Network_Security_v2.0.0.pdf

[15] Gu, M., X. Li, and Y. Cao, "Optical Storage Arrays: A Perspective for Future Big Data Storage," *Light: Science & Applications*, Vol. 3, No. 5, May 23, 2014, p. e177.

[16] https://www.ibm.com/docs/en/tarm/8.11.6?topic=infrastructure-disk-array.

[17] Chowdhury, M., R. Boutaba, and S. Hasan, "Security and Privacy in Cloud and Virtualization: A Survey," *Computer Networks*, Vol. 193, 2021, p. 108066.

[18] Zhang, Y., et al., "HomeAlone: Co-Residency Detection in the Cloud," *Proc. IEEE Symposium on Security and Privacy*, 2011, pp. 313–328.

[19] ISO/IEC, *ISO/IEC 27001:2022 – Information Security Management*, International Organization for Standardization, 2022.

[20] Gartner, *Best Practices for Securing Workloads in Virtualized Environments*, Gartner Research, 2022, https://www.gartner.com.

[21] SANS Institute, *Virtualization Security: Challenges and Solutions*, SANS Whitepaper, 2022, https://www.sans.org/white-papers.

CHAPTER 5

Virtualization Security in Cloud Computing

5.1 Introduction

Virtualization is fundamental to modern cloud computing technologies, efficiently using modern computer resources and being flexible, scalable, and innovative [1]. Virtualization, at a high level, can render virtual representations of physical resources including hardware platforms, storage triads, and network resources. The virtualization process in cloud computing is ultimately about establishing VMs so that multiple VMs can run independently on one physical machine and each operate as a fully independent computer [2].

The hypervisor is the heart of virtualization and serves as a software layer between the physical hardware and the VMs. It dynamically assigns phases, such as CPU, memory, and storage, to the individual VMs, while providing strong isolation [3]. This separation is vital for security and stability, as it prevents any single VM's operations from impacting others.

Virtualization is crucial for cloud computing, enabling cloud providers to deliver scalable services by securely allowing multiple users to share the same hardware through multitenancy [4]. This design isolates each user's data and applications, creating a consistent, secure environment within a shared infrastructure. Virtualization also supports elastic provisioning, allowing resources to scale up or down dynamically, ensuring minimal latency and cost-effectiveness.

A full virtualization environment is shown in Figure 5.1, with VMs running on top of a hypervisor that interfaces with the hardware. Each VM runs a full OS instance and interacts with the hypervisor, which manages the allocation of resources between the VMs and the physical hardware [5]. The hypervisor is the primary component of full virtualization as it manages VMs, creates VMs, maps the underlying hardware, and provides access to hardware resources. Hypervisors are either type 1 (also called a bare-metal hypervisor) or type 2 (also called a hosted hypervisor). Type-1 hypervisors install directly on the hardware of a host machine and command system resources; type-1 hypervisors have a smaller footprint than a traditional OS in system resources. Type-2 hypervisors run on top of an existing OS while providing access to the underlying hardware, making type-2 hypervisors

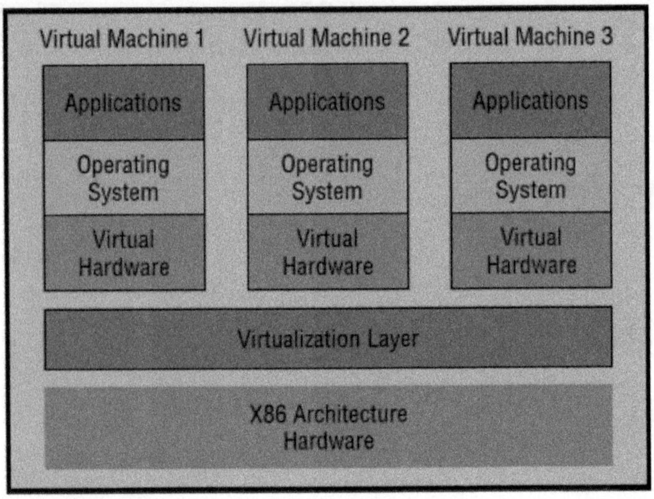

Figure 5.1 Full virtualization environment and have VMs running on a hypervisor that interacts with the hardware [5].

a less efficient system resource-wise than type-1 hypervisors. A few hypervisors include VMware ESXi, Microsoft Hyper-V, Xen KVM, and Oracle VirtualBox [3].

Furthermore, Figure 5.2 illustrates a full virtualization setup with a host OS, where the virtualization layer operates on top of the host OS. The key components include physical hardware, a host OS, a type-2 hypervisor, and VMs. The VMs run their own guest OS and applications, sharing hardware resources via the hypervisor and host OS. This setup introduces a host OS between the hypervisor and hardware, making it slightly less efficient than bare-metal hypervisors [6]. Additionally, virtualization improves resource utilization, letting information technology departments run multiple applications and OSs on fewer machines. This efficiency reduces hardware costs and power consumption, lowering operational expenses

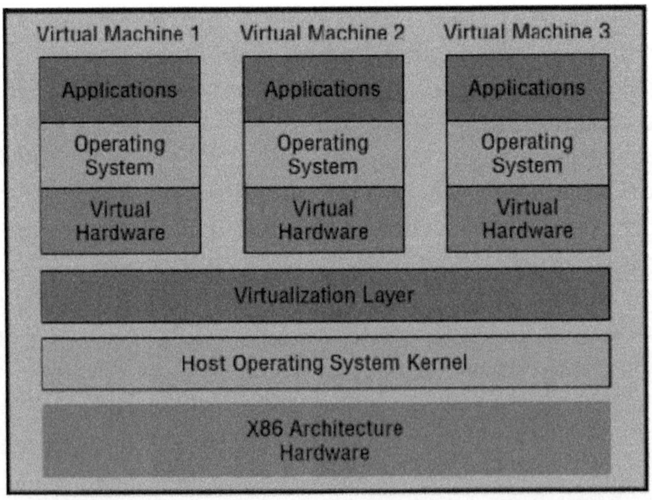

Figure 5.2 Full virtualization but works with a host OS instead of a hypervisor [5].

and supporting environmental sustainability by reducing the carbon footprint associated with large server farms [7].

Security also benefits from virtualization, as abstracting workloads from physical hardware can enhance disaster recovery processes. Features such as snapshots and cloning support rapid recovery, minimizing downtime during failures, a critical advantage for enterprises needing continuous operations [8].

Virtualization makes it possible to create controlled environments for testing and development so that developers can test software on various OSs without requiring separate physical machines [9]. This capability accelerates development cycles and enables agile methodologies that foster innovation.

Virtualization marks a shift from traditional IT infrastructure to more flexible, efficient, and scalable cloud-based solutions [10]. Decoupling applications and systems from specific physical devices maximizes hardware usage and enables new service models with economic advantages. Virtualization remains fundamental to cloud computing, driving the agility and cost efficiency that businesses need to compete in today's dynamic markets.

5.1.1 Types of Virtualizations in Cloud Computing

Virtualization is the primary technology in cloud computing that maximizes resource utilization, scalability, and management through partitioning and abstraction of physical resources [11]. We will discuss virtualization's four main types: server, network, storage, and desktop virtualization. We will look at the four main types of virtualizations of cloud computing (Figure 5.3): server virtualization, network virtualization, storage virtualization, and desktop virtualization.

5.1.2 Server Virtualization

Server virtualization allows the server to be divided into multiple isolated virtual servers (or simply VMs), where each VM can operate independently with its own OS, applications, and configurations, thereby optimizing resource utilization and management [3].

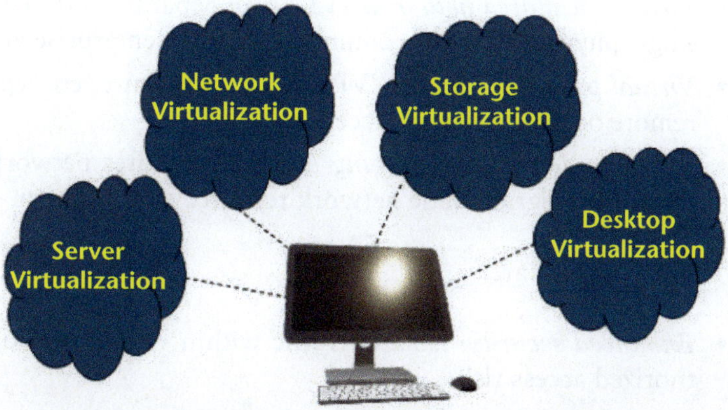

Figure 5.3 Types of virtualizations [11].

The key components are:

- *Hypervisor:* The software layer managing VMs on a physical server, with two main types:
  - *Type 1 (bare-metal):* Runs directly on hardware, offering high performance and efficient resource management;
  - *Type 2 (hosted):* Operates on a host OS, making it ideal for testing or development environments.

The advantages are:

- *Optimized resource utilization:* Reduces idle hardware, improving cost efficiency by consolidating workloads onto fewer physical servers.
- *Isolation and security:* VMs remain isolated from each other, ensuring that issues such as crashes or malware affect only the involved VM.
- *Scalability and flexibility:* VMs can be created, resized, or deleted dynamically based on demand.
- *Disaster recovery:* Server virtualization supports replication and migration, minimizing downtime during hardware failures.

With regard to use cases, server virtualization is widely used in data centers and Infrastructure as a Service (IaaS) environments, enabling providers such as Amazon Web Services (AWS), Google Cloud, and Azure to offer virtualized servers to customers.

5.2 Network Virtualization

Network virtualization abstracts and combines physical network resources, creating multiple virtual networks over the same physical infrastructure [12].

The key components are:

- *Virtual local area networks (VLANs):* Separate and manage traffic within a single physical network, commonly used in enterprise and cloud networks.
- *Virtual private networks (VPNs):* Create secure, encrypted connections for remote or intra-network access.
- *Software-defined networking (SDN):* Separates network control and data, enabling programmatic network resource management.

The advantages are:

- *Enhanced security:* Isolates traffic within virtual networks, reducing unauthorized access risk.
- *Flexibility and scalability:* Virtual networks can be created or adjusted without hardware changes, easily meeting shifting demand.

- *Efficient resource utilization:* Reduces latency and optimizes bandwidth use across VMs.
- *Centralized management:* Centralized control over policies, monitoring, and provisioning for easier network administration.

With regard to use cases, they are ideal for multitenant cloud environments, hybrid cloud setups, and VPN solutions requiring secure cloud connectivity.

5.3 Storage Virtualization

Storage virtualization consolidates storage from multiple devices into a single virtual resource, streamlining management, enhancing performance, and increasing resilience [13].

The key components are:

- *Virtual storage pool:* Aggregates storage capacity from various devices, enabling flexible and dynamic allocation.
- *Storage area network (SAN):* High-performance, centralized storage often used for VM data.
- *Network-attached storage (NAS):* Shared storage accessible over a network, supporting centralized data access.

The advantages are:

- *Improved storage utilization:* Optimizes storage by pooling resources and reducing physical storage requirements.
- *High availability:* Enables data replication across devices, increasing resilience and minimizing downtime.
- *Scalability:* Easily add or remove storage without disrupting operations.
- *Simplified management:* Centralized management tools reduce complexity and overhead.

With regard to use cases, common in cloud storage services such as AWS S3 and Google Cloud Storage, as well as in disaster recovery for data replication and backup.

5.4 Desktop Virtualization

Desktop virtualization separates desktop environments from physical devices, hosting them centrally and enabling secure remote access for users [14].

The key components are:

- *Centralized server:* Hosts the desktop environment, accessible remotely by users.

- *Remote display protocols:* Remote Desktop Protocol (RDP) and Independent Computing Architecture (ICA) facilitate remote access with optimized performance.
- *Endpoint devices:* Users access virtual desktops from thin clients, personal computers, or tablets connected to the central server.

The advantages are:

- *Enhanced security:* Data remains on the server, reducing loss or theft risk from endpoints.
- *Reduced hardware needs:* Reduces endpoint device costs since processing occurs on the server.
- *Centralized management:* Enables IT admins to efficiently manage, patch, and update desktops.
- *Remote access and flexibility:* Supports remote work by allowing access from any internet-connected device.

With regard to use cases, they are suitable for remote work environments, secure organizations, and educational institutions requiring standardized access.

5.5 Benefits

Virtualization in cloud computing has transformed how IT resources and services are managed and delivered, offering greater efficiency, flexibility, and performance across cloud environments. By abstracting physical resources into virtual instances, virtualization enables organizations to optimize operations and adapt swiftly to evolving business needs [15]. Here are the main benefits of virtualization in cloud computing:

- *Resource optimization and efficiency:* Virtualization increases hardware utilization by allowing multiple VMs to operate on a single physical server, improving efficiency and optimizing resource utilization. By consolidating VMs, many physical machines are no longer needed. This saves on hardware investments and maintenance costs.
- *Cost savings:* By consolidating workloads onto fewer servers, virtualization reduces direct costs (hardware purchase, management, and maintenance) and indirect costs (such as energy consumption for power and cooling). These savings create a more sustainable, cost-effective IT infrastructure.
- *Scalability:* Virtualization allows rapid scaling of IT resources to meet dynamic business demands without requiring new hardware. Organizations can scale up (add resources to a single VM) or scale out (add more VMs) to ensure optimal performance, thus providing agility to adapt to workload changes.
- *Enhanced disaster recovery:* Virtualization supports improved disaster recovery with features such as VM snapshots and cloning, facilitating swift

backup and recovery. Virtual environments can be replicated and migrated across data centers with minimal downtime, ensuring business continuity and quick restoration after a failure.

- *Simplified management and automation:* Centralized control panels simplify virtual environment management, allowing administrators to efficiently manage and allocate resources. Automation tools streamline provisioning, scaling, monitoring, and updating, easing the IT workload and reducing the potential for human error.
- *Flexibility and mobility:* Virtualization separates applications from physical hardware, enabling them to be moved across environments without disruption. This flexibility aids load balancing, maintenance, and migrations while supporting remote access, allowing users to access applications from any location or device.
- *Enhanced security:* Although virtualization has security considerations, it also provides improved security options. Virtual environments are isolated, which helps to prevent the spread of threats across systems. Centralized management and automated patching further enhance security, while features such as secure boot, data encryption, and role-based access control (RBAC) support compliance and protection.
- *Environmental impact:* Consolidating physical servers reduces the energy required for powering and cooling data centers, helping organizations to reduce their environmental footprint. This shift supports sustainability goals, which are increasingly important in today's business landscape.

In summary, virtualization in cloud computing provides substantial advantages from resource efficiency and cost savings to enhanced security and scalability. As a foundational technology, virtualization enables businesses to operate with greater agility, flexibility, and resilience, driving innovation and adaptation in an ever-evolving digital world.

5.6 Challenges

Virtualization transforms cloud computing, enhancing flexibility, cost-efficiency, and scalability. However, it also introduces complexities that must be managed to ensure secure, high-performing, and compliant virtual environments [16]. Here are some of the primary challenges and solutions in this domain. Furthermore, Figure 5.4 highlights the challenges in virtualization in cloud computing, including performance overhead, resource allocation, and security risk. Addressing these challenges is essential for improving virtualized cloud environments' performance.

5.6.1 Security Risks

Virtualized environments inherently involve shared infrastructure, increasing security vulnerabilities.

Figure 5.4 Challenges in virtualization in cloud computing [17].

- *Hypervisor vulnerabilities:* The hypervisor is the core software managing VMs, isolating them from each other. If compromised, it could expose all VMs to attack. "VM escape" attacks, where one VM gains access to others or the host, underscore the critical need for hypervisor security.
- *Shared infrastructure risks:* In multitenant setups, multiple users share the same hardware, creating cross-tenant attacks and data leakage risks.
- *Insider threats:* With numerous stakeholders, including cloud providers and administrators, insiders with access to the infrastructure may pose risks, intentionally or inadvertently.
- *Inter-VM communication vulnerabilities:* Unsegmented virtual networks allow attackers to move laterally across VMs, potentially compromising the entire environment.

The mitigations are:

- *Hypervisor hardening:* Regularly update hypervisors and restrict access, employing multifactor authentication for authorized personnel.
- *Isolation and segmentation:* Use network segmentation to separate VMs and restrict lateral movement.
- *Monitoring and intrusion detection:* Deploy real-time tools to detect and respond to malicious activities.

5.6.2 Resource Contention

Resource contention arises when multiple VMs share finite resources, impacting performance [18].

- *Overcommitment of resources:* Allocating more virtual resources than physically available can lead to contention if high-demand VMs compete simultaneously.
- *CPU and memory bottlenecks:* CPU-intensive or memory-intensive VMs may delay others, reducing efficiency.
- *Storage and I/O contention:* High I/O demands can lead to storage bottlenecks and slow data access.
- *Network bottlenecks:* Limited bandwidth can degrade performance when many VMs access the network.

The mitigations are:

- *Resource monitoring and management:* Track resource usage patterns to optimize allocation.
- *Dynamic resource allocation:* Adjust resources based on real-time demand.
- *Quality of service:* Prioritize critical applications to minimize contention.
- *Scaling infrastructure:* Add physical resources to meet demand effectively.

5.6.3 Complex Management

Managing virtual environments at scale demands specialized tools and expertise [19].

- *Resource allocation and optimization:* Efficiently allocating resources and balancing workloads becomes more complex as VMs scale.
- *Monitoring and performance management:* Real-time data on VM health and usage is critical but complex.
- *Configuration management:* Each VM must be correctly configured, updated, and secure, or it can become a vulnerability.
- *Backup and disaster recovery management:* Scheduling backups and ensuring data consistency across VMs is increasingly challenging at scale.

The mitigations are:

- *Automation and orchestration:* Automate resource allocation, monitoring, and configuration to streamline management.
- *Centralized management platforms:* Use management tools for resource and performance insights.
- *Virtualization management policies:* Define policies to ensure consistent resource management and security practices.
- *Training and expertise:* Build specialized skills within IT teams to handle complexities.

5.6.4 Compliance and Data Privacy

Handling regulated or sensitive data in virtualized environments brings unique compliance challenges [20].

- *Multitenancy and data isolation:* Data isolation becomes critical in shared infrastructure to prevent cross-tenant data access.
- *Data residency requirements:* Compliance regulations may require data to remain in specific regions, complicating migrations and replications.
- *Access control and auditing:* Enforcing access restrictions and maintaining logs can be challenging across multiple VMs.
- *Data encryption and protection:* Encryption at rest and in transit is essential but challenging to manage at scale.

The mitigations are:

- *Data segmentation and isolation:* Separate customers' data to prevent unauthorized access and ensure compliance.
- *Geographic data controls:* Many cloud providers offer options to restrict data location to comply with residency requirements.
- *Encryption and key management:* Secure encryption practices and key management solutions ensure data privacy.
- *Auditing and reporting tools:* Track data access and user activity for compliance reporting.

5.6.5 Performance Overhead

The hypervisor layer in virtualization can cause performance overhead, affecting resource-intensive applications. Optimizing performance requires balancing resource allocation and regularly monitoring workloads to prevent bottlenecks.

5.6.6 Licensing Costs and Constraints

While virtualization reduces hardware costs, software licenses for virtualization platforms and management tools can be expensive. Organizations may face complexities with licensing compliance, particularly in multicloud setups.

5.6.7 Backup and Recovery

Virtualized environments benefit from enhanced disaster recovery, yet managing backups across numerous VMs is complex. Automation and robust recovery solutions are essential to ensure reliable restoration.

5.6.8 Vendor Lock-In

Heavy reliance on a single virtualization vendor limits flexibility, particularly when integrating diverse systems in hybrid or multicloud environments. Vendor lock-in can also restrict pricing negotiations and system compatibility.

5.7 Summary

Virtualization brings vast potential to cloud computing but presents challenges around security, resource optimization, complexity, compliance, and costs. By proactively addressing these areas, organizations can leverage virtualization to its fullest potential, driving operational efficiency and maintaining a competitive edge.

5.7.1 Virtualization Management Tools in Cloud Computing

Virtualization management tools are vital to managing the complexity and dynamic nature of virtualized environments in cloud computing. These tools make it easier to manage VMs, optimize resource consumption, and optimize performance and security [21]. Here is a detailed description of the four most popular virtualization management tools: VMware vSphere, Microsoft Hyper-V, Citrix XenServer, and OpenStack.

5.7.1.1 VMware vSphere

Overview

VMware vSphere is one of the most widely adopted enterprise virtualization platforms. Renowned for its robustness and wide range of features, vSphere is suitable for businesses of all sizes, helping them to build cloud infrastructures, consolidate servers, and manage data centers more efficiently [22].

The key features are:

- *vMotion:* Allows live migration of VMs without downtime, facilitating maintenance activities and load balancing.
- *Distributed resource scheduler:* Automates resource allocation across VMs to ensure optimal performance and efficiency.
- *High availability:* Offers automatic restarts for VMs in case of hardware or server failure, reducing downtime.
- *Enhanced security:* Features such as VM Encryption and secure boot options protect data and the system's integrity.
- *Management interface:* vSphere Web Client provides a unified interface for managing large-scale deployments.

Its use cases are that it is ideal for data centers demanding high performance, availability, and security. It is extensively used in industries pursuing private cloud development and infrastructure consolidation.

5.7.1.2 Microsoft Hyper-V

Overview

Microsoft created the Hyper-V virtualization platform, which is integrated into Windows Server environments. It primarily helps businesses that use Microsoft products by offering smooth management and integration [23].

The key features are:

- *Live migration:* Supports moving VMs between physical hosts without downtime.
- *Dynamic memory:* Adjusts memory allocation to VMs in real time based on current demand, optimizing resource usage.
- *VM replication:* Provides disaster recovery through asynchronous replication of VMs.
- *Nested virtualization:* Allows running VMs inside other VMs, which is helpful for testing and development scenarios.
- *Integration services:* Enhances VM management by integrating with the host OS, ensuring increased performance and reliability.

Its use cases are that it is suited for firms already operating within the Microsoft ecosystem, offering a cost-effective and tightly integrated virtual infrastructure solution.

5.7.1.3 Citrix XenServer

Overview

Citrix XenServer is a high-performance virtualization platform known for its strong support of virtual desktop infrastructure (VDI) and application delivery. It aims to deliver cloud services and desktop virtualization solutions with scalability and ease of management [24].

The key features are:

- *XenMotion:* Enables live migration of VMs for load balancing and hardware maintenance.
- *Integrated Management XenCenter:* Provides a comprehensive management interface for managing virtual environments.
- *GPU passthrough:* Supports graphics-intensive applications by allocating a VM exclusive use of a graphics card.
- *High availability:* Ensures that critical applications and services remain available at all times.
- *Security:* Offers advanced security measures, including virtual Trusted Platform Module (TPM) and per VM firewalling capabilities.

Its use cases are that it is commonly used in enterprises focusing on VDI and applications that require robust performance, particularly those delivering complex graphics operations.

5.7.1.4 OpenStack

Overview

OpenStack is an open-source cloud platform that provides IaaS. It is highly customizable and used to manage and orchestrate cloud-based resources, making it a preferred choice for building private and public clouds [25].

Its key features are:

- *Modular architecture:* Offers flexibility through independently deployed modules, such as Nova for computing, Neutron for networking, and Swift for object storage.
- *Scalability:* Capable of scaling from simple setups to managing thousands of VMs across data centers.
- *Open source:* Supports a large community that continuously contributes to its development, ensuring that it stays current with technology trends.
- *Multitenancy:* Securely separates resources among different users/tenants, making it suitable for cloud service providers.

Its use cases are that it is suitable for organizations seeking a highly customizable cloud solution or those offering cloud resources to multiple tenants, such as service providers and large enterprises.

These virtualization management tools offer distinct features and benefits for different organizational needs and environments. While VMware vSphere and Microsoft Hyper-V are more traditional choices for enterprises focusing on robust integration and reliability, Citrix XenServer excels in VDI scenarios [26]. OpenStack provides a flexible framework for building and managing cloud resources. The choice of tool largely depends on specific business needs, existing IT infrastructure, and long-term cloud strategies.

5.7.2 Cloud Service Providers Offering Virtualization

Cloud service providers play a pivotal role in delivering virtualization solutions that enable businesses to leverage cloud computing's full benefits, such as scalability, efficiency, and reduced operational costs [27]. Each provider has different features and services that are tailored to different business needs. Examine virtualization services offered by AWS, Microsoft Azure, Google Cloud Platform, and IBM Cloud.

5.7.2.1 AWS

Overview

AWS is one of the largest and most widely used cloud service providers globally, known for its comprehensive suite of cloud products and services. Virtualization in AWS is primarily realized through its Elastic Compute Cloud (EC2) service [28].

Its key services are:

- *Amazon EC2:* Provides scalable virtual servers, dubbed instances, which run a large variety of operating systems and configurations. EC2 has the flexibility to allow the customer to select the storage, networking, and configurations that best suit their needs.

- *Elastic load balancing:* Automatically distributes incoming application traffic across multiple targets to ensure high availability and fault tolerance.
- *AWS auto scaling:* Ensures applications have the right resources by automatically adjusting capacity.
- *Security features:* Virtual Private Cloud (VPC), IAM roles, and security groups are included to secure virtual environments.

Its use cases are that AWS is ideal for startups and large enterprises looking to deploy scalable applications in the cloud, with flexibility in compute power and tailored configurations. Its global presence ensures low latency and high-performance applications worldwide.

5.7.2.2 Microsoft Azure

Overview

Microsoft Azure is a leading cloud service platform offering many cloud computing services. Azure is particularly popular for businesses utilizing Microsoft ecosystems, allowing seamless integration and migration [23].

Its key services are:

- *Azure Virtual Machines:* Offers scalable virtual servers on demand, running Windows and Linux OSs.
- *Azure Virtual Network:* Provides a secure, private network in the cloud, with options for connecting to on-premises environments.
- *Azure Kubernetes Service (AKS):* Simplifies deploying, managing, and scaling containerized applications using Kubernetes.
- *Hybrid Cloud Capabilities:* Through Azure Arc and Azure Stack, businesses can manage workloads across on-premises, multicloud, and edge environments seamlessly.

Its use cases are that Azure is suitable for businesses that favor Microsoft tools and solutions, offering deep integration with Office 365 and Windows Server and strong support for hybrid cloud models.

5.7.2.3 Google Cloud Platform

Overview

Google Cloud Platform (GCP) leverages Google's global infrastructure to offer a reliable and secure cloud environment. GCP is known for its strong emphasis on analytics, machine learning, and data management [29].

Its key services are:

- *Google Compute Engine:* Delivers VMs with customizable sizes and configurations to meet different workload needs.
- *Google Kubernetes Engine (GKE):* Provides a managed environment for deploying, managing, and scaling containerized applications using Kubernetes.
- *BigQuery:* An enterprise data warehouse that allows Structured Query Language (SQL)-like queries on large datasets and supports data analytics.
- *AI and machine learning:* GCP offers advanced AI tools like TensorFlow and AutoML to support AI projects.

Its use cases are that GCP is popular among data-driven organizations and developers focusing on AI, machine learning, and real-time data analytics due to its robust infrastructure and innovative solutions.

5.7.2.4 IBM Cloud

Overview

IBM Cloud offers a suite of cloud computing services with a strong focus on hybrid cloud solutions, integrating traditional IT environments with modern cloud-native applications [30].

Its key services are:

- *IBM Virtual Service:* Allows configurable compute capacity deployment on shared and dedicated public cloud environments.
- *IBM Cloud Kubernetes Service:* Provides a managed Kubernetes service for automating containerized application deployment, operation, and scaling.
- *IBM Watson:* Offers cognitive services for AI solutions, including natural language processing and machine learning.
- *Hybrid Cloud Solutions:* With IBM Cloud Satellite and Red Hat OpenShift, IBM provides strong hybrid and multicloud architecture capabilities, allowing seamless application deployment across diverse IT environments.

Its use cases are that IBM Cloud is aimed at enterprises with complex legacy systems that need to integrate into modern cloud solutions. It suits industries requiring robust, secure hybrid cloud platforms, such as finance and healthcare.

Each cloud service provider offers distinct advantages tailored to business needs and technological strategies. AWS and Azure are favored for their comprehensive ecosystem and integration capabilities, while GCP excels in data analytics and AI [31]. IBM Cloud focuses on hybrid cloud solutions and cognitive computing. What provider to use will often depend on the operational needs. The technology IBM Cloud is a cloud computing service and solution suite that offers traditional public and private cloud solutions. It offers various cloud models, which includes public, private, and hybrid cloud solutions. IBM Cloud Services include IaaS, Platform as a Service (PaaS), and SaaS [32]. The Public Cloud is a multitenant environment, where an organization uses computing resources in the pay-as-you-go model. A private cloud can be thought of as the same environment but is dedicated to one organization that requires additional security, regulations and compliance, and customization of their own environment. The Hybrid Cloud is optimized for the ability to integrate organizations on-premise infrastructure and private clouds with public cloud environments.

The key features of IBM Cloud include IBM Watson AI, IBM Kubernetes and Containerization, multicloud management, and IBM Cloud Foundry. The application is deployed using the PaaS model. IBM Cloud is integrated with Watson, IBM's AI and machine learning platform that allows organizations to incorporate AI into their applications [33]. It also provides managed Kubernetes services for container orchestration, offering customizable, single-tenant dedicated servers for high-performance computing and hardware control. IBM Cloud supports multicloud management, allowing users to manage workloads across different clouds, including third-party providers such as AWS, Azure, and Google Cloud stack, as well as the long-term strategic objectives of an organization.

5.7.3 Virtualization Security in Cloud Computing

Virtualization is a critical component of cloud computing, enabling efficient resource utilization and flexible service delivery. However, with these benefits come significant security challenges that require comprehensive strategies and solutions to ensure virtualized resources' integrity, confidentiality, and availability [34]. Here, we explore critical aspects of virtualization security, focusing on hypervisor, VM, and network security.

5.7.3.1 Hypervisor Security

Overview

The hypervisor, also known as a VM monitor, is a layer of software that enables multiple operating systems to share a single hardware host [35]. It manages the execution of VMs and thus is a crucial target for security attacks.

Its security challenges are the following:

- *Hypervisor attacks:* Include attempts to exploit the hypervisor to gain control over the host machine or other VMs. An attacker who compromises the hypervisor can access all VMs running on it.
- *Risk of VM escape:* A malicious VM breaks out of its isolated environment to interact with the hypervisor or other VMs, potentially leading to data breaches.

Its security measures are:

- *Regular updates and patch management:* Ensuring the hypervisor is updated with the latest security patches to protect against known vulnerabilities.
- *Access control:* Using robust authentication methods implementing strict access controls to limit who can interact with the hypervisor's management interface.

- *Security hardening:* Configuring the hypervisor according to best practices, such as turning off unnecessary services and installing minimal functionality to reduce the attack surface.

Hypervisor security is crucial in virtualized environments, as it manages VMs and controls access to physical hardware. Key aspects of hypervisor security include isolation and segmentation, hypervisor hardening, patching and updates, access control, VM escape prevention, secure boot and firmware protection, monitoring and auditing, encryption, security against hyperjacking, and virtual trusted platform module (vTPM). VM isolation ensures strong isolation between VMs, limiting the impact of a compromised VM. Hypervisor hardening reduces the hypervisor's features, removes unused components, and follows security best practices to minimize vulnerabilities. Access control, such as RBAC and two-factor authentication, limits administrative access to the hypervisor with strict permissions. VM escape prevention prevents VMs from bypassing the hypervisor layer, while secure boot and firmware protection ensure the hypervisor and firmware are authenticated and not tampered with at startup. Monitoring and auditing IDPS detect suspicious activities at the hypervisor level while logging and auditing keep logs for security audits and incident investigations. Encryption protects VM data at rest and in transit, while memory encryption protects VM memory from unauthorized access. Hyperjacking is an attack where a malicious actor gains control of the hypervisor, and vTPM provides cryptographic operations within virtualized environments. Hypervisor security is essential in preventing attacks in cloud and virtualized data centers, as compromising the hypervisor can give attackers control over multiple VMs and sensitive data.

5.7.3.2 VM Security

Overview

VMs are the building blocks of a virtualized environment and need specific security measures to prevent unauthorized access and data breaches [36].

Its security challenges are:

- *VM sprawl:* As the number of VMs increases, so does the complexity of managing them, which can lead to unpatched and poorly managed VMs becoming security vulnerabilities.
- *Inadequate isolation:* Flaws in VM isolation could allow malicious operations to affect other VMs or the host system.

Its security measures are:

- *Isolation techniques:* Ensuring strict isolation between VMs through policy enforcement and proper configuration to prevent unauthorized interaction.
- *Endpoint security:* Deploying antivirus, intrusion detection/prevention systems, and other endpoint security solutions within each VM to protect against malware and attacks.

- *Snapshot management:* Regularly create and manage VM snapshots to facilitate fast restoration in case of an attack while ensuring snapshot management itself remains secure.
- *Virtualized security:* Sometimes referred to as security virtualization, this represents a departure from static hardware-based approaches. Virtualized security is in the realm of software-based security explicitly designed for deployment in a virtualized IT environment. Unlike hardware-based security devices such as switches, routers, and firewalls, virtualized security solutions are flexible and adaptive. Just like on-demand computing, the security function and services can follow where the demand-created workloads and services go. When you recreate workloads and applications on demand, and with virtualized cloud computing, you can consider how virtualized security could apply in a multitenant public cloud. In private cloud computing, adversaries can more easily be isolated with machines that are running in the same environment; therefore, intrusions and impacts are contained within that private environment. In public cloud computing, where multitenancy may invite poor to moderate levels of isolation of workloads, it is even more essential that you consider how you will secure workloads and ensure the security service and function are not influencing the mission of your VMs. Hypervisors are categorized into two types: type-1 hypervisors and type-2 hypervisors. Type-1 hypervisors run directly on unmanaged systems, enabling greater interaction between systems. In contrast, type-2 hypervisors operate as applications on the host operating system, simulating the hardware that the system typically interacts with. Moreover, in type-1 virtualization, the virtual machine monitor (VMM) sits above the hardware and listens in on all actions initiated or performed on behalf of VMs and the hardware. The type-2 virtualized environment allows the VMM to act as an application on the host OS with the host's OS performing I/O drivers and manage the creation of guest VMs. Ensuring security for VMs hosted in cloud environments remains a significant focus for DevOps teams.

The DevOps Engineering: Planning to Production course offers hands-on examples of securing cloud infrastructure. Service provider security ensures that the system's virtualization hardware is not physically accessible to anyone not authorized, and each VM can be given access control that can only be established through the hypervisor to safeguard it against unwanted access by cloud administrators. Hyper-safe technology protects the hypervisor's code integrity through hyper-safe technology. To ensure VM security, four steps must be taken: segregate newly hosted components, test and review all components, isolate services from infrastructure management and orchestration, and use separate management APIs to protect the network. Following these steps, businesses can effectively manage their resources and preserve their virtualized networks from potential threats. A hypervisor is a software layer that allows virtualization by managing and provisioning VMs. The hypervisor creates a bridge between the physical hardware and virtual environment so that every VM can work independently of one another. Closed VMs utilize and convert physical resources into virtual resources. This allows for cloud providers and end users to better utilize resources and, consequently, lower costs.

There are two main classes of hypervisors: one is a type-1 hypervisor that runs directly on the physical host providing underlying hardware directly, and the other is a type-2 hypervisor that runs an OS while providing virtualization services to multiple VMs.

When we refer to hypervisor security, we are talking about controls implemented to secure the hypervisor and the VMs that it services against threats. Aspects of hypervisor security are access control, VM isolation, threat detection and mitigation, patch management, encrypted data, protecting sensitive data, system stability, compliance, protecting reputation, malicious attack, DoS, code execution, running services that should not be running, memory corruption, nonupdated hypervisor, patching and updating, reduction, and elimination. Organizations should take the necessary precautions to safeguard sensitive information such as financial, personal, and intellectual property. To accomplish this, organizations must maintain system stability, adhere to respective industry requirements and standards, and prevent malicious attacks. These hypervisor vulnerabilities can vary: DoS, code execution, running services that are unessential, memory corruption, having hypervisors that are not up-to-date, exploitations such as Spectre and Meltdown, patching and updating hypervisors on a regular basis, limiting access to hypervisor host management options, auditing access to hypervisor hosts, limiting network access to hypervisor host management options, utilizing VM encryption, Unified Extensible Firmware Interface (UEFI) Secure Boot, and virtualization-based security (VBS). Having organizations follow best practices can increase the security of their virtualized environment and help to defend against attacks. Organizations should review and reassess security measures on a regularly timed schedule to keep abreast of current attacks.

In conclusion, hypervisor security is a key part of any virtualized environment as it is the bridging point from the physical hardware to the virtualized environment. Protecting the hypervisor is important to protect sensitive data and personal information in order to be compliant with regulations, protecting reputations, and maintaining the stability of the virtualized environment. By using some of these best practices, organizations can help with increasing the security of their virtualized environment and defending against attacks.

5.7.3.3 Network Security in Virtualized Environments

Overview

Virtualized environments introduce new network dynamics, with VMs communicating over virtual networks. This requires securing both traditional network components and their virtual equivalents [37].

Its security challenges are:

- *Complex network configurations:* Virtual networks add layers of complexity that can obscure visibility and control, leading to potential misconfigurations and vulnerabilities.
- *Inter-VM traffic:* Traffic between VMs on the same host may not pass through traditional security appliances, rendering conventional security measures ineffective.

Its security measures are:

- *Virtual firewalls:* Implement virtual firewalls to monitor and control inter-VM traffic, ensuring that only authorized communications occur.
- *Network segmentation:* Use network segmentation to divide different VMs into distinct segments, limiting the spread of potential threats and reducing the attack surface.
- *Encryption and secure protocols:* Ensure that data is encrypted in transit using secure protocols to protect it from interception and eavesdropping.

Ensuring security in virtualized cloud computing environments is a multifaceted task that involves safeguarding the hypervisor, VMs, and the networks that connect them. Comprehensive security policies, regular updates, access controls, and the deployment of advanced security technologies are essential to mitigate the inherent risks of virtualization. By addressing these areas, organizations can protect their virtual infrastructures from attacks and ensure their cloud services' continued integrity, reliability, and efficiency.

5.7.4 Confidential Computing

Confidential computing is an emerging field focused on protecting data in use, ensuring that sensitive data processed in memory is protected from unauthorized access [38]. Confidential computing is a cloud computing technology that encapsulates data within a protected CPU, ensuring that only the data being processed and its processing methods are stored within the CPU's environment. This approach extends data protection beyond traditional measures, which typically focus on data at rest and in transit. By offering an additional layer of security during computation, confidential computing addresses vulnerabilities that could be exploited during data processing. Key to this effort are advances in hardware security technologies offered by various leading manufacturers. Here is a detailed exploration of these technologies. Confidential computing is a cloud computing technology that isolates data within a protected CPU while it is being processed [39]. This data is only accessible to specially authorized programming code, making the CPU's resources invisible and not discoverable by any program or person. As organizations increasingly turn to hybrid and public cloud services, finding data privacy solutions becomes more critical. The main objective of confidential computing is to provide companies with a greater sense of confidence in the security of their data, especially when it comes to sensitive or business-critical workloads.

Data encryption is not new to cloud computing, as cloud providers have been encrypting data at rest and in transit [40]. However, with confidential computing, data in use is also protected with encryption. This exposes data to threats such as memory dump attacks and root user compromises. Confidential computing addresses this issue by using a hardware-based architecture called a trusted execution environment (TEE), which is a secure coprocessor inside a CPU. Embedded encryption keys are used to secure the TEE, and attestation mechanisms embedded within the coprocessor ensure that the TEEs are only accessible to the authorized application code [40]. When an application tells the TEE to decrypt it, the data is released for processing. While the computer decrypts and processes the data, it is invisible to everyone, including the cloud provider, other computer resources, hypervisors, VMs, and even the OS.

Confidential computing is a breakthrough technology because it meets a need unique to cloud computing and increasing demand: trustless security in a cloud computing environment. Cloud computing will likely remain the go-to solution for private users who need to know that their software, computational workloads, and data are not left open for cloud providers or people whom they do not want to have contact with their computing [41]. In a conventional on-premises computing environment, when a bad actor captures or forges credentials from a cloud provider, they have access to sensitive processes, data, and software. We feel safe when we have internal data centers that we keep locked and behind safe doors. With confidential computing, we can achieve the same level of trust in a cloud environment, where digital assets are thousands of miles away. There are many upsides to using confidential computing, such as protection of sensitive data while processing, ability to collaborate with partners to deliver new cloud solutions, customers feeling good about selecting a cloud provider because the provider is reliable and trustworthy. In summary, confidential computing is a disruptive technology that uniquely addresses the needs of cloud computing; it provides an emerging opportunity for trustless security in a cloud computing environment. This means that organizations can adopt the latest cloud technologies without worrying about data privacy or possible compliance issues, allowing organizations to focus on their core competencies and operations.

5.7.4.1 Hardware Manufacturers and Confidential Computing

1. Intel Software Guard Extensions and Trust Domain Extensions

- *Intel Software Guard Extensions (SGX):* Intel's SGX technology allows applications to create secure enclaves and isolated regions of memory within which sensitive data can be processed while remaining protected from external access, even if the OS is compromised [40].
- *Functionality:* SGX enables developers to partition sensitive code and data into enclaves, shielding them with hardware-based encryption boundaries.
- *Applications:* SGX is particularly useful for cloud environments, blockchain, and systems requiring high levels of privacy, such as financial services.
- *Intel Trust Domain Extensions (TDX):* TDX build upon SGX's capabilities by enhancing the protection of VMs through isolated execution environments known as trust domains, expanding protection from just the application layer to include virtualized infrastructures.
- *Enhancements:* TDX aims to facilitate isolated execution in broader VM environments, improving multitenant security beyond what SGX provides.

2. ARM TrustZone and Confidential Computer Architecture

- *ARM TrustZone:* TrustZone technology creates a secure execution environment that partitions the system into secure and nonsecure worlds. This dual-execution environment minimizes the attack surface for sensitive operations.
- *Functionality:* TrustZone allows specific application components to run in a protected execution space, ensuring confidentiality and integrity of data.
- *Applications:* TrustZone is widely used in mobile devices, IoT, and increasingly in cloud computing, where protecting user credentials and DRM content is essential.
- *ARM Confidential Computer Architecture (CCA):* The CCA extends TrustZone's capabilities across more complex computing systems, addressing broader multitenancy and virtualization scenarios typical of modern cloud services.
- *New features:* The CCA is designed to enhance secure workload execution in virtualized multitenant cloud environments by tightly integrating with virtualization layers.

3. AMD Secure Encrypted Virtualization

- *AMD Secure Encrypted Virtualization (SEV):* SEV is AMD's approach to reinforcing VM security by providing memory encryption features that prevent unauthorized access to data while it is being processed [42].
- *Functionality:* By encrypting VM memory, SEV ensures that only the intended VM can access its data, preventing access at the hypervisor level.
- *Applications:* SEV is particularly beneficial in cloud environments, as it helps to protect tenant data from potential threats from untrusted hypervisors.

In the SEV-ES architecture, there are a number of components, namely, the AMD CPU, Platform Security Processor (PSP), Enlightened OS, VMM, VM executable (VMX), and the VMkernel driver. In order to configure and use SEV-ES, it must be turned on in the system BIOS settings and added to a VM via the vSphere Client, or using PowerCLI commands. SEV-ES can be used to create new VMs or to turn on existing VMs. Furthermore, the user privileges required to manage SEV-ES activated VMs are identical to user privileges required to manage standard VMs. SEV-ES activation does not support the following features: System Management Mode (SMM), vMotion, powered-on snapshots, hot add or remove of CPU or memory, suspend/resume VMware, fault tolerance clones and instant clones' guest integrity, UEFI secure boot, and vMotion.

4. IBM Protected Execution Facility

- *IBM Protected Execution Facility (PEF):* PEF is IBM's technology for ensuring the secure execution of workloads, focusing on isolating sensitive tasks from other operations [43].
- *Functionality:* This facility uses hardware-based mechanisms to segregate workload execution, ensuring that sensitive tasks remain secure even if a host is compromised.
- *Applications:* PEF is designed to cater to industries with stringent compliance and data protection needs, such as healthcare and financial services.

Confidential computing is crucial in enhancing data security in an increasingly digital and cloud-dominated world. By leveraging cutting-edge technologies developed by industry leaders such as Intel, ARM, AMD, and IBM, organizations can ensure that their data remains secure even while in use [44]. This advancement helps to reinforce trust in cloud computing, empowering companies to handle sensitive workloads with greater assurance of privacy and compliance. As threats evolve, these technologies will remain critical pillars in shaping secure computing environments.

5.7.5 Encryption in Virtualized Environments

Encryption is fundamental to securing data within virtualized environments, ensuring that sensitive information remains confidential and protected against unauthorized access [45]. Implementing robust encryption strategies is even more crucial in virtualized settings, where multiple VMs share the same physical hardware. Critical aspects of encryption in these environments include secure randomness generation, effective key management, and specific encryption techniques for VMs.

Figure 5.5 illustrates the encryption in virtualized environments. It shows how encryption is applied to enhance data security. It includes data encryption, which protects against unauthorized access, and encryption keys managed by a key management service [45]. Data in transit encryption uses secure protocols such as Secure Sockets Layer (SSL), Transport Layer Security (TLS), and Internet Protocol Security (IPsec) for protecting data transmitted between VMs, storage, and cloud services. Memory encryption protects sensitive data in multitenant environments. Hypervisor-level encryption ensures data confidentiality when moving or copying VMs. Encryption in virtualized environments ensures data protection, privacy, and compliance with security regulations across cloud infrastructures.

5.7.5.1 Randomness Generation

Overview

Randomness is essential in cryptographic systems for generating secure keys, initialization vectors, and other cryptographic parameters. The strength of encryption often relies on the unpredictability of these random values [46]. In virtualized en-

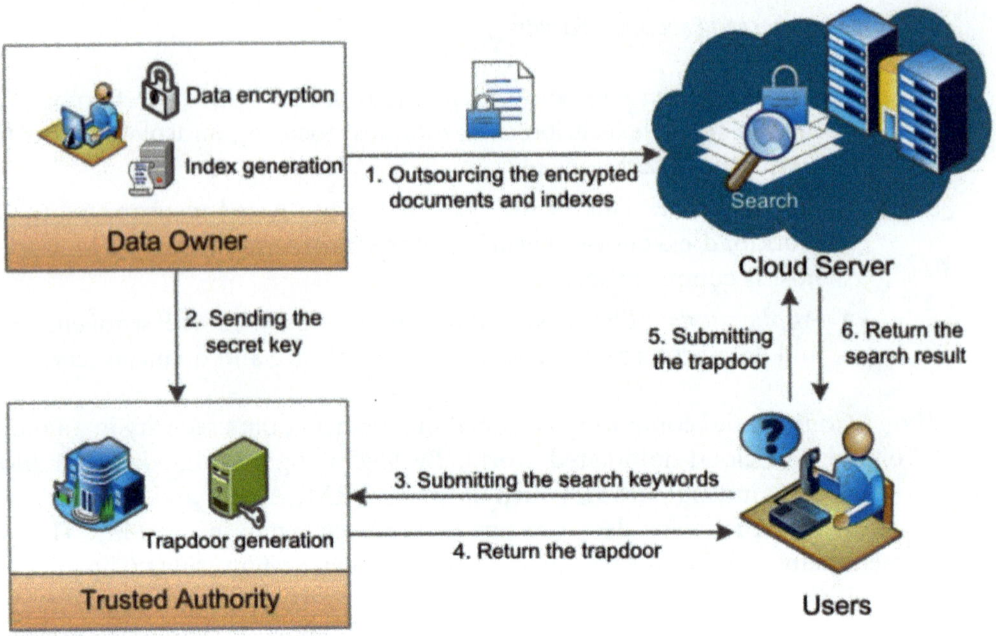

Figure 5.5 Encryption in virtualized environments [45].

vironments, ensuring high-quality randomness can be challenging due to resource sharing and potential entropy depletion.

Its challenges are:

- *Entropy pooling:* VMs often lack the direct hardware access that physical machines have, which can limit the availability of entropy from traditional sources such as disk activity or mouse movements.
- *Shared resources:* The shared nature of hardware in virtual environments can complicate the isolation and source of entropy, potentially leading to weaker cryptographic randomness.

Its solutions are:

- *Hardware random number generators (RNGs):* Using hardware-based RNGs can significantly improve the quality of randomness by providing a dedicated source of entropy independent of virtualized system constraints.
- *Enhanced software RNGs:* Employing enhanced algorithms and techniques that simulate high entropy conditions can also be effective, especially when hardware RNGs are unavailable.

5.7.5.2 Key Management

Key management is a critical component of any encryption strategy, encompassing the generation, distribution, storage, and destruction of encryption keys [47].

1. Key Management Server

A key management server (KMS) provides centralized control over keys, offering a secure repository where keys can be managed efficiently across multiple VMs and applications [47].

The benefits are:

- *Centralized management:* Simplifies the administration of keys and policies, reducing the complexity of handling encryption keys across large virtual environments.
- *Automated governance:* Implements policies for crucial rotation, expiration, and access permissions automatically, ensuring that keys remain secure without manual intervention.
- *Audit and compliance:* Provides logging and auditing capabilities to ensure compliance with regulatory requirements that mandate key management and data protection standards.

The considerations are:

- *Integration:* The KMS should integrate seamlessly with existing infrastructure and virtualization platforms for smooth key distribution and life-cycle management.
- *Redundancy and backup:* Ensuring that the KMS is resilient to failure with proper backup strategies is essential for maintaining continuous access to keys and, consequently, secure operations.

2. VM Encryption

VM encryption secures the data stored within a VM by applying disk encryption techniques to protect its contents [45].

The benefits are:

- *Data protection at rest:* By encrypting VM disks, data remains protected even if the disks are copied or stolen, ensuring confidentiality.
- *Compliance:* Helps organizations to meet data protection regulations by ensuring that sensitive data is encrypted and inaccessible without proper authorization.
- *Implementation:*
    - *Choice of encryption algorithms:* Selecting robust, industry-standard algorithms such as Advanced Encryption Standard (AES) is critical for effective VM encryption.
    - *Performance considerations:* While disk encryption can incur performance overhead, modern virtualization platforms often include hardware acceleration features to mitigate these impacts.

Its challenges are:

- *Key management:* Proper management of encryption keys is crucial; losing access to keys can mean losing access to encrypted data entirely.
- *Integration with cloud services:* In cloud environments, integrating VM encryption with existing cloud provider services (e.g., AWS KMS, Azure Key Vault) can streamline management and enhance security [48].

Figure 5.6 elaborates the KMS for smart cities, which involves key generation, distribution, storage, revocation, and renewal [49]. Key generation secures cryptographic keys for devices, applications, and users, while distribution ensures secure communication. Key storage prevents unauthorized access and tampering [50]. Key revocation removes compromised or outdated keys, while renewal updates keys for long-term security. The system ensures secure communication, data integrity, and privacy across interconnected devices in the smart city ecosystem. Encryption in virtualized environments involves a combination of randomness generation, robust essential management practices, and effective VM encryption strategies. Ensuring that these elements are correctly implemented can significantly enhance data security within virtual settings, protecting against unauthorized access and maintaining compliance with increasingly stringent data protection regulations. By leveraging hardware and software tools, organizations can secure their virtual environments effectively, safeguarding their most critical assets.

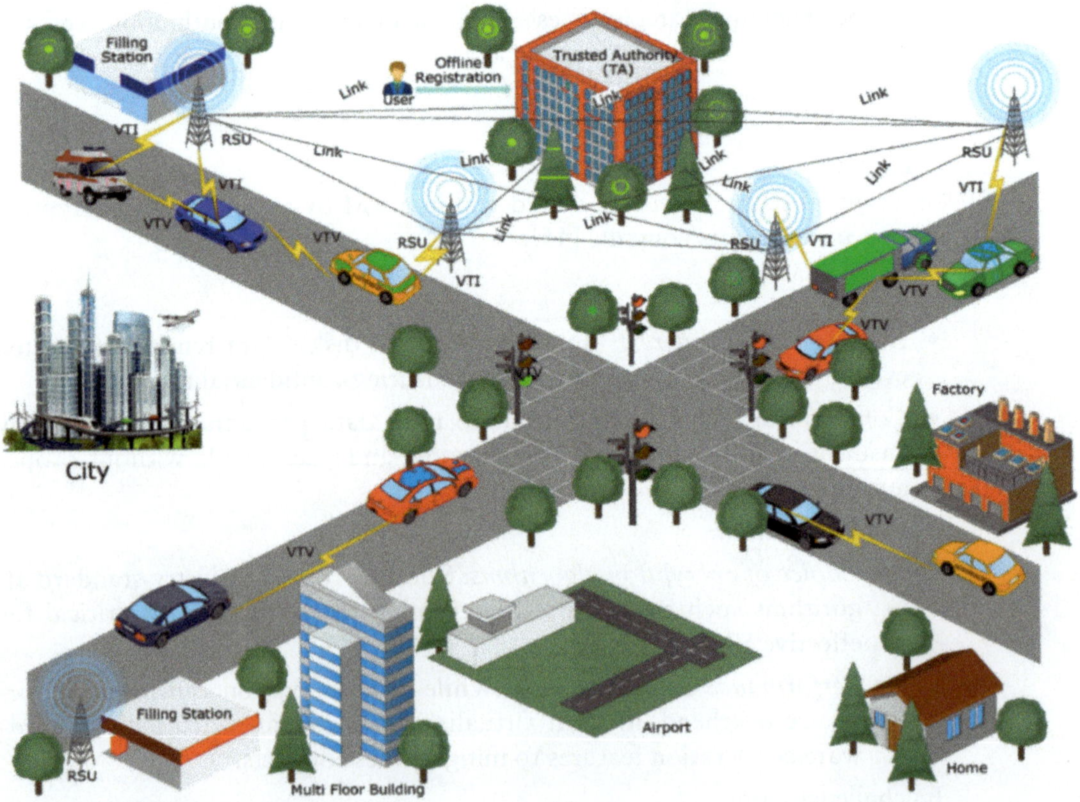

Figure 5.6 KMS for a smart city [49].

However, efficient management of large numbers of vehicles in Vehicle-Aware Networks (VANETs) is a challenge. VANETs are wireless networks that enable communication between vehicles and other entities, providing a promising solution for managing urban mobility [51]. These networks comprise trusted authority (TA), vehicles, and roadside unit (RSU). TA registers vehicle users, provides secret keys, and authenticates vehicles for communication. RSUs are immobile units installed along the roadside to facilitate vehicle-to-TA communication. VANETs communicate between vehicle to RSU (V2R) and vehicle to vehicle (V2V) using the IEEE 802.11p standard wireless channel access. Authentication is crucial for security, but message confidentiality remains challenging due to the unsecured wireless channel.

A group-key distribution approach has been proposed to address this issue, where the TA distributes a group key to each vehicle, ensuring encryption and dynamic updating [52]. Grover discussed the security and privacy challenges in VANETs, which can enhance road safety, traffic efficiency, and transportation services, and proposed various security mechanisms, including authentication, encryption, intrusion detection, and privacy protection, to ensure the integrity, confidentiality, availability, and authenticity of communication in VANETs. Advanced security mechanisms and protocols can mitigate these threats and ensure the safe operation of VANETs. Countermeasures include secure key management, message integrity checks, random oracle models, and time stamping [52]. Conditional privacy-preserving authentication schemes are used for security and privacy preservation, often utilizing bilinear pairing operations. Grover also addressed the problem of controlling the transmission rate in a communication network and proposes privacy-preserving route reporting schemes for traffic management. A novel technique with a moving-zone-based architecture is proposed, combining RSUs on static locations, public mobile transportation, and vehicles owned by local governments.

5.8 Conclusion

This chapter was about virtualization security in cloud computing. Virtualization was introduced, along with its types, benefits, challenges, and management tools. The major vendors are VMware vSphere, Microsoft Hyper-V, Citrix XenServer, OpenStack, AWS, Microsoft Azure, GCP, and IBM. This chapter also summarized hypervisor security, VM security, network security, hybrid security, confidentiality computing hardware providers, and encryption security method implementations, such as Intel SGX, TDX, ARM TrustZone, and CCA, AMD SEV, IBM PEF, random number generators, key management, and VM encryption. The section summaries defined each major topic of the chapter. In general, this chapter reviewed multiple aspects of virtualization in cloud computing. Creating a foundation for modern IT infrastructure, virtualization provides an abstraction layer to enable multiple VMs to share the same physical hardware. The chapter explored several topics, any of which are critical to comprehending how virtualization enablement and security facilitates cloud computing environments.

A primary focus was on the security dimensions of virtualization, highlighting the need to protect virtual environments against unique threats. This includes securing the hypervisor, which manages the execution of VMs and presents a critical target for attacks. Adequate hypervisor security involves access controls, regular updates, and robust configurations to prevent unauthorized access and ensure system integrity. Additionally, VM security is addressed, emphasizing the importance of isolating VMs to prevent unauthorized access and the spread of vulnerabilities. Security measures such as endpoint protection within each VM and snapshot management are crucial in safeguarding data integrity.

Network security in the context of virtualization is important as well. This chapter mentioned applying virtual firewalls, network segmentation, and encryption to ensure that when data is in transit, it is protected from interception and unauthorized access whether within a complex virtualized network or among virtual elements within heterogeneous networks.

This chapter highlighted the emerging field of confidential computing, which focuses on protecting data during use by leveraging advanced hardware security features. Key technologies include Intel's SGX and TDX, ARM's TrustZone and CCA, AMD's SEV, and IBM's PEF. These technologies provide secure enclaves, isolated execution environments, and memory encryption to ensure data remains protected even from the host systems, addressing privacy and data integrity concerns.

This chapter underscored the importance of encryption in protecting data within virtualized environments. It discussed randomness generation, highlighting the challenges of ensuring high-quality randomness in VMs and using hardware RNGs to mitigate them. Key management is another critical area, covering the role of key management servers and strategies for VM encryption to protect data at rest and ensure compliance with data protection regulations.

The examination of leading cloud service providers (AWS, Microsoft Azure, GCP, and IBM Cloud) illustrates the various ways that they utilize virtualization to provide scalable and secure cloud services. Each cloud provider features a distinct set of services including compute services, automated resource scaling, and security frameworks that accommodate various operational business models, from new startups to enterprise-scale applications.

This chapter reviewed virtualization management tools such as VMware vSphere, Microsoft Hyper-V, Citrix XenServer, and OpenStack, all embodying similar features that allow efficient management of diverse virtual environments. These tools all help to improve the use of resources, crushing operational processes, and efficiently managing security in virtualized infrastructures in general.

This chapter gave a broad understanding of the opportunities and pitfalls that you can design into your virtualization models from benefits to limitations and strategic use of virtualization technologies in cloud computing. With unique aspects such as security, confidentiality, management, and the features of the major platforms, this chapter provided understanding on how virtualization can assist with your daily use of IT operations and productively create a safer, flexible, and efficient computing environment in place.

References

[1] Josyula, V., M. Orr, and G. Page, *Cloud Computing: Automating the Virtualized Data Center*, Indianapolis, IN: Cisco Press, 2011.

[2] Najafizadegan, N., E. Nazemi, and V. Khajehvand, "An Autonomous Model for Self-Optimizing Virtual Machine Selection by Learning Automata in Cloud Environment," *Software: Practice and Experience*, Vol. 51, No. 6, June 2021, pp. 1352–1386.

[3] Thyagaturu, A. S., et al., "Operating Systems and Hypervisors for Network Functions: A Survey of Enabling Technologies and Research Studies," *IEEE Access*, Vol. 10, July 29, 2022, pp. 79825–79873.

[4] Battula, M., "A Systematic Review on a Multi-Tenant Database Management System in Cloud Computing," *2024 International Conference on Cognitive Robotics and Intelligent Systems (ICC-ROBINS)*, April 17, 2024, pp. 890–897.

[5] Wulf, C., M. Willig, and D. Göhringer, "A Survey on Hypervisor-Based Virtualization of Embedded Reconfigurable Systems," *2021 31st International Conference on Field-Programmable Logic and Applications (FPL)*, August 30, 2021, pp. 249–256.

[6] Baumgartner, J., C. Lillo, and S. Rumley, "Performance Losses with Virtualization: Comparing Bare Metal to VMs and Containers," *International Conference on High Performance Computing*, May 21, 2023, pp. 107–120.

[7] Katal, A., S. Dahiya, and T. Choudhury, "Energy Efficiency in Cloud Computing Data Centers: A Survey on Software Technologies," *Cluster Computing*, Vol. 26, No. 3, June 2023, pp. 1845–1875.

[8] Choi, S. H., and K. W. Park, "Cloud-BlackBox: Toward Practical Recording and Tracking of VM Swarms for Multifaceted Cloud Inspection," *Future Generation Computer Systems*, Vol. 137, December 1, 2022, pp. 219–233.

[9] Kumar, A., et al., "Virtual Environments Testing in Cloud Service Environment: A Framework to Optimize the Performance of Virtual Applications," *International Journal of System Assurance Engineering and Management*, Vol. 13, Suppl. 1, March 2022, pp. 1–5.

[10] Darwish, D., (ed.), *Emerging Trends in Cloud Computing Analytics, Scalability, and Service Models*, Hershey, PA: IGI Global Scientific Publishing, 2024.

[11] Karunamurthy, A., et al., "Cloud Database: Empowering Scalable and Flexible Data Management," *Quing: International Journal of Innovative Research in Science and Engineering*, March 30, 2023.

[12] Geetha, A., and P. Kumari, "Network Virtualization," in *Towards Wireless Heterogeneity in 6G Networks*, Boca Raton, FL: CRC Press, 2024, pp. 226–242.

[13] Gupta, D., *The Cloud Computing Journey: Design and Deploy Resilient and Secure Multi-Cloud Systems with Practical Guidance*, Birmingham, UK: Packt Publishing Ltd., 2024.

[14] Mansouri, Y., and M. A. Babar, "A Review of Edge Computing: Features and Resource Virtualization," *Journal of Parallel and Distributed Computing*, Vol. 150, April 1, 2021, pp. 155–183.

[15] Bartlett, L., K. A. Kabir, and J. Han, "A Review on Business Process Management System Design: The Role of Virtualization and Work Design," *IEEE Access*, October 10, 2023.

[16] Hamid, S. A., Y. Boujelben, and F. Zarai, "Enhancing Cloud Gaming Experience through Optimized Virtual Machine Placement: A Comprehensive Review," *Journal of Network and Systems Management*, Vol. 32, No. 4, October 2024, p. 80.

[17] Surya, P., et al., "Virtualization Risks and Associated Issues in Cloud Environment," *2021 International Conference on Technological Advancements and Innovations (ICTAI)*, November 10, 2021, pp. 521–525.

[18] Banerjee, S., S. Roy, and S. Khatua, "Towards Energy and QoS Aware Dynamic VM Consolidation in a Multi-Resource Cloud," *Future Generation Computer Systems*, Vol. 157, August 1, 2024, pp. 376–391.

[19] Delgado, J. M., et al., "A Research Agenda for Augmented and Virtual Reality in Architecture, Engineering and Construction," *Advanced Engineering Informatics*, Vol. 45, August 1, 2020, p. 101122.

[20] Thapa, C., and S. Camtepe, "Precision Health Data: Requirements, Challenges and Existing Techniques for Data Security and Privacy," *Computers in Biology and Medicine*, Vol. 129, February 1, 2021, p. 104130.

[21] Zolfaghari, R., et al., "Application of Virtual Machine Consolidation in Cloud Computing Systems," *Sustainable Computing: Informatics and Systems*, Vol. 30, June 1, 2021, p. 100524.

[22] Patrão, L., *VMware VSphere Essentials: A Practical Approach to VSphere Deployment and Management*, New York: Springer Nature, 2024.

[23] Mulder, J., *Multi-Cloud Architecture and Governance: Leverage Azure, AWS, GCP, and VMware vSphere to Build Effective Multi-Cloud Solutions*, Birmingham, UK: Packt Publishing Ltd., 2020.

[24] Docter, Q., and C. Fuchs, *CompTIA Cloud Essentials+ Study Guide: Exam CLO-002*, New York: John Wiley & Sons, 2020.

[25] Tomarchio, O., D. Calcaterra, and G. D. Modica, "Cloud Resource Orchestration in the Multi-Cloud Landscape: A Systematic Review of Existing Frameworks," *Journal of Cloud Computing*, Vol. 9, No. 1, September 10, 2020, p. 49.

[26] Fenton, T., and P. Kennedy, Running ESXi on a Raspberry Pi, https://doi.org/10.1007/978-1-4842-7465-1.

[27] Salama, R., et al., "Service Models for Internet of Things, Global Value Chains, and Mobile Cloud Computing," *Smart Global Value Chain*, August 1, 2024, pp. 121–136.

[28] Ulyanov, O., M. Schwartzman, and H. Sanku, *VMware Cloud on AWS Blueprint: Design, Automate, and Migrate VMware Workloads on AWS Global Infrastructure*, Birmingham, UK: Packt Publishing Ltd., 2024.

[29] Dantas, V., *Architecting Google Cloud Solutions: Learn to Design Robust and Future-Proof Solutions with Google Cloud Technologies*, Birmingham, UK: Packt Publishing Ltd., 2021.

[30] Ponnusamy, A., and A. Spanner, *Technology Operating Models for Cloud and Edge: Create Your Purpose-Built Distributed Operating Model for Public, Hybrid, Multicloud, and Edge*, Birmingham, UK: Packt Publishing Ltd., 2023.

[31] Musarat, M. A., et al., "Evaluating Cloud Computing in Construction Projects to Avoid Project Delay," *Journal of Open Innovation: Technology, Market, and Complexity*, Vol. 10, No. 2, June 1, 2024, p. 100296.

[32] Deb, M., and A. Choudhury, "Hybrid Cloud: A New Paradigm in Cloud Computing," *Machine Learning Techniques and Analytics for Cloud Security*, December 21, 2021, pp. 1–23.

[33] Petiwala, F. F., V. K. Shukla, and S. Vyas, "IBM Watson: Redefining Artificial Intelligence Through Cognitive Computing," *Proceedings of International Conference on Machine Intelligence and Data Science Applications: MIDAS 2020*, 2021, pp. 173–185.

[34] Mansouri, Y., and M. A. Babar, "A Review of Edge Computing: Features and Resource Virtualization," *Journal of Parallel and Distributed Computing*, Vol. 150, April 1, 2021, pp. 155–183.

[35] Wulf, C., M. Willig, and D. Göhringer, "A Survey on Hypervisor-Based Virtualization of Embedded Reconfigurable Systems," *2021 31st International Conference on Field-Programmable Logic and Applications (FPL)*, August 30, 2021, pp. 249–256.

[36] Saeed, A., P. Garraghan, and S. A. Hussain, "Cross-VM Network Channel Attacks and Countermeasures Within Cloud Computing Environments," *IEEE Transactions on Dependable and Secure Computing*, Vol. 19, No. 3, November 10, 2020, pp. 1783–1794.

[37] Alnaim, A. K., "Securing 5G Virtual Networks: A Critical Analysis of SDN, NFV, and Network Slicing Security," *International Journal of Information Security*, Vol. 23, No. 6, December 2024, pp. 3569–3589.

[38] Ali, B., M. A. Gregory, and S. Li, "Multi-Access Edge Computing Architecture, Data Security and Privacy: A Review," *IEEE Access*, Vol. 9, January 21, 2021, pp. 18706–18721.

[39] Jangjou, M., and M. K. Sohrabi, "A Comprehensive Survey on Security Challenges in Different Network Layers in Cloud Computing," *Archives of Computational Methods in Engineering*, Vol. 29, No. 6, October 2022, pp. 3587–3608.

[40] Chakrabarti, S., et al., "Trusted Execution Environment with Intel SGX," in *Responsible Genomic Data Sharing*, New York: Academic Press, 2020, pp. 161–190.

[41] Linthicum, D., *An Insider's Guide to Cloud Computing*, Reading, MA: Addison-Wesley Professional, 2023.

[42] Zhao, S., et al., "vSGX: Virtualizing SGX Enclaves on AMD SEV," *2022 IEEE Symposium on Security and Privacy (SP)*, May 22, 2022, pp. 321–336.

[43] Mohan, A., et al., "Securing AI Inference in the Cloud: Is CPU-GPU Confidential Computing Ready?" *2024 IEEE 17th International Conference on Cloud Computing (CLOUD)*, July 7, 2024, pp. 164–175.

[44] Teng, S. Y., et al., "Recent Advances on Industrial Data-Driven Energy Savings: Digital Twins and Infrastructures," *Renewable and Sustainable Energy Reviews*, Vol. 135, January 1, 2021, p. 110208.

[45] Seth, B., et al., "Integrating Encryption Techniques for Secure Data Storage in the Cloud," *Transactions on Emerging Telecommunications Technologies*, Vol. 33, No. 4, April 2022, p. e4108.

[46] Aumasson, J. P., *Serious Cryptography: A Practical Introduction to Modern Encryption*, San Franscisco: No Starch Press, Inc., 2024.

[47] Ahmad, S., S. Mehfuz, and J. Beg, "Hybrid Cryptographic Approach to Enhance the Mode of Key Management System in Cloud Environment," *The Journal of Supercomputing*, Vol. 79, No. 7, May 2023, pp. 7377–7413.

[48] Murthy, J. S., G. M. Siddesh, and K. G. Srinivasa (eds.), *Cloud Security: Concepts, Applications and Practices*, Boca Raton, FL: CRC Press, 2024.

[49] Lom, M., and O. Pribyl, "Smart City Model Based on Systems Theory," *International Journal of Information Management*, Vol. 56, February 1, 2021, p. 102092.

[50] Mousavi, S. K., et al., "Security of Internet of Things Based on Cryptographic Algorithms: a Survey," *Wireless Networks*, Vol. 27, No. 2, February 2021, pp. 1515–1555.

[54] Lee, M., and T. Atkison, "VANET Applications: Past, Present, and Future," *Vehicular Communications,* Vol. 28, 2021.

[55] Grover, J., "Security of Vehicular Ad Hoc Networks Using Blockchain: A Comprehensive Review," *Vehicular Communications*, Vol. 34, April 1, 2022, p. 100458.

CHAPTER 6

Application Security in Virtualized Environments

In today's digital world, every device and application uses a virtualized environment, which has become the foundation of sophisticated IT infrastructure. VMs have executed numerous applications on a single physical server [1]. However, the broad use of these systems poses several issues, including privacy and security dependability. Among them, security is one of the significant issues in which cybercriminals take advantage of the vulnerabilities in the many virtual environment platforms currently accessible [2]. By identifying and discussing countermeasures, this chapter's primary goal is to provide a broad overview of application security in a virtualized context. Although this environment improves scalability and resource efficiency, it poses unique security issues [3]. Maintaining system availability, avoiding unwanted access, and safeguarding sensitive data depend on the security of programs running in virtualized environments.

6.1 Overview of Virtualized Applications

One popular method that allows numerous VMs to operate on one or more physical machines while abstracting the underlying machine architecture to the VM is virtualization [4]. It generates virtual instances of system resources like servers, storage, networks, and applications. Essentially, you can host multiple OSs and applications on one physical server, which enhances the utilization of resources and provides flexibility [4].

Virtualization is the primary technology that enables the cloud, as shown in Figure 6.1 [5], which entails running several OSs on a single computer's hardware. This makes it simpler to add, remove, maintain, and troubleshoot new machines, services, and applications by enabling users to run multiple computers carrying out distinct tasks; hence, the VMs can be moved, copied, and backed up while they are operating, and thus require less maintenance and do not have any downtime [6]. It is to be noted that they are clustered. Therefore, migration is possible without requiring the VM to be shut down. Moving a live VM between clusters without shutting it down is called "live migration."

Virtualization reduces the overall system setup and maintenance cost by using a single physical machine to accommodate many VMs; for example, according to

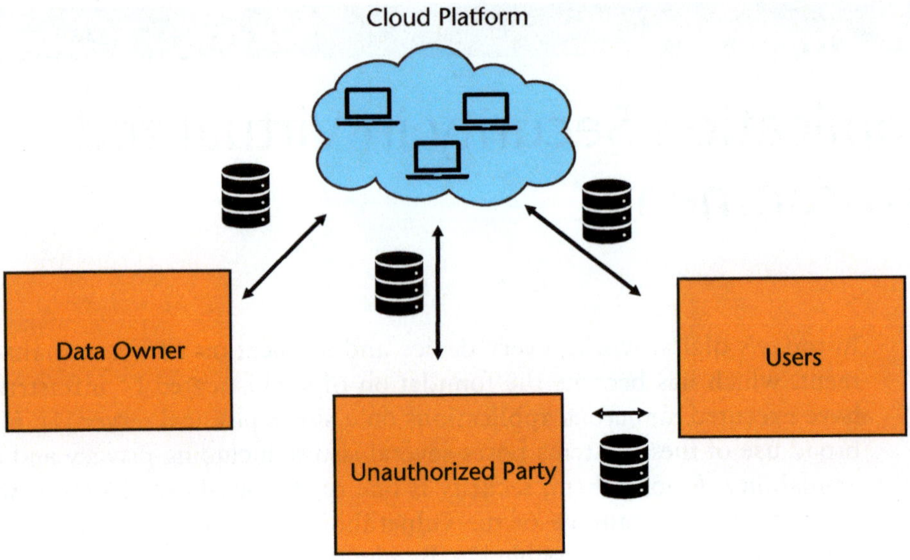

Figure 6.1 General overview of virtualized applications.

VMware, 15 VMs can be executed simultaneously [7]. Partitioning, which allows multiple VMs to share a physical server's resources, is one of the main characteristics of operating VMs [8]. This allows for lower power consumption and better use of the available hardware. Because of their hardware independence and encapsulation, VMs are easy to move, copy, and back up [9]. If necessary, they can also be easily moved to a physical server. The majority of businesses, according to Gartner, have a virtualization program.

6.2 Securing Web Servers

The widespread use of web applications and market competition brings a range of vulnerabilities and potential attacks [10]. Web server security is paramount for companies operating online businesses (Figure 6.2) [11], as evidenced by high-profile hacking incidents. The management of workloads across diverse web services is contingent upon web technologies, which serve as the intermediary between web servers and clients. These technologies fall into two categories: client-side services and server-side services. Web servers work with a high volume of sensitive data, making them key targets for attackers [12]. Consequently, safeguarding the website or web applications and the surrounding network becomes essential. An insecure web server and application can pose significant risks to a business [13].

Expertise and knowledge in the respective domain are required to protect web servers, and web server security is enhanced after taking necessary action. Moreover, attackers exploit the weaknesses and vulnerabilities of the design and implementation of the web server [14].

Web security comprises different activities, such as protecting data transmitted, preventing unauthorized access, and mitigating malicious attacks on websites, web applications, and their underlying web servers [15]. It ensures data protection during its transfer between a client and a server. Web technology facilitates the

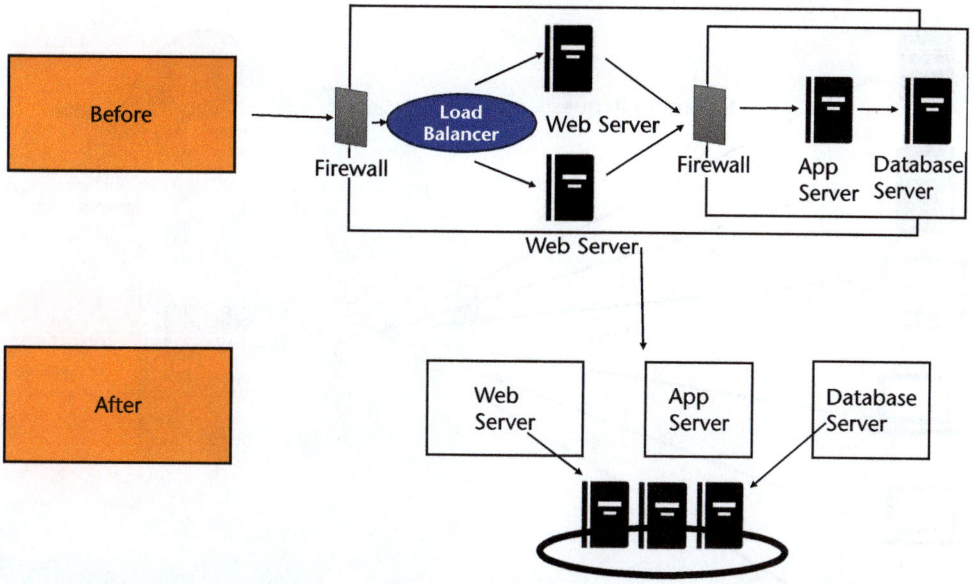

Figure 6.2 Securing web server in different scenarios.

connection between web servers and their clients, acting as an interface. The term "web technologies" aptly describes the collection of technologies necessary to manage the workload distribution among various web services in the modern era [16]. With many online services available, numerous technologies are continuously being developed to support them. Essentially, these services can be classified into two primary groups: client-side technologies and server-side technologies. The internet comprises a vast network of interconnected computers. The term "World Wide Web" denotes the websites that are publicly accessed and globally linked through the internet, as well as the client devices that access web content depicted in Figure 6.3 [17]. Its creation aimed to provide a visual means of sharing information. The World Wide Web (WWW) works over the Hypertext Transfer Protocol (HTTP), a web address (or URL) typically begins with "http://". HTTP functions as a subprotocol of Transmission Control Protocol/Internet Protocol (TCP/IP), the protocol governing the internet [18]. All the web pages that we visit are stored on web servers located worldwide. These servers are interconnected, allowing for seamless retrieval of web pages from one another. "Internet" refers to this interconnectedness and the entirety of the network. When a web address is entered into a web browser, the request is transmitted to an Internet Service Provider (ISP) [19]. The ISP locates the server hosting the requested web page, forwards the request to the server, and retrieves and delivers the page in response. Web pages contain HTML instructions that the web browser interprets and displays accordingly.

Communication on the WWW is accomplished by communicating information through HTTP. The web browser on the client side issues an HTTP request, which travels over the internet and is routed to the web server connected with the requested domain name [20]. The server then sends a formatted file back to that client. A web server sits in a bespoke application while it waits for a request (referred to as the client). However, once a client-side script made the request, the web server accepts the request and completes it by executing the server-side script. This

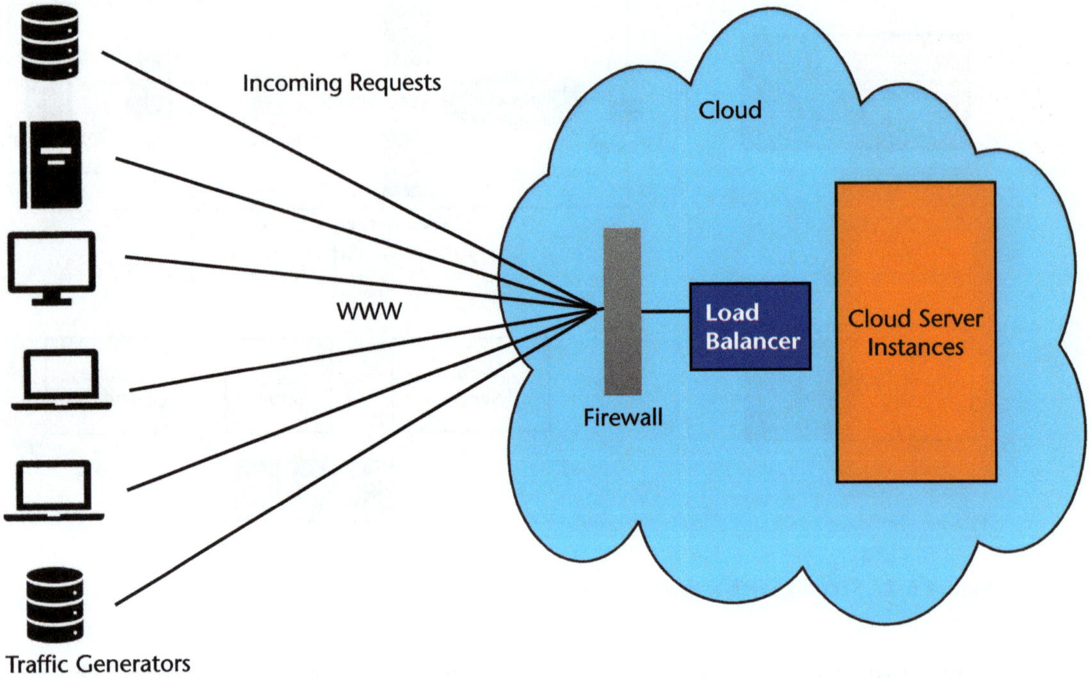

Figure 6.3 Securing web in cloud environments.

concept is very important in networking because it allows software programs that operate in different locations to interact with each other effectively. In a conventional model, a server (or daemon), is explicitly waiting for one or more client side requests [21]. Multiple client platforms can share the services provided by a standard server program, which is usually a component of a more extensive program or application. A web browser acts as a client program on the internet, requesting services from a web server. The TCP/IP protocol suite sends client requests for files following File Transfer Protocol (FTP) to the dedicated servers [22]. Other program relationship models include master/slave and peer-to-peer, where either program can initiate a transaction.

Client-side technologies operate on user computers, where browsers interpret and display content to the user. Some technologies, including HTML, CSS, JavaScript, and Flash, evolved as powerful tools for the development of web applications [23]. JavaScript has significantly evolved into a powerful tool for shaping user experience. Initially used for form validation and image rollovers, JavaScript now enables advanced operations due to innovative techniques [24]. One such technology is light-box, which displays images and content without loading a new web page. Unlike HTML and CSS, which are not executable and only provide instructions to the browser, JavaScript can send information, make requests to the server, and react to user behavior without server interaction. For instance, JavaScript can analyze text input, apply formatting, and verify if the entered text adheres to predefined formats [25]. This functionality helps to ensure accurate data transmission to the server.

Web servers have default procedures for retrieving web pages, which can be modified by incorporating server-side scripts [26]. When a server receives a request, it executes the script and appends the output to the web page. Server-side scripts are logical and sophisticated, capable of analyzing user behavior and interacting with databases to retrieve stored or stored user data. A combination of server-side scripting is Hypertext Preprocessor (PHP) and SQL, which is highly effective and sophisticated. It is frequently used for reading and writing data to a database, processing user input from forms, and interpreting and formatting complex content before sending it to the client [27].

Web development technologies include client-side technologies such as Asynchronous JavaScript and XML Ajax. It uploads and downloads the new data from the server without requiring a full page reload, which allows users to continue interacting with the page seamlessly [28]. Many frameworks come equipped with customizable, prebuilt widgets that perform everyday tasks, such as selecting a date from a calendar, displaying data charts, or creating tabbed panels [29].

On the server side, newer languages such as PHP and Ruby dynamically generate data by utilizing information from files and databases. The "participatory web" evolution has transformed how data is formatted and shared between websites [30]. While vulnerabilities represent weaknesses inherent in a system, attacks are the methods attackers employ to exploit those weaknesses. Understanding the attacker's perspective and likely strategies is crucial for effectively implementing security features and countermeasures during application design, implementation, and deployment [31]. Planned strategies effectively detect various potential threats by using the well-known acronym created by Microsoft: STRIDE [32]. S stands for "spoofing," in which an attacker pretends to get unauthorized access by using a fake IP address or stolen user credentials. T is "tampering," in which an unauthorized data change is often used; in contrast, the data is transmitted among systems over a network. R is for "repudiation," which represents the application or system's ability to properly log the actions of users. I is for "information disclosure," in which confidential information is accessed without authorization. D is for "denial of service," in which actions significantly degrade the overall quality of service for legitimate users by overwhelming the system with multiple copies in the network; it can manifest response delays, excessive data loss, or service interruptions. E stands for "elevation of privilege," in which vulnerabilities are exploited for unauthorized access or control; this generally happens when an attacker successfully logs as a legitimate user or host [32].

Web applications are susceptible to attacks like invalidated input and broken access control, highlighting the importance of addressing underlying vulnerabilities for adequate protection.

Web application attacks pose a significant threat to networks (Figure 6.4) [33], and securing systems against them is crucial. Attackers employ various techniques to exploit system vulnerabilities [34]. For instance:

- *Account lockout attacks:* This is where attackers attempt to lock out all user accounts by repeatedly exceeding the login failure threshold set by the authentication system [35]. This can lead to a large-scale DoS attack, especially if resetting accounts is resource-intensive.
- *Brute-force attacks:* These are primarily used to guess passwords, circumvent access control, or bypass security mechanisms with minimal knowledge.

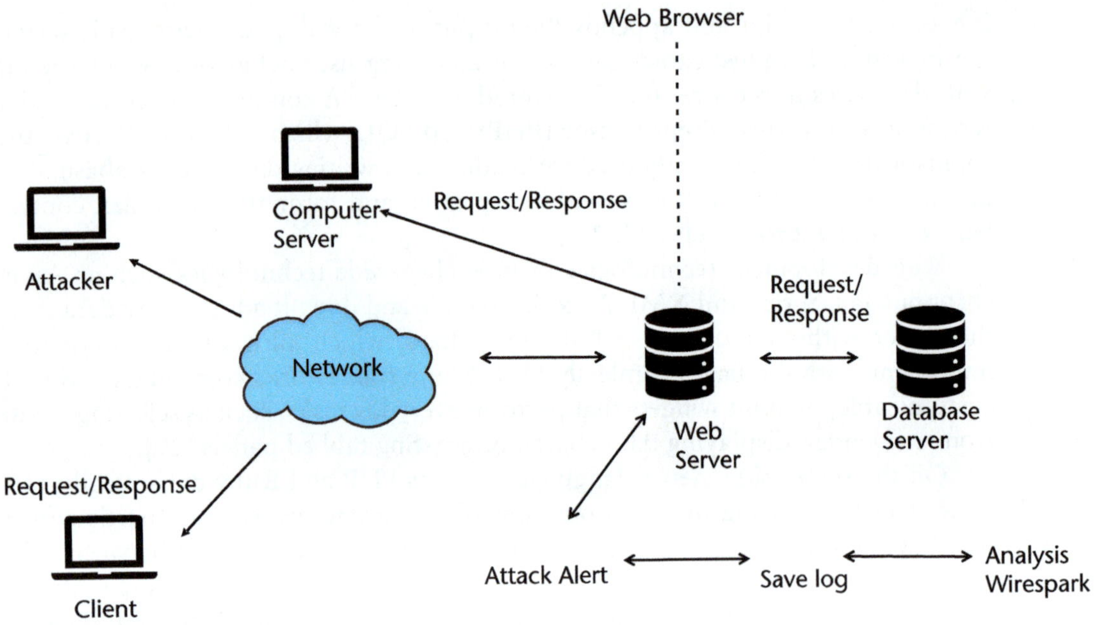

Figure 6.4 Security attack on a virtualized web environment.

Attackers utilize dictionary attacks or brute-force attempts using predefined character sets [36]. The attack duration is calculated based on the chosen method, the number of attempts, system efficiency, and the estimated efficiency of the targeted system. Non-brute-force attacks, which involve all possible characters, offer no guarantee of success. Form and session data attacks, targeting data submitted through forms (using GET/POST methods) and user session-level data.

- *Buffer overflow attacks:* These exploit memory vulnerabilities by overwriting memory fragments of a process that should not be modified [37]. Overwriting critical values such as the Instruction Pointer (IP) or Base Pointer (BP) can trigger exceptions, segment faults, and other errors, often leading to unexpected application termination. These errors, particularly stack or heap overflow errors, occur during operations on character-type buffers.
- *Cross-site request forgery (CSRF) attacks:* These force an authenticated end user to perform unintended actions on a web application [38] by sending malicious links via email or chat. A successful CSRF exploit can compromise end-user data and operations, especially if the targeted account has administrative privileges. CSRF attacks deceive victims into loading a page containing a malicious request, allowing the attacker to leverage the victim's identity and privileges to perform undesired actions. These attacks typically target functions that modify the server state but can also be used to access sensitive data. Web browsers automatically include site-associated credentials such as session cookies and authentication credentials [39]. The severity of a CSRF attack increases if the attacker can embed the attack on a vulnerable site, as the victim is more likely to visit a compromised page than a random web page.

- *Cache poisoning attacks:* These are an advanced method in which an attacker exploits the web server's behavior and the web cache to insert fake information so that malicious HTTP response splits and flows in web applications [40]. In contrast, only that user will be affected if the malicious response is stored in a user's browser cache. Executing a cache poisoning attack requires the attacker to identify vulnerable service code. This causes the cache server to first flush its current content, then send a crafted request, and finally send the request that contains the previously injected content in the cache. While more difficult to perform in practice, it is considered easier than cross-user defacement.
- *Code injection attacks:* These execute malicious code into an application and are carried out by adding strings of characters to cookies or URL argument values, exploiting inadequate input/output data validation [41]. Code injection is similar to command injection, but in code injection, the added code becomes part of the application itself.
- *Cross-site history manipulation breaches:* These exploit improper partitioning of client browser history objects per site. Manipulating the browser's history can compromise the Same-Origin Policy (SOP), enable bidirectional CSRF, and facilitate other exploits [42]. This manipulation can also violate user privacy. SOP is a critical security mechanism in modern browsers, preventing web pages from different origins from communicating with each other.
- *Cross-site scripting (XSS):* This is another class of injection attack in which a malicious script is inserted into what appears to be a harmless and trusted website [43]. The amount of XSS attacks have swelled due to the availability of the web application as a medium to deliver malicious code, often in browser side scripts, to unsuspecting end users. The end user's browser is not able to determine that the script is untrustworthy and thus the malicious script may gain access to sensitive information that the browser stores for use with the website, such as cookies, or session tokens (Figure 6.5).
- *DoS attacks:* These want to lower the quality of services for authorized users. These assaults may take advantage of flaws in programming logic, resource management, or network packet handling [44]. When a server is overwhelmed with many requests, it may cease to provide services to legitimate users. Similarly, exploiting a programming vulnerability or improper resource handling can allow an attacker to inject and execute arbitrary code, granting access to critical information or enabling command execution on the server. For example, if users can specify the number of objects to create on the application server without any enforced limit, an attacker could trigger excessive object creation, depleting available memory and potentially causing a DoS.
- *Double encoding attacks:* These employ multiple layers to bypass security controls or cause unexpected application behavior [44]. This technique can be used when web servers accept and process client requests in various encoded forms. The backend platform or modules responsible for handling encoded data may perform subsequent decoding steps without adequate

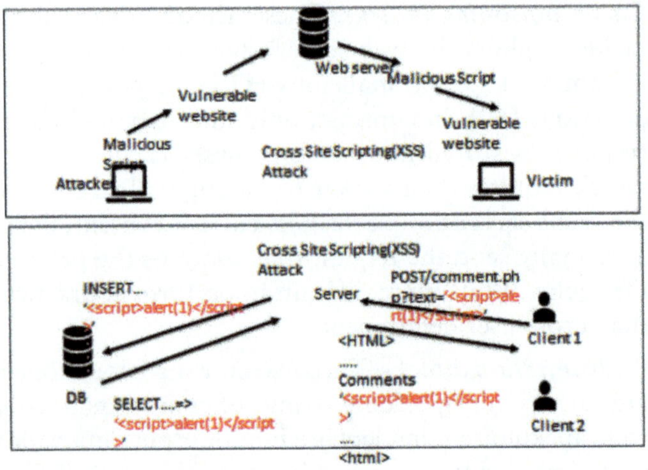

Figure 6.5 XSS attack in web base security.

security checks, creating exploitation opportunities. Attackers can inject double encoding into pathnames or query strings to circumvent web application validation schemes and security filters.

- *Forced browsing attacks:* These enumerate and access resources not referenced by the application but remain accessible [45]. These attacks can be performed manually if the application uses predictable patterns for indexing directories and pages or automated tools can be used to target standard files and directory names.
- *HTTP request smuggling attacks:* These exploit incomplete parsing of submitted data by intermediary HTTP systems acting as proxies.
- *LDAP injection attacks:* These target web applications building LDAP statements constructively based on user input. Inadvertent sanitizing of user input allows attackers to control LDAP statements using a local proxy to execute arbitrary commands. The commands can grant permissions for unauthorized LDAP queries or can change content in the LDAP tree. Like SQL injection, LDAP injection can use more sophisticated exploitation methods.
- *Man-in-the-middle (MITM) attacks:* The attacker intercepts any communication between two systems or a TCP connection between a client and server. When the sender and receiver link has been intercepted, the attacker behaves like a sender and receiver proxy and allows for different processes to read, insert, or change the data being transmitted between the two systems.
- *Network eavesdropping (or network sniffing) attacks:* These capture and analyze network packets from other computers to extract sensitive information. Attackers utilize network sniffers to collect packets and analyze their contents using protocol decoders or streaming reassembling techniques. The effectiveness of network eavesdropping relies on certain conditions, such as:
    - *LAN environments with hubs:* Hubs act as network repeaters, duplicating every received network frame to all connected ports, making capturing packets easier for an attacker.

- *LAN environments with switches:* Switches typically forward traffic only to the intended recipient, making eavesdropping more difficult. However, attackers may exploit vulnerabilities or misconfigurations in switches or employ techniques such as ARP spoofing to redirect traffic to their system for analysis.
- *SQL injection (SQLi) attacks:* These are presented in Figure 6.6 [46], introducing harmful SQL queries into an application through user input. A successful SQL injection can allow an attacker to read sensitive data, modify database data, perform administrative operations, read hidden data, and even execute commands to the OS. SQL injection vulnerabilities are a common find in PHP and ASP applications, particularly those that utilize an older, functional interface correctly. The scope of SQL injection attacks is primarily dependent on the skill and imagination of the attacker, although this can further be controlled by spending effort on applying countermeasures based on a defense-in-depth model, such as utilizing database connections that are low-privilege. SQL injection attacks can be used to:
  - Spoof identity;
  - Tamper with existing data;
  - Create repudiation issues;
  - Disclose sensitive data;
  - Destroy data;
  - Gain administrative control over the database server.
- *Unicode encoding attacks:* These exploit flaws in an application's Unicode decoding mechanism. Attackers can use this technique to encode specific characters in URLs or other input fields to access protected resources.

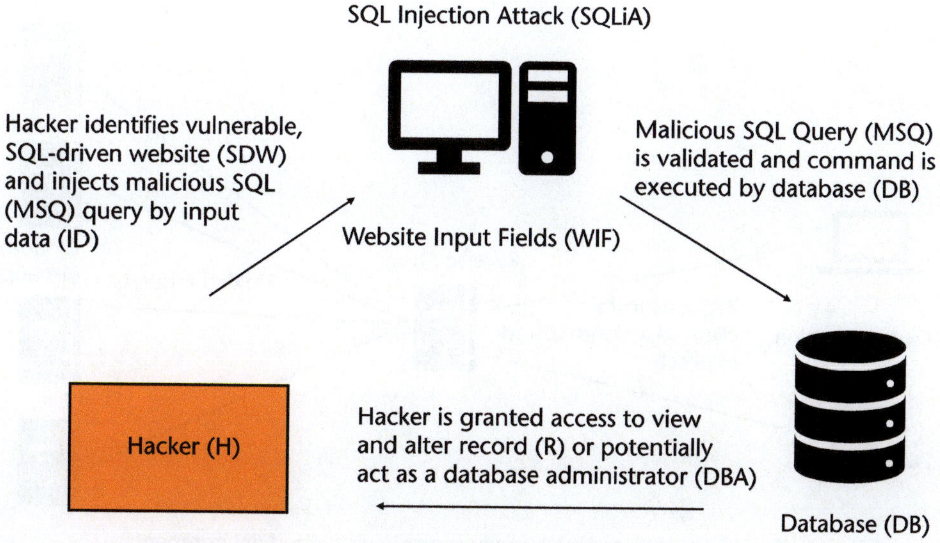

Figure 6.6 SQL injection attack in a virtualized web environment.

- *Web analysis:* This is essential in understanding and optimizing web usage (Figure 6.7) [47]. These measure website traffic, conduct business and market research, and provide valued data regarding website traffic and page views. It enables different tools to monitor traffic patterns, essential for market research. On-site web analysis is mainly focused on measuring visitor behavior and assessing the website's performance in a commercial context. It can be broadly categorized into two types:
  - *Off-site web analysis:* This measures a website's potential audience, share of voice, and online sentiment.
  - *On-site web analysis:* This tracks visitor behavior, conversion rates, and website performance. The distinction between these categories has become less clear in recent years as vendors increasingly offer tools that span both areas.

Logfile analysis and page tagging are the two main types of web traffic reporting. In the early days of the internet, website statistics primarily focused on counting the number of client requests (or "hits") to the web server, downstream of several other server metrics. However, as sites moved to multiple files and added images within HTML files, counting client requests proved to be a less reliable metric. Therefore the two new measures, page views and visits (or sessions), were introduced in the mid-1990s. While page views and visits are still the two most widely used measures in web traffic, they are understood to be relatively basic indicators.

Early web counters used images embedded in web pages to track the times that the image was requested. In the late 1990s, this concept evolved to incorporate invisible photos and JavaScript code, which could transmit information about the page and the visitor. Web analysis companies could then process this information remotely to generate comprehensive statistics.

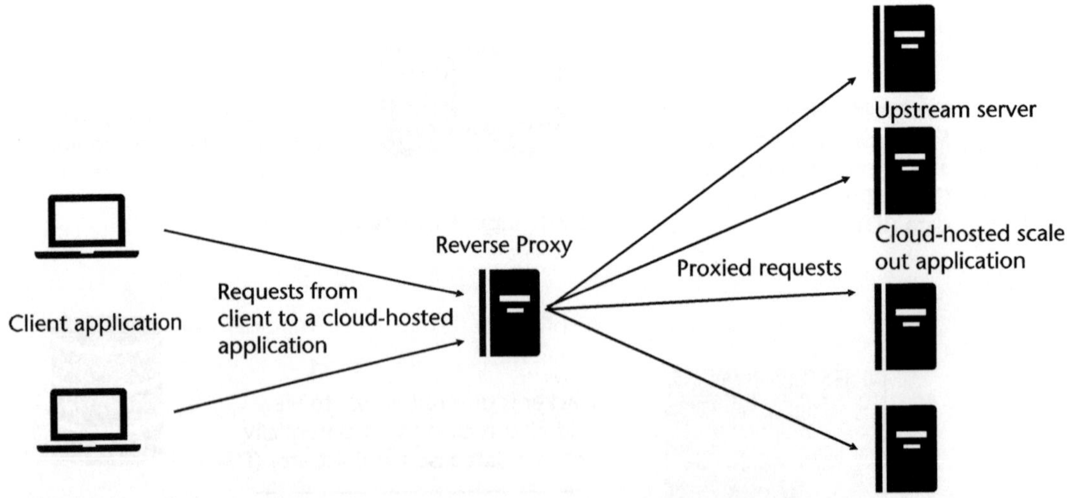

Figure 6.7 A web analysis service using a proxy server in virtualized environment.

Modern web analysis services often employ cookies to identify users uniquely during visits and subsequent sessions. However, cookie acceptance rates vary significantly across websites, potentially affecting collected and reported data quality. Using third-party or in-house data collection servers for website data collection introduces additional DNS lookups by the user's computer. With the growing popularity of Ajax-based solutions, an alternative approach to using invisible images has emerged, involving a callback to the server from the rendered page. Proxies, including request and reverse proxies, are commonly used.

Regular software updates are essential for maintaining security. Hackers often exploit known vulnerabilities in specific software versions to compromise systems and steal personal information.

6.3 Securing Database Servers

Database security is a key aspect of information security, which mainly focuses on protecting database from unauthorized access, security threats, and data breaches [48]. A database security breach occurs when the confidentiality of data in a database is compromised, causing harm to an enterprise. It can result in:

- Compromised intellectual property;
- Damage to brand reputation;
- Business continuity issues.

Noncompliance with data privacy regulations leads to financial penalties.

Database security enhances the capability of physical storage and the rising incidents of data breaches. Inadequate database security can have severe consequences for organizations, including:

- Financial losses due to theft, fines, and legal penalties;
- Reputational damage leads to loss of customer trust;
- Operational disruption caused by system failures and data loss.

Several factors contribute to database security breaches. Some common causes are:

- Software misconfigurations and vulnerabilities;
- Human error and negligence;
- Insider threats, including malicious insiders, negligent insiders, and infiltrators;
- Exploitation of database software vulnerabilities;
- SQL or NoSQL injection attacks;
- Buffer overflow exploitation;
- Malware infections;
- Attacks on backups.

Organizations can implement various security measures to mitigate these risks. These include access control, which restricts unauthorized access to the database by using different credentials. Auditing establishes security standards for the organization's database and performs regular checks to prevent failures. Authentication verifies the identification of users, computers, or processes that attempt to access the database. Encryption protects the confidentiality of data by converting it into an unreadable format. Integrity controls ensure the accuracy and consistency of data in the database. Backups are made regularly for the data and log files in case of data loss or system failures. Application security uses antivirus software and different protection measures to protect the database from various threats. Strong passwords enforce password complexity for preventing brute force attacks. Data validation tests the user's input to prevent inaccurate data from entering the system on both client and server sides. SQL injection prevention implements allowlisting or blocklisting to prevent attackers from manipulating database queries (see Figure 6.7). XSS prevention protects against attacks injecting malicious scripts into websites by implementing appropriate security measures.

In Figure 6.8, the DDoS attacks involve a human attacker leveraging a small group of masters, who deploy network scanners to identify poorly secured computers. The masters then install a script or service, a daemon, onto the poorly secured machines to create zombies capable of initiating an attack against any internet-connected machine or network with which they are paired. When the attacker has enough zombie machines, the attacker only needs to send packets to the chosen target, the victim. Because of the distributed nature of DDoS attacks, it is often difficult to track the attacker, as the real attacks are coming from zombie machines, and the owners of these machines are often unaware that they have been compromised. Most network packets used for DDoS attacks also use forged source addresses, which further makes the attacker's location difficult to track.

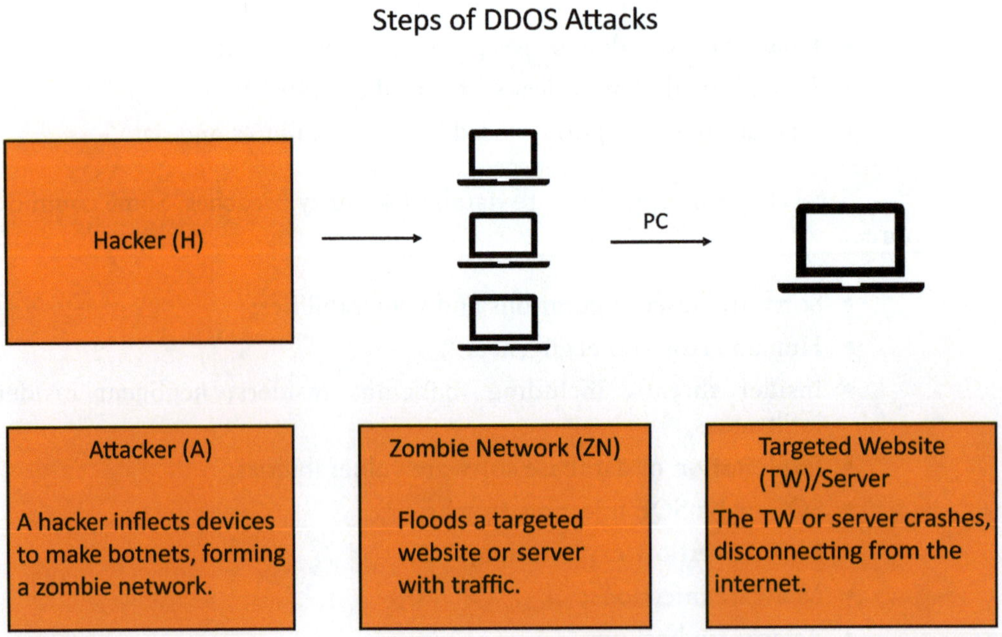

Figure 6.8 The steps of DoS attacks in a virtualized environment.

6.4 Securing Other Critical Applications

The rapid advancement of internet technologies has made web applications an integral part of modern life, offering unmatched convenience and accessibility. These applications are fundamental tools for communication, financial transactions, and accessing information. However, ensuring the security of web applications has become critically important, especially for businesses and organizations. Web security safeguards websites, applications, and APIs from cyberattacks, ensuring smooth performance and protection against data breaches or vandalism.

The international nonprofit Open Worldwide Application Security Project (OWASP) monitors vulnerabilities and publishes periodically a "Top Ten" list of security risks, which includes broken access control security, cryptographic failures, and injection [49]. The report details how these vulnerabilities arise, how they can be exploited, and measures that developers can implement to protect their applications. A security breach in web applications can have severe consequences, as organizations often store sensitive data, including financial details, personal information, and intellectual property. Data breaches can lead to financial fraud, identity theft, and other victim harm. Additionally, organizations risk reputational damage, legal penalties, and a loss of future business.

The OWASP Top Ten list is widely recognized as a comprehensive guide to identifying and addressing critical security threats. One significant security event happened in 2018 when Facebook's "View As" feature, designed to let users see their accounts from other people's viewpoints, was abused because access safeguards were not in place. By stealing access tokens, attackers might get around the requirement for login information. Over 10 million people's data was hacked by attackers, a significant security threat.

SQL injection attacks demonstrate the risk of web security vulnerabilities today. For example, in 2007, millions of credit and debit card credentials were stolen, and hackers took advantage of SQL flaws in several retail establishments in the United States. Financial data has also been stolen via XSS assaults. Attackers pretend to make it look authentic by directing users to a phony website with a Secure Socket Layer (SSL) certificate through the inclusion of malicious code that takes private financial information at risk.

Another well-known instance was in 2007 when Turkish hackers used SQL injection techniques to target US military servers. They routed users to websites with anti-Israeli and anti-American propaganda by obtaining administrator access. This instance demonstrates the various effects of SQL injection attacks, which can be used to disseminate ideological messages and steal confidential data. Secure web practices, such as HTTPS and SSL/TLS encrypted connections, are crucial for preventing attacks and mitigating these risks [50]. To guarantee the security and reliability of web applications, these examples highlight the need for proactive web security measures and the necessity for developers to fix vulnerabilities.

6.5 Best Practices for Application Security in Virtualized Environments

Improvement in the security system of virtualized environments protects the data and system from risks. It can be strengthened by techniques such as application isolation, in which every program is operated in a separate VM so that if any of the applications are attacked, the other applications operating in different VMs will not be affected by the security lapse. Another technique is enforcing security policy adaptation in which strong security rules are implemented to manage security credentials. Software is updated regularly to reduce vulnerabilities and control security attacks. Constant monitoring is performed to identify and address malicious activity quickly. Several tools are applied to locate irregularities that might point to a security breach. Patch management is vital to fixing known vulnerabilities. A comprehensive backup strategy is used to restore the data and provide a clear backup. Segmented security zones separate the virtual environments into separate areas, which lowers the possibility of a security breach in the entire system. The least privilege principle reduces the possibility of privileged accounts being abused or exploited. Hardening VMs turned off the unused services, installed the most recent patches, and set up firewalls, which secured the VMs. Snapshotting and cloning make regular snapshots or clones easier for backup and recovery procedures. Hypervisor security uses robust, authentic techniques, access controls, and frequent upgrades, which necessarily secures the hypervisor. Network segmentation is used for virtual switches and virtual local area networks (VLANs) for communication segregation between VMs, preventing lateral movement during a breach. Continuous security monitoring detects and resolves attacks using security tools, improving the system's performance.

6.5.1 Microsoft Application Virtualization 4.5

This focuses on the security configurations that preserve a reliable and effective environment by using best practices adopted by organizations to improve the services. Figure 6.9 highlights how organized implementation promotes productivity and security.

6.5.1.1 Key Security Aspects and Considerations in Application Virtualization Environments

A virtualized security development life cycle is a methodological approach that integrates security at every secure software system development stage. It consists of phases: the secure windows initiative, trustworthy computing, and the larger security development life cycle. Enhanced security features has several security measures for improving system defense such as internet-facing deployments that enable deployment in circumstances where the users use the internet; Kerberos authentication and authorization, which enhances the safe access control and identity validation; and the secure-by-default configuration, which reduces vulnerabilities by activating the security settings by default. Controlled log file access limits unauthorized access to log files known as controlled log file access, user permissions provides safe user permission settings, access control lists (ACLs) capture and secure file-based ACLs to manage permissions effectively, and certificate-based secure communication certificates are crucial in establishing encrypted and secure communication between servers and clients in application virtualization (App-V) environments. Certificates

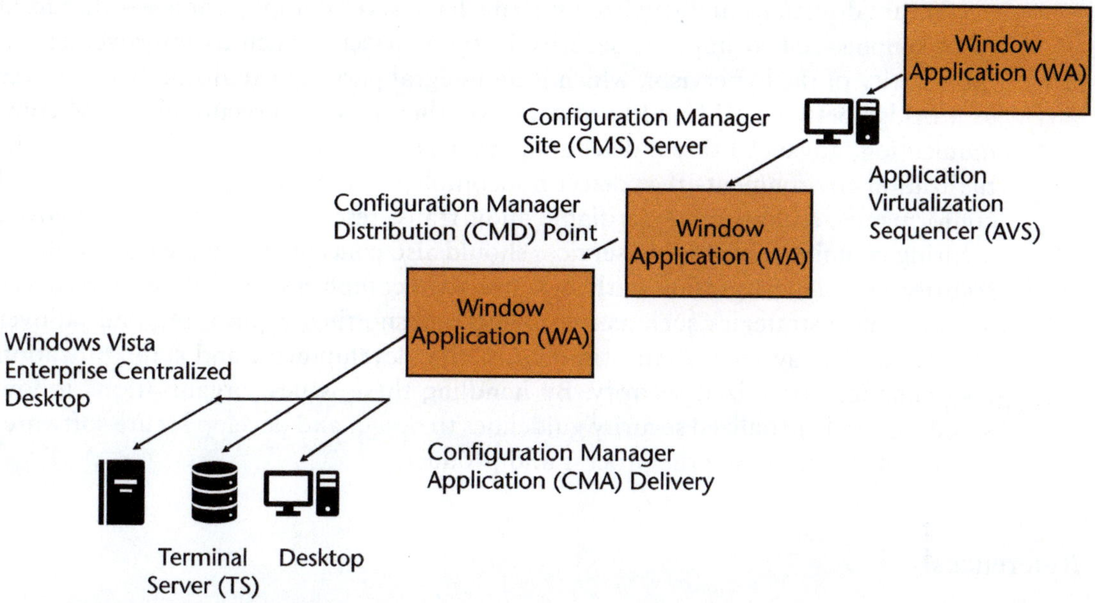

Figure 6.9 Architecture of App-V 4.5 in a virtualized environment [51].

validate identities and prevent data interception during communication. Data store security includes App-V management servers that interact with the database (data store) through SQL connections over TCP port 1433.

Client security configuration imposes security during the App-V Client installation process. Moreover, the ADM template permits centralized security setting management through group policy. This makes it easier to enforce uniform security settings for all clients. Sequencing security places a strong emphasis on preserving security when creating packages. With internet-facing scenarios, users outside the company network can access virtualized apps thanks to App-V's support for deployments for internet-based clients. It is advised that the App-V management server be situated in a demilitarized zone (DMZ) for increased protection. This configuration permits external access while adding a layer of security to segregate internal systems.

6.6 Summary

Virtualized environments have become an essential part of contemporary IT infrastructures because of their capacity to reduce overall costs, boost operational flexibility, and improve resource efficiency. This chapter overviews virtualized applications and securing web and database servers. Moreover, securing other critical applications is also elaborated to enhance virtualized security for different organizations. Furthermore, best practices for application security in virtualized environments are also discussed, continuously improving security practices' research and development program.

Future directions in virtualized systems have several important areas that need to be emphasized to improve security in these systems, such as improvement in the security of the hypervisor, which is an integral part of virtualization and serves as a bridge between VM and hardware. Another area is to secure inter-VM communication, advanced threat detection, and response compliance in cloud and virtualization environments that detect noncompliance concerns, guarantee standard conformance, and generate verifiable audit trails; research is required. Moreover, securing containers and micro-services should also concentrate on creating uniform security models, integration with IoT and edge computing, and disaster recovery and resilience strategies such as improving snapshotting, replication, and failover strategies. User awareness and training, policy development, and standardization also enhance virtualized security. By handling these issues, organizations follow standards and virtualized security guidelines to design and develop secure software, continuously improving the process and product.

References

[1] Del Campo, G., et al., "Digital Twins for Street Lighting: Challenges for a Virtual Reality Solution Based on Internet-of-Things Devices and Photometry Rendering," *2023 IEEE Sustainable Smart Lighting World Conference & Expo (LS18)*, June 8, 2023, pp. 1–6.

[2] Tabrizchi, H., and M. Kuchaki Rafsanjani, "A Survey on Security Challenges in Cloud Computing: Issues, Threats, and Solutions," *The Journal of Supercomputing*, Vol. 76, No. 12, December 2020, pp. 9493–9532.

[3] Haque, A. B., B. Bhushan, and G. Dhiman, "Conceptualizing Innovative City Applications: Requirements, Architecture, Security Issues, and Emerging Trends," *Expert Systems*, Vol. 39, No. 5, June 2022, p. e12753.

[4] Mansouri, Y., and M. A. Babar, "A Review of Edge Computing: Features and Resource Virtualization," *Journal of Parallel and Distributed Computing*, Vol. 150, April 1, 2021, pp. 155–183.

[5] Sharma, V. K., et al., "Introduction to Virtualization in Cloud Computing," in *Machine Learning and Optimization Models for Optimization in Cloud*, Longdon, UK: Chapman and Hall/CRC, 2022, pp. 1–14.

[6] Faruk, M. N., K. L. Prasad, and G. L. Prasad, "An Efficient VM Live Migration Through VM I/O Requests Using Live Scheduling Scheme (LSS)," *Smart Computing Techniques and Applications: Proceedings of the Fourth International Conference on Smart Computing and Informatics*, Volume 1, 2021, pp. 271–285.

[7] Zolfaghari, R., et al., "Application of Virtual Machine Consolidation in Cloud Computing Systems," *Sustainable Computing: Informatics and Systems*, Vol. 30, June 1, 2021, p. 100524.

[8] Abeni, L., A. Biondi, and E. Bini, "Partitioning Real-Time Workloads on Multi-Core Virtual Machines," *Journal of Systems Architecture*, Vol. 131, October 1, 2022, p. 102733.

[9] Srivastava, D. K., et al., "Virtualization Concepts and Industry Standards in Cloud Computing," in *Bio-Inspired Optimization in Fog and Edge Computing Environments*, Auerbach Publications, 2023, pp. 147–164.

[10] Schmitt, M., "Securing the Digital World: Protecting Smart Infrastructures and Digital Industries with Artificial Intelligence (AI)-Enabled Malware and Intrusion Detection," *Journal of Industrial Information Integration*, Vol. 36, December 1, 2023, p. 100520.

[11] Parast, F. K., et al., "Cloud Computing Security: A Survey of Service-Based Models," *Computers & Security*, Vol. 114, March 1, 2022, p. 102580.

[12] Kumar, A., and G. Somani, "Security Infrastructure for Cyber Attack Targeted Networks and Services," *Recent Advancements in ICT Infrastructure and Applications*, June 12, 2022, pp. 209–229.

[13] Sołtysik-Piorunkiewicz, A., and M. Krysiak, "The Cyber Threats Analysis for Web Applications Security in Industry 4.0," *Towards Industry 4.0—Current Challenges in Information Systems*, 2020, pp. 127–141.

[14] Muzammil, M. B., et al., "Unveiling Vulnerabilities of Web Attacks Considering Man in the Middle Attack and Session Hijacking," *IEEE Access*, January 5, 2024.

[15] Rani, S., A. Kataria, and M. Chauhan, "Cyber Security Techniques, Architectures, and Design," in *Holistic Approach to Quantum Cryptography in Cyber Security*, Boca Raton, FL: CRC Press, 2022, pp. 41–66.

[16] Naik, H. S., A. Fritzsche, and K. M. Moeslein, "Modularity in Making: Simplifying Solution Space for User Innovation," *R&D Management*, Vol. 51, No. 1, January 2021, pp. 57–72.

[17] Ayres, R. U., "The Internet and the World Wide Web," *The History and Future of Technology: Can Technology Save Humanity from Extinction?* Cham, Switzerland: Springer Nature, 2021, pp. 519–557.

[18] Rabadi, Y. E., and J. Lu, *Building a Secured XML Real-Time Interactive Data Exchange Architecture. Research Anthology on Architectures, Frameworks, and Integration Strategies for Distributed and Cloud Computing*, Hershey, PA: IGI Global, 2021, pp. 270–357.

[19] Cameron, N., "Updating a Web Page," *Electronics Projects with the ESP8266 and ESP32: Building Web Pages, Applications, and WiFi Enabled Devices*, 2021, pp. 181–222.

[20] Swamy, S. N., and S. R. Kota, "An Empirical Study on System Level Aspects of Internet of Things (IoT)," *IEEE Access*, Vol. 8, October 9, 2020, pp. 188082–188134.

[21] da Silva, T. B., et al., "Toward Future Internet of Things Experimentation and Evaluation," *IEEE Internet of Things Journal*, Vol. 9, No. 11, September 22, 2021, pp. 8469–8484.

[22] Choi, B., "Linux Fundamentals II–TCP/IP Services," in *Introduction to Python Network Automation Volume I-Laying the Groundwork: The Essential Skills for Growth*, Berkeley, CA: Apress, 2024, pp. 475–559.

[23] Singh, R. P., and B. R. Chandavarkar, "Dynamic Content Security Policy Generation at Client-Side to Mitigate XSS Attacks," *2024 15th International Conference on Computing Communication and Networking Technologies (ICCCNT)*, June 24, 2024, pp. 1–7.

[24] Song, A. H., et al., "Artificial Intelligence for Digital and Computational Pathology," *Nature Reviews Bioengineering*, Vol. 1, No. 12, December 2023, pp. 930–949.

[25] Kim, H., and J. S. Yi, "Image Generation of Hazardous Situations in Construction Sites Using Text-to-Image Generative Model for Training Deep Neural Networks," *Automation in Construction*, Vol. 166, October 1, 2024, p. 105615.

[26] Urbieta, M., et al., "MDWA: A Model-Driven Web Augmentation Approach—Coping with Client-and Server-Side Support," *Software and Systems Modeling*, Vol. 19, November 2020, pp. 1541–1566.

[27] Sahu, S. K., "Web Security for PHP Applications," in *Building Secure PHP Applications: A Comprehensive Guide to Protecting Your Web Applications from Threats*, Berkeley, CA: Apress, 2024, pp. 125–175.

[28] Loo, Z., et al., "GenDatr: Visualizing Probabilistic Data Generation in Medical Data Science," *Proceedings of the Future Technologies Conference*, November 8, 2024, pp. 373–378.

[29] Gole, V., and S. Shiralkar, *Empower Decision Makers with SAP Analytics Cloud*, New York: Springer, 2020.

[30] Ghosh, S., "Web3 Architectures," in *The Age of Decentralization*, New York: Productivity Press, 2025, pp. 172–212.

[31] Khanam, S., et al., "A Survey of Security Challenges, Attacks Taxonomy and Advanced Countermeasures in the Internet of Things," *IEEE Access*, Vol. 8, November 11, 2020, pp. 219709–219743.

[32] Sanfilippo, J., et al., "Stride-Based Threat Modeling for MYSQL Databases," *Proceedings of the Future Technologies Conference (FTC) 2019*, Volume 2, 2020, pp. 368–378.

[33] Upadhyay, D., and S. Sampalli, "SCADA (Supervisory Control and Data Acquisition) Systems: Vulnerability Assessment and Security Recommendations," *Computers & Security*, Vol. 89, February 1, 2020, p. 101666.

[34] Shafique, A., A. Mehmood, and M. Elhadef, "Survey of Security Protocols and Vulnerabilities in Unmanned Aerial Vehicles," *IEEE Access*, Vol. 9, March 17, 2021, pp. 46927–46948.

[35] Wang, X., et al., "Attacks and Defenses in User Authentication Systems: A Survey," *Journal of Network and Computer Applications*, Vol. 188, August 15, 2021, p. 103080.

[36] Por, L. Y., et al., "A Systematic Literature Review on the Security Attacks and Countermeasures Used in Graphical Passwords," *IEEE Access*, March 7, 2024.

[37] Liu, C., et al., "A Buffer Overflow Detection and Defense Method Based on RISC-V Instruction Set Extension," *Cybersecurity*, Vol. 6, No. 1, September 6, 2023, p. 45.

[38] Rankothge, W. H., and S. M. Randeniya, "Identification and Mitigation Tool for Cross-Site Request Forgery (CSRF)," *2020 IEEE 8th R10 Humanitarian Technology Conference (R10-HTC)*, December 1, 2020, pp. 1–5.

[39] Rao, M. S., et al., "Cross-Site Request Forgery as an Example of Machine Learning for Web Vulnerability Detection," *2023 3rd International Conference on Smart Data Intelligence (ICSMDI)*, March 30, 2023, pp. 422–426.

[40] Alharbi, F., et al., "DNS Poisoning of Operating System Caches: Attacks and Mitigations," *IEEE Transactions on Dependable and Secure Computing*, Vol. 19, No. 4, January 13, 2022, pp. 2851–2863.

[41] Kaur, M., M. Raj, and H. N. Lee, "Cross Channel Scripting and Code Injection Attacks on Web and Cloud-Based Applications: A Comprehensive Review," *Sensors*, Vol. 22, No. 5, March 2, 2022, 1959.

[42] Sandhu, P. S., and L. Banda, "Cross-Site Scripting Attack Prevention (On Application Layer)," in *Advanced Computer Science Applications*, Apple Academic Press, 2023, pp. 59–73.

[43] Hannousse, A., S. Yahiouche, and M. C. Nait-Hamoud, "Twenty-Two Years Since Revealing Cross-Site Scripting Attacks: A Systematic Mapping and a Comprehensive Survey," *Computer Science Review*, Vol. 52, May 1, 2024, p. 100634.

[44] Bhardwaj, A., et al., "Distributed Denial of Service Attacks in Cloud: State-of-the-Art of Scientific and Commercial Solutions," *Computer Science Review*, Vol. 39, February 1, 2021, p. 100332.

[45] Kowta, A. S., et al., "Analysis and Overview of Information Gathering & Tools for Pentesting," *2021 IEEE International Conference on Computer Communication and Informatics (ICCCI)*, January 27, 2021, pp. 1–13.

[46] Agbakwuru, A. O., and D. O. Njoku, "SQL Injection Attack on Web Base Application: Vulnerability Assessments and Detection Technique," *International Research Journal of Engineering and Technology*, Vol. 8, No. 3, 2021, pp. 243–252.

[47] Sun, Z., M. Anbarasan, and D. J. Praveen Kumar, "Design of Online Intelligent English Teaching Platform Based on Artificial Intelligence Techniques," *Computational Intelligence*, Vol. 37, No. 3, August 2021, pp. 1166–1180.

[48] Naguib, A., and K. M. Fouad, "Database Security: Current Challenges and Effective Protection Strategies," *2024 6th International Conference on Computing and Informatics (ICCI)*, March 6, 2024, pp. 120–130.

[49] Cruz, D. B., J. R. Almeida, and J. L. Oliveira, "Open Source Solutions for Vulnerability Assessment: A Comparative Analysis," *IEEE Access*, Vol. 11, September 14, 2023, pp. 100234–100255.

[50] Platenka, V., A. Mazalek, and Z. Vranova, "Attacks on Devices Using SSL/TLS," *2021 International Conference on Military Technologies (ICMT)*, June 8, 2021, pp. 1–6.

[51] Zacker, C., *Exam Ref MS-900 Microsoft 365 Fundamentals*, Seattle, WA: Microsoft Press, 2023.

CHAPTER 7

Compliance and Audit in Virtualized Environments

7.1 Introduction

The evolution of virtualization within enterprise IT environments has disrupted traditional paradigms of compliance. Historically, industry standards and governmental regulations assumed a relatively static landscape: data was stored on dedicated hardware, access was tightly regulated at the perimeter, and evidence of compliance could often be demonstrated through basic logs, static network maps, or lists of physical machines. Today, however, virtualization's dynamic nature, where workloads can move fluidly from one host to another, network boundaries are defined in software, and resources are abstracted from their underlying hardware, presents a far more challenging landscape for regulatory conformity.

Hypervisors are a vital aspect of virtualization environments, providing an abstraction layer between underlying hardware and OSs [1, 2]. As a point of control, the hypervisor will need to be audited for patch management, limited services, secured access, managed services, and secure remote management, among other areas. If there are any risks at the hypervisor level, all confidentiality and availability of hosted systems are no longer guaranteed. The layered architecture of virtualized environment is depicted in Figure 7.1. This architecture provides a brief overview of layered architecture in a virtualized secure environment to fulfill users' needs.

- *Payment Card Industry Data Security Standard (PCI DSS) in the virtual world:* The PCI DSS is a very prescriptive and widely adopted set of standards, especially for organizations that deal with credit card and debit card data. A summary of the PCI's security standards is summarized in Figure 7.2. The PCI DSS is effectively a set of requirements with many layers of guidance across a variety of areas such as encryption, network segmentation, access control, vulnerability management, logging and monitoring, and testing [3]. In terms of virtualization, each of these components is defined for a scenario where, in some cases, network segmentation may be implemented using software-defined networking (SDN), and multiple virtual instances may share

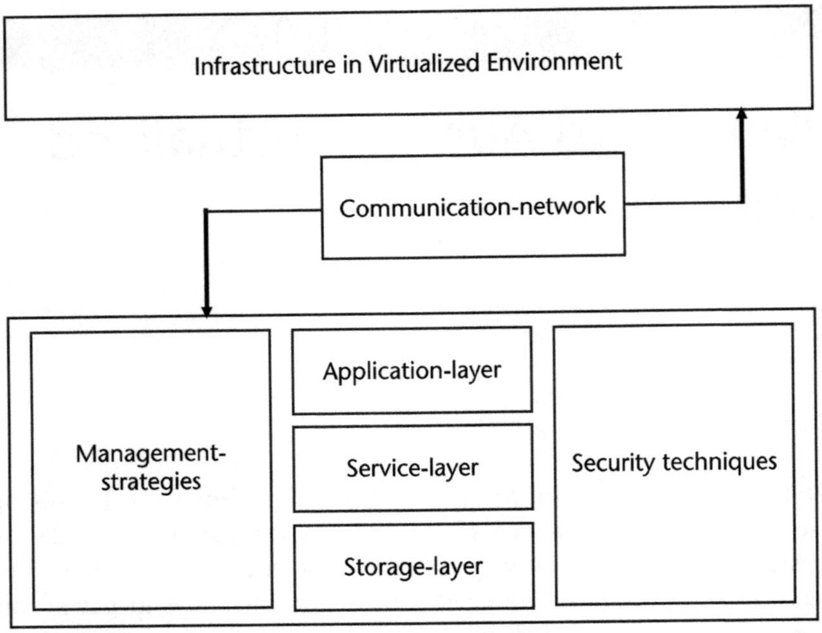

Figure 7.1 Layered architecture of virtualized environment.

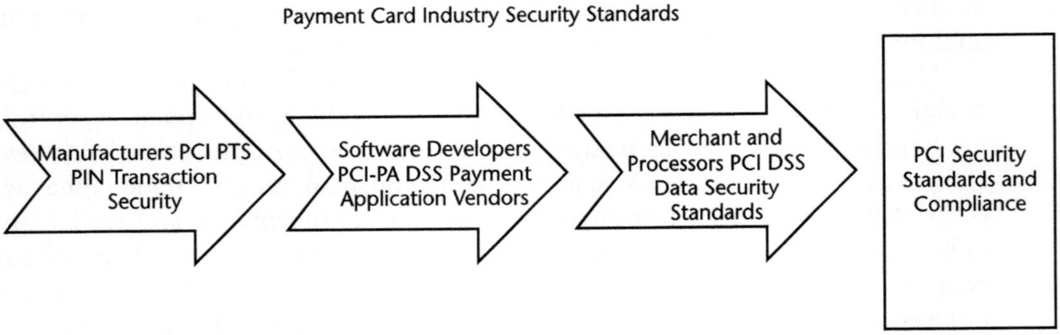

Figure 7.2 Overview of the security standards of the payment card industry.

the same hardware resources, potentially with different security postures. Compliance here demands logical isolation of the cardholder data environment (CDE), careful management of access to hypervisor consoles, and airtight control over orchestration APIs. Even a misconfigured management network or VM template can bring the CDE into the "compliance scope."

The PCI Security Standards Council has published supplementary guidance for virtualized systems, recognizing scenarios such as "VM escape" attacks, where a vulnerability in one VM can compromise adjacent workloads, and requiring detailed asset inventories, rigorous patching, and airtight change controls at every layer of the stack.

- *HIPAA and Protected Health Information (PHI) in virtualization:* The use, storage, transmission, and accounting of PHI is managed by HIPAA. HIPAA is associated with the healthcare sector, but also applies to internationally established standards [4]. Practically, in traditional settings, requirements could be met by physically locking down a database server or segmenting a network. In virtualized environments, the sheer flexibility of VMs, which can be easily cloned for test or development use, data moving automatically between data stores, and snapshots kept for disaster recovery, means that sensitive PHI could unintentionally proliferate or become exposed.

HIPAA's Security Rule mandates comprehensive audit controls for systems containing PHI. This obligation covers logs on both physical hosts and all virtual objects and demands precise access records. The identity tooling must be able to trace precisely who has accessed what data, when, and why, even as VMs are instantiated or destroyed, potentially hundreds in a single day. Encryption at rest and in transit, strong user authentication, automatic session termination, and robust incident response planning must be mapped not merely to servers, but to every virtualized element touching PHI, including orchestration and backup tools.

- *Sarbanes-Oxley Act (SOX), General Data Protection Regulation (GDPR), and the rising tide of international regulations:* The SOX is focused on the integrity of financial records and reporting. In virtual environments, the control requirements and audit requirements apply to application servers, database servers, the underlying orchestration tools used to provision the virtual resources, and the controls on the hypervisor console [5]. It is also an obligation to log and be able to review all privileged users who have ever accessed a financial system to configure it or access sensitive data. Ephemeral or improperly managed virtual resources pose a risk of undetected, unauthorized change and that risk is not tolerable.

  The European Union's GDPR and the UK Data Protection Act 2018 are even broader, prescribing stronger principles of transparency, data minimization, consent, erasure, notification, and data localization. In the cloud environment, which is highly dynamic, this means that the organization must be able to show the location of people's personal information at any moment in time, which parties can access that information, and for which purposes that data can be used. The simplistic act of cloning a VM for troubleshooting purposes, or moving a dataset to another cloud region for load balancing, runs the risk of inadvertently violating the GDPR unless managed appropriately. The GDPR also requires rapid breach notification (72 hours), thus making event correlation and log preservation critical.

- *From static security to dynamic compliance:* Most regulations, including emerging frameworks such as ISO 27001/27017 for information and cloud security, share foundational principles: strict access control, risk-centric policies, robust evidence production, and documented process management. The ISO process is briefly discussed in Figure 7.3. It consists of different units: confidentiality, risk analysis, internal processing, process requirement identification, record keeping and tracking, and control requirement identification. However, their enforcement requires different tools and considerable operational discipline in the virtual world. Automation, change tracking, asset tagging, network micro-segmentation, immutable logging, and real-time compliance dashboards are becoming expected, not optional.

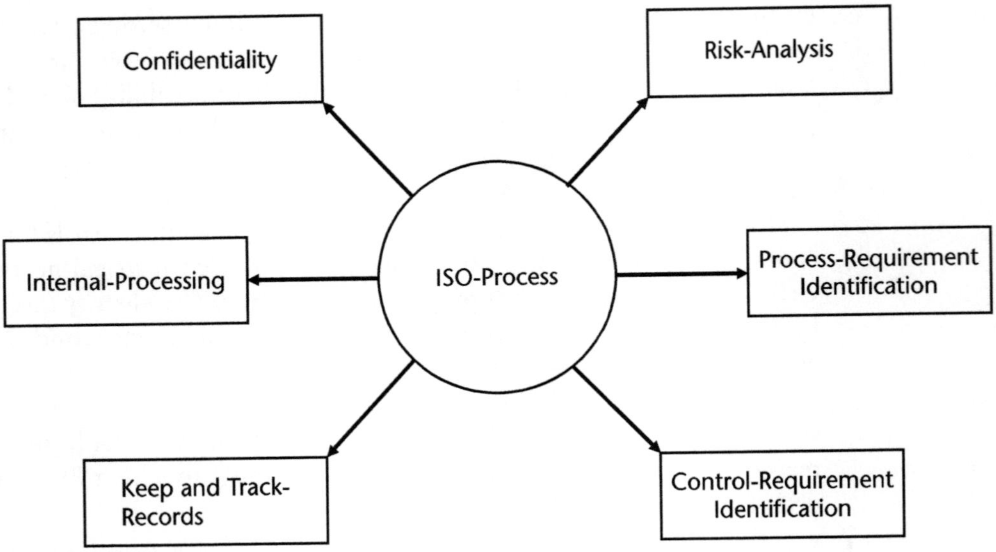

Figure 7.3 Brief description of the ISO process.

It is also critical to recognize that responsibility for compliance does not stop where the data center ends: virtualization is a key enabler of hybrid and cloud deployments, meaning that third-party attestation, auditable contracts, and ongoing due diligence of cloud service providers (CSPs) are increasingly required [6]. All regulatory obligations apply regardless of whether assets are on-premises, in the public cloud, or on a complex multitenant platform.

In summary, effective compliance in virtualized environments demands a holistic approach: a thorough understanding of applicable regulatory standards, accurate scoping of every asset and data flow, technological adaptation to new threats, and operational discipline to match regulatory intent with verifiable practice.

7.1.1 Impact of Shared Responsibility Models in Cloud Compliance

The introduction of cloud technologies has significantly altered the landscape of information technology compliance and audit. One of the most critical, and often misunderstood, elements of cloud compliance is the shared responsibility model. It is important to know where the compliance of the customer begins and ends, and the compliance of their cloud service provider at each environment level gets more complicated with IaaS, PaaS, SaaS, and hybrid or multicloud alternatives [7].

- What is the shared responsibility model? In a shared responsibility model, the CSP and the customer (also referred to as the tenant or subscriber) assume control over different parts of the virtualized and cloud-based ecosystem.
- Cloud providers own the "security of the cloud," meaning the underlying hardware, software, networking, and facilities that run the cloud services.
- Customers own the "security in the cloud," meaning data protection, endpoints, account management, and access configuration.

The partition of these responsibilities shifts depending on cloud service type:

- *IaaS (e.g., Amazon EC2, Azure VM):* Provider secures the infrastructure, and customer secures VMs, OSs, applications, data, and identities.
- *PaaS (e.g., Azure SQL Database, Google App Engine):* This also provides the OS and run time, leaving the provider primarily responsible for application security, data, and user management.
- *SaaS (e.g., Microsoft 365, Salesforce):* The provider controls nearly everything; the customer is mainly responsible for user access and specific data management/configurations.
- *Hybrid and multicloud scenarios:* Where some workloads run locally and others in various public clouds compound the complexity, as different segments of the infrastructure might fall under distinct compliance regimes and responsibility splits.
- *Audit and compliance implications:* A misunderstanding of shared responsibility is a well-known cause of compliance failures [8]. For example, an organization might incorrectly assume that their cloud provider encrypts data by default or that patch management is always handled by the provider, when these are customer responsibilities in many IaaS contexts.

Regulatory frameworks such as PCI DSS, HIPAA, or SOX all require clear lines of accountability:

- Who configures and monitors firewalls and network security groups?
- Who monitors access logs and performs security incident responses?
- Who ensures backup integrity, data retention, and right to erasure in multitenant environments?

Due diligence must include:

- Understanding "shared controls" (e.g., both CSP and customer have roles in monitoring or incident management);
- Reviewing the CSP's compliance certifications (e.g., SOC 2, ISO/IEC 27001) to ensure they align with your obligations;
- Updating internal controls and audit frameworks based on the precise demarcation of duties.

Audit preparation in cloud contexts demands documentation of each party's roles, evidence of continuous compliance by both parties, and contractual clarity (often referenced in data processing agreements and service level agreements).

A best practice is to regularly review the CSP's "shared responsibility matrix" documentation and ensure internal teams map all regulatory requirements to an accountable owner, provider, customer, or both, especially as new services are adopted [9].

IaaS tenants may mistakenly assume that their VM workloads are physically isolated. Without associated audit tools from CSPs that detect co-residency or cross-tenant VLAN leaks, such presuppositions may be untrue. Furthermore, the absence of, or violations of, "no co-residency" or "no shared owner" are often difficult to determine without automated validation systems that are part of the virtualization technology.

Hypervisors expose management interfaces that must be hardened to prevent unauthorized access. Only secure, encrypted remote access protocols (e.g., Secure Shell (SSH), hypertext transfer protocol secure (HTTPS)) should be enabled. Remote access must be logged separately, and administrative accounts should be tied to specific users for accountability. Disabling unused APIs and services minimizes attack surfaces.

7.1.2 Compliance Challenges in Containerization and Orchestration Platforms

While VMs have become widely accepted in compliance and security frameworks, the rapid rise of containerization and orchestration platforms, along with technologies such as Docker, Kubernetes, OpenShift, and serverless models, has introduced new complexities [10]. Regulators and auditors often lag behind technical innovation, leaving organizations with a lack of clear guidance for applying standards such as PCI DSS, HIPAA, or ISO/IEC 27001 to these newer paradigms.

What makes containers different?

- *Ephemeral and dynamic:* Containers are lightweight and highly transient, often created and destroyed within seconds. This volatility makes traditional audit trails and stateful monitoring much more complex.
- *Shared resources:* Containers on the same host share a single OS kernel, making strong isolation crucial; a misconfigured container can potentially impact others ("container escape").
- *Layered architecture:* Compliance must address not just running containers but also images, registries, orchestration configuration (Kubernetes manifests, Helm charts), and the underlying nodes.

Orchestration platforms and compliance gaps are the following:

- *Distributed control:* In clustered environments (e.g., Kubernetes), the attack surface and complexity multiply: security, insecure control planes, vulnerable APIs, and misconfigured secrets management can all lead to compliance failures.
- *Lack of prescriptive guidance:* Most regulatory frameworks are written for server-centric environments. PCI DSS, for example, refers to "servers" and "network segments," rather than pods, namespaces, and clusters.
- *Shadow IT risk:* Developers can easily spin up containers outside of formal controls, increasing the risk of noncompliant workloads going undetected.

Compliance approaches for container and orchestration deployments are:

- *Policy-as-code:* Tools such as Open Policy Agent (OPA), Kubernetes Admission Controllers, and Pod Security Policies can enforce compliance at deployment time, ensuring that only secure, well-configured resources enter production.

- *Immutable infrastructure:* Containers enable repeatable, controlled builds and deployments; compliance scanning at the image build phase (using tools such as Aqua, Twistlock, Trivy) is essential.
- *Comprehensive logging:* Orchestrators should forward logs from all nodes and containers to a central repository, with consistent time-stamping and immutability. Activity in registries (including pulls, pushes, and deletions) must also be tracked.
- *Network segmentation and least privilege:* Apply namespace segmentation, network policies (e.g., Calico), and role-based access controls (RBACs) aggressively within clusters to isolate sensitive workloads.

With regard to audit readiness, as standards evolve (e.g., the PCI SSC's Container Supplement), stay abreast of new guidance and document all compensating controls, security design choices, and hardening routines for auditor review. The security attack scenario in a virtualized environment is discussed in Figure 7.4.

7.1.3 Cross-Border Data Transfers and Virtual Infrastructure Compliance

What is particularly intriguing is that, as cloud computing and distributed virtual environments continue to emerge across the globe, factors relating to the location, transmission and processing of data have become governing compliance issues in themselves. Compliance issues that include, but are not limited to, regionally based data protection law, legislation such as the EU's GDPR, California's CCPA, Brazil's General Data Protection Law (LGPD), and similar draft legislation in various regions around the world [11].

Key regulatory principles are:

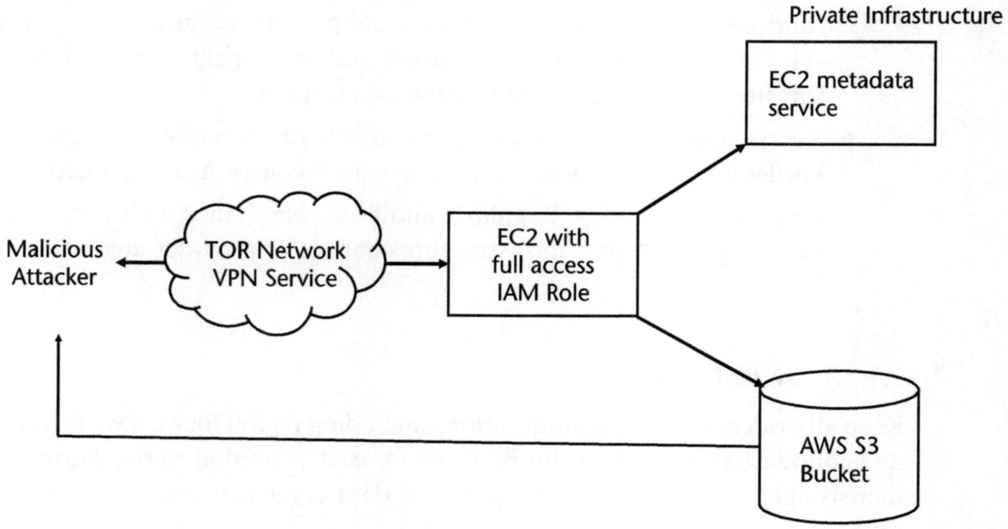

Figure 7.4 Security attacks scenario in a virtualized environment.

- *Data localization:* Many laws now condition certain processing activities on the data remaining within specific national or regional boundaries.
- *International transfers:* GDPR imposes restrictive rules for transferring personal data outside the European Economic Area (EEA). Some examples include evaluating standard contractual clauses, making adequacy decisions, or obtaining explicit user consent.

Virtualization complicates data geography:

- *VM and container mobility:* VMs, containers, and storage can be migrated automatically between global cloud regions to balance load or optimize cost, sometimes with no direct user involvement or awareness.
- *Hybrid and multicloud challenges:* Enterprises may run sensitive workloads on-premises, in public/private clouds, or at the edge, creating a patchwork of legal obligations.
- *Backup/replication:* Backups and disaster recovery solutions may routinely copy regulated data to geographically dispersed locations, raising potential compliance risks.

Compliance strategies for cross-border data challenges are:

- *Data mapping and classification:* Maintain detailed inventories of all personal and regulated data, mapped to the specific geographic locations and legal jurisdictions in which data is stored or processed, including backup and failover sites.
- *Region-aware orchestration:* Use cloud-native features (such as AWS Regions, Azure's geographical policies, Google's organization policies) and automation to ensure that new workloads or migrations abide by data residency requirements.
- *Contractual controls:* GDPR's international transfers require you to take precautions to ensure that all vendors, subprocessors, and partners enter into suitable data processing agreements and implement approved methods of transfer (e.g., EU Standard Contractual Clauses).
- *Access restrictions:* Enforce strict controls to prevent cross-region or cross-border administrative access that may itself constitute a regulated "transfer."
- *Ongoing monitoring:* Regularly audit for compliance with data localization rules, especially after infrastructure changes or provider upgrades.

7.1.3.1 Audit Preparation

Keep all evidence system configurations, including region locks, data flow mapping, and contractual artifacts, well-organized for easy provision to regulators, who will increasingly request on-demand proof of data residency and movement controls [12].

These three intertwined areas, shared responsibility models, container/orchestration platforms, and cross-border data compliance, are among the most pivotal and rapidly evolving domains in the compliance and audit landscape for virtual environments. A mature compliance framework today must account for shifting duties between providers and customers, technological advances beyond classic VMs, and the legal complexities of a truly global infrastructure.

7.2 Guidelines for Compliance and Audit

Virtualized environments offer enormous agility and scale, but they also introduce new layers of complexity and risk. Robust compliance and audit management in these dynamic landscapes is only possible through a blend of technical solutions, operational processes, and a forward-thinking governance framework. This section outlines practical steps, controls, and modern tools to fulfill regulatory obligations and ensure sustained audit readiness in virtualized and multicloud settings.

7.2.1 Structural Versus Operational Properties in Cloud Compliance

Cloud compliance checks must audit both the structural properties (e.g., VM placement, VLAN assignments, and consistency of network topology) and the operational properties (e.g., reachability, firewall rule application) [13]. There may be many tools that only audit real-time traffic and/or audit for misconfiguration; however, structural misalignment, such as shared compute nodes with untrusted tenants, is equally essential and can be the most problematic aspect, particularly if there is no structural auditing. The architecture of compliance and auditing is elaborated in Figure 7.5.

A comprehensive audit of a virtualization implementation should cover:

- Documenting the virtualization management architecture;
- Verification of hypervisor version and vendor support;
- Patch management procedures and service limitations;
- The audit process around provisioning/deprovisioning of administrative accounts;
- The management of VM sprawl and software license consumption;
- Capacity and performance monitoring;
- Secure remote access and logging;
- Encryption of VM's machine data at rest and in transit;
- Separation of sensitive VMs;
- Use of secure VM templates and a standardized approach to provisioning.

7.2.2 Automated Compliance Tools and Solutions for Virtual Environments

Modern compliance in virtualized infrastructures depends increasingly on automation, due to the scale and velocity at which workloads are created, modified, and

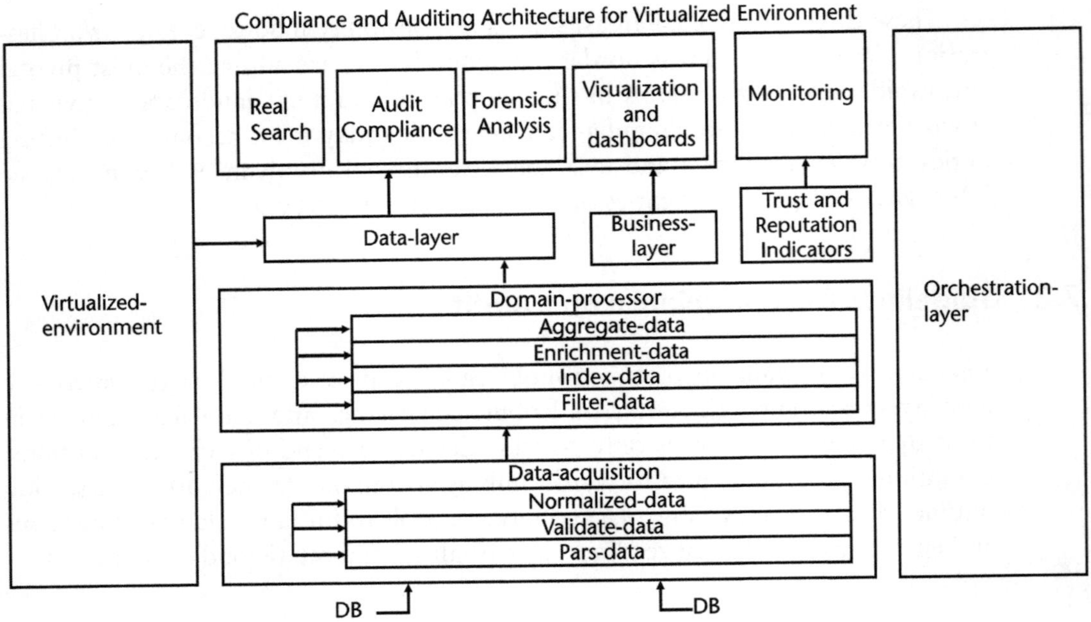

Figure 7.5 Architecture of compliance and auditing.

deleted. Manual tracking is simply not feasible [14]. Automated compliance platforms facilitate real-time policy enforcement, continuous monitoring, and proactive risk identification.

The key components and best practices are:

- *Continuous integration (CI) and continuous deployment (CD):* Incorporating compliance checks into CI and CD testing pipelines will ensure that new VMs, containers, and code releases adhere to required configurations and policies before they are deployed to production. Some commonly used tools for this purpose include Chef InSpec, HashiCorp Sentinel, and Aqua Security for Terraform and Kubernetes.
- *Continuous compliance monitoring:* Dedicated tools (AWS Config, Azure Policy, Google Security Command Center) automatically evaluate cloud and virtual assets to compliance frameworks (PCI DSS, ISO 27001, NIST) and provide alerts and auto-remediation for drift.
- *Artificial intelligence (AI)/machine learning in compliance:* Machine learning can highlight anomalous patterns and predict where controls might be weak based on historical deviations, enabling more intelligent alerting and prioritization.
- *Centralized dashboards:* Single-pane-of-glass views provide real-time metrics, policy audit trails, and evidence for regulators, which are crucial to prompt successful audit outcomes.

A practical tip is to always select compliance tools and platforms that allow for customization to your specific regulatory needs and harmonize evidence gathering across both on-premises and cloud virtual resources.

Modern cloud compliance requires both operational monitoring and structural validation of the live configuration of virtual resources across multiple control layers. An example of this might include a configuration check of the infrastructure management layer (OpenStack Nova), the type of SDN controller (Open Day light), and the configuration on the live virtual switch (Open vSwitch) to ensure no violations of a security policy that could go unnoticed (VM co-residency, VLAN leaks).

7.2.3 Auditing APIs and Management Consoles in Virtual Infrastructures

APIs and management consoles are the "nervous system" of every virtual and cloud infrastructure. Their security and auditability directly underpin the overall compliance posture.

The key guidelines are:

- *Comprehensive logging:* All API calls, configuration changes, login attempts, and privilege escalations in management consoles (such as vSphere, Azure Portal, and AWS Console) must be logged, with logs harvested in real time to a central, immutable system.
- *Privilege control:* Limit direct access to management consoles and APIs on a least-privilege basis. Use RBACs, enforce multifactor authentication, and regularly review access rights.
- *API security:* Secure all API endpoints via transport encryption (TLS), robust authentication, rate limiting, and input validation. Rotate API keys regularly and disable default/admin accounts wherever possible.
- *Change reconciliation:* Periodically reconcile logged API events with intended changes and associated approval records to detect shadow IT or unauthorized activity.
- *Audit consideration:* Ensure logs are retained according to your regulator's requirements, are time-synchronized, and are backed up in a way that preserves evidence integrity for forensic review.

7.2.3.1 Practical Auditing Complexity and Layering Example

On platforms like OpenStack, audit evidence for a single virtual resource may be stored across Neutron, Nova, and Open vSwitch. To verify security compliance based on the tenant's virtual router, for example, we need to relate the tenant's virtual router (and interfaces); and from the Open vSwitch storage, the VM MAC address and VLAN tag; to demonstrate (no common ownership or tenant-specific separation) compliance, all of which is impossible without automated correlation and formal verification capability.

7.2.4 Handling and Reporting Security Incidents in a Compliance Context

Incident response in virtual environments must be swift, precise, and thoroughly documented, as regulatory timelines for notification can be strict (e.g., GDPR's 72-hour window for personal data breaches).

The core procedures are:

- *Incident response plan:* Establish and regularly test a documented incident response plan specifically adapted for virtual infrastructures, including roles, escalation paths, and integration with cloud provider incident workflows.
- *Chain of custody and forensic readiness:* Capture and protect logs, VM snapshots, and network traces in a way that preserves evidential value. Forensic processes should be designed to avoid contamination and provide clear timelines of events.
- *Notification and escalation:* Understand and document the legal requirements for breach notification in all operational jurisdictions. Ensure upstream providers and relevant authorities/partners are notified as stipulated in contracts and laws.
- *Post-incident review:* After every incident, conduct a root-cause analysis, update response plans, and retrain staff on revised procedures.
- *Compliance insight:* Properly handling incident evidence and breach reporting can mitigate penalties and demonstrate organizational maturity to regulators.

7.2.5 Data Life-Cycle Management, Archiving, and Right to Erasure

Virtualized and cloud environments can result in data sprawl, snapshots, clones, backups, and orphaned storage containing sensitive data. Compliance requires a clear and enforceable data life-cycle policy.

The steps for control are:

- *Data mapping:* Maintain up-to-date records of where all regulated data resides, including transient copies in archives or backups.
- *Retention policies:* Automate the application of data retention periods corresponding to regulatory mandates (e.g., finance, health, or privacy law durations).
- *Right to erasure:* Procedures must exist to locate and fully erase personal or sensitive data on request ("right to be forgotten"), including from backups, inactive VMs, and ancillary storage.
- *Secure deletion:* Implement secure wipe or cryptographic erasure processes where practical to ensure that data is irrecoverable following decommissioning.
- *Archiving practices:* Archived virtual resources must be treated as in-scope for compliance, with access controls, monitoring, and retention limits applied as rigorously as to live data.

On a practical note, data life-cycle automation tied to both virtual and cloud orchestration prevents accidental noncompliance and reduces administrative burden.

7.2.5.1 VM Life-Cycle Management

The life cycle of VMs must be managed to prevent VM sprawl. Policies should be established to manage provisioning, allocate licenses, manage usage duration, and facilitate decommissioning [15]. The audit should focus on whether the organization is correctly removing dormant or orphaned VMs in a timely fashion, and whether the provisioning tools place restrictions on time allocation or chain of authority on VM creation.

7.2.6 Third-Party Vendor and Supply Chain Compliance in Virtualized Ecosystems

Today, many organizations exist within a complicated framework of external vendors, partners, and cloud providers. Regulatory requirements necessitate strong controls in their environment and assurance that partner environments are compliant and secure.

The controls and contractual safeguards are:

- *Due diligence and onboarding:* It will be crucial to evaluate the compliance posture of all suppliers who access sensitive data or operate parts of your virtual environment. Require proof of certifications (e.g., ISO 27001, SOC2), recent audit reports, and the results of penetration testing.
- *Contractual clauses:* Embed clauses mandating specific security controls, data protection standards, breach notification timelines, and audit rights in every supplier or cloud contract.
- *Continuous monitoring:* Where possible, use automated tools (e.g., cloud access security broker (CASB), third-party risk management platforms) to continuously monitor vendor compliance and receive timely alerts about changes in their security posture.
- *Right to audit:* Periodically exercise your contractual right to audit vendor controls and work collaboratively to remediate findings.
- *Clear termination protocols:* Ensure that supplier offboarding includes the verified erasure of data and the revocation of access across all virtualized assets.
- *Audit success factor:* Document all supplier assessments, communication logs, and remediation actions to supply strong evidence during compliance audits.

7.2.6.1 Real-World Insight

When integrating with public or private clouds, you often inherit a complex web of infrastructure, which means that transparency must take precedence when it comes to the vendor. For example, clouds based on OpenStack must expose tenant resource mappings and audit trails from the control plane to the virtual switch to meet ISO 27017 or CCM standards on logical isolation and network segmentation.

7.2.7 Privacy Impact Assessments and Compliance by Design

Future-ready compliance means integrating privacy and security insight from project conception through deployment and beyond, a philosophy increasingly formalized in global privacy laws.

The systematic procedures are:

- *Conducting data protection impact assessment (DPIAs):* For any new virtualized initiative (e.g., migration, SaaS adoption, container deployment), carry out a DPIA to systematically identify and mitigate privacy risks.
- *Embedding in DevOps:* Leverage compliance-as-code principles, integrating policy enforcement (access controls, encryption, logging) directly into infrastructure manifests and build pipelines.
- *Default security configurations:* Use hardened VM images, secure baseline templates, and mechanisms enforcing least-privilege and denial-by-default models.
- *Documentation and traceability:* Keep design artifacts, threat models, and DPIA outputs well-documented, available to regulators and internal auditors.
- *Iterative review:* Continually reassess and adjust during regular change cycles, especially when introducing new technology or significant configuration changes.
- *Strategic impact:* Embedding compliance by design reduces costly later remediation and demonstrates auditability and due diligence from the outset.

7.2.7.1 Audit Considerations in Virtual Networks

VMs as files can be accessed and copied without access control. Access control, segregation, or encryption should be enforced on shared storage systems to ensure data security. Audit checks considered for secure encryption key storage should include secure key handling restrictions and disaster recovery verification.

In summary, effective compliance and audit in virtualized environments must shift from episodic, manual controls to an integrated, automated, and dynamic approach, one that extends across the technical stack, vendor ecosystem, and data life cycle [16]. By following these guidelines, organizations not only reduce regulatory risk but also position themselves for scalable, secure, and resilient digital operations. Guidelines for compliance and audit in virtualized environments derive from both regulatory obligations and operational necessities. While the high-level aims remain consistent, protecting sensitive data, ensuring transparency, and enabling continuous oversight, the means to achieve these aims must account for the speed, complexity, and abstraction of virtualization technology.

7.2.7.2 Comprehensive Scoping and Intelligent Asset Management

The first and essential task is precise scoping. In virtual environments, this involves continuous discovery not only of VMs and their associated storage but also of hypervisors, management servers, orchestration scripts, network overlays, and, increasingly, containers and ephemeral workloads. Automated tools, tightly integrated with your virtualization stack, should maintain a real-time inventory of all assets: who owns them, what data they process, where they reside, and which regulatory boundaries apply. Tagging, labeling, and metadata enrichment are vital: a VM storing patient records must always be flagged PHI-regulated, wherever it migrates within your environment [17].

This intelligent asset management underpins all subsequent compliance activities. Without it, organizations risk scope drift where assets containing sensitive data move in or out of their compliance boundaries without detection, creating regulatory blind spots and audit failures.

7.2.7.3 Segmentation, Isolation, and Data Control

With accurate inventories in place, the following primary guideline is granular segmentation. Virtual environments excel in flexibility, but this can be a liability if not properly regulated. Regulatory requirements mandate that sensitive data environments, such as PCI cardholder segments or zones containing regulated financial data, are strictly segregated from less-trusted systems. This implies using virtual LANs (VLANs), software-defined networks, and micro-segmentation to isolate regulated workloads. Management and orchestration traffic must always be kept on dedicated, access-controlled networks with encrypted transport [18].

Storage isolation is equally critical: storage volumes or datastores holding PHI or cardholder data should never be shared with less secure workloads. Where possible, use disk encryption, snapshots, and backup images, ideally with keys managed outside the virtualization environment by a dedicated key management system.

7.2.7.4 Robust Access and Privilege Management

Access controls should be multilayered and dynamically adaptable. In a virtualized environment, administrative privileges extend deeply: one hypervisor administrator could have the ability to access, change, or destroy hundreds of virtualized environments and assets at once. Implement RBAC vigorously, with federated identity management and multifactor authentication for all administration (and hopefully all) tasks on the hypervisor and hypervisor host platform environments. Never allow default accounts or credentials to exist: automate credential changes and treat least privilege as the default [19].

Regularly review all access grants, tying them back to current employment status, project need, and compliance scoping. Automate the removal of obsolete or orphaned accounts, and require multiple-person control or oversight ("four-eyes principle") for all significant configuration changes.

7.2.7.5 Logging, Audit Trails, and Central Analytical Oversight

Logging presents unique challenges in virtualized environments due to their distributed and dynamic nature. Ensure that all events, including host configuration changes, hypervisor access requests, guest VM life-cycle actions, and network policy updates, are captured and aggregated into a central, immutable log repository. Timestamp synchronization is essential for reliable forensic and compliance reporting; employ Network Time Protocol (NTP) or an equivalent across all layers [19].

Logs must not only be retained in accordance with regulatory requirements (sometimes for up to 7 years) but also be reviewable by both internal and external auditors. Set up triggers and analytic rules to provide real-time alerts for suspicious activity (such as privilege escalation, failed authentication attempts, or unplanned VM provisioning) and conduct regular manual reviews, supplemented by machine learning or SIEM tools for pattern recognition and anomaly detection.

7.2.7.6 Agile Change and Configuration Management

Because virtual resources are easily altered, change management processes must be formal, automated where possible, and always auditable. Document and peer-review every proposed change to in-scope systems, enforce configuration drift detection, and ensure that all production deployments pass through automated compliance checks before going live.

Apply configuration baselines to all VM templates, hypervisors, and network devices. These should be enforced and continuously checked, for example, using Infrastructure as Code principles or configuration management systems such as Ansible, Puppet, or Chef. Any deviation from the baseline (such as enabling prohibited services, reducing logging verbosity, or changing firewall policy) should trigger an immediate review [19].

7.2.7.7 Embedded Continuous Compliance

Perhaps most critical is the principle of continuous compliance. Because virtualized estates change constantly, compliance is not an annual or quarterly event, but a day-to-day (and often minute-to-minute) discipline. Leverage continuous compliance tools that integrate directly with your platform APIs and generate two forms of output: (1) dashboards and near-time reports for operational staff; and (2) historical artifacts and structured evidence trails for future audits.

Finally, document every policy and procedure, and train staff regularly, not just on technical controls, but on the importance of compliance to the organization's reputation and regulatory risk profile. Foster a culture of openness and responsiveness: prompt reporting and resolution of compliance exceptions are markers of operational maturity.

7.2.7.8 Virtual Environment Monitoring

Effective monitoring in virtual environments includes log review, anomaly detection, and intrusion prevention system (IPS). The audit should include verification of log reviews by administrators on a scheduled basis, responses to flagged events, and testing of alerting systems to ensure their effectiveness. Consistent near-real-time monitoring is essential in environments involving financial transactions or regulatory requirements.

7.3 Importance of Compliance and Audit in Virtualized Environments

The importance of compliance and audit in the context of a virtualized ecosystem is far greater than just regulatory obligation. It should now be clear that in a global trading environment, where data can cross boundaries, and transactional activities no longer require geographic boundaries, good compliance and audit practices imply operational state resilience and sustained operational value and trust. Two dimensions typically overlooked here are human factors and compliance culture, and the role of the auditor, whose job it is to scrutinize or criticize and raise the level of accountability of the organization [20].

7.3.1 Human Factors and Compliance Culture in Virtualized Operations

While technology forms the backbone of virtualization security and compliance, the most sophisticated infrastructure can be undermined by lapses in behavior, misunderstanding, or disengagement at the human level. People, culture, and awareness ultimately determine the success or failure of compliance efforts. In a virtualized environment, where abstracted systems, rapid automation, and complex control planes accelerate both opportunity and risk, the human element becomes both a potential vulnerability and a powerful force for resilience.

The human element in risk and noncompliance is:

- *Complexity and skill gaps:* Virtual environments require administrators, developers, and analysts to master new concepts, including SDN, automated provisioning, and distributed storage. Without comprehensive training, staff may misconfigure controls, misuse privileges, or overlook new threats. Many high-profile breaches (such as misconfigured cloud storage or open management consoles) have their roots in human error or misunderstanding.
- *Insider threats and privilege misuse:* The flexibility of virtual platforms also complicates the management of privileged accounts. Individuals with broad access, developers with the ability to spin up VMs, or operators with hypervisor-level control, represent a potent risk if not carefully monitored and regularly rotated. Malicious insiders, or simply careless actors, can bypass or subvert technical controls.
- *Awareness and continuous reinforcement:* Regulatory requirements and best practices are continually evolving. Staff who are unaware of new policies, or who view compliance exercises as merely a tick-box burden, are less likely to report anomalies, escalate issues promptly, or contribute to an open compliance culture.

In order to build a culture of compliance, establishing security and compliance as shared values, rather than obligations dictated from above, must be a deliberate, multifaceted effort:

- *Ongoing training:* Regular, role-specific training sessions are vital: administrators need deep technical guidance; end users require clear, accessible instructions focused on practical risks (such as phishing, credential hygiene, and shadow IT).

- *Clear communication:* Policies should be written in language accessible to all, supplemented by concise how-to-comply guides and reminders embedded within day-to-day tools.
- *Positive reinforcement:* Recognizing and rewarding staff who follow procedures, report near-misses, or improve processes fosters engagement and a sense of ownership.
- *Incident handling and learning:* Every compliance lapse, audit finding, or security incident should be treated as an organizational learning opportunity. Root cause analysis that focuses on process and cultural factors rather than blame helps to prevent repetition and deepens collective competence.
- *Leadership involvement:* When senior leaders champion compliance (by engaging in audits, funding training, and demonstrating transparency), buy-in cascades through the organization.

For the strategic benefits of compliance culture, a strong compliance culture does more than reduce risk of breaches, or fines. It encourages accountability and transparency across the organization. It:

- *Builds trust:* Customers and partners increasingly demand evidence not just of policy, but of genuine commitment to governance and stewardship.
- *Enables agility:* When compliance is embedded in workflows and viewed as everyone's responsibility, product launches, migrations, and audits proceed more quickly and with less friction.
- *Enhances audit outcomes:* Auditors often cite culture and staff competence as intangible, but vital, markers of an organization's maturity and control.

In virtualized operations where technology can blindside inattentive or unprepared humans, culture and compliance norms are the ultimate last line of defense.

7.3.2 Auditor's Perspective: Preparing for and Managing Virtualization Audits

From the auditor's point of view, virtualization presents new opportunities and new headaches. The very attributes that make virtualized environments attractive, elasticity, abstraction, and automation, render them opaque and potentially unpredictable. This section demystifies what auditors seek, how organizations can prepare, and the wider business value of audit readiness.

What do auditors look for?

- *Asset inventory and scope:* Auditors require clear, continuously updated lists that show which virtual resources (VMs, containers, hypervisors, storage, and network overlays) are within regulatory scope, what data they contain, and how responsibilities are assigned. Disjointed or ad hoc inventories are red flags.

- *Segmentation and isolation controls:* Demonstrable and enforceable network and data segregation across logical, not just physical, boundaries is a central compliance expectation (e.g., PCI DSS, GDPR). Auditors look for evidence of micro-segmentation, clear change logs, and periodic testing of segmentation controls.
- *Access management and privilege review:* Role-based access, least-privilege allocation, multifactor authentication, and timely deprovisioning are scrutinized. Detailed logs and attestation of access reviews are required, sometimes going back years.
- *Logging, monitoring, and forensics:* Centralized, immutable audit trails for all administrative and sensitive actions are essential. Auditors will verify the completeness, retention, and recovery of logs.
- *Automated controls and policy enforcement:* Auditors are increasingly requiring assurance that automated compliance checks are integrated through CI/CD pipelines, infrastructure-as-code templates, and security "gates" to report compliance as a continuous process instead of an episodic process.
- *Incident response, evidence chain, and reporting:* Rapid breach notification, well-drilled forensics protocols, and documentation of response steps matter hugely, as regulations (such as GDPR) increasingly penalize not just breaches, but the failure to respond or report adequately.

How to prepare for virtualization audits:

- *Maintain live documentation:* Automated asset management, compliance dashboards, and current network/data flow diagrams simplify both the scoping and day-of-audit logistics.
- *Conduct mock audits:* Regular test runs, "tabletop" scenarios, or preaudit workshops ready teams for real-world scrutiny, surface overlooked issues, and condition staff for evidence requests.
- *Audit evidence readiness:* Store all compliance artifacts, fact policies, training logs, access reviews, breach notifications, technical diagrams, and attestation reports in clearly structured, rapidly accessible repositories.
- *Foster auditor collaboration:* Open, timely, and transparent communication with auditors improves outcomes and builds a reputation for good faith and control.

Items of strategic importance of audit readiness are:

- *Risk reduction:* Proactive audit preparation limits surprises and reduces the likelihood and impact of negative findings.
- *Competitive advantage:* Certification and clean audit histories can open doors in regulated industries, making audit outcomes directly relevant to winning new business or entering new markets.
- *Operational fitness:* The discipline required for audit readiness (up-to-date inventories, tested incident response) overlaps with and directly strengthens robust IT and business operations.

- *Continuous improvement:* Auditors often provide insights and recommendations that drive incremental improvements in controls and posture, often at less cost than learning from incidents.

In essence, approaching audits as a collaborative, continuous process underpinned by a strong compliance culture and active, prepared teams elevates compliance from regulatory minimum to strategic asset. The importance of compliance and audit in virtualized environments is both technical and profoundly human. The interplay between policy, process, technology, and people underpins not only the avoidance of fines but also the achievement of trust, agility, and enduring resilience in the face of constant change [21].

At the heart of every compliance program, especially within the context of virtualized environments, lies a deeper set of business, operational, ethical, and strategic imperatives. Compliance in these settings is not simply a regulatory burden. Instead, it is fundamental to trust, risk management, resilience, and competitive advantage.

7.3.2.1 Foundation of Trust in an Interconnected World

In the digital economy, where businesses routinely operate across borders, sectors, and platforms, trust is the foundational currency. Trust enables customers to share sensitive data. Trust is what partners and suppliers depend on before interconnecting systems or sharing intellectual property. Without robust compliance and auditable assurance, that trust evaporates. Breaches of data privacy and regulatory mandates today rarely remain hidden; news spreads rapidly, regulatory proceedings are often public, and customers' tolerance for lapses is low. Transparent, repeatable, and independently validated compliance efforts, demonstrated through clean audit reports, visible certifications, and a rapid incident response, act as credentials of reliability and professionalism [22].

7.3.2.2 Risk Mitigation in a Complex, Fluid Landscape

Virtualized environments heighten every traditional risk of IT data loss, privilege misuse, service outage, and cyberattack while introducing new ones. The sheer ease with which a privileged operator might inadvertently or maliciously impact multiple workloads, the way a single unpatched vulnerability can cross logical boundaries, and the possibility of rapid, uncontrolled sprawl of sensitive data across virtual disks or cloud providers all demand new risk management approaches. Regular audits serve as both early warning systems and diagnostic tools, surfacing problems before they escalate into crises and providing paths for improvement.

7.3.2.3 Penalty and Sanction Avoidance

Noncompliance now carries not just reputational or operational costs, but also severe legal and financial liabilities. Fines for data breaches, especially under GDPR, but also under PCI, HIPAA, and SOX, can run to millions or tens of millions of pounds or dollars. In some cases, regulators may even restrict or revoke an organization's right to conduct business altogether. Clean, well-documented, and easily accessible audit trails are vital legal evidence in the event of investigation or dispute and may significantly mitigate penalties where these nonetheless occur.

7.3.2.4 Operational Hygiene and Business Resilience

The compliance disciplines of inventorying assets, monitoring logs, reviewing access rights, and simulating disaster recovery are core to meeting auditing requirements the cornerstones of effective IT operations high-maturity organizations, that compliance and operational resilience often converge: the same processes that prepare you for regulatory real so view improve your ability to survive ransomware, recover from hardware failures, or accommodate rapid staff turnover. Internal and third-party audits expose inefficiencies, uncover "shadow IT," and reinforce best practices, making day-to-day service delivery more predictable and robust.

7.3.2.5 Catalyst for Continuous Improvement and Innovation

Organizations that treat compliance actively, not passively, frequently discover its value as a catalyst for improvement and innovation. For instance, the requirement to automate asset discovery and log correlation may spur wider adoption of DevOps and infrastructure as code, enhancing agility. The drive to regularize access controls may accelerate cloud migration, as hyperscale providers can offer managed services with built-in compliance tooling. Moreover, demonstrating compliance and audit maturity is often a precondition for attracting new kinds of clients, entering regulated markets, or leveraging sensitive data analytics at scale.

7.3.2.6 Adaptability in a Shifting Regulatory Environment

The global regulatory landscape is not static; with every technological innovation comes new scrutiny, revised rules, and changed expectations from customers, regulators, and partners. Organizations that automate evidence production, distribute responsibility for compliance, and maintain close alignment with audit outcomes are inherently more agile, capable of rapidly accommodating new laws, customer concerns, or risk discoveries. Auditing is thus both a snapshot of current posture and a practice run for the next wave of regulatory requirements.

In conclusion, compliance and audit, when performed comprehensively in virtualized environments, are investments in trust, resilience, efficiency, and sustainable competitive differentiation. They should be valued as foundational business enablers, never relegated to a mere after-the-fact tick-box exercise.

7.4 Best Practices for Compliance and Audit in Virtualized Environments

As organizations accelerate their transformation through cloud and virtualization, the landscape of compliance is undergoing a significant evolution. Standards, laws, and best practices that were designed for traditional, perimeter-bound IT environments are being rewritten in light of borderless networking, decentralized architectures, and new threat models. Staying ahead in compliance is no longer about reacting to today's requirements, but anticipating tomorrow's regulatory, technological, and operational shifts [23]. This section explores the emerging standards, future trends, and next-wave best practices that will shape virtual environment compliance in the coming decade.

7.4.1 The Move to Zero Trust Architectures

For decades, a castle-and-moat model shaped IT security, relying on hardened perimeters and trusted zones. In today's dynamic virtual environments, such trust assumptions are obsolete. Enter the zero trust model, the principle that no network, user, or device (inside or outside organizational boundaries) is trusted by default. Every interaction, access request, and data movement must be continuously authenticated, authorized, and audited.

Implications for compliance are:

- *Micro-segmentation:* Zero trust relies heavily on deep network segmentation, applied not only to physical networks but also to virtual networks, containers, and even API interactions. Compliance with PCI DSS and similar standards is increasingly tied to demonstrating robust, granular segmentation and access control.
- *Identity-centric controls:* Regulations and standards will increasingly expect organizations to implement identity-driven policies. Authentication and authorization become integral audit trails for every workload, device, and automated process.
- *Continuous monitoring:* Zero trust assumes that breaches will occur; thus, real-time monitoring and behavioral analytics become mandatory for proving compliance, not just for security.

7.4.1.1 Future Standards Influence

Frameworks such as the US NIST 800-207 on zero trust architecture and the growing adoption by ISO/IEC are providing blueprints for audit and compliance standards that move away from perimeter-based trust models.

7.4.2 Confidential Computing and Trusted Execution Environments

With virtualized workloads in public clouds, standard concerns very much include confidentiality and integrity of data "in use," when at rest or in transit. Confidential computing utilizes hardware-based Trusted Execution Environments (TEEs), such as Intel SGX and AMD SEV, to separate sensitive code and data from everything else, including a hacked hypervisor and/or cloud administrator [24].

Key compliance implications are:

- *Enhanced data protection:* Regulations such as GDPR, HIPAA, or PCI DSS may soon require or incentivize confidential computing to ensure data separation and mitigate risks of cloud-provider access or cross-tenant leakage.
- *Auditable assurance:* TEEs provide cryptographic proofs (attestation) that compliance controls are not just policy, but technologically enforced and verifiable even across borders or provider boundaries.
- *Supply chain security:* Confidential computing extends to software life-cycle trust, enabling compliance with emerging standards around provenance, integrity, and anti-tampering.

Emerging standards are the Confidential Computing Consortium (CNCF) and various ISO/IEC working groups, which are developing frameworks to standardize and audit the use of TEEs for regulatory compliance.

7.4.3 The Shift to Privacy-First Standards: ISO/IEC 27701 and Beyond

The GDPR and its global kin have brought privacy to the forefront of compliance, driving the creation of new, privacy-centered standards. ISO/IEC 27701 ("Privacy Information Management") augments ISO/IEC 27001 to align with privacy law requirements and enhance data subject rights (such as access, correction, and erasure) within virtual and cloud environments.

Key developments include:

- *Privacy by design:* Future compliance will expect privacy to be built in at every layer, from VM image to API endpoint to backup repository. Privacy impact assessments and design documentation will be required evidence in audits.
- *Data minimization and localization:* New standards are moving towards stricter controls on data residency, automatic deletion, and reduction of unnecessary data flows, especially in hybrid and multicloud settings.
- *Auditability and transparency:* Organizations will need to produce granular records detailing where data resides, who has accessed it, and how long it is retained on demand for both regulators and consumers.

National and regional standards, including the upcoming EU NIS2 Directive for essential services and updates to Australia's Privacy Act, will introduce new controls determined by risk profile, sector, and event impact.

7.4.4 Towards Integrated, Automated Compliance Platforms

With the pace of change in virtualized environments, compliance is shifting from point-in-time reporting to continuous, real-time assurance. Next-generation compliance tools are leveraging AI/machine learning, automation, and platform-native APIs to enforce controls, report on compliance posture, and respond to violations without human intervention.

Directional trends are:

- *Compliance as code:* Embedding regulation, policy, and control assertions directly into infrastructure definitions (e.g., in Terraform or Kubernetes manifests).
- *Automated evidence and attestation:* As regulators require proof on demand, systems will automatically document, sign, and submit audit records.
- *Cross-cloud standardization:* With multicloud and hybrid operations now the norm, standards will increasingly focus on interoperability and federated compliance (the ability to prove compliance across multiple providers in concert).

7.4.5 The Influence of Evolving Regulatory Ecosystems: NIS2, DORA, and Others

The EU's NIS2 Directive (in effect since 2023), the Digital Operational Resilience Act (DORA), and similar laws are increasing the stakes for critical infrastructure and digital supply chain security [25]. These regulations will extend compliance obligations to virtualized environments involved in essential services, requiring:

- End-to-end auditability along the supply chain;
- Mandatory incident reporting windows;
- Demonstrable business continuity in the event of a virtualized service outage.

International harmonization is also underway, meaning that compliance controls built for one territory are more likely to be recognized, or demanded, worldwide.

For organizations to accomplish and maintain regulatory compliance in virtual environments, they must not only escape from reactive, checklist-orientated approaches, but they must also adopt a practiced set of interrelated best practices in culture, process, and technology to embed compliance and audit functions at the core of their IT and business landscape.

7.4.5.1 Proactive, Risk-Based Compliance Management

The most successful organizations treat compliance like a living system. They begin with regular risk assessments that incorporate evolving threats, regulatory updates, business changes, and lessons learned from incidents. Risks are quantified and prioritized, with controls (technical, procedural, and organizational) mapped directly to the most critical workloads, data, and system components. For example, VM templates and golden images are reviewed and hardened upfront; access policies are tailored to the sensitivity of the data; and continuous improvement is mandated through frequent control testing and review.

7.4.5.2 Automation Across All Compliance Functions

Virtualized environments simply move too quickly for manual oversight to be adequate. Employ automated tools for asset discovery, access management, configuration compliance, and log aggregation. Integration with orchestration and deployment tools ensures that every new or changed resource is brought under compliance governance from inception. Automated compliance scans validate patch levels, configuration states, and network segmentation every time code is deployed or infrastructure is altered. Real-time dashboards give both operational and compliance teams instant insight into the state of the environment.

7.4.5.3 Segregation of Duties and Strong Access Controls

Enforce granular roles and permissions using RBAC and multifactor authentication throughout the entire virtual architecture, from orchestration platforms to hypervisor consoles to guest VMs. Segregate duties not only administratively, but technically: require multiple approvers for sensitive changes, and rotate administration tasks to avoid overfamiliarity or insider threats. Utilize just-in-time access provisioning for temporary privileges, ensuring that all access is time-limited and auditable.

7.4.5.4 Immutable and Centralized Logging

Deploy a central log repository, ideally with immutability features such as Write Once, Read Many (WORM) storage or managed cloud data lakes for event correlation and evidence preservation. Logs must cover every security-relevant event: from user authentication, configuration changes, and resource life-cycle events, to data access and network policy updates. Develop standard operating procedures to review logs both in real time (using SIEM/analytics tools) and in batch (for compliance audits). Regularly test log integrity, backup, and restoration procedures to ensure optimal performance.

7.4.5.5 Continual Education and Compliance Culture

Mandatory, regular training, allied to clear and accessible policy documentation, is essential. Extend training beyond technical staff to business leaders and end users, ensuring everyone understands not just the what, but also the why of compliance. Foster a culture that views compliance issues or audit findings as learning opportunities, not blame exercises. Celebrate clean audit outcomes and visible improvement; empower staff to flag potential gaps or propose improvements.

7.4.5.6 Regular, Iterative Audit, and Penetration Testing

Move away from an "audit as event" mindset to one of "audit as process." Schedule internal audits at frequent and predictable intervals, adjusting themes and sample sizes based on past findings and changing environmental conditions. At least annually, engage independent auditors to challenge and validate your posture. Include penetration tests and red-team scenarios targeting both technical controls and personnel, simulating real-world attack tactics across hybrid environments.

7.4.5.7 Defense in Depth: Layered Controls and Monitoring

Recognize that no single layer will offer complete security. Implement multitiered controls: segmentation, access management, encryption, monitoring, logging, endpoint protection, and incident response. Cross-validate controls; for example, detect failed changes to configuration management as both process anomalies and as triggers for automated security review.

7.4.5.8 Third-Party and Supplier Compliance Management

Vetting, contracting, and ongoing assurance processes should be established for every supplier or service provider that participates in the virtualization stack or data flow. Require evidence of their controls (through third-party attestations, certifications, or direct audits), and ensure your obligations (such as breach reporting timelines or data location requirements) are contractually flowed down the supply chain.

7.4.5.9 Continuous Improvement

Finally, treat every audit, incident, control breach, or "near miss" as fuel for improvement. Track findings to timely closure. Use key performance indicators and metrics dashboards to monitor progress. Remain vigilant for advances in automation, analytics, or compliance tooling that may reduce cost, complexity, or risk.

By systematically enacting these best practices tailored to the realities of your own virtualized estate, organizations can not only satisfy regulators but also build robust, agile, and secure foundations for business success in an increasingly compliance-driven landscape.

7.4.6 Preparing for the Future: Best Practice Takeaways

To remain compliant amid rapid change, organizations should:

1. Continuously monitor regulatory developments and participate in standards working groups.
2. Adopt zero trust and privacy-by-design as the default architectural principles.
3. Invest in confidential computing capabilities and review cloud providers' support for TEEs and attestation.
4. Automate compliance checking and evidence generation as part of CI/CD and operational pipelines.
5. Map and track supply chain dependencies, and prepare to demonstrate security across vendors and partners.
6. Anticipate the convergence of cyber and privacy regulation, treating data protection as both a security and business continuity imperative.
7. Train leadership, compliance staff, and engineers on emerging standards; future-proof the compliance culture.

7.5 Case Studies

7.5.1 Case Study 1: Capital One Cloud Data Breach and Compliance Gaps (2019)

In 2019, Capital One, a major US financial institution, experienced a data breach incident that exposed data for over 100 million customers. The breach derived from a misconfigured AWS Web Application Firewall operating on a VM. The actor exploited this misconfiguration to access sensitive data stored in the cloud. This incident highlighted how lapses in configuring, indeed, resource configuration audit and monitoring, could cause catastrophic exposures, even when formal compliance attestations with regulations, such as PCI DSS, existed [26, 27].

In a compliance/audit context:

- Weaknesses in firewall configurations and overly permissive AWS IAM roles went undetected.
- Audit processes did not identify the virtualization-layer misconfigurations.
- The incident exposed the inadequacy of reviewing virtual network and access controls only during annual compliance checks.

The outcome was that Capital One paid an $80 million fine to the US Treasury for failing to establish effective risk management in its virtual/cloud estate and faced significant lawsuits and reputational damage.

7.5.2 Case Study 2: British Airways GDPR Fine and Virtualized Infrastructure Gaps (2018–2020)

British Airways experienced a cyberattack in 2018 that compromised personal and payment-related information for approximately 500,000 customers. The attack likely targeted vulnerabilities in web and application servers hosted in a virtualized environment and went unnoticed for weeks, according to estimates. The following regulatory investigation revealed significant weaknesses in the areas of network segmentation, logging, and monitoring [28, 29].

In a compliance/audit context:

- British Airways had inadequate audit trails between virtualized application environments.
- There was insufficient network segregation, allowing attackers to move laterally across the estate.
- The ICO singled out "poor security arrangements," demonstrating that surface-level regulatory compliance (e.g., basic access control) is insufficient without comprehensive, auditable virtualization controls.

The outcome was that British Airways was fined £20 million under GDPR for failing to implement appropriate technical and organizational measures and for delayed breach notification.

7.5.3 Case Study 3: Equifax Data Breach—Patch Management Failures in a Virtualized Context (2017)

Equifax, a leading US credit reporting agency, experienced one of the most significant data breaches in 2017, affecting approximately 147 million people. Attackers exploited an unpatched Apache Struts vulnerability running on virtualized infrastructure. The company's internal audits failed to confirm whether all VMs running vulnerable middleware had correctly been patched [30, 31].

In a compliance/audit context:

- Ineffective audit and patch management processes did not surface gaps in virtualized server configurations.
- Regulatory agencies found that Equifax lacked automated controls and a dependable, audit-ready inventory of virtualized servers.
- Lapses breached both data protection laws and sector-specific compliance rules for financial data.

The outcome was that Equifax paid up to $700 million in settlements and fines. Regulatory reports cited failures in internal audit and virtualization policy enforcement.

7.5.4 Case Study 4: VMware ESXiArgs Ransomware—Patch Audit Gaps Exposed (2023)

In February 2023, thousands of servers running VMware ESXi were hit by the ESXiArgs ransomware attack. Attackers leveraged a known, unpatched vulnerability (CVE-2021-21974) in the ESXi hypervisor, a core component of many virtual data centers, to remotely execute code and encrypt all hosted VMs. Many affected organizations had not completed or audited the application of the VMware security update [32, 33].

In a compliance/audit context:

- Organizations failed to maintain accurate, up-to-date inventories of virtualized estates.
- Audit processes failed to identify overdue patches for ESXi servers, exposing a critical compliance gap.
- The scale and speed of attacks demonstrated the inadequacy of one-off or spreadsheet-based virtual asset auditing.

7.5.5 Case Study 5: Tesla Insider Data Leak—Virtual Desktop Audit Weakness (2023)

In 2023, Tesla disclosed a massive data leak involving over 100 gigabytes of sensitive internal data, including employee information and customer contacts. German regulators later reported that the data was exfiltrated by insiders who had access to company resources, including data residing in virtual desktop and cloud workspace environments [34, 35].

In a compliance/audit context:

- Investigations suggested that there was an insufficient audit of virtual desktop infrastructure (VDI) sessions and data flows.
- There was a lack of automated monitoring and real-time control of insider activity within virtualized environments.
- Weak detection controls delayed breach discovery and contributed to a GDPR inquiry against Tesla for compliance failings.

The outcome was that German data protection authorities launched an investigation; Tesla faced both reputational damage and potential regulatory fines, and the case highlighted the critical importance of a comprehensive virtual environment audit and monitoring.

7.6 Summary

This chapter has traversed the complex landscape of compliance and audit for today's virtualization environments. We began by establishing the context: the growing regulatory expectations (PCI DSS, HIPAA, SOX, GDPR) fully observable against the rapid change, pace, and complexity as private, public, and hybrid clouds now typify the virtualization landscape. We next established a clear and detailed roadmap for achieving compliance, which outlined processes in asset management, segmentation, access management, automation, logging, change and incident management, documentation, and ongoing management.

We spent time defining why compliance and audit are critical, not just as a regulatory obligation, but as a chief enabler of trust, operational excellence, business agility, and risk reduction. We also integrated these best practices and further observed that doing so continues to require automation, a relevant culture, flexible processes, and competent personnel.

The modern reality is stark and clear to see: only those organizations that make compliance dynamic, strategic, and an integral part of day-to-day operations will thrive in a world shaped by relentless digital change, increasing regulatory scrutiny, and evolving compliance expectations. In brief, compliance and audit are foundational to securing, building trust, and maintaining competitiveness in virtualized enterprises.

In optimizing audits of virtualized environments:

- Secure baseline VM templates.
- Use strong segmentation of VMs across sensitivity levels.
- Keep accurate documentation of virtualization infrastructure.
- Encryption is a best practice for sensitive data at rest and in transit.
- Use regular patching and vulnerability scans.
- Access controls with individual accountability.
- Secure all remote access paths.
- Perform regular backup and recovery drills, including encrypted key recovery.

References

[1] Thyagaturu, A. S., et al., "Operating Systems and Hypervisors for Network Functions: A Survey of Enabling Technologies and Research Studies," *IEEE Access*, Vol. 10, July 29, 2022, pp. 79825–79873.

[2] Tiburski, R. T., et al., "A Lightweight Virtualization Model to Enable Edge Computing in Deeply Embedded Systems," *Software: Practice and Experience*, Vol. 51, No. 9, September 2021, pp. 1964–1981.

[3] Williams, B., and J. Adamson, *PCI Compliance: Understand and Implement Adequate PCI Data Security Standard Compliance*, Boca Raton, FL: CRC Press, 2022.

[4] Essefi, I., et al., "HIPAA-Controlled Patient Information Exchange and Traceability in Clinical Processes," *2022 IEEE 9th International Conference on Sciences of Electronics, Technologies of Information and Telecommunications (SETIT)*, May 28, 2022, pp. 452–460.

[5] Bajra, U. Q., et al., "The Impact of the Sarbanes–Oxley Act on the Integrity of Financial Reporting: Was It Meritorious?" *Journal of Corporate Accounting & Finance*, Vol. 34, No. 3, July 2023, pp. 184–196.

[6] Mishra, P., E. S. Pilli, and R. C. Joshi, *Cloud Security: Attacks, Techniques, Tools, and Challenges*, London, UK: Chapman and Hall/CRC, 2021.

[7] Mathur, P., "Cloud Computing Infrastructure, Platforms, and Software for Scientific Research," *High Performance Computing in Biomimetics: Modeling, Architecture and Applications*, March 21, 2024, pp. 89–127.

[8] Thompson, J., "Compliance," in *The Experience of Illness*, Oxon, UK: Routledge, 2022, pp. 109–131.

[9] Singh, U. K., and A. Sharma, "Cloud Computing Security Framework Based on Shared Responsibility Models: Cloud Computing," in *Cyber-Physical, IoT, and Autonomous Systems in Industry 4.0*, Boca Raton, FL: CRC Press, 2021, pp. 39–55.

[10] Mahavaishnavi, V., R. Saminathan, and R. Prithviraj, "Secure Container Orchestration: A Framework for Detecting and Mitigating Orchestrator-Level Vulnerabilities," *Multimedia Tools and Applications*, Vol. 84, No. 17, May 2025, pp. 18351–18371.

[11] Rong, K., et al., "Cross-Border Data Transfer: Patterns and Discrepancies," *Journal of International Business Policy*, Vol. 8, No. 1, March 2025, pp. 10–32.

[12] Kumar, M., G. Kaur, and P. S. Rana, "Performance, Portability, Productivity, and Security in HPC Cloud: A Systematic Literature Review," *The Journal of Supercomputing*, Vol. 81, No. 11, July 29, 2025, p. 1197.

[13] Anand, N., et al., "Securing Software Defined Networks: A Comprehensive Analysis of Approaches, Applications, and Future Strategies Against DoS Attacks," *IEEE Access*, December 19, 2024.

[14] Szmeja, P., et al., "ASSIST-IoT: A Modular Implementation of a Reference Architecture for the Next Generation Internet of Things," *Electronics*, Vol. 12, No. 4, February 8, 2023, p. 854.

[15] Swathi, T., B. Swathi, and P. Sunanda, "Mitigating VM Sprawl: Strategies for Effective Resource Management in Cloud Environments," *2024 IEEE 6th International Conference on Cybernetics, Cognition and Machine Learning Applications (ICCCMLA)*, October 19, 2024, pp. 148–151.

[16] Anirudh, U. N., and S. S. Darshan, "Role-Based Virtuosity in Virtual Environments: A Technical Exploration of Access Control and Authentication Mechanisms," in *Cloud Security*, London, UK: Chapman and Hall/CRC, 2024, pp. 183–196.

[17] Vermesan, O., et al., "Internet of Things Beyond the Hype: Research, Innovation and Deployment," in *Building the Hyperconnected Society: Internet of Things Research and Innovation Value Chains, Ecosystems, and Markets*, Gistrup, Denmark: River Publishers, 2022, pp. 15–118.

[18] Dasher, G., I. Envid, and B. Calder, "Architectures for Protecting Cloud Data Planes," arXiv preprint arXiv:2201.13010, January 31, 2022.

[19] Tayouri, D., et al., "White Paper-Cybersecurity in Agile Cloud Computing—Cybersecurity Guidelines for Cloud Access," *Cybersecurity in Agile Cloud Computing—Cybersecurity Guidelines for Cloud Access*, September 28, 2022, pp. 1–36.

[20] Yuan, Q., and T. Chen, "Holding AI-Based Systems Accountable in the Public Sector: A Systematic Review," *Public Performance & Management Review*, February 23, 2025, pp. 1–34.

[21] Joshi, V. C., *Changing Dimensions of Financial Services and Banking Regulation*, New York: Springer Books, 2025.

[22] Nandan Prasad, A., "Regulatory Compliance and Risk Management," in *Introduction to Data Governance for Machine Learning Systems: Fundamental Principles, Critical Practices, and Future Trends*, Berkeley, CA: Apress, 2024, pp. 485–624.

[23] Alevizos, L., V. T. Ta, and M. Hashem Eiza, "Augmenting Zero Trust Architecture to Endpoints Using Blockchain: A State-of-the-Art Review," *Security and Privacy*, Vol. 5, No. 1, January 2022, p. e191.

[24] Zobaed, S. M., and M. Amini Salehi, "Confidential Computing Across Edge-to-Cloud for Machine Learning: A Survey Study," *Software: Practice and Experience*, Vol. 55, No. 5, May 2025, pp. 896–924.

[25] Pierides, M., and J. Mulligan, "Key Themes of Resiliency, Outsourcing and Third-Party Risk Management Regimes," *Journal of Securities Operations & Custody*, Vol. 17, No. 2, January 1, 2025, pp. 102–118.

[26] Schroeder, P., "Capital One to Pay $80 Million Fine After Data Breach," *Reuters*, August 6, 2020.

[27] Khan, S., et al., "A Systematic Analysis of the Capital One Data Breach: Critical Lessons Learned," *ACM Transactions on Privacy and Security*, Vol. 26, No. 1, November 7, 2022, pp. 1–29.

[28] Tidy, J., "British Airways Fined £20m over Data Breach," *BBC News*, October 16, 2020.

[29] Voss, W. G., *Airline Commercial Use of EU Personal Data in the Context of the GDPR, British Airways and Schrems II*, Colo. Tech. LJ, Vol. 19, 2021, p. 377.

[30] Ahir, K. J., S. Sajjala, and B. Pandurangan, "Breaking Trust: The Equifax Breach and Software Failures."

[31] Bond, M., K. Human, and N. Kwon, "Analysis and Implications for Equifax Data Breach," 2022, . https://cs.ucf.edu/~mohaisen/doc/teaching/cap5150/fall2022/cap5150-proj2.pdf.

[32] Kaur, G., and V. Grover, "Detection and Prevention of Hypervisor and VM Attacks," *2021 IEEE International Conference on Nanoelectronics, Nanophotonics, Nanomaterials, Nanobioscience & Nanotechnology (5NANO)*, April 29, 2021, pp. 1–5.

[33] Halikias, H., "Preparation, Response, and Recovery," in *Digital Shakedown: The Complete Guide to Understanding and Combating Ransomware*, Cham: Springer Nature Switzerland, 2024, pp. 49–65.

[34] Schweitzer, H., et al., *Data Access and Sharing in Germany and in the EU: Towards a Coherent Legal Framework for the Emerging Data Economy: A Legal, Economic and Competition Policy Angle-Final Report (Expertenstudie im Auftrag des Bundesministeriums für Wirtschaft und Klimaschutz)*, 2022, https://pure.mpg.de/rest/items/item_3457829/component/file_3457831/content.

[35] Coppens, B., and O. Zendra, "Is Privacy Possible in a Digital World?" *The HiPEAC Vision 2023*, 2023, pp. 145–162.

CHAPTER 8

Disaster Recovery and Business Continuity in Virtualized Environments

8.1 Overview of Disaster Recovery and Business Continuity Planning

In this chapter, we explore the essential practices for ensuring service reliability and resumption in an IT environment. We begin by observing disaster recovery and business continuity planning, focusing on analyzing how business operations depend on IT and the effects of an outage. This analysis helps in identifying the strategies and investments necessary to achieve an acceptable level of reliability in the environment.

We will explore several common backup strategies for data protection and their application in recovery scenarios. Disaster recovery practices rely on these backups and other data replication techniques. Lastly, we will investigate how to incorporate high availability into computers and networks to minimize the risk of outages.

Disaster recovery and business continuity planning are distinct but interconnected concepts. Disaster recovery is a component of business continuity planning. Disaster recovery focuses on recovering the technical aspects of a business, including computers, software, networks, and data. Business continuity planning encompasses disaster recovery and includes procedures to restore business operations, the necessary business infrastructure, and the daily work of employees. Business continuity planning is crucial for maintaining business operations and returning to business as usual during a disaster. Disaster recovery and business continuity planning professionals collaborate to ensure the recoverability and continuity of all organizational aspects affected by outages or security events. Figure 8.1 demonstrates the disaster recovery in physical environments.

An overview of disaster recovery and business continuity planning in virtualized environments is outlined.

8.1.1 Disaster Recovery

Disaster recovery in virtualized environments includes a set of policies, tools, and procedures considered to enable the recovery or continuation of vital technology

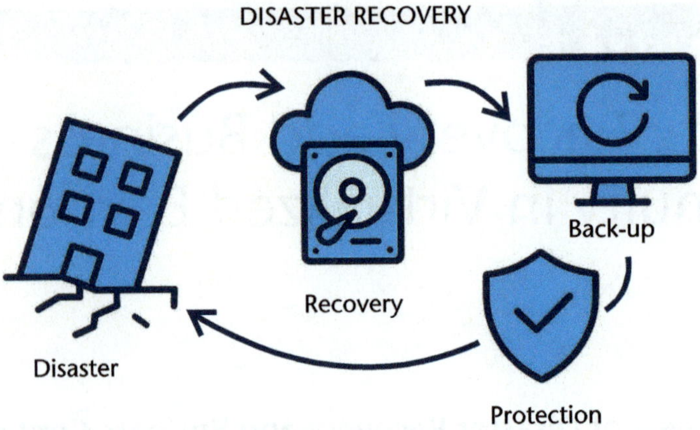

Figure 8.1 Disaster recovery in physical environments.

infrastructure and systems resulting in a natural or human made disaster such as cyberattacks and hardware failures. In a virtualized setup, this process typically leverages virtualization technology to create snapshots, backups, and replicas of VMs and data, ensuring that they can be quickly restored or moved to another placement in the event of a disruption.

Key components of disaster recovery include automated failover procedure, risk assessment, business impact analysis including financial and operational consequences, data replication of systems, the ability to spin up VMs on backup hardware of critical data, regularly test the disaster recovery plans involved, and ensure that it works as expected and train staff to execute the plan.

The benefits of these key components of the disaster recovery encompass minimizing downtime and data loss, ensuring rapid recovery of IT services and safeguarding the organization's reputation and financial stability.

When developing a disaster recovery plan, it is essential to comprehend how your organization's IT infrastructure, applications, and network underpin its business operations. For example, while a specific business unit might assert that a particular application or function is not necessary until day 3 of a disaster, technological dependencies may necessitate its availability from day 1. In such cases, the disaster recovery planner should collaborate with and inform the business unit to clarify the need for day 1 recovery over day 3 recovery. The business unit's budget typically allocates a substantial expense for the IT department, which may lead them to believe that any disaster recovery or business continuity efforts are very expensive. Collaborating with IT subject matter experts (SMEs) can sometimes reveal ways to circumvent specific electronic feeds or file dependencies required for system recovery. However, successful execution hinges on understanding who and what is being recovered. The responsible business continuity or disaster recovery professional should collaborate with both the IT group and the business unit to achieve the overarching goal of maintaining a robust, productive, and profitable organization. Identifying who and what needs recovery is facilitated by assembling a team of experts, such as programmers, business analysts, system architects, system administrators, or any other necessary SMEs. These experts play a vital role in crafting the disaster recovery plan, possessing the technical know-how to operate the business systems in question and justifying the costs associated with specific disaster recovery processes. This information is crucial for the business unit manager to make well-informed decisions. Figure 8.2 illustrates the disaster recovery steps in virtualized environments.

8.1.2 Planning for Business Continuity

Business continuity in virtualized environments encompasses the strategies and procedures implemented to guarantee continuous operations for an organization during disruptions. Within a virtualized framework, business continuity planning leverages virtual infrastructure to sustain crucial business functions without interruption. This extends beyond mere disaster recovery tactics to encompass proactive measures ensuring redundancy, high availability, and the smooth functioning of IT services. Techniques such as live migration, load balancing, and routine testing of business continuity plans are employed to fortify business operations, enabling swift recovery from various incidents while upholding productivity and service standards.

Key components of business continuity include risk assessment, continuity strategies such as preventive and mitigation measures, recovery strategies, plan development, training and awareness of all employees' responsibilities, and finally testing the business continuity plan to identify the weakness. The benefits of these key components involve reducing both financial and operational impacts, improve organizational resilience and readiness, and guarantees the uninterrupted operation of essential business functions.

The business continuity professional focuses more on the business functions performed by employees rather than the underlying technologies. To devise strategies for resuming normal operations during a disaster, the business continuity professional collaborates closely with each business unit. This entails engaging with decision-makers, managers responsible for implementing decisions, and the frontline staff, often referred to as "power users." These power users possess intimate knowledge of applications, understanding their intricacies and nuances at a granular level. This perspective is crucial in crafting the business unit's continuity plan, and their involvement in disaster recovery rehearsals and tabletop exercises

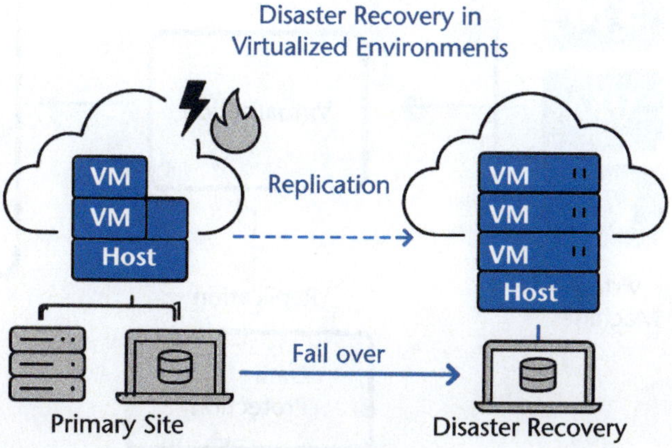

Figure 8.2 Disaster recovery in virtualized environments.

is essential. The business unit management team plays a pivotal role as they offer a broader business perspective and assist in determining the significance of applications based on the unit's mission. Moreover, the business unit must consider the necessity for a disaster recovery plan when introducing new or upgraded program applications. It is imperative for the disaster recovery or business continuity professional to stay informed about such changes.

For example, a business unit manager may explore a product with a vendor to enhance a current business function without involving the IT department or the disaster recovery or business continuity professional. Therefore, maintaining relationships with all stakeholders within the business unit is essential for the business continuity professional. This ensures that the knowledge and capability to recover new products are taken into account should they be introduced into the organization. Figure 8.3 illustrates an overview of the business continuity in virtualized environments.

In virtualized environments, a disaster recovery and business continuity plan utilizes virtualization technologies to bolster resilience and recovery capabilities. The key strategies include:

- *VM snapshots:* Recording the status of VMs to promptly recover them following a disturbance.
- *VM replication:* Generating instantaneous duplicates of VMs in various locations.
- *Automated failover:* Instantly transitioning to backup VMs upon the failure of primary VMs.
- *Load balancing:* Equitably distributing workloads among numerous servers to ensure optimal availability.
- *Live migration:* Relocating VMs between hosts seamlessly, without any interruption, thus upholding business continuity during maintenance or failures.

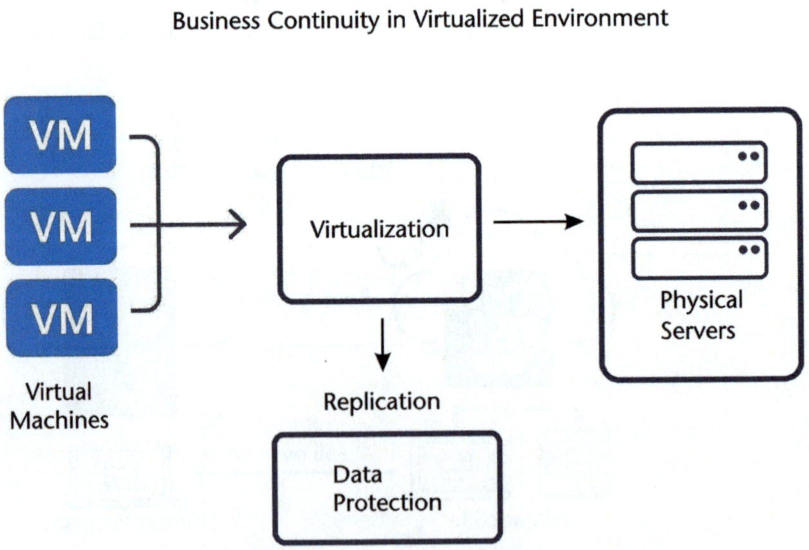

Figure 8.3 Overview of business continuity in virtualized environments.

By utilizing these technologies, organizations can significantly enhance their disaster recovery and business continuity capabilities, thus ensuring robust protection against a wide array of disruptions.

8.1.3 Case Study: For Disaster Recovery

A case study on disaster recovery in virtualized settings recently highlighted a financial firm that adopted sophisticated disaster recovery solutions to maintain uninterrupted business operations. Next is a summary of this case study.

8.1.3.1 Case Study: Financial Services Company Implements Advanced Disaster Recovery for Virtualized Environments

The context is that, as a prominent financial services provider, the company is dependent on its IT framework to sustain essential business functions. It encountered challenges in maintaining continuous availability and effective disaster recovery, attributed to the intricate and extensive nature of its virtualized systems. The significant materials for this case study include:

- Introduction of the company's virtualized infrastructure (VMware, vSphere, cloud-based virtualization);
- Current disaster recovery challenges including (recovery time, data reliability, agreement);
- Used Technology, which is Veeam's SureBackup technology;
- Governing and financial agreement.

The challenges were:

- Guaranteeing the uninterrupted operation of vital applications and services;
- Controlling and safeguarding a substantial volume of confidential financial information;
- Adhering to rigorous regulatory standards for data security and disaster recovery;
- Reducing the amount of operational disruption and data loss in a disaster scenario.

As a solution, the company established a comprehensive disaster recovery plan, which encompassed the following elements:

1. *Virtualization platform:* The company utilized VMware vSphere to virtualize servers, which improved resource management and simplified administration of VMs.
2. *Backup and replication:* The firm employed Veeam Backup & Replication for its swift and adaptable backup, replication, and recovery features for VMs, guaranteeing quick data retrieval after any system failures.
3. *Automated disaster recovery testing:* Regular and automated disaster recovery tests were conducted using Veeam's SureBackup technology, enabling

the company to confirm the restorability of its VMs and the efficiency of its disaster recovery plans.

4. *Cloud-based disaster recovery:* The company embraced a hybrid cloud model, integrating AWS for remote disaster recovery, adding an extra layer of defense, and facilitating swift cloud failover in the event of local disasters.
5. *Data encryption and security:* The company made sure that all data involved in backup and replication was encrypted during transfer and while stored, safeguarding sensitive financial records.

The outcomes were:

- *Improved recovery time objective (RTO) and recovery point objective (RPO):* The company significantly improved its RTO and RPO of the existing disaster recovery challenges, which allowed for the rapid reinstatement of essential services with minimal data disruption.
- *Improved regulatory adherence:* The disaster recovery solution adopted by the company facilitated compliance with legal standards for data safeguarding and disaster recovery.
- *Strengthened disaster recovery plan assurance:* The consistent automated tests bolstered confidence that the disaster recovery plan would be effective during an actual emergency.
- *Financial benefits:* The adoption of a hybrid cloud strategy reduced the necessity for costly alternative data centers, leading to financial savings while still providing robust protection.

The technical and scientific thinking for this example through deploying a sophisticated disaster recovery system designed for its virtualized framework, the financial services company ensured operational continuity, secured sensitive data, and complied with regulatory mandates. Also, evaluating of potential risks including hypervisor failures, challenges maintaining data integrity during replication, and possible network congestion or bottlenecks that could affect system performance and recovery effectiveness. The strategic application of contemporary disaster recovery technologies, including VMware vSphere, Veeam Backup & Replication, and AWS cloud solutions, was instrumental in realizing these outcomes. The case study underscores the criticality of implementing a solid and all-encompassing disaster recovery approach in virtualized settings to protect essential business functions and improve its virtual environment's resilience and ensure that they are prepared to handle disasters effectively.

As discussed in Section 8.1.2, business continuity is a crucial concept in virtualized environments. Despite companies' best efforts to prevent disasters and data loss, it is impossible to foresee every potential scenario. Therefore, companies must have robust plans to ensure business continuity under any circumstances.

Business continuity controls extend beyond merely backing up data and providing redundant hardware. Key considerations should include:

- Documenting system configurations;
- Establishing alternative communication channels;
- Ensuring a reliable power supply;
- Identifying all dependencies for applications and processes;
- Knowing how to manually perform automated tasks.

For effective business continuity planning, companies should adhere to the following best practices:

1. Develop a policy that guides the creation of the business continuity plan and assigns responsibilities.
2. Identify and prioritize critical systems and processes according to their importance.
3. Assess vulnerabilities, threats, and calculate associated risks.
4. Implement controls and countermeasures to mitigate risks.
5. Create strategies to quickly restore critical systems.
6. Establish procedures to maintain operations during a crisis.
7. Test the plan to ensure its effectiveness.
8. Regularly update the plan to reflect any changes.

8.2 Importance of Disaster Recovery and Business Continuity

Disaster recovery and business continuity are significant components for continuing the resilience and operational strength of organizations, specifically in virtualized environments.

These strategies from research studies indicated enable businesses to swiftly recover from disruptions, ensuring minimal downtime and data loss while continuing operations. Also, lowering expenses, facilitating off-site data replication, and improving overall resilience and adaptability.

1. Importance of disaster recovery and business continuity in modern IT:
   - The growing reliance on digital data emphasizes the need for strong disaster recovery and business continuity strategies to ensure data resilience and compliance with legal obligations [1].
   - Effective IT disaster recovery planning and business continuity are critical for reducing downtime and preventing data loss, ensuring the continuity of IT operations [2].
2. Role of virtualization in disaster recovery and business continuity:
   - Virtualization allows dynamic resource allocation, enabling rapid recovery and minimizing service disruptions, which is particularly vital in industries such as banking [3].
   - It facilitates real-time application migration and off-site data replication, improving disaster recovery and business continuity.

3. Cost efficiency and resource optimization:
   - Virtualized environments enable SMEs to cut down on costly IT infrastructure while meeting recovery targets via risk assessment.
   - Multicloud disaster recovery services leverage virtualization to manage cross-cloud disaster recovery efficiently, optimizing resources and reducing costs [4].
4. Challenges and strategies:
   - Implementing IT disaster recovery plan and business continuity faces challenges such as advancing technology, complex IT systems, limited budgets, and a lack of skilled personnel.
   - Developed technologies, cloud computing, and virtualization are key technologies for creating more effective recovery and continuity plans [2].
5. Legal and regulatory compliance:
   - Many industries and businesses are legally required to have disaster recovery and business continuity plans, making these strategies not just beneficial but mandatory [1].

Based on the significant insights and strategies, we consider that disaster recovery and business continuity are essential for maintaining resilience and operational stability in organizations, especially within virtualized environments. Virtualization technologies are key to enabling quick recovery, optimizing resource allocation, and lowering costs. Although challenges exist, the successful implementation of advanced technologies and a thorough understanding of the IT infrastructure are vital for successful disaster recovery and business continuity planning.

Figure 8.4 highlights the contrasting importance of disaster recovery and business continuity in virtualized environments, emphasizing their distinct roles in maintaining operational resilience.

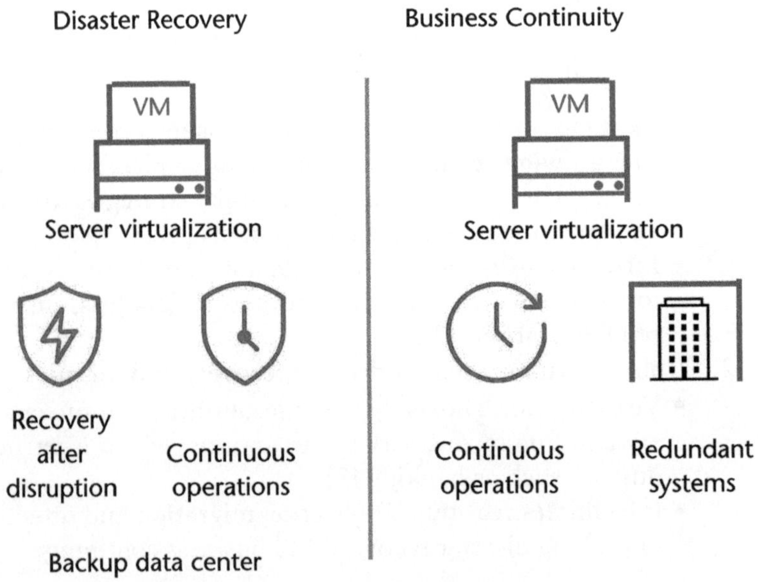

Figure 8.4 Comparing disaster recovery versus business continuity in virtualization.

8.2.1 The Connection Between Disaster Recovery and Business Continuity

Disaster recovery and business continuity are closely connected, with disaster recovery focusing on the repair of IT systems, data, and infrastructure after a disruption, while business continuity encompasses the broader effort to maintain ongoing business operations during and after a disaster. Disaster recovery is a critical component of business continuity, ensuring that technical systems are quickly repaired to support the overall goal of minimizing downtime and maintaining business resilience. Together, they form a comprehensive strategy to safeguard both IT systems and essential business functions. In Table 8.1, the relationship between disaster recovery and business continuity in virtualized environments is demonstrated. This emphasizes how various elements of disaster recovery and business continuity work together to enhance overall resilience and maintain operational stability. Disaster recovery focuses on restoring IT systems, while business continuity covers the wider scope of sustaining and resuming overall business operations. This shows how the two are interconnected, with disaster recovery being a critical part of the broader business continuity framework.

8.3 Guidelines for Implementing Disaster Recovery and Business Continuity

Ensuring the effective guidelines for implementing disaster recovery and business continuity in virtualized environments include conducting a risk assessment, developing a comprehensive disaster recovery plan, and acquiring appropriate virtualization and disaster recovery tools, regularly testing the plan, and provide training for the IT team on best practices and tools.

Virtualization introduces unique challenges and opportunities for disaster recovery and business continuity planning. Overcoming these challenges in IT disaster recovery plan and business continuity requires a comprehensive understanding of the organization's IT infrastructure, risk assessment, and the development of robust recovery strategies and plans.

The guidelines for implementing disaster recovery and business continuity in virtualized environments for any organization are outlined as follows:

1. Assess risks and prioritize systems:
    - Identify potential risks, threat, vulnerabilities, and the criticality of different VMs that could impact your virtualized systems.
    - Prioritize systems based on their importance to business operations.
2. Develop a comprehensive disaster recovery/business continuity plan:
    - Create detailed plans for both disaster recovery and business continuity fitted to your organization's needs and virtual infrastructure, outlining roles, responsibilities, and procedures.
    - Ensure alignment between IT recovery and overall business continuity needs.
3. Implement backup and replication:
    - Use regular backups and real-time replication of VMs and data to secondary locations.

Table 8.1 Relationship Between Disaster Recovery and Business Continuity in Virtualized Environments

Feature	*Disaster Recovery*	*Business Continuity*	*Relation*
Definition	Recovering VMs, data, and virtual infrastructure following a disaster	Maintaining continuous operation and minimizing disruption to business functions despite a disaster	Disaster recovery recovers virtual infrastructure following a disaster, business continuity maintaining ongoing operation in the event of a disaster
Scope	Focused on recovering virtual systems, virtual networks, and data	Encompasses maintaining operational processes, communication, and business functions in a virtualized setup	Disaster recovery supports business continuity by ensuring that IT systems are recoverable, which is essential for maintaining business operations
Objective	To restore virtualized IT infrastructure and data as quickly as possible	To ensure that business operations continue smoothly even when virtualized systems face issues	Disaster recovery is a component of business continuity, focusing on IT systems; business continuity encompasses disaster recovery and broader operational continuity
Replication	Continuous or scheduled replication of VMs and data to a backup location	Replication can involve not only data but also processes and personnel roles to ensure the continuity of business operations	Disaster recovery replication ensures rapid access to data and systems, aiding in the achievement of business continuity objectives
Planning	Involves creating recovery plans for VMs, virtual networks, and data backup	Involves developing strategies for maintaining business operations, including managing virtual environments	Disaster recovery plan is part of the broader business continuity plan, detailing how to recover IT systems specifically
Focus areas	VM snapshots and backups; restoration of virtual infrastructure; redundant virtual network configurations; recovery of virtualized applications	Continuity of virtualized services; management of virtual resources; communication strategies during virtual outages; continuation of business processes within virtual environments	Disaster recovery deals with the recovery of technical aspects; business continuity focuses on overall business operations and resilience
Approach	Reactive: focuses on recovering from virtual system failures or data loss	Proactive: ensures that virtualized systems support ongoing business operations even during disruptions	Approach in disaster recovery supports business continuity by ensuring quicker and more reliable recovery of IT systems, facilitating ongoing business operations
Testing	Involves testing VM recovery, backup restores, and virtual infrastructure restoration	Involves testing the effectiveness of business continuity strategies in maintaining virtualized operations	Testing disaster recovery plans supports business continuity by verifying that IT systems can be recovered as part of the overall business operations
Updates	Updated based on changes in virtual infrastructure, new virtual threats, and results from recovery tests	Updated to reflect changes in virtualized business processes, new technologies, and lessons learned from continuity tests	Disaster recovery failover ensures IT systems are available, supporting the continuity of business processes
Backup strategies	Regular backups, snapshots, and offsite storage for VMs and data	Backup strategies are part of the overall business continuity plan, including data, personnel, and operational backups	Effective disaster recovery relies on good backup practices, which contribute to overall business continuity

Table 8.1 (continued)

Feature	*Disaster Recovery*	*Business Continuity*	*Relation*
Integration	Should be integrated with business continuity plans to ensure IT recovery supports overall business functions in a virtualized environment	Should incorporate disaster recovery strategies to ensure that virtualized systems can support uninterrupted business operations	Disaster recovery documentation supports business continuity by providing a clear plan for IT recovery, which is integrated into the broader business continuity plan
Examples and compliance	Restoring a failed VM; reconfiguring a disrupted virtual network; recovering lost virtual data; compliance with IT-related regulations and standards for data protection	Maintaining access to virtual applications during a virtual infrastructure outage; ensuring virtual communication channels remain operational during a crisis; continuation of virtualized business processes; compliance with broader regulatory requirements related to business operations and continuity	Compliance in disaster recovery ensures that IT recovery practices meet regulatory standards, supporting overall business continuity compliance

- Store backups offsite or in the cloud to safeguard against regional disasters.

4. Automate failover and recovery:
   - Set up automated failover for mission-critical VMs to minimize downtime.
   - Implement recovery tools to streamline and speed up restoration processes.
5. Test and update plans regularly:
   - Conduct regular testing of disaster recovery and business continuity plans to ensure they work as expected effectiveness, of their, and address any issues.
   - Update plans based on the results of tests, changes in the environment, or emerging risks.
6. Ensure scalability and resource availability:
   - Check that backup environments have sufficient resources (compute, storage, network) to handle failovers.
   - Plan for future scalability based on predictable growth or changes in the business.
7. Secure data and systems:
   - Protecting data with encryption during backups and replication.
   - Ensure robust access controls to prevent unauthorized access to disaster recovery and business continuity systems.
8. Document everything:
   - Keep complete documentation of your disaster recovery and business continuity processes, including configurations, contact information, and step-by-step recovery instructions.
9. IT team training:
   - Train your IT staff on best practices and tools related to disaster recovery and business continuity to ensure they are prepared to respond effectively.

Following these guidelines, an organization can establish an effective disaster recovery and business continuity strategy in virtualized environments, proving resilience and minimum interruption to business operations.

Recent studies [5, 6] have indicated that the successful implementation of disaster recovery and business continuity in virtualized environments necessitates a thorough understanding of IT infrastructure, risk evaluation, and the creation of strong recovery strategies and plans, complemented by strategic guidelines to optimize organizational processes and ICT strategies. Focusing on information and communication technology systems, a framework for business continuity management, is needed to address gaps in the existing knowledge. Therefore, the authors of [7] identified gaps in business continuity management knowledge and recommended a framework applicable for all organizations.

8.3.1 Implementing Disaster Recovery and Business Continuity

8.3.1.1 Case Study for the ABC Group Company

In the modern digital era, organizations depend extensively on IT systems to sustain their operations. The growing complexity and interconnectivity of these systems demand effective disaster recovery and business continuity strategies. The following case study examines the implementation of a disaster recovery plan and business continuity in virtualized environments, emphasizing the challenges faced, the strategies employed, and the advantages of these practices.

Let's examine a particular business as an example, which we will call the ABC Group, as it is not a publicly traded company. The ABC Group is a manufacturer of consumer goods, producing a range of products including food and beverages, fabric care, home care, and personal care items. The key elements of the ABC Group's business model are customer segments, value scheme, customer details and relationships, revenue, resources, and cost structure. Given the uncertainties and potential future challenges, the ABC Group will encounter several obstacles that must be addressed in order to implement effective disaster recovery and business continuity plans as follows.

- *Significance of IT disaster recovery plan and business continuity:* IT Disaster Recovery Planning (IT DRP) is centered on the recovery and restoration of IT systems, infrastructure, and services after a disruptive event or disaster. Its main objective is to reduce downtime and prevent data loss, ensuring that critical IT functions are swiftly restored. However, business continuity takes a broader approach by focusing on the organization's capacity to sustain essential operations and deliver critical services both during and after a disruption. Together, IT DRP and business continuity are crucial elements of an organization's resilience strategy.
- *Challenges in implementation:* In virtualized environments, the implementation of effective IT DRP and business continuity strategies faces various challenges. These challenges include the rapid evolution of technology, the growing complexity of IT systems, budget limitations, resistance to change within the organization, and the need for skilled professionals. Moreover, integrating IT DRP and business continuity with broader organizational risk

management, along with addressing the influence of emerging technologies such as cloud computing and virtualization on recovery strategies, are key areas that require focus.

- *Strategies for successful implementation:* To address these challenges, organizations need to gain a deep understanding of their IT infrastructure and perform detailed risk assessments. Creating strong recovery plans and strategies is essential [8, 9]. Major approaches include:
  - *Integrated operating environment (IOE):* Creating an IOE within an enterprise information system by embedding business continuity factors can improve resilience. This approach encompasses identifying critical disconnection points and using systems integration technologies to unify platforms, data, protocols, and application formats.
  - *Continuous computing technologies:* Utilizing continuous computing technologies strengthens business continuity by supporting uninterrupted operations, even during failures or disasters.
  - *Holistic approach:* Taking a comprehensive, top-down approach to developing and implementing IT DRP and business continuity frameworks make sure that all operational aspects of the organization are addressed.

8.3.2 Advantages

Virtualized environments offer several benefits for disaster recovery and business continuity, including enhanced scalability, cost optimization, and improved resource efficiency. These advantages enable organizations to respond more effectively to disruptions, as illustrated in Figure 8.5, by agreeing flexible infrastructure management and more efficient allocation of computing and storage resources.

- *Flexibility and scalability:* Virtualization enables the fast placement and scaling of IT resources, which is crucial for efficient disaster recovery and business continuity.
- *Cost-efficiency:* Virtualized environments lower the expenses tied to retaining physical hardware and infrastructure, making it more affordable for organizations to implement comprehensive DRP and business continuity strategies.

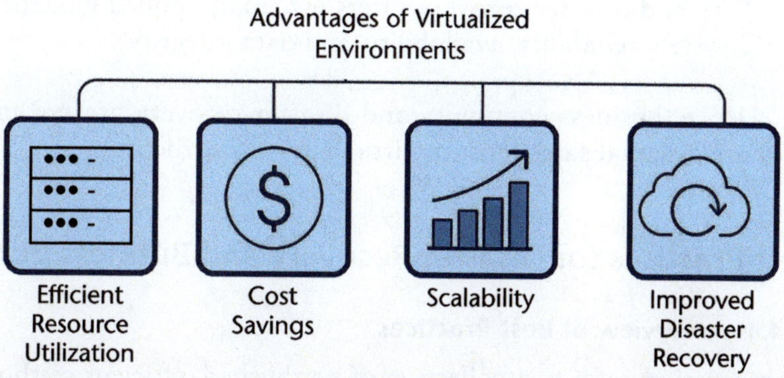

Figure 8.5 Advantages of virtualized environments.

- *Advanced recovery times:* Virtualization significantly improves recovery times by enabling the instant repair of VMs and applications. It also ensures efficient utilization of resources, allowing businesses to recover functions quickly while optimizing computing power and storage. This restructured approach reduces downtime and enhances overall resilience in disaster recovery scenarios.

Thus, considering that the ABC Group may encounter significant risks from uncertainties such as climate change, shifting business environments, cyberattacks, new competitors, reputational issues, and natural disasters due to insufficient focus on technological security, it is important to note that these risks are not unique to the ABC Group. Many other major companies and industries face similar challenges. Most organizations have integrated technology into their operations, management systems, marketing, and other areas. Consequently, competitive advantage will largely depend on the sophistication of their cutting-edge technologies and the efficiency of their operations. The conclusion of the ABC Group case study, which highlights the importance of implementing DRP, and business continuity in virtualized environments to make sure organizational resilience in place. Although challenges exist, the use of integrated operating environments, continuous computing technologies, and a complete approach can greatly improve an organization's capacity to recover from interruptions and sustain essential operations. As technology advances, continuous research and development will be crucial to overcoming new challenges and enhancing the effectiveness of IT DRP and business continuity strategies.

To conclude, business continuity and disaster recovery are fundamental rocks of robust IT infrastructure for organizations. In virtualized environments, however, they introduce both enhanced capabilities and unique difficulties:

- Virtualization supports accelerated recovery, dynamic resource management, and improved fault tolerance, making business continuity and disaster recovery strategies more responsive and efficient.
- These environments also present new risks, such as hypervisor-level vulnerabilities, misconfigurations, and potential single points of failure, necessitating a revised approach to continuity planning.
- As this chapter focuses on virtualization, the inclusion of business continuity and disaster recovery offers essential, applied guidance for maintaining system reliability, availability, and data integrity.

Hence, business continuity and disaster recovery are not marginal concerns; they are essential safeguards in virtualized infrastructures.

8.4 Best Practices for Disaster Recovery and Business Continuity

8.4.1 Overview of Best Practices

Best practices refer to a collection of established, efficient methods, techniques, or procedures that are broadly recognized and recommended within a specific industry or field. They represent the most effective and reliable ways to achieve desired results, drawing on collective experience, research, and expertise [9]. Implementing best practices assist organizations to maintain reliable quality, performance, and consistency among various processes and operations. As illustrated, best practices help to maintain consistent quality and efficiency by utilizing well-established methods based on professional experience, thorough research, and accepted industry standards. These approaches are widely adopted to ensure reliable outcomes and improve overall performance across various processes and operations as illustrated in Figure 8.6.

A best practice is an exceptional or innovative method that consistently outperforms standard performance levels. For a method or approach to qualify as a best practice, several of the following criteria must be met:

- There is evidence of an expert review, such as an independent assessment, award, or audit.
- Significant improvement in performance compared to standard levels is demonstrated.
- The results consistently surpass those of similar organizations.
- Multiple independent sources concur that the practice is superior.

The advantages of sharing best practices include serving as effective tools for driving organizational change, especially when integrated into a strategic plan to enhance preparedness, and deliver high-quality products and services. Before starting your own process, it is beneficial to review existing benchmarking studies and best practice case studies to identify current processes and practices that can be adjusted to fit your organization's needs, ultimately saving time. Sharing benchmarking data and best practices highlights innovative organizations that are:

As illustrated, ensure consistent quality and performance by applying proven methods grounded in experience, research, and industry standards

Figure 8.6 Best practices outline.

- Increasing customer and employee satisfaction;
- Enhancing management practices;
- Adopting new technologies;
- Ensuring best value.

One key benefit of benchmarking and sharing outcomes is the validation of business processes. By using proven methods, initiatives, and processes, your organization can achieve:

- Improved organizational preparedness;
- Significant cost avoidance;
- Major cost or time savings;
- Enhanced customer service.

Overall, benchmarking and sharing best practices provide a valuable opportunity to learn from others' experiences, apply that knowledge, and greatly improve operational performance.

8.4.2 Best Practices for Disaster Recovery and Business Continuity

Best practices for disaster recovery and business continuity in virtualized environments are suggested approaches and strategies aimed at ensuring an organization's IT systems can swiftly and efficiently recover from disruptions, while maintaining critical operations without major interruptions. These advanced best practices include:

1. *Automated arrangement and management:* Utilize automation tools to streamline and coordinate disaster recovery processes, ensuring a swift and precise response during disruptions.
2. *Comprehensive data backup and replication:* Employ advanced technologies for data backup and replication to keep up-to-date copies of critical information at multiple locations, enhancing data protection and accelerating recovery.
3. *Continuous monitoring and analytics:* Implement continuous monitoring and analytics tools to provide real-time insights into system performance and potential issues, enabling proactive management and timely identification of recovery needs.
4. *Regular testing and validation:* Perform frequent and thorough testing of disaster recovery and business continuity plans to confirm their effectiveness and make necessary adjustments based on test outcomes.
5. *Multitiered recovery strategies:* Create multitiered recovery strategies that cover different levels of IT infrastructure and services, from VMs to applications, ensuring inclusive disaster coverage.
6. *Integration with cloud services:* Use cloud-based disaster retrieval solutions to increase flexibility and scalability, facilitating seamless failover and recovery without dependence on physical infrastructure.

7. *RBAC and security:* Apply RBACs and security measures to safeguard sensitive data and ensure that only authorized personnel can access critical systems during recovery.
8. *Clear communication protocols:* Set up clear communication protocols and channels to ensure stakeholders are kept updated and that coordination efforts are effective both during and after a disruption.
9. *Regular training and awareness:* Offer ongoing training and awareness programs to ensure staff are well-versed in disaster recovery procedures and best practices, enhancing their ability to respond effectively in emergencies.
10. *Adaptive and scalable solutions:* Implement adaptive and scalable disaster recovery solutions that can adjust to evolving technologies and organizational needs, ensuring long-term effectiveness and resilience.

These best practices enable organizations to sustain operational resilience, reduce downtime, and swiftly recover from unexpected disruptions in virtualized environments as shown in Figure 8.7.

8.5 Summary

In this chapter, we defined and discussed disaster recovery and business continuity and implementation of best practices. Disaster recovery involves various risks that stem from natural events, human actions, and environmental factors. Additionally, IT services have different levels of criticality.

In virtualized environments, disaster recovery and business continuity plans leverage virtualization technologies to enhance resilience and recovery capabilities. By integrating these technologies, organizations can significantly improve their disaster recovery and business continuity effectiveness, providing robust protection against diverse disruptions.

Figure 8.7 Best practices for disaster recovery and business continuity in virtualized environments.

Table 8.1 can be used to demonstrate how disaster recovery and business continuity are interconnected, thereby boosting overall resilience and maintaining operational stability.

Best practices for disaster recovery and business continuity in virtualized environments involve recommended strategies and methods that ensure an organization's IT systems can recover quickly and effectively from disruptions while keeping critical operations running with minimal interruptions.

Developing a robust disaster recovery and business continuity strategy in virtualized environments is essential to ensuring organizational resilience and minimizing downtime during unplanned disruptions. To achieve this, organizations must adopt a comprehensive, methodical approach that encompasses a thorough understanding of their virtual IT infrastructure, detailed business impact analyses, and risk assessments tailored to virtualization technologies. Effective disaster recovery and business continuity planning should include the implementation of redundant systems, automated failover mechanisms, continuous data replication, and snapshot technologies that are native to hypervisors such as VMware vSphere or Microsoft Hyper-V.

Furthermore, aligning recovery strategies with international standards such as ISO/IEC 22301 for business continuity and ISO/IEC 27031 for IT disaster recovery ensures adherence to globally recognized frameworks. It is equally important to consider the influence of emerging technologies such as cloud computing, hybrid environments, and software-defined storage, which can introduce both opportunities and complexities into disaster recovery/business continuity planning.

Lastly, addressing operational challenges including the rapid pace of technological change, system interoperability, resource limitations, and budget constraints is critical for sustaining resilience. Regular testing, employee training, and continuous improvement cycles are also considered best practices to validate the effectiveness and reliability of disaster recovery and business continuity strategies in virtualized infrastructures.

References

[1] Pearce, M., S. Zeadally, and R. Hunt, "Virtualization: Issues, Security Threats, and Solutions," *ACM Computing Surveys,* Vol. 45, 2013, pp. 17:1–17:39.

[2] Hoesing, M., "Virtualization Security Assessment," *Information Security Journal: A Global Perspective,* Vol. 18, 2009, pp. 124–130.

[3] Khan, A., "Virtual Machine Security," *International Journal of Information and Computer Security,* Vol. 9, 2017, pp. 49–84.

[4] Han, Y. -N., et al., "A Centralized Monitoring Mechanism in Virtualized Environments," *DEStech Transactions on Engineering and Technology Research*, April 10, 2017.

[5] Kesa, D., "Ensuring Resilience: Integrating IT Disaster Recovery Planning and Business Continuity for Sustainable Information Technology Operations," *World Journal of Advanced Research and Reviews,* 2023.

[6] Russo, N., et al., "Exploring a Multidisciplinary Assessment of Organisational Maturity in Business Continuity: A Perspective and Future Research Outlook," *Applied Sciences,* Vol. 13, 2023, p. 19.

[7] Tiwary, R. K., and R. Sandhane, "Designing Business Continuity Plan for It Organizations: A Systematic Literature Review and Meta-Analysis," *Cardiometry,* 2022.

[8] Bajgoric, N., and Y. B. Moon, "Enhancing Systems Integration by Incorporating Business Continuity Drivers," *Industrial Management and Data Systems,* Vol. 109, 2009, pp. 74–97.

[9] Ashford, W., "Daily News for IT Professionals," *ComputerWeekly.com*, 2011, pp. 13–19.

CHAPTER 9

Best Practices for Virtualization Security

Virtualization security is crucial for protecting virtual environments, VMs, hypervisors, storage, and networks, from threats and vulnerabilities [1]. Organizations should implement best practices, including securing the hypervisor, hardening templates, segmenting traffic types, implementing storage security encryption, monitoring and logging, endpoint security with anti-malware, access control and authentication, disaster recovery, and providing education on virtualization security best practices. Routine updates and patches mitigate vulnerabilities, restricting hypervisor access to authorized users through role-based access control (RBAC) and multifactor authentication [2]. Virtual storage encryption helps to protect sensitive data, while access control limits access by the proper method of authentication. Routine backups and testing of recovery systems are essential. Casual monitoring and log management tools operationalize the detection of anomalies, as well as execute intrusion detection software (IDS)/intrusion prevention software (IPS) for the virtual environment. Endpoint security solutions, such as anti-malware or host intrusion detection systems, would typically be installed and never removed from the VMs. Access control and authentication adhere to the principle of least privilege [3].

9.1 Overview of Best Practices

To ensure the integrity, availability, and confidentiality of these systems, organizations should implement best practices such as securing the hypervisor, hardening VM templates, segmenting and isolating traffic types, implementing storage security encryption, monitoring and logging, endpoint security anti-malware, access control and authentication, disaster recovery, and business continuity, protecting virtual network traffic encryption, and providing education and awareness training on virtualization security best practices, which are shown in Figure 9.2 [5]. Multiple OSs can be installed on a single host computer thanks to VMs, which can be exploited as entry points for malicious software attacks. The hypervisor, which manages VMs, often uses services running on the VM's OS to inject malicious code into the host system [6]. To protect against such security threats, security features on both the host and guest systems, such as SELinux or Quick Emulator (QEMU) sandboxing, can be utilized. These features make it harder for malicious code to attack the hypervisor and transfer between the host and VMs. Many of the features

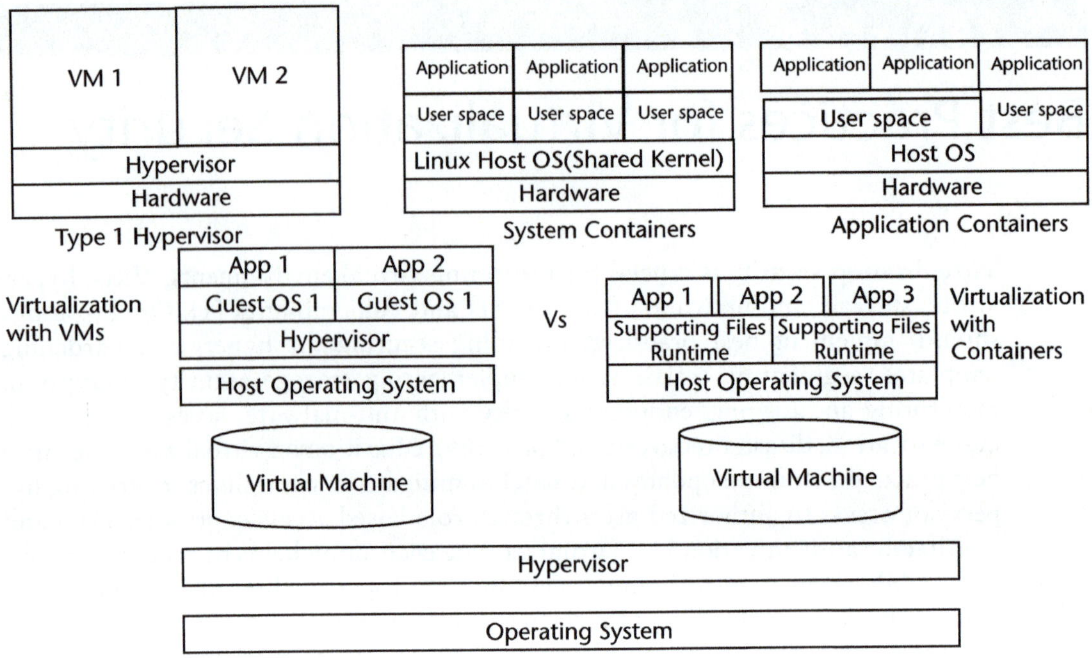

Figure 9.1 Overview of virtualized security.

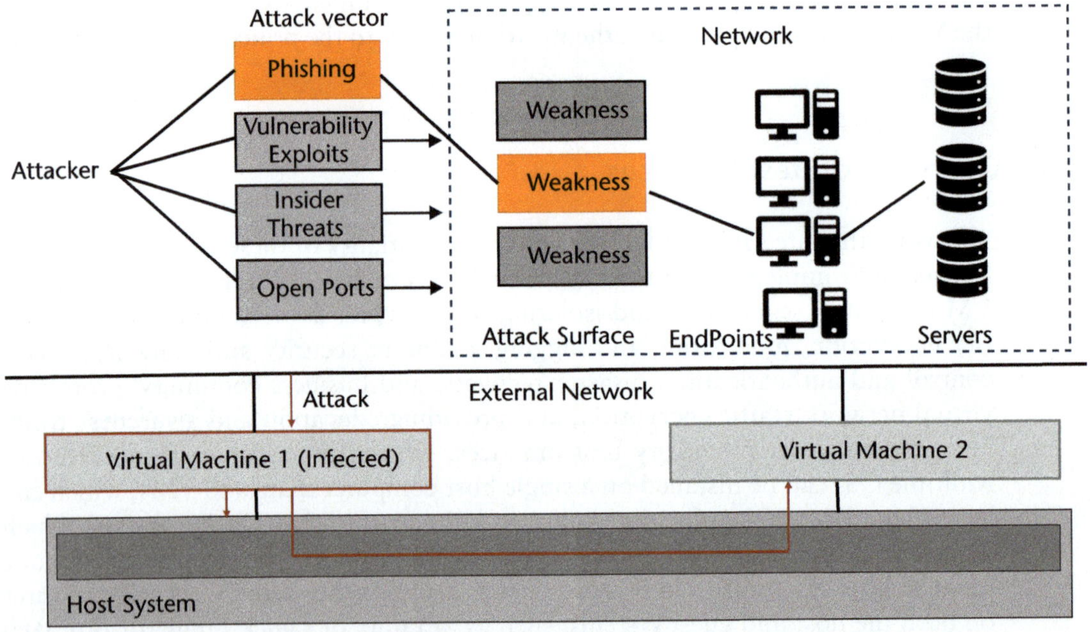

Figure 9.2 Overview of security attacks in the VM scenario.

provided by Red Hat Enterprise Linux (RHEL) 8 for VM security are always active and do not require enabling or configuration. Adhering to best practices can minimize the vulnerability of VMs and the hypervisor, ensuring a secure environment for both the host and VMs [7].

Virtualization technology provides the ability to create and run multiple VMs from a single physical server. This brings numerous benefits, including cost savings, improved scalability, and enhanced resources. However, to protect a cloud provider or organization's virtualization security from issues unique to virtualization, each of these issues must be addressed in each virtualized environment. Following best practices associated with virtualization security is vital to protect the repeatability and availability of the virtualized environment, as well as the confidentiality and integrity of the environment and data information.

Staying current with updates and patches is crucial to hypervisor security, as many attacks target unpatched hypervisors [9]. A minimal configuration disables unnecessary services and capabilities, limits access to hypervisor consoles, and restricts access to hypervisors from VMs and infrastructure components. Using VM isolation and segmentation, tasks are moved to new VMs, and they have limited interaction with one another, thereby mitigating an adversary's ability to perform lateral movement after a VM has been compromised [7]. Data encryption and protection are the process of protecting data in transit, at rest, and moving the VMs in their whole state from one host to another. We aim to prevent unauthorized access and system integrity breaches through access control and authentication, utilizing RBAC, multifactor authentication, and continuous monitoring of access within a virtualized environment [10]. Because virtualized environment behavior is prone to different vulnerabilities that attackers can exploit, other techniques such as patch management and vulnerability screening are essential for protecting virtualized infrastructure. Implementing these precautions helps to protect the system from any threats.

The hypervisor, also known as the VMM, is the primary software responsible for managing the implementation of VMs. It is crucial to protect the hypervisor as soon as virtualized resources are activated. The hypervisor acts as a bridge between the VM and the physical host. Some examples of best practices for securing the hypervisor include effective management, minimal configuration, proper segmentation, and maintaining VM isolation [6].

The best practices for task separation in distinct VMs are data segregation, network segmentation, least privilege, and discrete critical systems. Encryption technologies can be used to secure virtual and physical devices and other private data stored in VMs [11]. Secure protocols such as HTTPS, TLS, and SSH are used to encrypt communication between VMs. Migration security of VM makes sure that the migration process is encrypted for the protection of data in transit. Key management is done using a centralized, secure key management system.

Access control and authentication are crucial for preventing unauthorized access and maintaining the system's integrity [12]. The best practices include RBAC, which limits hypervisor control to administrators only, and implement multifactor authentication to access hypervisor management interfaces and perform administrative actions within the virtualized environment. The vehicular ad hoc networks (VANET) model, as shown in Figure 9.3 [13], comprises board units on vehicles and roadside units on the roadside, enabling the deployment of VANET infrastructure. Each car has sensors for collecting mapping data, which is processed by the on-board unit (OBU). The OBU then sends and receives data to other vehicles.

Virtualization security includes real-world implementation using standard industry tools for production environments:

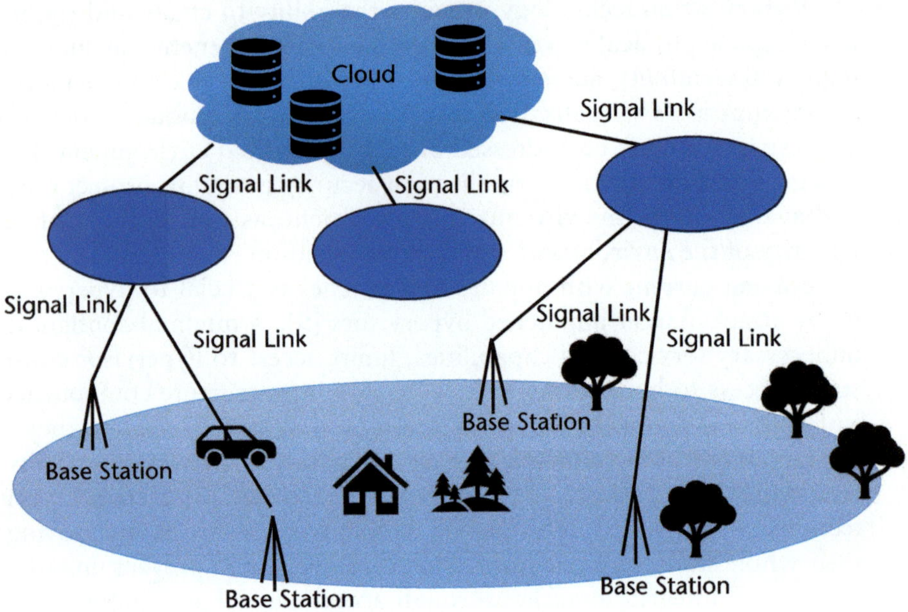

Figure 9.3 General overview of VANET in virtualized security practice.

- *Network segmentation:* Utilizing Cisco Nexus switches and 802.1Q VLAN tagging to segment traffic lanes for management, production, and storage purposes.
- *Micro-segmentation:* VMware NSX-T or Cisco ACI will provide ongoing, unambiguous policies controlling traffic between front-end, app, and database VMs.
- *Patch management:* VMware Update Manager (VUM), WSUS for Windows, apt-cron for Linux automation of patch cycle and management.
- *Centralized logging:* vCenter integration with SIEM products (Splunk, Elastic Stack, vRealize Log Insight) to analyze vCenter and ESXi logs in real time and respond quickly to troublesome situations.

Summarizing, securing the hypervisor, VM isolation, encryption, and access control is necessary to maintain the integrity of cloud and virtualized environments. After best practices are followed, organizations can enhance their security measures and protect virtualized resources from threats.

9.2 Guidelines for Implementing Best Practices

Implementing security in virtualized environments requires a structured approach to address unique vulnerabilities while ensuring compliance, performance, and scalability [14]. Key guidelines contain hypervisor, deploying secure VMs, and resource isolation. Security of the network encompasses the segmentation of networks using VLANs and software-defined networking (SDN), implementing secure communication protocols, monitoring and filtering traffic, and deploying tools for monitoring virtual network activity. Access control is critical, with RBAC and multifactor authentication required to access virtualized management consoles [15]. Data security encompasses data encryption at rest and in transit, automating backup and recovery procedures, and utilizing secure storage systems with RBACs and encryption. Automated patching is used for patch deployment, ensuring version compatibility. Centralized monitoring and incident response are achieved using tools such as SIEM for centralized logging and analysis. Anomaly detection and incident response plans are defined and tested to minimize downtime in the event of a breach [16]. Compliance and governance align with industry standards, and policy enforcement is done regularly. Audit trails are maintained to maintain logs of administrative activities for compliance verification and forensic analysis. User and administrator awareness training programs are conducted, and policy communication is clear and concise. Regular assessments are performed to identify and mitigate new risks [17].

Figure 9.4 presents an overview of the best practices for implementing a virtualized security infrastructure [18]. The layer of hypervisor security ensures that the hypervisor is protected with limited access, current patches, and a small attack surface. With isolation, to stop cross-VM attacks, implement robust VM isolation policies. In resource segmentation, give important tasks specific resources. For the security of networks, applying micro-segmentation enables more precise network controls. To examine the East-West traffic in the environment, use virtualized firewalls. Data in transit between VMs should be encrypted [19]. Give users particular roles and minimal privileges. With authentication, to access virtualized environments, use multifactor authentication.

Real-time events must be logged and probed consistently. Consistent invocation of snapshot-based backup and test recovery processes ensures that all pertinent data is encrypted during transmission and storage [20]. Stored private information should also be applied in general. Utilize endpoint security, which includes

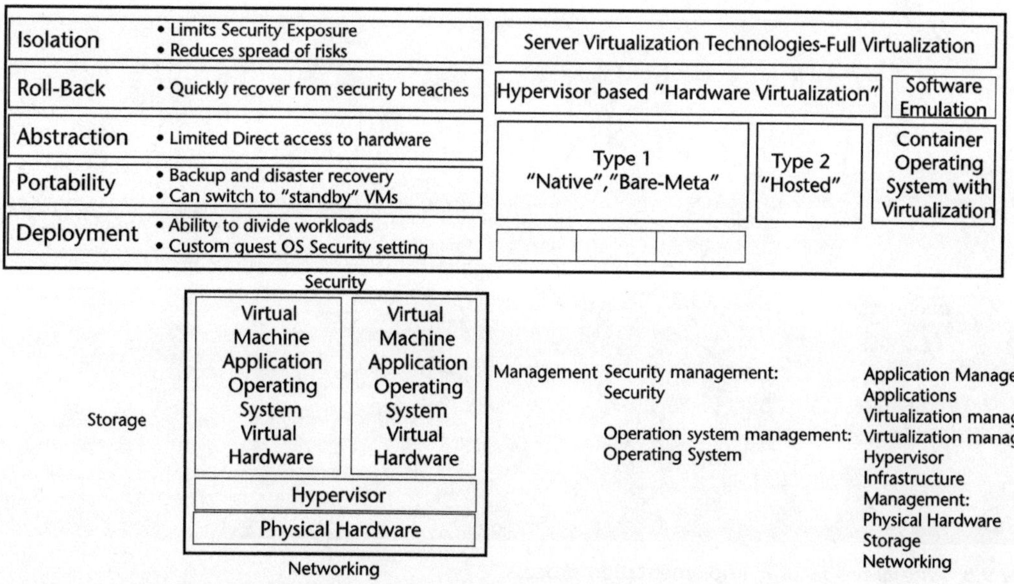

Figure 9.4 General overview for implementing best practices.

antivirus and anti-malware software, on VMs and update them regularly. A policy-driven configuration baseline strategy provides consistent VM security settings. It automates the patch updates and is monitored consistently. Utilize SIEM for continuous monitoring [21]. Use behavior-based technologies to identify anomalous activity. Ensure that you have a well-tested and documented incident response process. Comply with any applicable regulatory requirements, including GDPR, HIPAA, or PCI-DSS. Regularly review security policies and procedures to ensure that they are up-to-date and aligned with emerging threats. Train and raise awareness among administrators and users on the risks posed by virtualized environments, along with best practices through training and awareness initiatives.

The implementation process of virtualized security involves assessing and planning virtual assets, conducting risk assessments, meeting compliance requirements, defining objectives, and designing a security framework, as illustrated in Figure 9.5 [22], as well as selecting security tools, segmenting network architecture, developing a backup and recovery plan, formulating policies, implementing controls and configurations, integrating monitoring and response systems, testing and validating vulnerability assessments, conducting regular configuration audits, maintaining and updating systems through regular patching, providing periodic training for administrators and users on security protocols, reviewing and revising security policies to address new threats and technological changes, and continuously monitoring for the detection and mitigation of emerging threats [23]. The outcomes of the procedure serve as a detailed framework for security. This framework encompasses hypervisor hardening, VM security, and network protections. Maintaining secure and up-to-date virtualized environments relies on continuous monitoring, regular vulnerability assessments, backup testing, and configuration audits, among other measures. These practices ultimately contribute to a dynamic and evolving security posture.

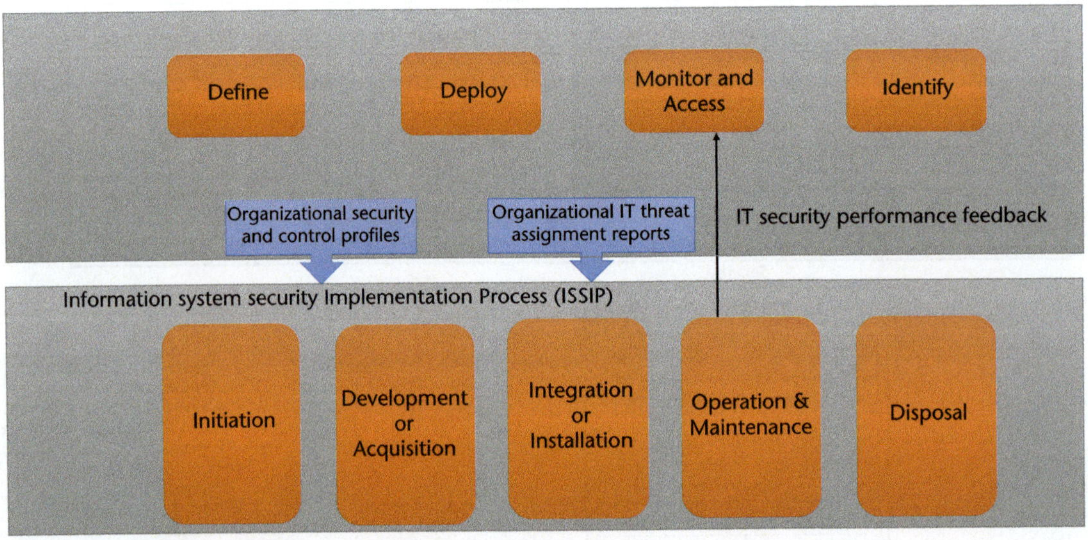

Figure 9.5 Virtualized security implementation process.

9.2.1 Security Framework Guidance

When implementing virtualization security, the target must be based on a recognized framework, such as:

- NIST SP 800-125: Security Guidelines for Virtualization Technologies;
- ISO/IEC 27001 & 27017: Information Security Controls and Cloud Specific Controls;
- DISA STIGs: Secure Configuration Checklists for Hypervisors (VMware ESXi, for example);
- CIS Benchmark: Configuration Baselines for Virtual Systems.

These standards can help you to create secure designs, ensure compliance, enforce encryption, and monitor the environment in real time to minimize attack surfaces.

9.3 Importance of Best Practices

Security for virtualization is essential for protecting VMs, hypervisors, and their constituents against security risks and weaknesses. These have several issues like poor VM separation, inter-VM attacks, and weaknesses in the hypervisor [1]. Meanwhile, they can undermine the hypervisor and lead to data theft and illegal access. Hypervisor attacks are a significant risk. Inter-VM attacks are malicious VMs interacting with one another across the same network, which can lead to unauthorized access between virtual environments and leakage of data [24]. Inadequate isolation could lead to unauthorized access between virtual environments, resulting in data leakage. It can also explore and exploit the vulnerabilities caused by misconfiguration.

Inter-VM attacks occur between malicious VMs on the same network, making them highly vulnerable to data theft and unauthorized access. This interaction can lead to unauthorized access within virtual environments and potential data leakage [25]. Insufficient isolation can result in unauthorized access between virtual environments and potential data leakage. With the increasing use of cloud-based virtualization, it is important to recognize the specific security concerns involved with cloud systems. Various methods for addressing these concerns are recommended by cloud providers. One crucial aspect of cloud security is the need to encrypt data both in transit and at rest [26].

Cloud-native security technologies from your cloud provider ensure that you are employing the best solutions and simplify the security of virtual environments. New threats and weaknesses are identified through regular policy reviews and their subsequent modifications [27].

Veeam offers a variety of ways to improve security for the virtualized environment by integrating automatic recovery testing, customer data platform (CDP), end-to-end encryption, artificial intelligence (AI)-enabled malware detection, immutable backup copies, and advanced monitoring and reporting to help to provide proactive security management with complete visibility into your virtual infrastructure [28]. By implementing these solutions, organizations can safeguard their virtual environments against both internal and external threats, thereby protecting their data and applications. VMs are not inherently more or less secure than hardware, but their added complexity can introduce specific vulnerabilities [1]. These vulnerabilities include obsolete or incorrectly configured software, inadequate isolation, or vulnerabilities that are shared through the hypervisor. However, there are benefits to virtualization, including faster provisioning and de-provisioning of secure environments, more straightforward implementation of uniform security policies, and better isolation from other VMs. Figure 9.6 shows the general overview of infrastructure security [18].

The dynamic, fluid nature of virtual environments, combined with the additional layer of the hypervisor, makes protecting virtualized resources distinct from typical IT security. Physical borders often define security perimeters, but virtualized systems are more fluid, making it more challenging to build and monitor them, as VMs can be quickly created, moved, or deleted [29]. A new attack surface is introduced by the hypervisor, raising the possibility of dangers such as hyperjacking, where an attacker takes control of the hypervisor.

Top virtualization security issues include external attacks, hypervisor attacks, sharing files between VMs and hosts, keeping snapshots of VMs, VM sprawl, malware, and security tools to protect your virtualized environment. External attacks can result in data breaches and service disruptions. While hypervisor attacks target the core element of any virtualized environment, other attacks aim to disrupt and cause reputational harm [30]. Strong access restrictions, encryption for data in transit and at rest, and routine system updates and patches to address known vulnerabilities are essential for reducing these risks.

VM escape happens when an attacker escapes a VM and communicates with the hypervisor or with other VMs on the same host [31]. This risk can be lowered

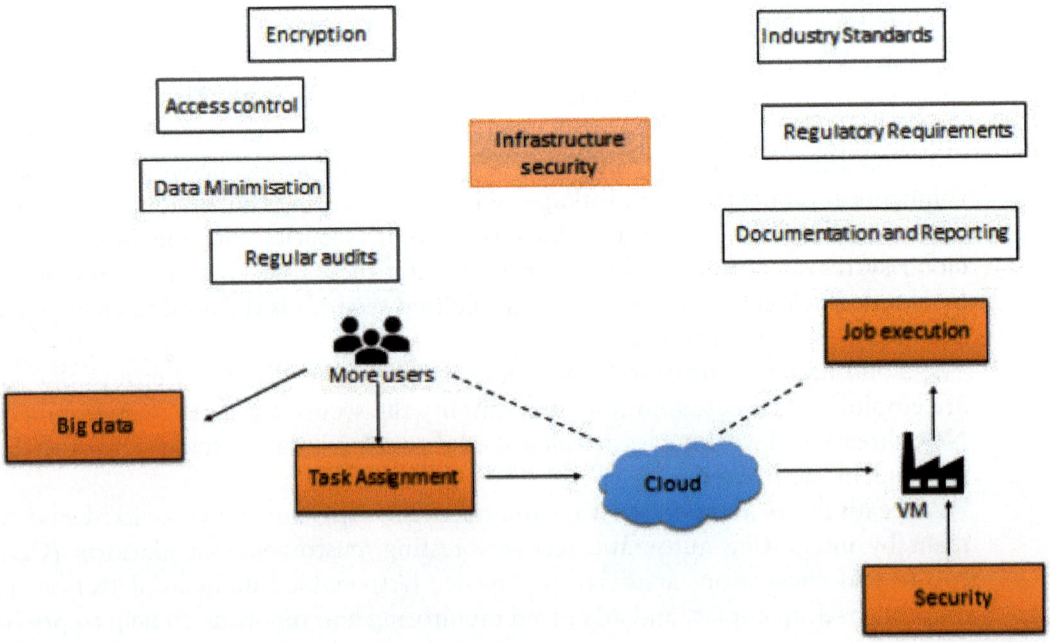

Figure 9.6 General overview of infrastructure security.

by performing an upgrade; the hypervisor and VMs must be patched, and strong isolation between VMs must be guaranteed. By conducting security evaluations and adhering to best practices for virtualization, the likelihood of VM escape occurrences can be reduced.

The hypervisor is the central constituent of any virtualized system, which targets the attacks on hypervisors that seek to seize complete control of VMs [32]. Important defenses against hypervisor attacks include using reliable computing-based and hardware-assisted virtualization, minimizing the attack surface of the hypervisor by shutting down unused services or processes, and keeping the hypervisor software updated with the most recent security patches. Because an attacker may be able to access the VM's files if they successfully gain access to the host, sharing files between hosts and VMs can also pose security problems.

Subsequently, snapshots of VMs may contain private information that hackers could use against you, and maintaining them is one of the significant security risks. Moreover, VM sprawl is the term used to describe the situation where an environment's VMs get so numerous that they become difficult to secure and administer [33]. Malware, which may infect and damage computers, is another significant threat to virtualized security. The integrity of VMs and the underlying hypervisor, antivirus, and anti-malware software, all crucial for safeguarding your virtualized environment, may be jeopardized by the detection and removal of threats.

Vulnerability management and scanning tools can perform continuous intelligence gathering on VMs, hypervisors, and associated network devices to identify publicly disclosed vulnerabilities and score risk [33]. While improving security and preventing lateral movement within the virtualized environment, firewalls and network segmentation technologies can limit and monitor traffic flow to and from VMs. Conducting real-time analysis requires a SIEM that can correlate many security alerts generated from network hardware and applications. Having tools that can identify active security threats while the application is in run time is paramount in virtualized systems.

9.4 Best Practices for Monitoring and Reporting

We examine the scope of monitoring design for an Azure Virtual Desktop workload, reviewing health and availability monitoring, performance monitoring, security monitoring, and reporting. An overview of Azure is illustrated in Figure 9.7 [34]. To start using Azure Monitor for Azure Virtual Desktop, the user must configure, at a minimum, one Log Analytics workspace, ideally dedicated to session hosts, and then enable the collection of diagnostics, performance counters, and Windows event logs data.

Azure offers multiple services, such as Azure Service Health and Azure Resource Health, to assist users in keeping informed about the health status of their cloud resources. Service Health provides views of the health for Azure services and regions, alerting users to any events that could impact their services, such as planned maintenance and service outages [35]. Health advisory notifications are provided about any effects on your Azure Virtual Desktop environment and connected subscriptions. The most proactive thing to do is to set up Service Health

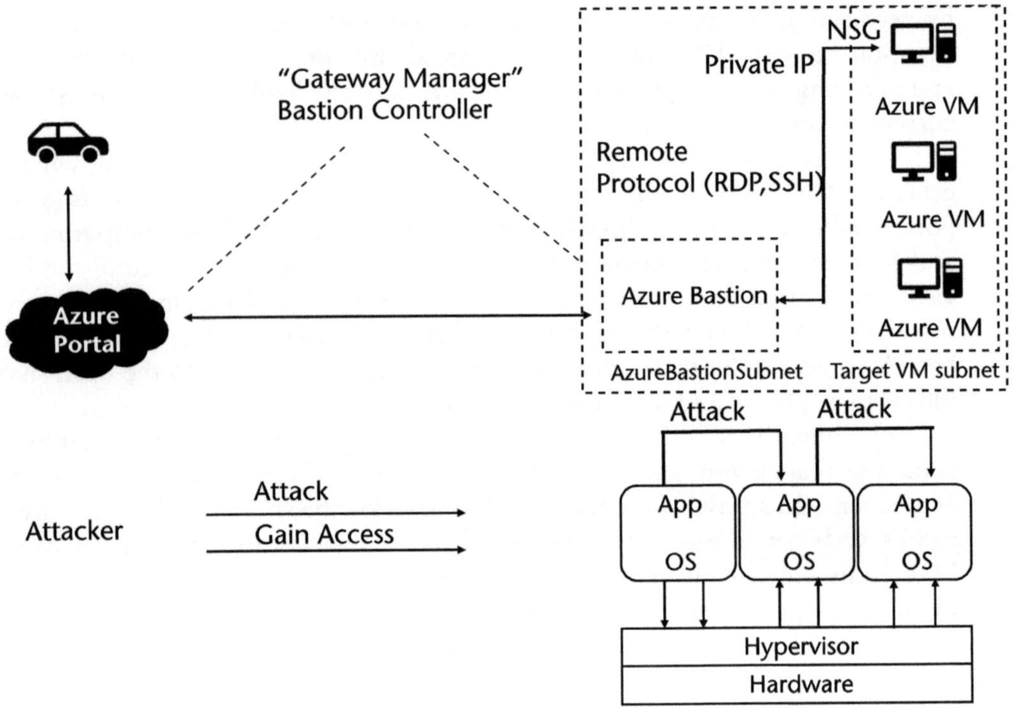

Figure 9.7 Overview of Azure best practices.

notifications so that you will be notified of planned maintenance, service problems, or other changes that might impact your Azure Virtual Desktop resources.

When service issues arise that impact your Azure resources, Resource Health helps to diagnose and obtain support [36]. It provides details about the health of your resources, both now and in the past. It is recommended that you set up proactive alerts to be informed of any unfavorable resource health conditions.

Users need essential important elements in their Azure Virtual Desktop environment to gain visibility and also gain some peace of mind regarding performance. The user can also follow the health of Azure Regional services through Service Health, to set Service Health Alerts, and Resource Health to monitor the critical components of VMs and storage solutions [37].

To achieve the key performance indicators and the required logs from Azure Virtual Desktop entities, diagnostics data should be routed to Log Analytics. This will include Azure Virtual Desktop application Group diagnostics, diagnostics data from storage, diagnostics data or host data from VMs, and additional logs submitted from a Monitor Agent or Log Analytics agent. VM Insights data can also be configured via various options [34].

Azure Virtual Desktop Insights is a dashboard based on the Monitor workbooks, designed to help users to understand Azure Virtual Desktop environments. The workbook, which configures diagnostics for the host pool and workspace, enables monitoring agents on session hosts, and configures the recommended performance counters and event logs to monitor environments, is included [38]. Azure Policy can also be used to confirm that tracking agents are installed in the VMs that support Monitor agents and Microsoft monitoring agents.

You can deploy Azure Virtual Desktop using deployment configurations and templates. You need to ensure that you are deploying diagnostic settings with your deployment configuration and that you are deploying VMs with either the Microsoft Monitoring Agent or Monitor Agent extensions. Performance counters measure how system resources are being utilized and send data to the Monitor interface after regularly defined intervals of time. Log analytics diagnostic tables can be used to query and analyze network data related to connections established from Azure Virtual Desktop [37]. The WVD Connection Network Data set includes a correlation identification that can be used to map to the specific Azure Virtual Desktop connection. The Azure Virtual Desktop network performance data provides useful performance metrics, including estimated round-trip time (in milliseconds) and estimated available bandwidth (in kilobits per second).

Windows event logs are data sources obtained on Windows VMs by Log Analytics agents [39]. It is helpful to monitor the Azure storage solution that contains FSLogix profiles or App Attach shares so that any limits that may negatively impact the user experience do not exceed a threshold. There are service limits on Azure Virtual Desktop that should be looked at during the design phase of your deployment. While these limits are substantial, monitoring them is still beneficial for larger developments, as it is easier to exceed them [34]. Diagnostic data should be configured to be sent to Log Analytics as part of improving security, and performance counters should be set up to track how system resources are being used. Event logs should be monitored not only for connection problems with the Azure Virtual Desktop agent, but also for the Azure storage solution containing FSLogix profiles or App Attach shares, and for how often the service is used, so that your workloads do not exceed the supported limits.

When addressing security in your workload, ensure that Microsoft Defender for Cloud and Microsoft Sentinel are enabled on the subscription and Azure Virtual Desktop session hosts that you deploy. You can manage vulnerabilities and compliance with commonly used standards and frameworks, such as the Payment Card Industry (PCI) and ISO 27001 [40], using Defender for Cloud. It is also a good idea to collect Microsoft Entra ID (Azure Active Directory) authentication and audit logs from your Azure Virtual Desktop session hosts and compile them in a central repository for security events involving your Azure virtual desktop hosts.

It is essential to remain compliant for Azure Virtual Desktop for the long-term health and security of your Azure Virtual Desktop delivery environment. You should continually deploy new images or utilize an update management tool to keep your environment up to date. You should run a compliance report (monthly) to keep an eye on the overall update compliance for your environment (which thereby keeps your administrator and security team apprised of the overall security compliance position of your environment) [41].

Alerts have two main purposes: to enhance operational excellence and to improve performance efficiency. To support security and performance in Azure Virtual Desktop, it is advisable to use the Monitor Alerts framework or a similar monitoring tool.

For Azure Virtual Desktop diagnostics, you should consider events and resources, including recommendations from Microsoft Defender for Cloud, VM performance metrics, critical events, service and resource health, AVD diagnostic information, as well as profile and App Attach packages.

In summary, Azure Virtual Desktop provides numerous benefits that enhance operational efficiency, security, and performance. By following these best practices, you can ensure that your workloads remain secure and effective. VANETs have received considerable attention in the past decade.

Other virtualization tools offer these types of considerations beyond Azure:

- *Integrated monitoring tools:* Utilize solutions such as vRealize Operations or Elastic Security for telemetry across layers, including VM, hypervisor, and network.
- *Scalable monitoring frameworks:* Event-driven systems provide deeper telemetry with a minimal performance footprint while tracking a live system.
- *Dynamic security assessment:* Tools need to provide detection on lateral VM traffic anomalies and privilege escalations accelerated in East-West traffic.

Advanced sensors in these cars provide assistance functions including suggestive lane changing, automatic lane tracking, front collision prevention, and partially autonomous driving [42]. In addition to offering drivers and passengers more services, these technological developments improve the driving experience. Nevertheless, ensuring safe message transmission and authentication with privacy are key issues that need to be addressed, among other challenges, for widespread VANET use. VANETs are a promising technology that enhances and increases roadway safety and improves the driving experience. With VANETs, warnings can be sent ahead of time for road construction, crashes, weather hazards, merge lane problems, speed limits, pedestrian traffic, and many other circumstances. Other options include infotainment for the driver and passengers and help with parking and toll payments, updating your navigation system, downloading music, video, and software updates. The VANET technology can assist law enforcement with tasks, such as accident investigations, accident reconstruction, and quickly locating an accident scene.

The VANET comprises OBUs located in vehicles and roadside units along the road, which together provide the necessary infrastructure for VANET implementations, as illustrated in Figure 9.8 [43]. Each vehicle is equipped with sensors that collect and receive data, that is then transmitted to the OBU. The OBU processes this information and facilitates communication with other vehicles as needed.

There are two essential types of communication in VANETs: Vehicle-to-Vehicle (V2V) communication and Vehicle-to-Infrastructure (V2I) communication. Both types can support various applications as outlined by the IEEE 802.11p specification, which offers low-latency and secure transport, as well as rapid network acquisition. The ability to handle fast and frequent handovers is also a crucial aspect of the basic functionality of VANETs. These capabilities result from the extensive work carried out by the IEEE 802.11 Task Group in standardizing communication protocols for VANETs, as highlighted in a best practice (Figure 9.9) [44].

Key management is a necessary aspect of a crucial encryption scheme that encompasses the distribution, storage, and destruction of encryption keys. Key management servers provide centralized control over keys, offering a secure repository for efficient management across multiple VMs and applications. Benefits

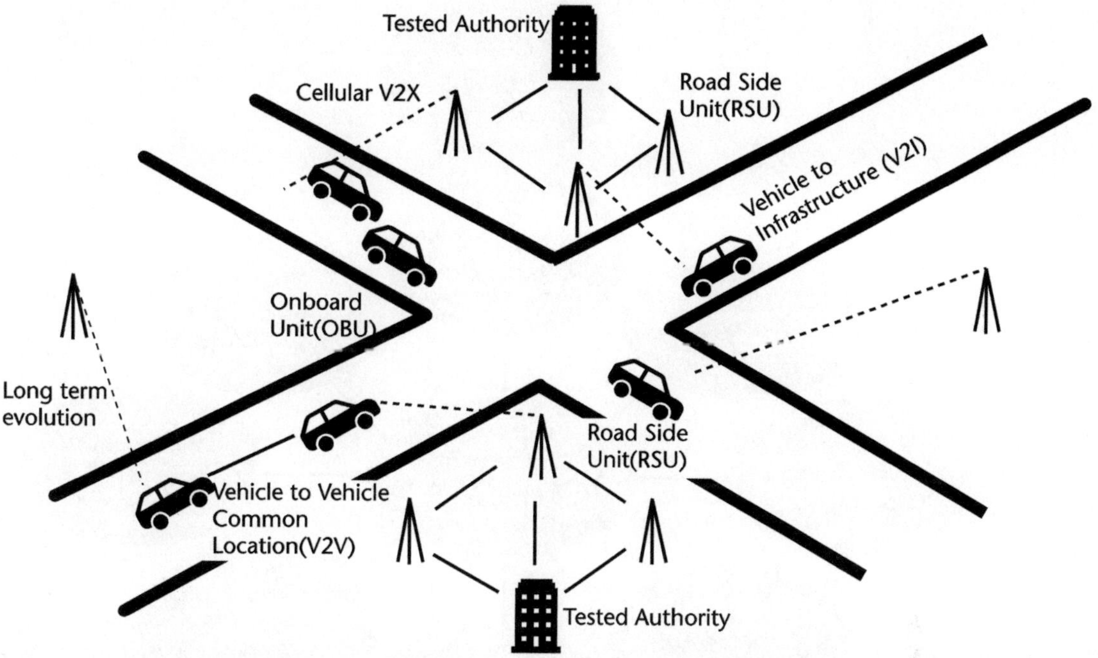

Figure 9.8 VANET.

include centralized management, automated governance, audit, and compliance with regulatory requirements.

Key management servers simplified the entire distribution life cycle by integrating platforms and infrastructure. Consistency in securing operations is provided through redundancy and backup [45]. However, disk encryption techniques such as VM encryption are required for protecting data stored in VVMs. It offers numerous stages, including protection, compliance, and proper securement of sensitive data.

Moreover, robust encryption methods such as AES are used for installation for effective encryption of the VM. Several challenges are faced in maintaining key management, resulting in data loss. However, it can be made easier by integrating VM encryption with cloud services such as Azure Key Vault and AWS key management servers.

Virtualization security is an essential aspect in every organization; therefore, best practices must be used to ensure its security, for example, patch management, vulnerability scanning, regular patching, system hardening, monitoring and logging, and incident response procedures [14]. Patch management ensures that virtual appliances, guest OSs, and hypervisors are protected from attacks.

Virtualized systems should have two components: disaster recovery and backup. An automated backup ensures that your data can be recovered in the event of a failure or corruption. In contrast, off-site backup allows backup copies to be stored off-site, protecting your data from site-specific disasters [46]. Disaster recovery testing is typically conducted to verify that backup and recovery procedures function as expected. In-depth monitoring and logging are necessary for detecting, stopping, and responding to attacks. It is essential to continually and consistently monitor your network traffic, VM activity, and hypervisor performance to help to

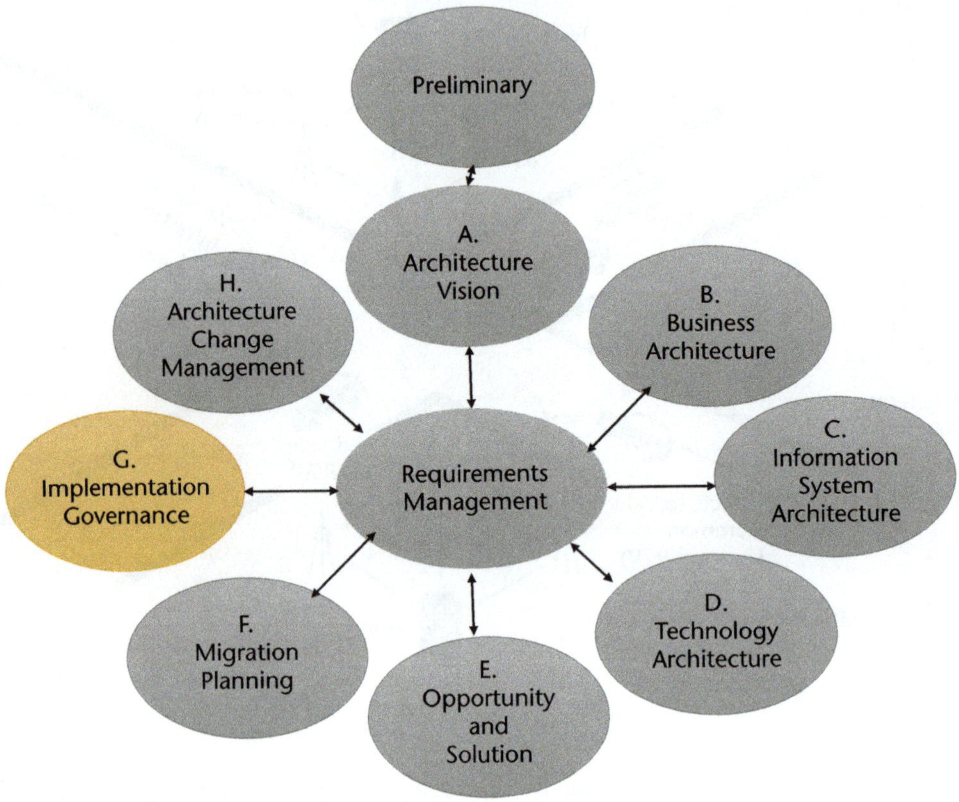

Figure 9.9 Best practices in VANET.

identify any aberrations or unauthorized access. Intrusion detection systems (IDS/IPS) can be used to monitor network traffic between virtual systems, identifying security threats such as malware, unauthorized access, or unusual communication patterns [47]. Another aspect of in-depth logging is centralized logging, such as a SIEM system, which collects and analyzes logs from the hypervisors, VMs, and virtual networks that may include configuration changes and system anomalies. Logging is determined by collecting and aggregating logs from VMs, hypervisors, and virtualized networks into the central system for analysis and auditing [48]. For detecting odd or suspicious activity, automatic alerts are generated to security staff. A security audit verifies that all security patches are implemented and comply with security rules. Various anomalies or unlawful communication between VMs or external sources are identified, and a report is generated on dashboards that provide all the data about the security posture of virtualized environments.

A few case studies related to this are briefly discussed here. The first one includes the VMware Hypervisor Security Breach [4], in which VMware vCenter Server, a popular tool for managing virtualized systems, was found to have several vulnerabilities. The security breach was caused by unpatched flaws in the vSphere client that an attacker might use to access virtualized computers without authorization. It impacts thousands of organizations around the world. Attackers may compromise hypervisors that oversee vital company resources. The security of virtualization infrastructure became a major worry as a result of the exploit. VMware urged users to update their systems by releasing essential fixes. Implementing firewalls, limiting network access to management interfaces, and enabling multifactor authentication were among the suggested measures.

The second case study reported was on the Target Corporation Security Breach [49], in which 40 million customers' credit card information and 70 million others' names, phone numbers, and email addresses were stolen by cybercriminals. Credentials taken from a third-party vendor (a heating ventilation and air conditioning (HVAC) contractor) were the initial source of the hack. The attackers used these to gain access to Target's network. Once inside, they used malware to obtain credit card information from point-of-sale systems. It resulted in a financial loss estimated at $162 million, as well as a loss of customer trust, reputational damage, and regulatory scrutiny. It targets the implemented chip-and-PIN (personal identification number) technology on payment cards, improved vendor management, and initiated a significant upgrade to its security infrastructure. The company faced several lawsuits and paid substantial settlements.

The third case study reported was the Cloud Hopper Campaign [50] in which a Chinese threat organization (APT10) was implicated in a highly skilled cyber espionage operation. Targets included managed IT service providers (MSPs) and their customers, with the intention of stealing confidential information and intellectual property. Attackers utilized phishing emails and remote access tools to breach MSPs and gain access to customer data kept on cloud servers. They gained permanent access to networks by exploiting flaws in third-party software. It impacted more than 100 businesses worldwide, including international corporations in the technology, healthcare, and defense industries. Trade secrets, confidential company information, and government data were among the stolen material. It affects businesses that were advised to strengthen their security posture by implementing stricter network monitoring procedures, enhancing cloud security, and better managing third-party vendors.

The fourth case study reported was ESXiArgs ransomware attacks [51], which involved a ransomware attack that encrypted VM files on VMware ESXi hypervisors, rendering systems unusable. It spread by enabling attackers to remotely execute malicious payloads due to flaws in the ESXi software. The attackers exploited VMware ESXi vulnerabilities, specifically CVE-2021-21974, a critical weakness in the vSphere Client (HTML5) that enabled remote code execution. Once inside, the attackers encrypted VMs using the ESXiArgs ransomware. Organizations that relied on ESXi-based infrastructures encountered operational issues due to the ransomware. Companies across various industries, from startups to established organizations, were affected. To address the vulnerabilities, VMware provided fixes. To mitigate the impact of ransomware, businesses were advised to promptly update to the latest versions of VMware ESXi and establish robust backup and disaster recovery protocols.

The fifth case study reported, the Capital One data breach [52], involved a former employee of AWS who used a vulnerability within Capital One's systems to obtain personally identifiable information for 106 million customers in the United States and Canada. These records exposed sensitive information, including names, addresses, credit scores, and Social Security numbers. A Social Security vulnerability was a misconfigured firewall that allowed an attacker to exploit an AWS functionality (AWS's metadata service) to gain unauthorized access to data that existed in the cloud. Additionally, data associated with approximately 106 million people was also compromised. Capital One received an $80 million fine from the US Treasury for failing to appropriately safeguard customer data. Capital One provided free credit monitoring and quickly informed those who were impacted. The company significantly bolstered its cloud security and vulnerability management practices, emphasizing stricter security controls and ongoing risk assessments.

The key findings from the case studies venture into several major themes:

- *Supply chain vulnerabilities:* Several of the incidents (Target and Cloud Hopper) were caused by loose systems at third-party vendors that allowed things such as poor procedures and employee overexposure of systems.
- *Value of patching:* This key theme is the timely patching of known vulnerabilities (i.e., VMware ESXiArgs, Capital One).
- *Cloud security issues:* The importance of robust cloud security processes and procedures is underscored by several high-profile breaches (Cloud Hopper, Capital One).
- *Advanced persistent threats:* The complicated breaches (Cloud Hopper) in other cases involved multiple nation-states seeking access to government data and priceless intellectual property.

The malware ESXiArgs highlights that malware targeting virtualized systems is becoming a growing threat. The case studies illustrate various attack vectors, including the exploitation of software vulnerabilities, misconfigurations, and phishing. These studies demonstrate the necessity of securing the entire IT ecosystem, encompassing internal systems, third-party providers, and cloud infrastructures.

9.4.1 Technical Case Studies

Case Study: FortiGate-VM Firewall in a SaaS Business

A technology business on AWS deployed FortiGate-VM instances in all its VPCs. They enabled deep SSL inspection, intrusion prevention, and log aggregation to Splunk Cloud. As a result, they prevented malicious IPs from launching SSH port scans. They were able to defend against these types of attacks by employing a proactive defense model. This picture helped to mitigate multitenant workloads.

Case Study: Micro-Segmentation in Banking

A large bank leveraged the VMware NSX-T Distributed Firewall to ensure that zero trust policies were enforced. The product even enabled the bank to review its environment in the event of a ransomware attack. Lateral movement between compromised and noncompromised VMs was blocked, which proved the value of micro-segmentation as a defense-in-depth strategy.

9.5 Summary

Virtualized security is widely used to protect secured different applications. In this chapter, we summarized the overview of best practices that should be used to provide a secure environment, as well as guidelines for implementing these best practices. These best practices enhance the security measures that protect the virtualized environment from attacks. A systematic strategy was discussed that is used to address vulnerabilities, strengthen and enhance compliance, and improve performance in virtualized security environments. Moreover, the importance of best practices was also discussed to represent the effectiveness of best practices in virtualized security, which various organizations widely adopt. It is necessary to protect VMs, hypervisors, and their parts from threats and vulnerabilities such as inter-VM assaults, hypervisor attacks, and insufficient VM isolation. To mitigate these risks, it is recommended to implement robust access controls, regular updates, and various security tools, such as Veeam Data Platform.

Furthermore, this chapter discussed the monitoring, auditing, and reporting of best practices in virtualized environments, enabling us to track and continuously improve the best practices as well as the process and system to adopt in an agile environment. Securing virtualized environments requires a blend of advanced monitoring systems, mandatory access controls, trusted computing technologies, and comprehensive security frameworks that incorporate both technical and organizational measures. Real-world examples, such as micro-segmentation, hypervisor hardening, and SIEM in real time, demonstrate methods from best practices that can successfully deter attacks across various sectors, including healthcare, finance, and cloud service providers.

Aligning security with global standards, such as NIST SP 800-125, ISO/IEC 27001, and CIS Benchmark, helps organizations build resilience, compliance, and reduce their attack surface in virtualized infrastructures. Virtualization can introduce risks such as VM escape, hypervisor attacks, and lateral movement, hence the requirement for layered defenses, continuous monitoring, and policy-based access control to ensure that integrity and availability are still intact. Establishing and executing regular patch management, network segmentation, and SIEM-driven logging allow for enabled detection and alerting on sequences, providing visibility into the complex virtual ecosystems.

References

[1] Compastié, M., et al., "From Virtualization Security Issues to Cloud Protection Opportunities: An In-Depth Analysis of System Virtualization Models," *Computers & Security*, Vol. 97, October 1, 2020, p. 101905.

[2] Lekkala, S., and P. Gurijala, "Endpoint and Mobile Security Imperatives," in *Security and Privacy for Modern Networks: Strategies and Insights for Safeguarding Digital Infrastructures*, Berkeley, CA: Apress, 2024, pp. 155–165.

[3] Vasani, V., et al., "Comprehensive Analysis of Advanced Techniques and Vital Tools for Detecting Malware Intrusion," *Electronics*, Vol. 12, No. 20, October 17, 2023, p. 4299.

[4] Sharma, S., D. L. Kumar, and E. A. Vijay, "Introduction to Virtualization, Security and Cloud Security," in *Machine Learning Hybridization and Optimization for Intelligent Applications*, Boca Raton, FL: CRC Press, 2025, pp. 108–126.

[5] Aslan, Ö., et al., "A Comprehensive Review of Cyber Security Vulnerabilities, Threats, Attacks, and Solutions," *Electronics*, Vol. 12, No. 6, March 11, 2023, p. 1333.

[6] Thyagaturu, A. S., et al., "Operating Systems and Hypervisors for Network Functions: A Survey of Enabling Technologies and Research Studies," *IEEE Access*, Vol. 10, July 29, 2022, pp. 79825–79873.

[7] Gurrala, R. R., T. S. Kumar, and K. Anuradha, "Virtual Machine Security Issues and Solutions When It Is in Host," *2024 10th International Conference on Advanced Computing and Communication Systems (ICACCS)*, Vol. 1, March 14, 2024, pp. 441–449.

[8] Sharma, V. K., et al., "Introduction to Virtualization in Cloud Computing," in *Machine Learning and Optimization Models for Optimization in Cloud*, London, UK: Chapman and Hall/CRC, 2022, pp. 1–14.

[9] Ngoc, T. D., et al., "Mitigating Vulnerability Windows with Hypervisor Transplant," *Proceedings of the Sixteenth European Conference on Computer Systems*, April 21, 2021, pp. 162–177.

[10] Anirudh, U. N., and S. S. Darshan, "Role-Based Virtuosity in Virtual Environments: A Technical Exploration of Access Control and Authentication Mechanisms," in *Cloud Security,* London, UK: Chapman and Hall/CRC, 2024, pp. 183–196.

[11] Seth, B., et al., "Integrating Encryption Techniques for Secure Data Storage in the Cloud," *Transactions on Emerging Telecommunications Technologies*, Vol. 33, No. 4, April 2022, p. e4108.

[12] Qiu, J., et al., "A Survey on Access Control in the Age of Internet of Things," *IEEE Internet of Things Journal*, Vol. 7, No. 6, January 24, 2020, pp. 4682–4696.

[13] Sharma, S., et al., "A Detailed Tutorial Survey on VANETs: Emerging Architectures, Applications, Security Issues, and Solutions," *International Journal of Communication Systems*, Vol. 34, No. 14, September 25, 2021, p. e4905.

[14] Cunha, J., et al., "Enhancing Network Slicing Security: Machine Learning, Software-Defined Networking, and Network Functions Virtualization-Driven Strategies," *Future Internet*, Vol. 16, No. 7, June 27, 2024, p. 226.

[15] Bhuiyan, Z. A., et al., "On the (In) Security of the Control Plane of SDN Architecture: A Survey," *IEEE Access*, August 22, 2023.

[16] Al-Dahasi, E., and F. A. Khan, "Automating Security Incident Response in SCADA Systems Through SIEM-ML Integration," *2024 29th International Conference on Automation and Computing (ICAC)*, August 28, 2024, pp. 1–10.

[17] Landoll, D., *The Security Risk Assessment Handbook: A Complete Guide for Performing Security Risk Assessments*, Boca Raton, FL: CRC Press, 2021.

[18] Chowdhury, N., and V. Gkioulos, "Cyber Security Training for Critical Infrastructure Protection: A Literature Review," *Computer Science Review*, Vol. 40, May 1, 2021, p. 100361.

[19] Benamrane, F., and R. Benaini, "An East-West Interface for Distributed SDN Control Plane: Implementation and Evaluation," *Computers & Electrical Engineering*, Vol. 57, January 1, 2017, pp. 162–175.

[20] Guptha, A., H. Murali, and T. Subbulakshmi, "A Comparative Analysis of Security Services in Major Cloud Service Providers," *2021 5th International Conference on Intelligent Computing and Control Systems (ICICCS)*, May 6, 2021, pp. 129–136.

[21] Gnatyuk, S., et al., "Software System for Cybersecurity Events Correlation and Incident Management in Critical Infrastructure," in *Data-Centric Business and Applications: Advancements in Information and Knowledge Management, Volume 1*, Cham: Springer Nature Switzerland, 2024, pp. 247–269.

[22] Wang, X., et al., "Design and Implementation of SecPod, a Framework for Virtualization-Based Security Systems," *IEEE Transactions on Dependable and Secure Computing*, Vol. 16, No. 1, March 2, 2017, pp. 44–57.

[23] Edwards, D. J., "Vulnerability Assessment and Penetration Testing," in *Mastering Cybersecurity: Strategies, Technologies, and Best Practices*, Berkeley, CA: Apress, 2024, pp. 371–412.

[24] Benzidane, K., S. Khoudali, and A. Sekkaki, "Secured Architecture for Inter-VM Traffic in a Cloud Environment," *2nd IEEE Latin American Conference on Cloud Computing and Communications*, December 9, 2013, pp. 23–28.

[25] Saeed, A., P. Garraghan, and S. A. Hussain, "Cross-VM Network Channel Attacks and Countermeasures Within Cloud Computing Environments," *IEEE Transactions on Dependable and Secure Computing*, Vol. 19, No. 3, November 10, 2020, pp. 1783–1794.

[26] Singh, A., and K. Chatterjee, "Cloud Security Issues and Challenges: A Survey," *Journal of Network and Computer Applications*, Vol. 79, February 1, 2017, pp. 88–115.

[27] Falk, T., C. Rollenhagen, and B. Wahlström, "Challenges in Performing Technical Safety Reviews of Modifications–A Case Study," *Safety Science*, Vol. 50, No. 7, August 1, 2012, pp. 1558–1568.

[28] Patrão, L., "vSphere Backup and Disaster Recovery," in *VMware vSphere Essentials: A Practical Approach to vSphere Deployment and Management*, Berkeley, CA: Apress, 2024, pp. 631–641.

[29] Zolfaghari, R., and A. M. Rahmani, "Virtual Machine Consolidation in Cloud Computing Systems: Challenges and Future Trends," *Wireless Personal Communications*, Vol. 115, No. 3, December 2020, pp. 2289–2326.

[30] Butt, U. A., et al., "Cloud Security Threats and Solutions: A Survey," *Wireless Personal Communications*, Vol. 128, No. 1, January 2023, pp. 387–413.

[31] Sierra-Arriaga, F., R. Branco, and B. Lee, "Security Issues and Challenges for Virtualization Technologies," *ACM Computing Surveys (CSUR)*, Vol. 53, No. 2, May 17, 2020, pp. 1–37.

[32] Anumukonda, N. S., and R. K. Yadav, "Detection of Suspicious Activities at Hypervisor in Cloud Computing: A Brief Study," *International Conference on Intelligent Systems Design and Applications*, December 11, 2023, pp. 72–85.

[33] Rishiwal, V., et al., "Blockchain-Secure Gaming Environments: A Comprehensive Survey," *IEEE Access*, December 2, 2024.

[34] Soh, J., et al., "Overview of Azure Infrastructure as a Service (IaaS) Services," in *Microsoft Azure: Planning, Deploying, and Managing the Cloud*, Apress, 2020, pp. 21–41.

[35] Murthy, J. S., "Decoding the Cloud: A Comprehensive Exploration of Data Loss Scenarios, Resilient Storage Architectures, and Advanced Backup Strategies in Cloud Environments," in *Cloud Security*, London, UK: Chapman and Hall/CRC, 2024, pp. 52–75.

[36] Zaki, J., et al., "Introducing Cloud-Assisted Micro-Service-Based Software Development Framework for Healthcare Systems," *IEEE Access*, Vol. 10, March 22, 2022, pp. 33332–33348.

[37] Udayakumar, P., and D. R. Anandan, "Design and Deploy Azure IoT Security," in *Design and Deploy IoT Network & Security with Microsoft Azure: Embrace Microsoft Azure for IoT Network Enhancement and Security Uplift*, Berkeley, CA: Apress, 2024, pp. 319–418.

[38] Darr, S., "Monitor and Maintain an Azure Virtual Desktop Infrastructure," in *Azure Virtual Desktop Specialist: Exam Study Guide-AZ-140*, Berkeley, CA: Apress, 2022, pp. 213–256.

[39] Suvarna, S. A., "Live Monitoring of Malware Attacks on Cloud Using Windows Agent-Based Solution," in *Implementing Enterprise Cyber Security with Open-Source Software and Standard Architecture: Volume II*, Gistrup, Denmark: River Publishers, 2023, pp. 115–132.

[40] Cochran, K. A., "Securing the Cloud: A Comprehensive Guide to Cloud Security," in *Cybersecurity Essentials: Practical Tools for Today's Digital Defenders*, Berkeley, CA: Apress, 2024, pp. 327–363.

[41] Manzoor, J., et al., "Cybersecurity on a Budget: Evaluating Security and Performance of Open-Source SIEM Solutions for SMEs," *PLOS One*, Vol. 19, No. 3, March 28, 2024, p. e0301183.

[42] Sheikh, M. S., J. Liang, and W. Wang, "Security and Privacy in Vehicular Ad Hoc Network and Vehicle Cloud Computing: A Survey," *Wireless Communications and Mobile Computing*, Vol. 2020, No. 1, 2020, p. 5129620.

[43] Abdulkadhim, F. G., et al., "Optimizing the Roadside Unit Deployment Mechanism in VANET with Efficient Protocol to Prevent Data Loss," *Wireless Personal Communications*, Vol. 127, No. 1, November 2022, pp. 815–843.

[44] Mahi, M. J., et al., "A Review on VANET Research: Perspective of Recent Emerging Technologies," *IEEE Access*, Vol. 10, June 16, 2022, pp. 65760–65783.

[45] Somasekaram, P., R. Calinescu, and R. Buyya, "High-Availability Clusters: A Taxonomy, Survey, and Future Directions," *Journal of Systems and Software*, Vol. 187, May 1, 2022, p. 111208.

[46] Ramesh, G., J. Logeshwaran, and V. Aravindarajan, "A Secured Database Monitoring Method to Improve Data Backup and Recovery Operations in Cloud Computing," *BOHR International Journal of Computer Science*, Vol. 2, No. 1, 2022, pp. 1–7.

[47] Hassan, S. K., and A. Ibrahim, "The Role of Artificial Intelligence in Cyber Security and Incident Response," *International Journal for Electronic Crime Investigation*, Vol. 7, No. 2, July 3, 2023.

[48] Hongkamnerd, W., et al., "Effects of SIEM Recovery Time: Case Study on Security Onion," *2024 21st International Conference on Electrical Engineering/Electronics, Computer, Telecommunications and Information Technology (ECTI-CON)*, May 27, 2024, pp. 1–6.

[49] Tai, X., and H. Zhang, "Target Corporation," in *Information Technology Security and Risk Management*, Boca Raton, FL: CRC Press, 2024, pp. 11–17.

[50] Miadzvetskaya, Y., "EU Sanctions in Response to Cyber-Attacks as Crime-Based Emergency Measures," *Computer Law & Security Review*, Vol. 54, September 1, 2024, p. 106010.

[51] Malatji, M., "Cybersecurity Alerts and Advisories: Leveraging Artificial Intelligence to Secure Digital Assets," *2024 IEEE Technology and Engineering Management Society (TEMSCON LATAM)*, July 18, 2024, pp. 1–7.

[52] Naseema, N., S. Akhtar, and A. A. Al Hinai, "Disrupting Financial Services: A Case Study on Capital One's Fintech Odyssey," in *Harnessing Blockchain-Digital Twin Fusion for Sustainable Investments*, Hershey, PA: IGI Global, 2024, pp. 363–383.

CHAPTER 10

Emerging Trends in Virtualization Security

The ubiquitous technology can be used to enhance lives in modern world. It dynamically changes the emerging trends in information and communication technology [1]. Adoption and updating to stay with these trends are successful in the competitive global market. The virtualized security is an evolving field driven by the increasing adoption of virtualized environments, cloud computing, and hybrid infrastructures [2]. As organizations continue to virtualize more workloads, the attack surface grows, prompting the need for innovative and adaptive security solutions. One way for users and apps to share physical resources in contemporary clouds is through virtualization. It improves process reliability and fault tolerance by combining underutilized machines into a single system, maximizing data center resources [3]. Full virtualizations and para-virtualizations are two categories of conventional virtualization. Full virtualization enables the operation of multiple guest OSs on a single platform by generating virtual versions of the hardware resources such as processors and servers. Para-virtualizations give commands to the host OS directly and run guest applications in separate domains [4]. Container-based virtualization, sometimes called visualization or containerization, can boost data center utilization while lowering the resource overheads associated with conventional virtualization. This resource management solution is a well-liked substitute for hypervisor-based virtualization since it is economical, scalable, and effective [5].

10.1 Overview of Emerging Trends (Containers and Micro-Services)

Although computers have been around for a while, new projects and technologies are being developed daily. It is crucial to watch new trends to comprehend current advancements and technologies [6]. These are cutting-edge technologies that become more well-liked and create new user trends. Emerging trends that will significantly affect the digital economy and interactions in digital societies will be examined in this chapter. Some trends may persist and draw user attention, while others may eventually fade.

The complexity of monoliths is decreased by the architecture that facilitates containerization. It features lightweight, more adaptable distributed systems with carefully analyzed independent services for communication, such as remote procedure call (RPC), TCP, or HTTP [7]. Containerization has grown in popularity in industrial applications due to its cross-platform compatibility, portability restrictions, and efficient orchestration and management tools. However, problems such as poorer container isolation techniques, no persistent storage, and support for various clouds limit its widespread use in industrial operations [8]. A Linux host is required for containerization, and moving containers from one OS family to another is more difficult than moving VMs. Because there is no native support for Dockerization on macOS, it is challenging.

Workloads can be decreased by sharing containers across several tasks, but security breaches are more likely. Regular security updates are essential for containerization to remain successful in industrial applications [9]. To keep it moving forward in the industrial sector, it is crucial to examine its advantages and disadvantages and deal with these problems.

10.1.1 Container and Kubernetes Security

Because of technological advancements and cyberthreats, the virtualization landscape is evolving. Containers and micro-services are crucial for creating and implementing modern applications because they ensure consistency across different contexts. However, there are additional security dangers associated with this technology [10]. Sharing the host OS kernel across containers could be a security risk if isolation techniques are ineffective. A container escape occurs when an attacker gains access to the host OS by using a compromised container. Additionally, base images rely on vulnerabilities if they are not updated and inspected on a regular basis. The micro-services architecture divides applications into smaller, modular services, which requires secure communication channels between containers to prevent unauthorized access and data interception [11]. Although these technologies increase scalability and agility, they present new security risks.

Although containers are frequently used in virtualization, there are special security issues because of their transient nature and dependence on shared resources [12] with adoption of frameworks for different container security. It enables applications to run consistently across different computing environments. Containers are more resource-efficient than traditional VMs because they share the same OS kernel. The container security necessitates both ongoing monitoring and preventative actions. Using reliable sources for container images, routinely checking them for vulnerabilities, and quickly installing updates are all best practices [13]. Runtime security tools monitor container behavior and instantly identify any irregularities. Network policies that are defined and enforced regulate container traffic and reduce exposure to possible dangers restricting access to platforms for container orchestration and managing permissions with RBAC. The Kubernetes is an open-source, portable, and extensible platform that makes declarative configuration and automation easier for containerized workloads and services [14]. It has a vast ecosystem that is expanding quickly. Kubernetes tools, services, and support are widely accessible. Containers can have associated different risks, such as vulnerable container images, insecure configurations, and untrusted networks. They require strong isolation mechanisms, proper access controls, and image scanning [12].

10.1.2 Micro-Services

Small autonomous services that carry out a distinct task are known as micro-services, as shown in Figure 10.1 [15]. Using lightweight application programming interfaces (APIs), these services exchange information. Because they are independent, teams can focus on the service of which they are in charge without affecting the application as a whole. In addition to the programming language used, each micro-service may have different data storage options.

Access requests from outside users and other services are managed by micro-service application security. An Open Policy Agent (OPA) or other sidecar authorization engine can handle all access control requests [16]. To manage client requests from the outside, applications may also have a monolithic API gateway that spans the whole micro-service layer.

10.1.3 Micro-Service Security

As shown in Figure 10.2, we can identify two security levels that must be implemented in a typical micro-services-based application [17]. Implement interservice communication through a messaging platform. Thus, East-West traffic security is implemented between the micro-service and the messaging platform. Security must be implemented at the micro-services layer if such a messaging platform is unavailable.

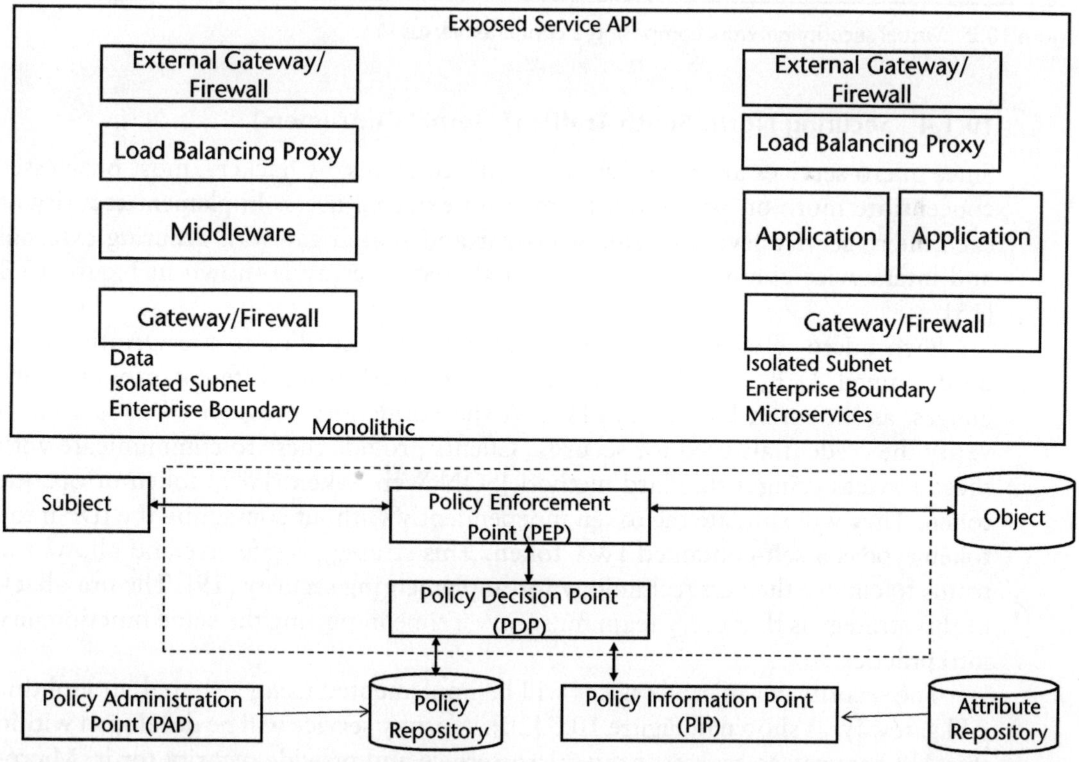

Figure 10.1 Securing application using micro-services.

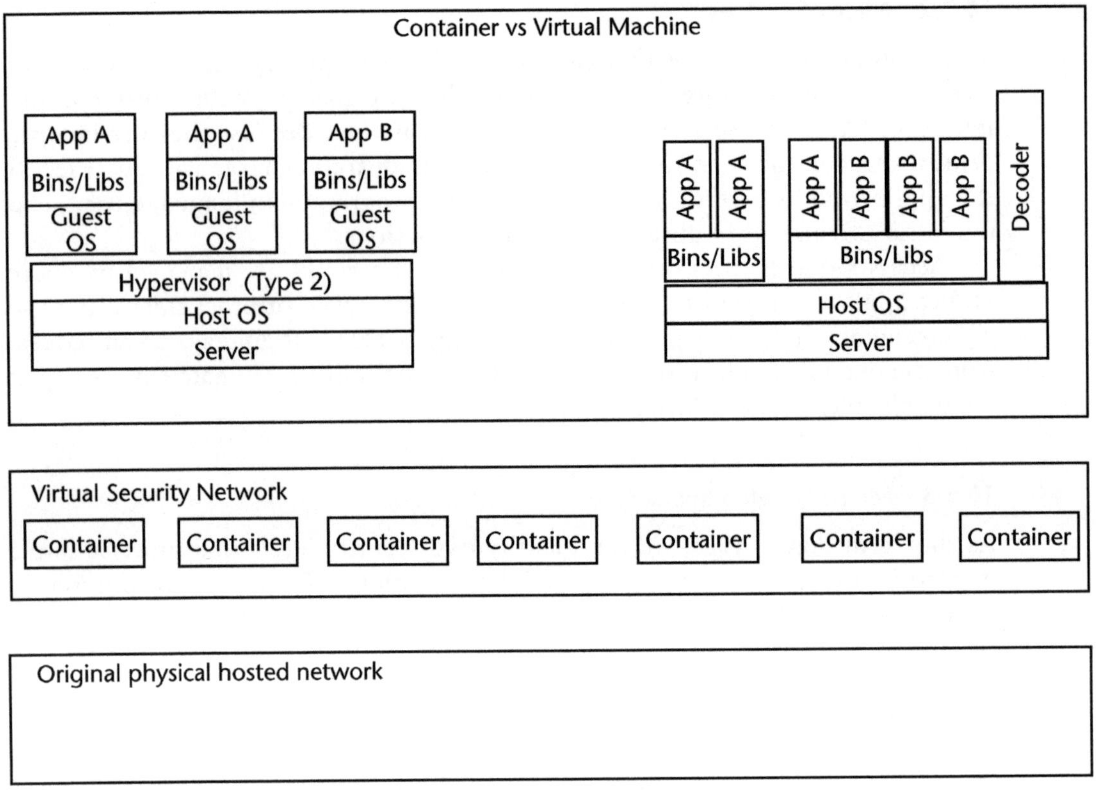

Figure 10.2 Virtual security network comprising a container versus VM.

10.1.4 Securing North-South Traffic (External Consumers)

Since micro-services are the most vulnerable to attack by hackers, most businesses concentrate more on protecting them from external users. Implement security at each micro-service level by using a sidecar and shared gateway. Securing external and interservice communication using a shared gateway is shown in Figure 10.3 [18].

Each micro-service has security implemented according to the OAuth2 standard, named A, B, and C. These are implemented using different program languages, as shown in Figure 10.3 [16]. A shared identity provider (IDP) is used to verify the credentials used for security. Clients provide these to communicate with these services using a standard method JSON Web Token (JWT) token or opaque token. They will validate the token independently without contacting the IDP if the token type is a self-contained JWT token. This strategy is effective and allows the teams to choose the best technology for implementing security [19]. The drawback of this strategy is that every team must invest time in putting the same functionality into practice.

The security for micro-services will be implemented using a shared, monolithic API gateway, as shown in Figure 10.3 [20]. A proxy service will be developed within this API gateway to represent the micro-service and provide security for it. Micro-services do not need to be touched if security configurations need to be changed. This method has the disadvantage of adding a monolithic element to the overall architecture. According to the token or authentication method used to implement

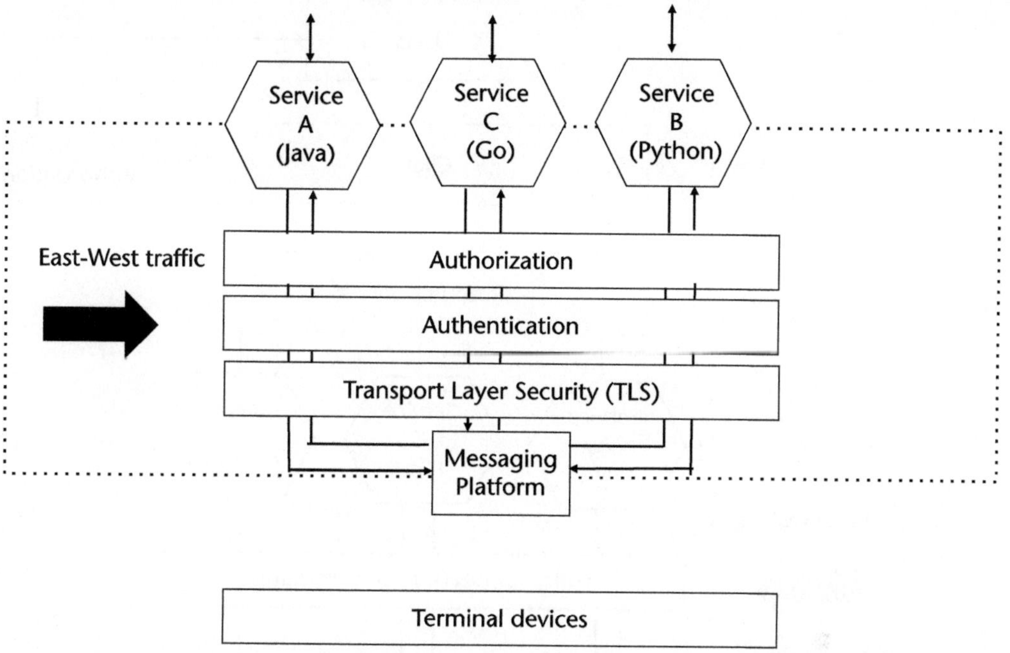

Figure 10.3 Securing external and inter-service communication using a shared gateway.

security, the API gateway will speak with the IDP to verify the client's credentials. With this architecture, there are more secure methods where OAuth 2.0-based security is used to protect both the API gateway and individual micro-services [21]. In this case, the API gateway can verify the client request and produce the necessary tokens following back-end authentication, or if the token is legitimate for backend authentication, it can send it straight to the back end.

10.1.5 Securing Traffic Going East-West

Securing interservice communication, or communication between micro-services, is the next security stage, as shown in Figure 10.4 [22]. As stated at the outset, we are decoupling interservice communication using a messaging platform to improve the overall architecture. Let's examine how interservice communication security can be implemented in a micro-services architecture.

This is the least secure method when communication is enabled using SSL between the micro-service and the messaging platform. We can employ this strategy if the micro-service and the messaging platform are located within a secured LAN. This idea is illustrated in Figure 10.4 [23]. The micro-services will use TLS to communicate with the messaging platform, which will be signed and encrypted in transit, as shown in Figure 10.4. The highest level of security offered by this method is that no third party can access the data. The messaging platform (such as Kafka or NATS) will communicate between the services. Implementing authentication for communication between the micro-services and the messaging platform is an option if the prior method is insufficiently secure for organization [16]. As a result, only micro-services with legitimate credentials can interact with the messaging platform and, eventually, with other micro-services. To offer enhanced security,

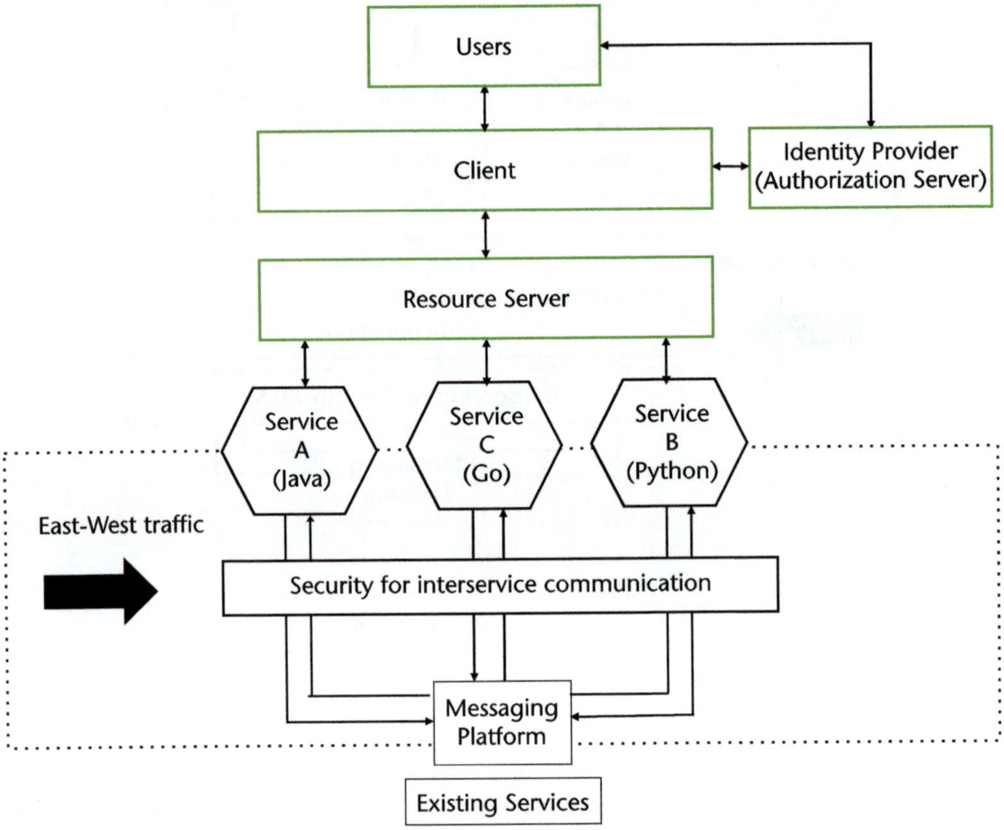

Figure 10.4 Securing interservice communication through TLS and MLS.

micro-services are given the credentials to verify their communication with the messaging platform, as shown in Figure 10.4. The messaging platform will determine whether to use a mechanism such as token-based methods or basic authentication [24].

An authorization scheme specifies which micro-services can access others. Channels provide the most secure method for interservice communication. Figure 10.4 illustrates this concept [25].

Micro-services are outfitted with credentials that contain the service's identity and the right to retrieve information from other services using this method. Users can manage access with wildcard subscriptions on a messaging platform such as NATS, which allows users to restrict who can access what. This is the most secure interservice communication system that we can put in place [26]. An emerging trend in cloud and virtualization security is confidential computing, which protects the data in use. Traditional security mechanisms provide data at rest and data in transit security; however, data processing in memory is not secured [27]. Using specialized hardware-based technologies such as trusted execution environments (TEEs), confidential computing bridges this gap by protecting data in use.

Enhancing data security in virtualized environments involves sensitive data processing in shared environments, such as cloud platforms, within which several VMs use the same physical hardware [28]. With confidential computing, sensitive workloads running in VMs, or containers, are isolated so that they are invisible to malicious insiders, such as a cloud administrator, or an external attacker. TEEs such as Intel Software Guard Extensions (SGX) or AMD Secure Encrypted Virtualization (SEV), create an isolated execution environment in hardware. Such environments guarantee that data and code in the TEE are not accessible to the OS, the hypervisor, or other VMs even in case of a breach. Protecting multitenant architectures typically employs multitenant architectures, where many customers and/or applications may share physical resources. Data is encrypted during processing, reducing the attack surface, thereby minimizing the risk on the data leakage between tenants under confidential computing. Addressing insider threats administrators with elevated privileges are especially present for virtualized infrastructures, particularly for the public cloud. With confidential computing, data is encrypted while compute means that administrators cannot access sensitive information even if they have full control over the infrastructure. Integrating virtualization security tools with this secure isolation, the existing virtualization security practices such as encryption, RBAC, and container isolation can be integrated with confidential computing [29]. Methods of virtualized workload protection can be combined to achieve a zero trust security model, providing maximum protection.

Virtualization security across a range of industries is enhanced by confidential computing. In financial services, it guarantees the protection of sensitive customer data that is being processed in a cloud-hosted virtualized environment because it prevents sensitive data from being breached or accessed by unauthorized third parties. Confidential computing is critical in healthcare for allowing organizations to adhere to stringent regulations such as HIPAA that require sensitive patient data to remain secure during its analysis and processing on virtualized infrastructures. It enables the same ability in government and defense applications where secure processing of classified information can be performed in VMs and containers using TEEs, protecting against both internal and external threats [30]. The transformational use cases demonstrate the powers of confidential computing in protecting sensitive workloads in the wide range of virtualized environments.

10.2 Guidelines for Preparing for the Future

Preparing for the future in a rapidly evolving technological and business landscape involves strategic planning, skill development, and adaptability [31]. Here are key guidelines to help individuals and organizations stay ahead.

Organizations increasingly use virtualization in private or public clouds to maximize hardware utilization and optimize performance through effective load distribution. Sensitive data loss and serious data breaches may result from not securing these systems. A system that maximizes resilience and offers safe, long-term benefits of virtualization must have security and assurance of the virtualized environment.

10.2.1 Evaluating the Risks

The system compartmentalization is made possible by VMs and containers. By doing this, a system can be isolated and segregated, preventing hackers from infiltrating the entire system when one component is vulnerable to an attack.

There are several risks to consider, and security is crucial for businesses, IT managers, and service providers who want to prevent significant repercussions. The responsibility is shared when relying on a third party for a secure processing environment [32]. Using trusted computing when sharing a cloud system enables users to monitor the data and software security in their VM or container.

10.2.2 Protecting VMs

VMs need safeguards different from hardware, and it can be challenging to determine the level of (cyber) security in a VM. In a public cloud scenario, anyone utilizing a virtualized environment must trust the service provider. The providers themselves can confirm the authenticity and condition of their virtualization infrastructure [33]. Sharing crucial security data, like the security status of VMs and the virtualization infrastructure, is made possible by trusted computing.

It is essential to ensure that VMs and containers only run on reliable systems because virtual environments are only as safe as their hosted infrastructure. Users can build trust in their VM and the underlying virtualization infrastructure by putting trusted virtual platforms into place.

Furthermore, as cloud services become more virtualized, attackers may access the systems more efficiently. Hacking, already a lucrative profession, has become more sophisticated, automated, and profitable in recent years, and it now more closely resembles real business than before. For this reason, the industry must create a reliable way to confirm the integrity and legitimacy of the VMs and containers involved.

A common platform to consider cloud computing and virtualization is the personal computer client. However, other platforms, such as storage and network devices, also use virtualization. Trusted computing guidance is necessary for the implementation of all virtualization uses.

10.2.3 The Future of Virtualization Security

Implementing trusted computing guidance is necessary for all virtualization applications. As virtualized environments evolve, the TCG Virtualized Platform workgroup understands that trusted computing needs more robust security measures. To maximize resilience and provide safe, long-term benefits of virtualization, a system must have security and assurance of the virtualized environment [34].

10.2.4 Container Scanning Tools

In virtual environments, container security is important and can only be handled proactively using container scanning tools and run-time security. Aqua Security, Trivy, and other tools automate the vulnerability scanning of image, integrity checking of images at run time, and threat detection at run time. These tools guarantee vulnerability and a misconfiguration-free container in deployment and continuously monitor the run-time behavior of a container to detect and mitigate anomalies. In this case, ZTA comprises an added layer of security that verifies all access attempts inside the containerized environment [35]. ZTA means that only authenticated and authorized entities can interact with container workloads using principles of least privilege, identity-based access, and network segmentation. One such case study is the 2019 Kubernetes security breach wherein the attackers were able to take advantage of an unprotected Kubernetes API server to deploy malicious containers for crypto mining. One example of a case study is the 2019 Kubernetes security breach in which the attackers were able to use an unprotected Kubernetes API server to run malicious containers to create crypto miners. Mitigation was done by restricting API server access, implementing RBAC, enabling logging and monitoring, as well as scanning images (base image) with Trivy regularly. As a result, this breach highlights the need for a multilayered approach to securing containerized environments involving tools, ZTA principles, and continuous monitoring.

10.3 Importance of Staying Ahead of Emerging Trends

The future perspective of emerging trends is critical in today's fast-paced and ever-changing world. This practice can have a transformative impact on individuals, businesses, and organizations. Here is why it is essential.

10.3.1 Virtual Memory Manager Implementation Issues

A hardware interface that is approximately equal to raw hardware must be exported to the software in a VM by the virtual memory manager (VMM). It must be able to deny hardware access while maintaining control of the computer. There are several ways to accomplish this, each with unique design trade-offs. When weighing these tradeoffs, integrity, performance, and simplicity are the main design objectives for VMMs [36]. The ability of the VMM to run legacy software is by far its most significant advantage, so compatibility is crucial. Virtualization overhead measurement and performance aim to make the VM run as quickly as the software on the physical machine.

10.3.2 CPU Virtualization

Direct execution in VMM involves running the VM on the hardware, which permits it to maintain vital control over the CPU, indicating that CPU architecture is virtualizable. To implement essential direct execution, privileged mode is required for the VMM to operate, although the privileged and unprivileged code of the VM must run in the CPU's unprivileged mode. The CPU will trap the VMM, simulating the privileged operation on the VM state for which the VMM is responsible each time the VM tries to execute a privileged operation. Although VMM was not able to take control over the CPU, in a guest OS, it is unsafe to run disabling interruptions. Instead, the VMM would record that the VM's interrupts were disabled after trapping the interrupt-disabling operation.

After that, until the VM reenables interruptions, the VMM would delay sending it more interruptions. Therefore, the secret to creating a virtualizable architecture is to include trap semantics that enable a VMM to run the VM directly, safely, and transparently using the CPU which is given in Figure 10.5 [37, 38]. Using these semantics, the VMM can make the software operating inside the VM appear to be running on a real computer using direct execution. A difficulty for advanced

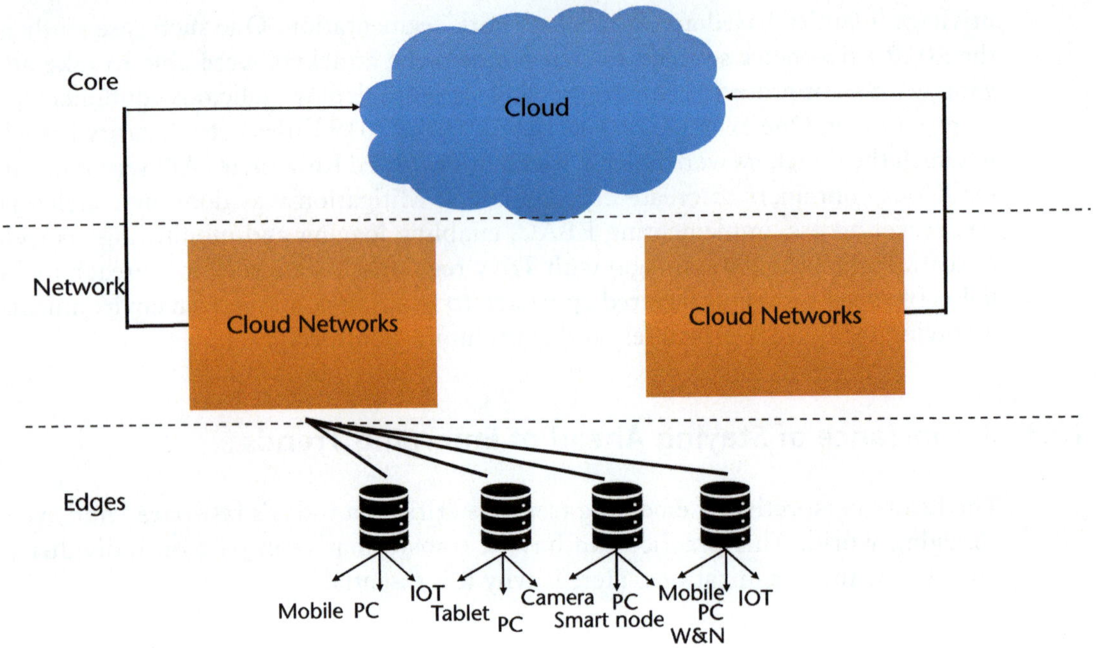

Figure 10.5 Resource usage in a virtualized environment.

architectures is the ability of the CPU to read privileged state by using unprivileged instructions, for example, the ability of software in the VM to read the code segment register to determine the CPU's current privilege level.

Additionally, this replacement reduced virtualization overhead, including privileged instruction traps, leading to improved performance. Afterward, the designers altered an Irix OS to utilize this para-virtualized version of the MIPS architecture. Compatibility issues are the main disadvantage of para-virtualization. An OS must be ported to a para-virtualized VMM to run there. Older OSs cannot function, vendors must work together, and old computers cannot simply switch to VMs. Because so much legacy software is still in use despite years of great backward-compatible x86 hardware, it is not easy to give up backward compatibility.

Academic research projects have supported para-virtualization despite these disadvantages because it is a significant engineering challenge to create a VMM with all-around great performance. In order to allow speedy, compatible virtualization of the x86 architecture, VMware created a new virtualization method that accomplishes rapid, on-the-fly binary translation with traditional direct execution. Nearly all modern OSs can support direct execution because the processor mode to run typical application programs can be virtualized.

The binary translator can function in privileged modes that are not virtualizable by patching the nonvirtualizable x86 instructions. The outcome is a high-performance VM that maintains full software compatibility since it is compatible with the hardware.

AMD has announced short-term hardware support for Intel's Vanderpool technology and VMMs for x86 CPUs with its Pacifica technology. A VMM can employ direct execution to run safely and transparently, thanks to a new execution mode introduced by AMD and Intel Technologies' VMs instead of making the current execution modes virtualized [39]. The effort in this mode seeks to cut down on the execution trap overhead as well as the total number of traps to exercise VMs, in order to improve performance. In theory, direct execution-only VMMs on x86 processors could be realized once the technologies become available, certainly for OS environments that do not utilize these new modes of execution. If this hardware support works out as well as the early IBM mainframe virtualization support, it should be possible to further cut the performance overhead and simplify the implementation of virtualization mechanisms. Our experience has indicated that, even without para-virtualization, beneficial hardware support can cut overhead enough that the benefits of a fully compatible VM abstraction greatly outweigh any lost performance benefit from losing compatibility.

10.3.3 Challenges

The virtual memory system (VMS) manages the memory assigned to a VM. To maintain a reasonable balance between the memory allocated to a VM and the memory that the VMS has at its disposal, the VMS must periodically reclaim some of that memory by paging a portion of the VM to disk. However, the OS running (Guest-OS) in the VM has a much better idea of which pages are potential candidates to be paged out, and it is possible that the VMM is unaware of these pages. To overcome this issue, VMware's server is used to adopt para-virtualization. A troubleshooting process runs to assign additional memory, communicating with each other for reallocation. OSs frequently update their page tables, causing software to be overloaded. Hardware-managed shadow page tables could accelerate x86 CPU virtualization. Future research should focus on cooperative resource management choices for guest OSs, VMMs, and the data center as a whole. Since resource management is a promising field for future research, significant advancements are anticipated in this field during the next 10 years.

10.3.4 I/O Virtualization

IBM's mainframe channelized the I/O system in the last two decades, which allows it to communicate with a separate channel processor. It works well for I/O devices, such as text terminals and disks [41]. However, pervasive computing makes virtualizing much more difficult because of the varied assortment of I/O devices. It takes a lot of work to write a VMM layer that communicates with the diverse range of I/O devices supported by x86-based computing systems, which come from a variety of manufacturers and have varying programming interfaces.

10.3.5 Challenges

To provide these capabilities, the hosted architecture was developed by VMware Workstation. This architecture utilizes host OS (HostOS) device drivers, such as Windows or Linux, to access devices. Since most devices have drivers that run on these OSs, the virtualization layer can support any I/O device. Because the VMM renders the VM's virtual display card in a window on the HostOS, the HostOS can control, operate, and manage what I/O display devices the VM thinks are present.

Its comprehensive compatibility, scheduling, resource management, and other HostOS environment features, as well as its ease of installation, are just a few of its numerous advantages. It also has certain disadvantages. For example, the hosted architecture raises the performance overhead for I/O device virtualization considerably, which is too high for server environments with high-speed disk and network subsystems.

10.3.6 Future Support

Industry trends are focusing on physical support for virtualization of high-performance I/O devices. Channels such as Universal Serial Bus (USB) and Small Computer System Interface (SCSI) are replacing discrete devices. These interfaces reduce virtualization overhead and ease implementation complexity. With efficient hardware support, channel input and output devices can safely pass to the software in the VM, eliminating all input and output virtualization overhead. I/O devices must know about VMs and support multiple virtual interfaces, allowing the VMM to safely map the interface into the VM [42]. I/O devices performing direct memory access require address remapping to ensure that memory addresses are mapped to the locations specified by shadow page tables. In systems with multiple VMs, the VMM requires an effective method to route device completion interrupts to the appropriate VM utilizing the same I/O device. By reducing virtualization overhead, this capability enables VMs to handle even the most I/O-intensive applications.

Maintaining shadow copies in software can result in undesired overhead because OSs frequently alter page tables. Mainframe virtualization architectures have long included hardware-managed shadow page tables, which would be helpful in speeding up the virtualization of x86 CPUs.

Future studies in resource management have a lot of potential. There is still much to learn about how guest OSs and VMMs can collaborate to manage resources. Furthermore, research needs to examine resource management from the perspective of the entire data center, and we anticipate that this field will see significant advancements over the next 10 years.

It is impossible to exaggerate the significance of virtualized security. Strong virtualized security measures are becoming more and more necessary as we depend more on the internet for everything from social interaction to banking. People and businesses need to stay up to date with the latest advancements in virtualization security since cyber threats are dynamic and ever-evolving. A secure online experience and the protection of private information depend on this attention to detail [43]. Understanding how cyber threats are always changing is crucial. Professionals in virtualization security must be alert and make necessary adjustments because hackers are constantly inventing new ways to take advantage of vulnerabilities. This dynamic ecosystem includes threats such as ransomware, phishing attempts, data breaches, and more. To effectively combat these threats, it is imperative to understand their nature and evolution.

Future-proofing through continuous learning and adaptation is the final step in staying up to date with virtualized security trends. Individuals and organizations need to be ready to invest in ongoing education and training in order to address the challenges of a rapidly changing digital landscape. This commitment to lifelong learning includes attending conferences and seminars, staying up to date on the latest advancements in virtualization security, and maybe going back to school to complete an online master's degree. By fostering an environment of learning and flexibility, people and organizations may protect themselves against attacks and prepare for upcoming advancements in virtualized security. Everyone should be concerned about the significance of organizational and personal accountability in virtualized security, not just IT experts. People must practice good digital hygiene, including creating strong passwords, updating software frequently, and exercising caution when disclosing personal information online. Businesses are more obligated to safeguard their information, customers, and staff. Virtualized security must be incorporated into daily life beyond sporadic software updates or password changes. The community component of virtualized security depends on cooperation and information exchange. Sharing expertise and experiences in the battle against cyber threats is crucial. This covers collaboration between people, groups, businesses, and even countries. Cyber resilience can be improved through partnerships between public and private organizations.

It is essential to embrace virtualized security in the era of remote work. The distinction between personal and professional digital security has become hazier as more workers work from home. Securing home networks, being aware of the dangers of using personal devices for work, and keeping an eye out for emerging cyberattacks that target remote workers are all part of addressing the particular virtualized security issues that remote work environments present [44]. Companies must give their remote workers clear policies and resources to guarantee safe access to company networks, and workers must keep their homes safe for work.

10.4 Best Practices for Addressing Emerging Trends in Virtualization Security

10.4.1 Protect VMs by Using Authentication and Access Control in Windows-Azure

Create customized Windows-Azure policies and set resource conventions for the company to manage VM access. A level of scope beyond subscriptions is offered by Windows-Azure management groups, enabling effective control over policies, compliance, and access. Large-scale enterprise-grade management is provided by automatically transferring the group's conditions to every subscription under the management group. By strengthening deployment decisions and making it easier to understand and inventory VMs, Windows-Azure Resource. Users can access and configure VMs with secure privileged access by utilizing built-in Windows-Azure roles and the least privilege technique [45].

The Security Administrator, Developer Test Labs, VM Contributor, and Classic VM Contributor Users can control VMs but not the storage account or virtual network to which they are connected. By altering this setting, subscription administrators and co-administrators can take control of every VM within a subscription. Using availability sets or availability zones in Windows Azure and utilizing multiple VMs are advised to guarantee high availability for critical applications. When deployed in a Windows-Azure data center, this logical grouping guarantees that VM resources are isolated. It is recommended that anti-malware protection be installed, such as Microsoft anti-malware or a Microsoft partner's protection package. It offers features such as real-time protection and signature and engine updates. An anti-malware extension can be used for environments hosted separately from the production environment. Figure 10.6 shows the protection of malware against threats [46].

10.4.2 Manage VM Updates

Windows-Azure VMs are intended for user management and they should be regularly updated. The Update Management solution in Windows-Azure Automation is currently used to manage the OS updates for Windows and Linux personal computers that are installed in Windows-Azure. The Update Management solution in Windows-Azure Automation is what is currently being used to manage VMs with on-premises settings or other cloud providers. Examples of update settings in both OSs include Microsoft Monitoring Agent (MMA) for Windows or Linux, Automation Hybrid Run-book Worker, PowerShell Desired State Configuration (DSC) for Linux, and Microsoft Update or Windows Server Update Services (WSUS) for Windows Computers [48]. Check for and install all updates as a first step, and make sure the images created contain the most recent version of Windows upon deployment. Use a Windows-Azure Resource Manager template to periodically redeploy VMs to impose a new OS version. Rapidly apply security updates to VMs by enabling Microsoft Defender for Cloud to identify and apply missing updates. Install the latest security updates, especially for labs and external-facing systems hosting applications or services that need internet accessibility. Deploy and test a backup solution, following backup strategies that provide restore capabilities similar to users' experience with on-premises environments.

When transferring production workloads to Windows-Azure, they should either use Windows Azure Backup to handle backup needs or integrate it with current backup solutions. Threats that exploit known vulnerabilities are more likely to

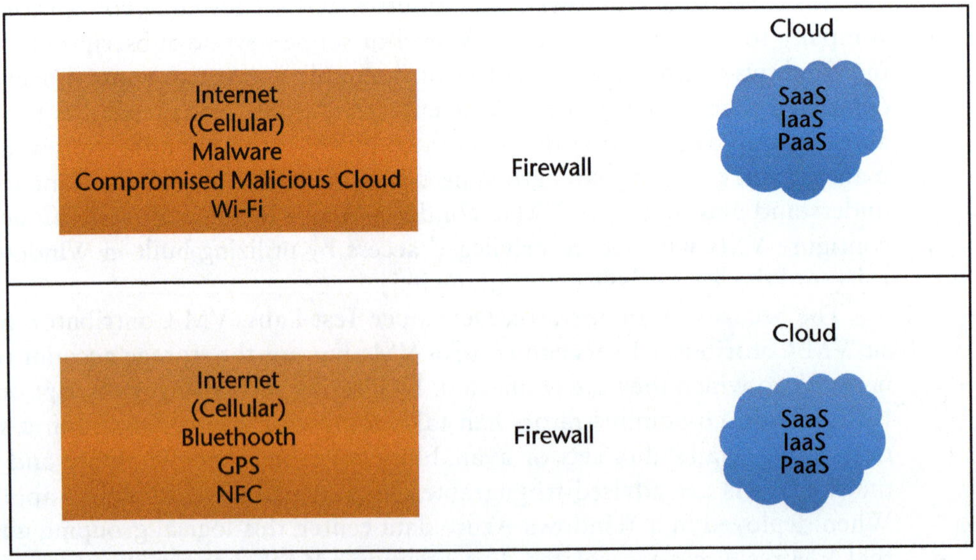

Figure 10.6 Protection of malware against threats.

target organizations not enforcing software update policies. Businesses must demonstrate diligence and implement the appropriate security controls to guarantee the security of their cloud-based workloads to adhere to industry regulations. Because Windows-Azure IaaS and traditional data-center software update best practices are very similar, it is advised that current software update policies be reviewed to incorporate Windows-Azure VMs.

10.4.3 Manage VM Security Posture

Microsoft Defender for Cloud is an application made to keep an eye on Linux and Windows VMs' security. It offers various features such as applying OS security settings, identifying and downloading missing important updates and system security, implementing endpoint anti-malware protection suggestions, and verifying disk encryption, assessing and remediating vulnerabilities, and detecting threats [48]. The tool actively monitors for potential threats, exposing them in security alerts, which aggregate into a single view known as security incident. Data is stored in Windows-Azure Monitor logs, providing insights into application and resource operations. This shared functionality helps organizations to form a complete picture of their environment. Without strong security measures, organizations may remain unaware of potential unauthorized user attempts to bypass security controls.

10.4.4 Monitor VM Performance

When VMs use more resources than necessary, it disrupts service and goes against the availability security principle. For VMs running web servers or IIS, this is particularly crucial as excessive CPU or memory utilization may indicate a DoS attack. Monitoring VM access both reactively and proactively is crucial. The Windows-Azure Monitor offers visibility into resource health, including resource diagnostic log files and the Windows-Azure Diagnostics extension, which can be enabled as part of the Windows-Azure Resource Manager template [49]. Because a VM using more resources could be a sign of an external resource attack, organizations that do not monitor VM performance are unable to determine whether variations in performance patterns are typical or indicative of a damaged process.

10.4.5 Encrypt Virtual Complex Disk Files

To protect the boot volume, the data volume at storage, the encryption keys, and any secrets, it is necessary to encrypt virtual hard disks. To encrypt the disks of both Linux and Windows IaaS VMs, we will utilize Linux's industry-standard DM-Crypt features and Windows' Bit-Locker features. Windows-Azure has an IaaS that provides Microsoft-Disk Encryption for Linux VMs. Figure 10.7 is a very high-level overview of Microsoft Azure [49]. For Windows-Azure disk encryption, as a best practice, we return the actions earlier to encrypt a VM using disk encryption: encrypting the VMs, creating a Microsoft Entra application for authentication, using a key encryption key for security, capturing a snapshot/backup before encrypting a disk, and ensuring that the key vault and the VMs are in the same region where the encryption secrets do not cross regional boundaries, they will stay inside the region. As we explore these features, it is possible to see how Azure Disk Encryption could

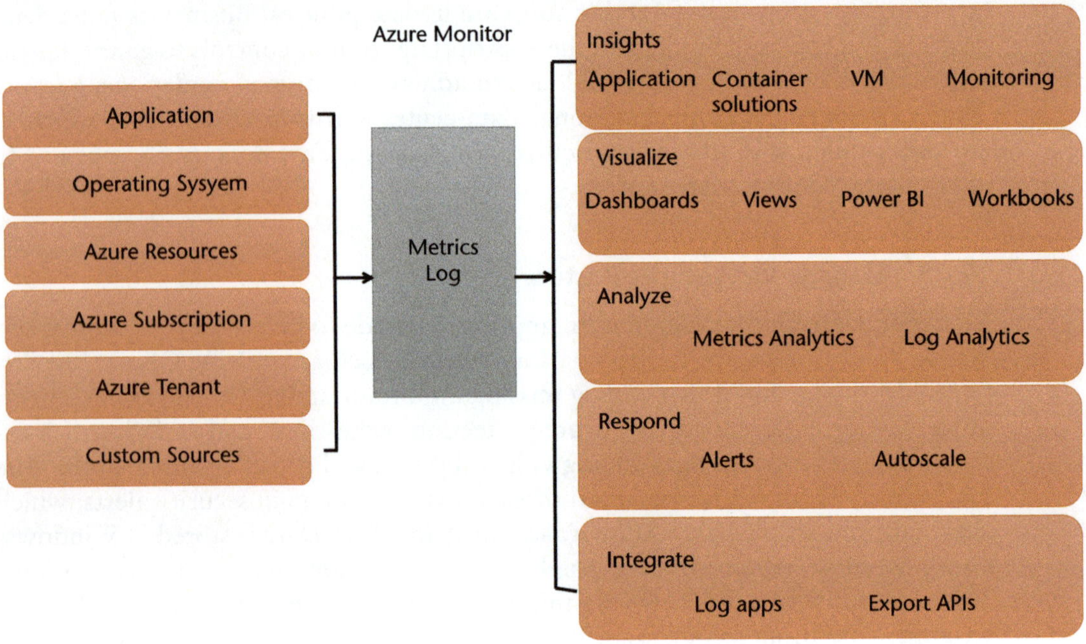

Figure 10.7 Generalized overview of Microsoft Azure.

help to achieve business objectives through IaaS VMs, enterprise security and compliance, as well as customer-controlled keys and policies. To sum up this section, encrypting virtual hard disks is critical to safeguarding boot volume, data volumes, encryption keys, and secrets in storage.

The internet connectivity Windows-Azure VMs must have their direct internet connectivity monitored and restricted to defend against attacks. Attackers attempt "easy" attacks, such as using popular passwords and unpatched vulnerabilities, and continuously search IP ranges for public cloud management ports that are open. To ensure that networking resources are only available to the core networking group, use Windows-Azure RBAC to avoid unintentional network routing and security exposure [50]. Find and fix vulnerable VMs that can be accessed from any IP address. If any network securities groups use Microsoft Defender for Cloud and set up incoming rules that allow access from any source IP address to limit access through internet-facing endpoints:

- *Security risks and requirements of radio interference signal (RIS)-assisted 6G:* The introduction of RIS in 6G radio communications presents new security threats, as it can be unlawfully misused for malevolent intent or exploited by attackers. The reconfiguration of the meta-surface is crucial for optimizing performance in energy, communication, and security. However, changing the electromagnetic properties of a new channel is created by reflected or refracted signals for hostile actions if RIS is used maliciously.
- *Eavesdropping:* Remote sensing arrays (RSAs) are useful for improving secure communications because they are open and broadcast, but they can also be abused to reduce secrecy performance. By placing RIS near the transmitter, passive attackers can intercept signals that are being transmitted. To

minimize the secrecy rate and increase the received signal power, the RIS's phase shift can be adjusted. Illegal usage of RIS has increased information leakage and the eavesdropping data rate. For instance, a drone equipped with a lightweight, power-free diffractive meta-surface to create a remote eavesdropping attack [51]. The remotely positioned metasurface drone (RMD) attack minimizes interference with normal communication while eavesdropping on backhaul connections with nearly 0% bit error rate (BER).

- *Jamming:* A DoS attack can be launched by an attacker using an RIS to disrupt everyday communication in a wireless communication system. The RIS can cause performance loss by inducing more reflecting signals to jam authorized users [52]. The inference signal strength at the authorized receiver can be greatly enhanced by optimizing the RIS's phase shift, which lowers the signal power. By intensifying the false noise produced by the jammer, this method can impair the regular communication of authorized users.
- *Pilot contamination/spoofing:* A lot of research has been done on the pilot contamination attack (PCA) on multiple-antenna systems and the real-time integrated system (RTIS) is opening up new possibilities for more potent attacks. A unique PCA that poses a serious danger to multiple-input multiple-output (MIMO) wireless communications by allowing the attacker to begin a PCA during the pilot training phase by taking advantage of RIS [53].

The reflection coefficients that are sent to the RIS controller from the base station are necessary for the RIS to function at its best, via a backhaul link. Feedback from the backhaul link is crucial for determining these coefficients. If the backhaul link's vulnerability is intruded, an attacker can create a hostile configuration using user CSI. Unauthorized access to the RIS controller and RIS microcontrollers may be vulnerable due to hardware or software loopholes, which can allow unauthorized access through malware injection. This can lead to malicious manipulation of tunable elements, modifying parameters to steer sensitive information distant from the path of dissemination that was intended. The shift of phase produced by RIS elements can be altered by manipulating the RIS controller once it has been intruded. The RIS controller manipulation attack (CMA), which is initiated by hacking or infecting the controller with malware, combines fake data injection and pilot contamination. To reduce the data rate at authorized receivers while limiting the likelihood of an attack, Acharjee and Chattopadhyay suggested a RIS controller manipulation assault [54]. Wireless environment reconfiguration RIS based on a meta-surface enhances wireless communication security and performance by adjusting electromagnetic propagation functions such as reflection, polarization refraction, and absorption. However, these functions can be reconfigured maliciously, altering signal behavior, for example, a meta-surface-enabled sideband steering attack, manipulating spectral-spatial characteristics of reflected waves to covertly establish a sideband channel for malevolent intent [55].

10.4.6 Manipulation Attack

Figure 10.8 illustrates the performance of RIS-assisted 6G in relation to security threats and requirements [56]. By rapidly altering the downlink and uplink

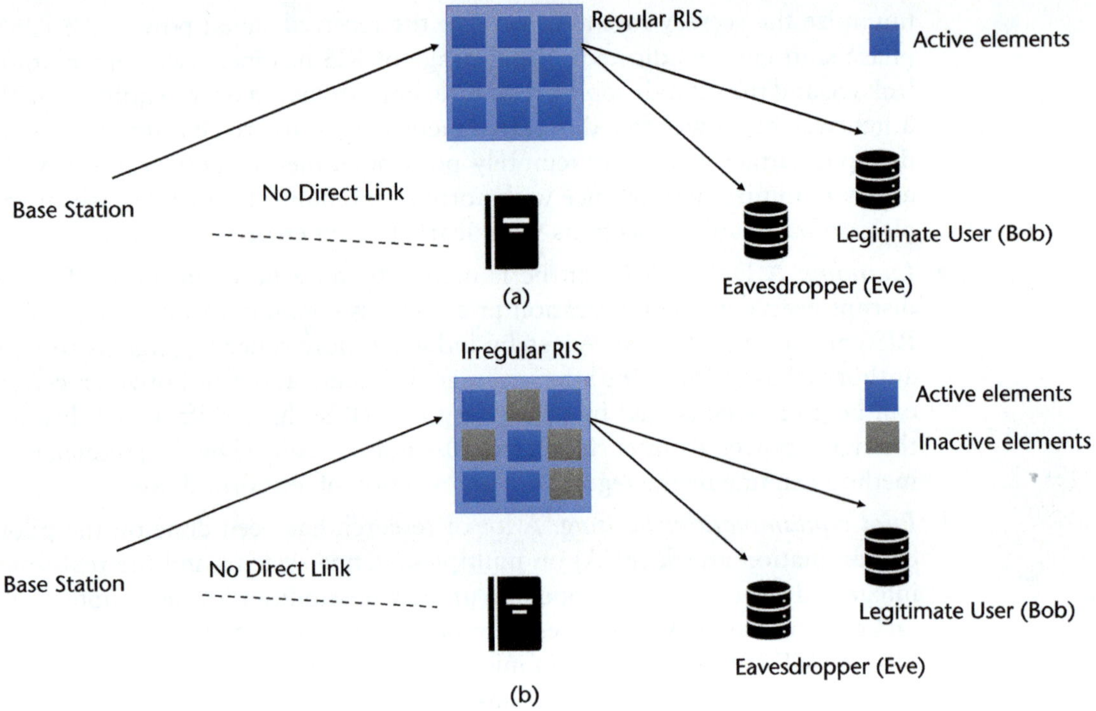

Figure 10.8 Security risks and requirements of RIS-assisted 6G.

reflection coefficients during the physical layer key (PLK) generation process, RIS-enabled manipulation can undermine channel reciprocity. This attack examines the vulnerabilities of traditional methods by targeting the PLK generation based on the channel frequency response. As a result, it is possible to reduce the key generation rate to nearly zero.

10.4.7 Security Requirements and Challenges to 6G

6G technologies are undergoing significant advancements due to new uses, hazards posed by novel methods, and different dangers. Using innovative security solutions to meet stringent security and privacy requirements is crucial. Figure 10.9 shows how to secure 6G technology in a virtualized environment [57]. Confidentiality is essential for wireless communication, ensuring that only legitimate transmitters and receivers can access the information. Traditional mobile communication systems typically ensure confidentiality through encryption at upper layers. Still, this physical layer information, which may contain private user information and activity data, cannot be ensured to be private using techniques. For mission-critical IoT applications, such as the internet used by the wireless sector, their integrity is essential. High computing overhead and latency may lead from 5G's optional integrity protection at the data link layer. To solve this problem, a more effective and efficient physical layer integrity protection technologies are required.

Authenticity is another critical aspect of 6G technology. Receivers verify the transmitter's identity to differentiate between authentic and fraudulent colleagues when communicating. Conventional mobile communication systems use non-access

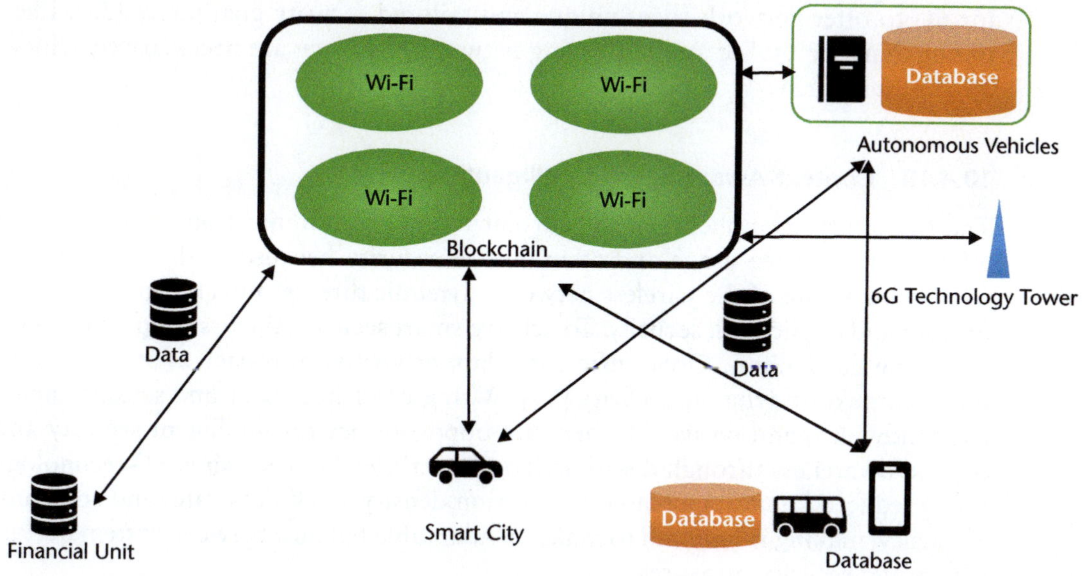

Figure 10.9 Securing 6G technology in a virtualized environment.

stratum (NAS) protocols, leading to false base station attacks. To address this issue, a solution known as physical layer channel-based authentication (PLA) has been introduced. Ensuring availability is crucial for legitimate users to access wireless communication systems anytime and from anywhere. However, DoS attacks can significantly undermine this availability, preventing authorized users from accessing network services when needed. This is especially critical for applications that require low latency and high reliability, such as industrial IoT and autonomous driving. Recent advancements in techniques like adversarial machine learning and real-time intelligence have revealed increasingly sophisticated and damaging jamming attacks, which pose new threats to the 6G network.

10.4.8 Post-Quantum Resilience

Quantum computing advancements have made classical cryptographic algorithms in 5G security systems unsafe, necessitating the redesign of cryptographic methods and protocols to give the system quantum resistance. New post-quantum cryptography methods have been assessed by the National Institute of Standards and Technology (NIST), which could in wireless communication networks in place of public key encryption techniques [58]. However, these options might make implementation more difficult, especially for low-end IoT devices. Because physical layer security measures are independent of computing complexity, they present promising options.

10.4.9 Differentiated and Customized Security

The traditional one-size-fits-all security strategy is ineffective since 6G is anticipated to serve a variety of applications with varying quality-of-service (QoS) and security requirements. Inspired by the DiffServ QoS paradigm, QoSec is being researched for 6G to offer network slices unique and tailored security guarantees [55]. Identifying dynamic QoSec and improving network efficiency are necessary to achieve intelligent security.

10.4.10 Context-Aware-Based Intelligent Security

The fixed security policies of the current mobile communication system are not efficient in resource usage and assurance of security because of the time-varying combinate nature of the wireless network, dynamic threats, and changing demands for user and application security. To achieve smart security, the first step involves establishing the dynamic QoSec using an adapt protective approach of security levels to the context of dynamic security [59]. With greater frequency and sensing capacity, bandwidth, and native AI, there are opportunities for intelligent security and context awareness through distributed or centralized AI processing. 6G technology offers reduced latency, increased connection density, peak data rate, and spectrum efficiency, making it essential to make an adaptable balance between system performance and security measures.

10.5 Summary

In this chapter, an overview of emerging trends of virtualized security was elaborated, as it is a rapidly growing field driven by the increasing adoption of cloud computing and hybrid infrastructures. Many solutions are available; however, container-based virtualization solutions surge data center utilization while minimizing resource overheads. Moreover, future guidelines along with the importance of virtualized security were also discussed. Continuous monitoring and preventative measures are necessary for container security, including applying updates, utilizing trustworthy sources for container images, and scanning for vulnerabilities. Runtime security tools and network policies regulate container traffic and reduce exposure to potential dangers. Kubernetes is an open-source platform that simplifies containerization and automation, offering security controls and APIs. Micro-services are small, autonomous services that perform distinct tasks using lightweight APIs. Access requests from outside users and other services are managed by micro-service application security, with an Open Policy Agent or sidecar authorization engine handling all access control requests. Micro-service security involves East-West traffic security between micro-services and messaging platforms and North-South traffic security for external consumers.

Best practices for addressing emerging trends in virtualization security were also discussed in this chapter as the implementation of best practices for all virtualization applications is necessary for the security of virtualization in the future. As we depend more on the internet for social contact and banking, virtualized security is essential. Protecting private information and guaranteeing a safe online experience require an understanding of and ability to adjust to changing cyber threats. To guarantee safe access to corporate networks and the security of remote workers' residences, businesses must offer clear policies and resources.

References

[1] Hidayat, D. N., et al., "Digital Technology Supporting English Learning Among Indonesian University Students," *Research and Practice in Technology Enhanced Learning*, Vol. 17, No. 1, June 8, 2022, p. 23.

[2] Li, J., et al., "CyberGuarder: A Virtualization Security Assurance Architecture for Green Cloud Computing," *Future Generation Computer Systems*, Vol. 28, No. 2, February 1, 2012, pp. 379–390.

[3] Sun, X., N. Ansari, and R. Wang, "Optimizing Resource Utilization of a Data Center," *IEEE Communications Surveys & Tutorials*, Vol. 18, No. 4, April 25, 2016, pp. 2822–2846.

[4] Thyagaturu, A. S., et al., "Operating Systems and Hypervisors for Network Functions: A Survey of Enabling Technologies and Research Studies," *IEEE Access*, Vol. 10, July 29, 2022, pp. 79825–79873.

[5] Alyas, T., et al., "Container Performance and Vulnerability Management for Container Security Using Docker Engine," *Security and Communication Networks*, Vol. 2022, No. 1, 2022, p. 6819002.

[6] Gill, S. S., et al., "AI for Next Generation Computing: Emerging Trends and Future Directions," *Internet of Things*, Vol. 19, August 1, 2022, p. 100514.

[7] Kaiser, S., et al., "Container Technologies for Arm Architecture: A Comprehensive Survey of the State-of-the-Art," *IEEE Access*, Vol. 10, August 8, 2022, pp. 84853–84881.

[8] Khan, A. A., and M. Zakarya, "Energy, Performance and Cost Efficient Cloud Datacentres: A Survey," *Computer Science Review*, Vol. 40, May 1, 2021, p. 100390.

[9] Sultan, S., I. Ahmad, and T. Dimitriou, "Container Security: Issues, Challenges, and the Road Ahead," *IEEE Access*, Vol. 7, April 17, 2019, pp. 52976–52996.

[10] Al-Doghman, F., et al., "AI-Enabled Secure Microservices in Edge Computing: Opportunities and Challenges," *IEEE Transactions on Services Computing*, Vol. 16, No. 2, March 1, 2022, pp. 1485–1504.

[11] Pereira-Vale, A., et al., "Security in Microservice-Based Systems: A Multivocal Literature Review," *Computers & Security*, Vol. 103, April 1, 2021, p. 102200.

[12] Vs, D. P., S. C. Sethuraman, and M. K. Khan, "Container Security: Precaution Levels, Mitigation Strategies, and Research Perspectives," *Computers & Security*, September 22, 2023, p. 103490.

[13] Wong, A. Y., et al., "On the Security of Containers: Threat Modeling, Attack Analysis, and Mitigation Strategies," *Computers & Security*, Vol. 128, May 1, 2023, p. 103140.

[14] Eyvazov, F., et al., "Beyond Containers: Orchestrating Microservices with Minikube, Kubernetes, Docker, and Compose for Seamless Deployment and Scalability," *2024 11th International Conference on Reliability, Infocom Technologies and Optimization (Trends and Future Directions) (ICRITO)*, March 14, 2024, pp. 1–6.

[15] Taha, M. B., S. Alrabaee, and K. K. Choo, "Efficient Resource Management of Micro-Services in Vanets," *IEEE Transactions on Intelligent Transportation Systems*, Vol. 24, No. 7, March 20, 2023, pp. 6820–6835.

[16] Hannousse, A., and S. Yahiouche, "Securing Microservices and Microservice Architectures: A Systematic Mapping Study," *Computer Science Review*, Vol. 41, August 1, 2021, p. 100415.

[17] Nasab, A. R., et al., "An Empirical Study of Security Practices for Microservices Systems," *Journal of Systems and Software*, Vol. 198, April 1, 2023, p. 111563.

[18] Haindl, P., P. Kochberger, and M. Sveggen, "A Systematic Literature Review of Inter-Service Security Threats and Mitigation Strategies in Microservice Architectures," *IEEE Access*, May 28, 2024.

[19] Demchenko, Y., et al., "Finding Data on the Web, Data Sets, Web Scraping, Web API," in *Big Data Infrastructure Technologies for Data Analytics: Scaling Data Science Applications for Continuous Growth*, Cham: Springer Nature Switzerland, 2024, pp. 417–446.

[20] Blinowski, G., A. Ojdowska, and A. Przybyłek, "Monolithic vs. Microservice Architecture: A Performance and Scalability Evaluation," *IEEE Access*, Vol. 10, February 18, 2022, pp. 20357–20374.

[21] Akon, M., et al., "Formal Analysis of Access Control Mechanism of 5G Core Network," *Proceedings of the 2023 ACM SIGSAC Conference on Computer and Communications Security*, November 15, 2023, pp. 666–680.

[22] Pereira-Vale, A., et al., "Security in Microservice-Based Systems: A Multivocal Literature Review," *Computers & Security*, Vol. 103, April 1, 2021, p. 102200.

[23] Li, F., et al., "Information Security Protection Techniques for Substation Operation and Maintenance Edge Gateway," *International Congress on Communications, Networking, and Information Systems*, March 25, 2023, pp. 68–80.

[24] Harisha, A., et al., "Open Standard Authorization Protocol: OAuth 2.0 Defenses and Working Using Digital Signatures," in *Advancements in Cybercrime Investigation and Digital Forensics*, Palm Bay, FL: Apple Academic Press, 2023, pp. 319–344.

[25] El Akhdar, A., et al., "Exploring the Potential of Microservices in Internet of Things: A Systematic Review of Security and Prospects," *Sensors*, Vol. 24, No. 20, October 21, 2024, p. 6771.

[26] Kim, J., et al., "Enhancing Security in SDN: Systematizing Attacks and Defenses from a Penetration Perspective," *Computer Networks*, January 23, 2024, p. 110203.

[27] Parast, F. K., et al., "Cloud Computing Security: A Survey of Service-Based Models," *Computers & Security*, Vol. 114, March 1, 2022, p. 102580.

[28] Kaur, H., and A. Anand, "Review and Analysis of Secure Energy Efficient Resource Optimization Approaches for Virtual Machine Migration in Cloud Computing," *Measurement: Sensors*, Vol. 24, December 1, 2022, p. 100504.

[29] Anirudh, U. N., and S. S. Darshan, "Role-Based Virtuosity in Virtual Environments: A Technical Exploration of Access Control and Authentication Mechanisms," in Cloud Security Chapman and Hall/CRC, 2024, pp. 183–196.

[30] Hayes, J., "Towards Private and Robust Machine Learning for Information Security," doctoral dissertation, University College London, 2021.

[31] Dishon, G., and T. Gilead, "Adaptability and Its Discontents: 21st-Century Skills and the Preparation for an Unpredictable Future," *British Journal of Educational Studies*, Vol. 69, No. 4, July 4, 2021, pp. 393–413.

[32] Akhtar, S. I., et al., "Inter-Cloud Data Security Framework to Build Trust Based on Compliance with Controls," *IET Information Security*, Vol. 2024, No. 1, 2024, p. 6565102.

[33] Tabrizchi, H., and M. Kuchaki Rafsanjani, "A Survey on Security Challenges in Cloud Computing: Issues, Threats, and Solutions," *The Journal of Supercomputing*, Vol. 76, No. 12, December 2020, pp. 9493–9532.

[34] Amiri, Z., et al., "Resilient and Dependability Management in Distributed Environments: A Systematic and Comprehensive Literature Review," *Cluster Computing*, Vol. 26, No. 2, April 2023, pp. 1565–1600.

[35] Syed, N. F., et al., "Zero Trust Architecture (zta): A Comprehensive Survey," *IEEE Access*, Vol. 10, May 12, 2022, pp. 57143–57179.

[36] Rodríguez-Molina, A., J. A. Mejía-de-Dios, and E. Mezura-Montes, "Evolutionary Semi-Vectorial Bilevel Optimization in the Mechanical and Control Design of Systems," *Engineering Applications of Artificial Intelligence*, Vol. 133, July 1, 2004, p. 108640.

[37] Randal, A., "The Ideal Versus the Real: Revisiting the History of Virtual Machines and Containers," *ACM Computing Surveys (CSUR)*, Vol. 53, No. 1, February 5, 2020, pp. 1–31.

[38] Moti, N., R. Salkhordeh, and A. Brinkmann, "Protected Functions: User Space Privileged Function Calls," *International Conference on Architecture of Computing Systems*, September 13, 2022, pp. 117–131.

[39] Sá, B., J. Martins, and S. Pinto, "A First Look at RISC-V Virtualization from an Embedded Systems Perspective," *IEEE Transactions on Computers*, Vol. 71, No. 9, November 8, 2021, pp. 2177–2190.

[40] Sha, S., et al., "Hardware-Software Collaborative Tiered-Memory Management Framework for Virtualization," *ACM Transactions on Computer Systems*, Vol. 42, No. 1-2, February 13, 2024, pp. 1–32.

[41] Sinha, P. K., and P. Sinha, *Foundations of Computing: Essential for Computing Studies, Profession and Entrance Examinations*, New Dehli, India: BPB Publications, 2022.

[42] Thyagaturu, A. S., et al., "Operating Systems and Hypervisors for Network Functions: A Survey of Enabling Technologies and Research Studies," *IEEE Access*, Vol. 10, July 29, 2022, pp. 79825–79873.

[43] Yadav, U., and A. Sharma, "Network Security in Evolving Networking Technologies: Developments and Future Directions," *Evolving Networking Technologies: Developments and Future Directions*, May 15, 2023, pp. 75–95.

[44] Jafar, U., and H. A. Hussain, "Addressing Unique Cybersecurity Challenges in Telehealth and Remote Physiologic Monitoring," *Secure Health*, 2025, pp. 124–168.

[45] Saha, S., and B. Mazumdar, "Towards Resolving Privacy and Security Issues in IoT-Based Cloud Computing Platforms for Smart City Applications," in *Integration of IoT with Cloud Computing for Smart Applications*, London, UK: Chapman and Hall/CRC, 2023, pp. 53–80.

[46] Sharmeen, S., et al., "Avoiding Future Digital Extortion Through Robust Protection Against Ransomware Threats Using Deep Learning Based Adaptive Approaches," *IEEE Access*, Vol. 8, January 30, 2020, pp. 24522–24534.

[47] Buchanan, S., and J. Joyner, *Azure Arc-Enabled Kubernetes and Servers*, Berkeley, CA: Apress, 2021.

[48] Sandbu, M., *Windows Ransomware Detection and Protection: Securing Windows Endpoints, the Cloud, and Infrastructure Using Microsoft Intune, Sentinel, and Defender*, Birmingham, UK: Packt Publishing Ltd., 2023.

[49] Bauer, D., et al., "Building and Operating a Large-Scale Enterprise Data Analytics Platform," *Big Data Research*, Vol. 23, February 15, 2021, p. 100181.

[50] Corno, F., L. De Russis, and L. Mannella, "Helping Novice Developers Harness Security Issues in Cloud-IoT Systems," *Journal of Reliable Intelligent Environments*, Vol. 8, No. 3, September 2022, pp. 261–283.

[51] Kline, K., et al., "Security, Privacy, and Compliance with the Law," in *Pro Database Migration to Azure: Data Modernization for the Enterprise*, Berkeley, CA: Apress, 2022, pp. 201–240.

[52] Khoshafa, M. H., et al., "RIS-Assisted Physical Layer Security in Emerging RF and Optical Wireless Communication Systems: A Comprehensive Survey," *IEEE Communications Surveys & Tutorials*, October 28, 2024.

[53] Das, S. K., et al., "Comprehensive Review on ML-Based RIS-Enhanced IoT Systems: Basics, Research Progress and Future Challenges," *Computer Networks*, Vol. 224, April 1, 2023, p. 109581.

[54] Acharjee, S. S., and A. Chattopadhyay, "Controller Manipulation Attack on Reconfigurable Intelligent Surface Aided Wireless Communication," *2022 IEEE International Symposium on Information Theory (ISIT)*, June 26, 2022, pp. 1247–1252.

[55] Zhang, S., W. Huang, and Y. Liu, "A Systematic Survey on Physical Layer Security Oriented to Reconfigurable Intelligent Surface Empowered 6G," *Computers & Security*, September 4, 2024, p. 104100.

[56] Naeem, F., et al., "Security and Privacy for Reconfigurable Intelligent Surface in 6G: A Review of Prospective Applications and Challenges," *IEEE Open Journal of the Communications Society*, Vol. 4, May 9, 2023, pp. 1196–1217.

[57] Aman, M. N., U. Javaid, and B. Sikdar, "Security Function Virtualization for IoT Applications in 6G Networks," *IEEE Communications Standards Magazine*, Vol. 5, No. 3, September 2021, pp. 90–95.

[58] Saarinen, M. J., "Mobile Energy Requirements of the Upcoming NIST Post-Quantum Cryptography Standards," *2020 8th IEEE International Conference on Mobile Cloud Computing, Services, and Engineering (MobileCloud)*, August 3, 2020, pp. 23–30.

[59] Fadlullah, Z. M., B. Mao, and N. Kato, "Balancing QoS and Security in the Edge: Existing Practices, Challenges, and 6G Opportunities with Machine Learning," *IEEE Communications Surveys & Tutorials*, Vol. 24, No. 4, July 18, 2022, pp. 2419–2448.

CHAPTER 11

Conclusion

11.1 Final Thoughts and Recommendations

The virtualization technologies have fundamentally transformed IT infrastructures, significantly enhancing scalability, efficiency, and innovation. While there are important security challenges to address, they can be effectively managed through proactive measures such as thorough threat analysis, real-time monitoring, and robust automated response mechanisms. Achieving seamless operations is not just an option; it requires a strong balance between security and performance, along with a commitment to innovation. This approach is essential for fostering collaboration among stakeholders and driving success. In addition to this, it has revolutionized IT infrastructures, enhancing scalability, efficiency, and innovation. However, several significant security challenges require proactive processes such as threat analysis, real-time monitoring, and automated response mechanisms. A seamless operation requires balanced security and performance with innovation, which is needed for collaboration among stakeholders.

11.2 Future Outlook for Virtualization Security

Modern IT infrastructure, which facilitates cloud computing, containerized apps, and hybrid environments, prioritizes virtualized security. However, there are both novel potential and problems for future virtualized security. Nevertheless, enhanced isolation and microsegmentation will offer more precise control over container and virtual machine traffic.

Zero trust architecture guarantees no implicit trust between entities and is the foundation of future virtualization security solutions. Another strategy that lowers unwanted access and boosts security is authenticated and authorized access to virtualized resources. Serverless computing and edge virtualization are important security domains, with solutions protecting thin virtual machines and containers at the edge.

Compliance and regulation will require stricter controls over virtualized environments, emphasizing data protection, access control, and real-time threat monitoring. Quantum-safe security will also become significant and incorporate quantum-resistant algorithms. Adopting specific measures will ensure resilience and trustworthiness in virtualized infrastructures.

About the Authors

Rajkumar Singh Rathore currently serves as a senior lecturer (associate professor) and program director for the MSc in Computing and IT within the School of Technologies at Cardiff Metropolitan University, United Kingdom. He leads the Cyber-Physical and Networked Systems group at the CeRISS Research Centre and heads the Cybersecurity initiatives for Connected and Autonomous Systems at the CINC Research Centre. As a Fellow of the Higher Education Academy (HEA) in the United Kingdom, Dr. Rathore has amassed several years of experience in the scholarship of teaching learning and research excellence. He is the cluster head of a Responsible and Transparent Artificial Intelligence Research Cluster (RTAR-C), consisting of 15 international universities for joint research endeavors.

An accomplished academic, he has coauthored multiple textbooks tailored for BSc and MSc programs in computer science. Dr. Rathore actively contributes to the academic community, having served as a Technical Program Committee chair and as a keynote speaker at several esteemed international conferences.

Dr. Rathore is a founding member of the IEEE Trustworthy Internet of Things (TRUST-IoT) Working Group and is a member of the ACM Europe Technology Policy Committee for AI, Data Science, Autonomous Systems and Cybersecurity. His research interests are diverse and include responsible AI, Internet of Things/cyber physical systems, cybersecurity and privacy, connected and autonomous vehicles (CAVs), EV charging infrastructure management, Smart Grid, intelligent networking of drones, and use cases of artificial intelligence and machine learning.

Liqaa Nawaf is a senior lecturer and research leader in the field of cyber security. She is the program director for the MSc Advanced Cyber Security and BSc Applied Cyber Security Apprentices with the School of Technologies at Cardiff Metropolitan University (CMU) and a coleader of Cybersecurity and Information Networks Centre (CINC). She holds a BSc (Hons) and an MSc Eng. in electrical and computer engineering from the New York Institute of Technology and a PhD in distributed and scientific computing from the School of Computer Science and Informatics at Cardiff University. She holds a Fellowship of the Higher Education Academy.

Dr. Nawaf has more than 18 years of experience in industry and academia as an expert in networks, AI, and cyber security. She is particularly interested in understanding how AI techniques could be used to support in distributed systems and cyber security, and the use of these techniques in various application areas. Dr. Nawaf is a founding member of the Women in Cyber (WiCys) Society at CMU and an active member of Women in Cyber Wales Cluster in the United Kingdom. She has been successful in securing several externally funded projects exploring different aspects of cyber security; the latest project is the Partnership for Education and Research (PER) Programme for Women in Cyber funded by the British Council UK Saudi Challenge Fund. Dr. Nawaf has authored numerous research papers published in a range of peer-reviewed international journals and academic transactions.

Shiv Prakash received a MTech and PhD in computer science and technology from Jawaharlal Nehru University, New Delhi, India, in 2010 and 2014, respectively. He had an excellent educational record throughout. He has more than two decades of experience in industry and academia as a senior subject matter expert and a faculty member in various organizations. He is currently associated with the Department of Electronics and Communication, University of Allahabad, Prayagraj, Uttar Pradesh, India. He has published more than 80 research papers in various peer-reviewed international journals and transactions (including the IEEE, Taylor and Francis, Elsevier, Springer, Wiley, and American Scientific Publishers) and around more than 50 research papers in proceedings of various peer-reviewed conferences in India and abroad. His current research interests include the Internet of Connected Vehicles (IoV), electric vehicles (EV), AI, big data analytics, biometric security, cloud computing, computer networks, machine learning, network security, and IoT use cases of sensor networks. Dr. Prakash is a reviewer of several international journals of repute (including those from the ACM, IEEE, Taylor and Francis, Elsevier, Springer, and Wiley).

Index

A

Access control
  hypervisor security in cloud computing, 118
  importance of, 209
  role-based (RBAC), 92, 97, 100, 109, 207, 210–11
  in securing guest OSs, 61
  virtual disk, 92
  virtualization in cloud computing and, 112
  virtual networks and, 40
  in Windows-Azure, 239–40
Access control lists (ACLs), 31
Account lockout attacks, 139
Agile change and configuration management, 170
Alerting, security monitoring plane, 6
AMD Secure Encrypted Virtualization (SEV), 124
APIs, auditing, 165
Application security
  best practices, 147–49
  critical applications and, 147
  database servers and, 145–46
  overview, 135–36
  summary, 149–50
  in virtualized environments, 135–50
  web servers and, 136–45
Application virtualization, 12
Archiving, 166
ARM Confidential Computer Architecture (CCA), 124
ARM TrustZone, 124
Artificial intelligence (AI), 72–73
Attacks
  account lockout, 139
  brute-force, 139–40
  buffer overflow, 140
  cache poisoning, 141
  code injection, 141
  cross-site request forgery (CSRF), 140
  DDoS, 21, 146
  DoS, 16–17, 34, 63, 141, 146
  double encoding, 141–42
  escape, 13–14
  guest OS, 14–15
  HTTP request smuggling, 142
  hypervisor, 13–14, 21
  inter-VM, 15–16, 213
  LDAP injection, 142
  man-in-the-middle (MITM), 142
  manipulation, 243–44
  network eavesdropping, 142–43
  SQL injection (SQLi), 143, 147
  Unicode encoding, 143
  XSS, 141, 142
Auditing
  APIs and management consoles, 165
  iterative, 179
  preparing for and managing, 172–75
  in virtual networks, 168
  vulnerability audits, 41, 43, 47
  See also Compliance and audit
Automated compliance platforms, 177–78
AWS, 115–16

B

Behavioral analytics, 83
Best practices
  for addressing emerging trends, 239–46
  advantages of sharing, 201
  application security, 147–49
  compliance and audit, 175–80
  disaster recovery and business continuity, 200–203
  general overview for implementing, 211
  guidelines for implementing, 210–13
  importance of, 213–15

Best practices (continued)
for monitoring and reporting, 215–22
for network security, 41–46
overview of, 207–10
storage security, 96–100
VANET, 220
for virtualization security, 207–23
for VM security, 69–72
British Airways case study, 181
Brute-force attacks, 139–40
Buffer overflow attacks, 140
Business continuity. *See* Disaster recovery and business continuity

C

Cache poisoning attacks, 141
CapitalOne Data Breach, 17–18, 181, 221–22
Case studies
best practices, 220–22
compliance and audit, 181–83
disaster recovery and business continuity, 191–93
guest OS attack, 14–15
hypervisor attack, 13–14
inter-VM attack, 15–16
securing a virtual switch, 34
securing VSA, 99–100
virtual firewall implementation, 36
virtual network architecture, 31–32
virtual router security, 38
virtual storage, 81–82
Citrix XenServer, 9, 114
Cloud computing
securing web in, 138
virtual machines (VMs) in, 103
VM security in, 119–21
See also Virtualization in cloud computing
Cloud Hopper Campaign case study, 221
Cloud-native security controls, 83
Cloud service providers
AWS, 115–16
Google Cloud Platform (GCP), 116–17
IBM Cloud, 117–18
Microsoft Azure, 116
See also Virtualization in cloud computing
Code injection attacks, 141
Compliance, security monitoring plane, 6
Compliance and audit
adaptability and, 175
APIs and management consoles, 165
architecture of, 164
automated compliance platforms and, 177–78
automated tools and solutions, 163–65
best practices, 175–80
case studies, 181–83
challenges in containerization and orchestration platforms, 160–61
confidential computing and TEEs and, 176–77
continuous improvement and, 175, 180
cross-border data transfers and virtual infrastructure, 161–63
data life-cycle management, archiving, right to erasure, 166–67
evolving regulatory ecosystems and, 178–80
guidelines for, 163–70
handling and reporting security incidents and, 165–66
human factors and compliance culture and, 171
importance of, 171–75
layered controls and monitoring and, 180
operational hygiene and business resilience and, 175
penalty and sanction avoidance and, 174–75
preparing for the future and, 180
privacy-first standards and, 177
privacy impact, 168–70
risk-based management, 178
risk mitigation and, 174
shared responsibility and, 158–60
structural versus operational properties, 163
supplier compliance management and, 180
third-party vendor and supply chain, 167
trust and, 174
in virtualized environments, 155–83
zero trust model and, 176
Confidential computing
about, 122
AMD Secure Encrypted Virtualization (SEV) and, 124

ARM Confidential Computer Architecture (CCA) and, 124
ARM TrustZone and, 124
as breakthrough technology, 123
data encryption and, 122–23
hardware manufacturers and, 123–25
IBM Protected Execution Facility (PEF) and, 125
Intel Software Guard Extensions (SGX) and, 123
Intel Trust Domain Extensions (TDX) and, 123
TEEs and, 176–77
Configuration management
agile change and, 170
complex management and, 111
as loophole, 17
OS hardening and, 59–60
virtualization technology management plane, 6
Container and Kubernetes security, 228
Container scanning tools, 234–35
Context-aware-based intelligent security, 246
Continuous verification, 75
Controller manipulation attack (CMA), 243
CPU virtualization, 235–37
Cross-border data transfers, 161–63
Cross-site request forgery (CSRF) attacks, 140
Cross-site scripting (XSS) attacks, 141, 142

D

Database servers, securing, 145–46
Data encryption
cloud computing and, 122
compliance and data privacy and, 112
database servers and, 146
measures, 41
OS hardening and, 60
storage security and, 98
strategies, 42
virtual complex disk file, 241–43
virtual machine, 127–28
Data life-cycle management, 166–67
Data protection impact assessment (DPIAs), 168
Data virtualization, 12
Demilitarized zones (DMZs), 70, 149
Denial-of-service (DoS) attacks, 16–17, 34, 63, 141, 146
Desktop virtualization
about, 9, 107
advantages of, 9, 108
effectiveness, 9
key components, 107–8
use cases, 9–10
DevOps Engineering, 120
Differentiated and customized security, 245–46
Digital Operational Resilience Act (DORA), 178
Disaster recovery, virtualization technology management plane, 6
Disaster recovery and business continuity
advantages of virtualized environments for, 199–200
best practices, 200–203
case study, 191–93
disaster recovery versus business continuity comparison and, 194
as fundamental, 200
guidelines for implementing, 195–200
implementing, 198–99
importance of, 193–95
overview, 187–93
in physical environments, 188
planning for, 189–91
relationship between, 195, 196–97
summary, 203–4
in virtualized environments, 187–204
Distributed denial-of-service (DDoS) attack, 21, 146
Double encoding attacks, 141–42

E

Eavesdropping, 16, 142–43, 242–43
Embedded continuous compliance, 170
Emerging trends
about, 227
best practices for addressing, 239–46
container and Kubernetes security, 228
container scanning tools and, 234–35
CPU virtualization, 235–37
east-west traffic security, 231–33

Emerging trends (continued)
future support and, 238–39
guidelines for preparing for, 233–35
I/O virtualization, 237–38
micro-services, 229
north-south traffic security, 230–31
overview, 227–33
risk evaluation, 233–34
staying ahead of, 235–39
VM protection and, 234
Encryption in virtualized environments
about, 125
key management, 126–29
randomness generation, 125–26
See also Data encryption
Entropy pooling, 126
Equifax case study, 182
Escape attack, 13–14
ESXiArgs case study, 221, 222

F

Failover measures, 45–46
File Transfer Protocol (FTP), 138
Firewall rules, 40
FortiGate-VM Firewall case study, 222
Future support, 238–39

G

General Data Protection Regulation (GDPR), 157
Google Cloud Platform (GCP), 116–17
Guest OSs
about, 56
access control mechanisms and, 61
attack case study, 14–15
benefits of, 56–57
critical functions of, 57
hardening, 70
IDPS and, 60–61
OS hardening and, 59–60
securing, 59–62
security policies and awareness training and, 62

H

Healthcare facility virtualization, 8
HIPAA (Health Insurance Portability and Accountability Act), 156–57
Host OS, 4
HTTP request smuggling attacks, 142
Hypertext Transfer Protocol (HTTP), 137
Hypervisor attacks
about, 13
case studies, 13–14
risks, *xv*, 21, 213
types of, 13, 118
Hypervisors
about, 53, 62, 209
auditing, 155
core functions, 53–54
hardening, 110
incident response, 65–66
maintenance, 18–19
monitoring and auditing, 64–65
secure configuration of, 63–64
securing, 62–66, 70–71
security in cloud computing, 118–19
type-1 (bare-metal), 54–55, 56, 121
type-2 (hosted), 55–56, 121
types of, 54, 121
in virtual network architecture, 30
vulnerabilities due to, 62–63, 110

I

IBM Cloud, 117–18
IBM Protected Execution Facility (PEF), 125
Identity and access management (IAM), 42–43, 75, 83
Inspecting, security monitoring plane, 5
Intelligent asset management, 169
Intel Software Guard Extensions (SGX), 123
Intel Trust Domain Extensions (TDX), 123
Internet of Things (IoT), 2
Interservice communication, 231–32
Inter-VM attacks, 15–16, 213
Intrusion detection and prevention systems (IDPS), 52, 60–61, 92, 98, 119
I/O virtualization, 237

ISO/IEC 27001, 177
ISO process, 157–58

J

Jamming, 243, 245
JSON Web Token (JWT) token, 230

K

Key management, 126–29, 218–19
Key management server (KMS), 127, 128, 219
Kubernetes, 228

L

LDAP injection attacks, 142
Legal/regulatory obligations, 20
Logging, 38, 59, 64–65, 169–70, 179
Logical domain channel (LDC), 91

M

Machine learning (ML), 72–73
Malware, protection against threats, 240
Management consoles, auditing, 165
Management interfaces, 57
Management plane, 6–7
Man-in-the-middle (MITM) attacks, 142
Manipulation attack, 243–44
Micro-segmentation, 75, 83
Micro-services
  about, 229
  east-west traffic security, 231–33
  inter-service communication, 231–32
  north-south traffic security, 230–31
  securing application using, 229
  security monitoring plane, 229–31
Microsoft
  App-V, 12, 148–49
  Defender, 217, 241
  Hyper-V, 8–9, 44–45, 114, 204
  Sentinel, 217
Microsoft Azure
  about, 116
  best practices, 216
  generalized overview of, 242
  Key Vault, 219
  monitoring storage solutions, 218
  Resource Health, 215, 216
  Service Health, 215, 216
  Virtual Desktop, 215, 216–18
Microsoft Monitoring Manager (MMA), 240
Microsoft Windows-Azure, 239–40, 241–42
Misconfiguration vulnerabilities, 17–18
Monitoring and reporting, 57, 215–22

N

Network address translation (NAT), 58–59
Network-attached storage (NAS), 107
Network eavesdropping attacks, 142–43
Network interface cards, 30
Network interface virtualization, 58–59
Network security
  best practices in virtualized environments, 41–46
  data encryption strategies and, 42
  failover measures and, 45–46
  identity and access management (IAM), 42–43
  importance of, 27–28
  introduction to, 25–27
  network segmentation approach, 44
  securing virtual switches and, 32–34
  software patching and updating and, 41
  summary, 46–47
  virtual firewalls in, 35–36
  virtualization in cloud computing and, 121–22
  in virtualized environments, 25–47
  virtual network architecture and, 30–31, 32
  virtual networks and, 39–41, 44–45
  virtual routers and, 37–38
  vulnerabilities, 15–16
  vulnerability audits and, 43
Network security groups (NSGs), 30
Network segmentation, 148, 161, 210
Network virtualization, 12, 26, 33, 45, 106–7
NIS2 Directive, 178

O

OpenStack, 115
Open Worldwide Application Security Project (OWASP), 147

Oracle VM VirtualBox, 11
Orchestration platforms, 160
Organization, this book, *xv–xvi*
OS hardening, 59–60
OS virtualization, 11

P

Patch management, 82, 92, 98
Payment Card Industry Data Security Standard (PCI DSS), 155–56
Performance monitoring, virtualization technology management plane, 6
Pilot contamination/spoofing, 243
Policy enforcement points (PEPs), 75
Post-quantum resilience, 245
Privacy impact assessment and compliance, 168–70
Privilege escalation, 43, 61, 63, 66, 170
Protected Health Information (PHI), 156–57
Provisioning and deployment, virtualization technology and management plane, 6

R

Randomness generation, 125–26
Random number generators (RNGs), 126
Red Hat Enterprise Linux (RHEL), 208
Reporting, security monitoring plane, 5
Resource-sharing vulnerabilities, 63
Right to erasure, 159, 166
Risk-based compliance management, 178
Robust access and privilege management, 169
Role-based access control (RBAC), 92, 97, 100, 109, 203, 207, 210–11

S

Sarbanes-Oxley Act (SOX), 157
Scalability
  network virtualization, 106
  storage array, 95
  storage virtualization, 107
  virtualization in cloud computing, 108
  virtual storage architecture (VSA) and, 88
  VSA and, 86–87
School management use case, 10
Secure Encrypted Virtualization (SEV), 233
Security breaches, impact on businesses, 19
Security culture, 71–72
Security monitoring plane, 5–6, 7
Server virtualization
about, 7, 105
  advantages of, 106
  importance in business, 7–8
  key components, 106
  use cases, 8–9
Service-level agreement compliance, 87
Shared responsibility models, 158–60
6G security requirements and challenges, 244–45
Snapshot management, 120
Software-defined networking (SDN), 106, 210
Software-defined security, 83
Software-defined storage (SDS), 80
SQL injection (SQLi) attacks, 143, 147
Storage area networks (SANs), 80, 89, 97, 107
Storage arrays
  benefits of, 95–96
  introduction to, 94–95
  as robust storage solution, 94, 96
Storage limitation, 99
Storage networks, securing, 93–94
Storage security
  best practices, 96–100
  introduction to, 96–99
  storage arrays and, 94–96
  storage limitation and, 99
  storage networks and, 93–94
  virtual disks and, 89–93
  VSA and, 79–89, 99–100
Storage virtualization, 12, 79, 80, 87–88, 97, 107
Supplier compliance management, 180
Supply chain compliance, 167

T

Target Corporation Security Breach, 221
Tesla insider data leak, 182–83
Third-party vendor compliance, 167
Traffic limiters, 34
Transmission Control Protocol/Internet Protocol (TCP/IP), 117, 118
Trusted execution environments (TEEs), 176–77, 232

Type-1 (bare-metal) hypervisor, 54–55, 56, 121
Type-2 (hosted) hypervisor, 55–56, 121

U

Unauthorized access, 17
Unicode encoding attacks, 143

V

Veeam, 213–14
Vehicle-Aware Networks (VANETs)
  about, 129, 218
  best practices, 220
  communication types, 218
  illustrated, 219
  OBUs, 218
  in virtualized security practice, 209–10
Virtual disks
advantages of securing, 90–92
  concept, 89–90
  introduction to, 89
  with logical domain channel progress, 91
  secure techniques, implementing, 92–93
  technical example, 91–92
  See also Storage security
Virtual disk server (VSD) and client (VCD) drivers, 91
Virtual firewalls
  implementation case study, 36
  potential vulnerabilities and risks, 35–36
  role in network security, 35
  techniques for security, 36
Virtual hard disk (VHD), 89
Virtual hardware, 57
Virtualization audits
  preparing for, 173
  readiness items, 173–74
  what auditor's look for and, 172–73
  See also Compliance and audit
Virtualization in cloud computing
  backup and recovery and, 112
  benefits of, 108–9
  challenges, 109–13
  complex management and, 111
  compliance and data privacy and, 112
  conclusions, 129–30
  confidential computing, 122–25
  desktop virtualization, 107–8
  encryption, 125–29
  hypervisor security, 118–19
  introduction to, 103–6
  licensing costs and restraints and, 112
  management tools, 113–15
  network security and, 121–22
  network virtualization, 106–7
  performance overhead and, 112
  providers offering, 115–18
  resource contention and, 110–11
  security risks and, 109–10
  server virtualization, 105–6
  storage virtualization, 107
  summary, 113–29
  types of, 105
  vendor lock-in and, 113
  virtualization security, 118–22
  VMs and, 103
  VM security, 119–21
Virtualization management policies, 111
Virtualization management servers
  about, 66
  best practice, 70–71
  incident response, 68–69
  monitoring and auditing, 67–68
  risks and vulnerabilities, 66
  security controls, 67
  See also VM security
Virtualization management tools, in cloud computing, 113–15
Virtualization(s)
  application, 12
  in cloud computing, 103–30
  CPU, 235–37
  data, 12
  defined, 2
  desktop, 9–10, 107–8
  full, 104–5
  I/O, 237
  network, 12, 106–7
  network interface, 58–59
  OS, 11
  as paradigm shift, 1
  role in enhancing cybersecurity, 18–19

Virtualization(s) (continued)
roles and significance in IT infrastructure, 5–7
security risks associated with, 13–18
server, 7–9, 105–6
storage, 12, 80, 87–88, 97, 107
types, 7–12
which type to use, 21–22
Virtualization security
about, *xiii,* 1–2
emerging trends in, 227–46
as essential, 219
future of, 234, 251–52
introduction to, 1
role integrity and reliability of IT infrastructure, 19–20
specific issues and, 20–21
VANETs in, 209–10
Virtualization security best practices
about, 207
general overview for implementing, 213
guidelines for implementing, 210–13
implementation process, 212
importance of, 213–15
for monitoring and reporting, 215–22
overview, 207–10
security attacks and, 208
security framework guidance, 213
summary, 222–23
top issues, 214
Virtualization technology
brief history of development, 2–4
framework, 3
framework with IT infrastructure, 6
host OS, 4
management plane, 6–7
overview, 2–7
reservoir, 7
security monitoring plane, 5–6
VM architecture, 58
Virtualized applications. *See* Application security
Virtualized environments
application security in, 135–50
automated compliance tools for, 163–64
compliance and audit in, 155–83
disaster recovery and business continuity in, 187–204
encryption in, 125–29
importance of maintaining security in, 19–20
monitoring, 170
network security in, 25–47, 121–22
security attacks scenario in, 161
storage security in, 79–101
traditional physical environments versus, 26
Virtual local area networks (VLANs)
network interface virtualization and, 58–59
network segmentation and, 148
in network virtualization, 106
potential risks in, 21
private, 34
Virtual machines (VMs)
about, 1, 4
architecture, 52–59
architecture illustration, 53
best practices and, 208–9
closed, 120
in cloud computing, 103
creation and management of, 28
failover options, 45–46
guest OSs, 56–57
hypervisor, 53–56
isolation, 18, 93
life-cycle management, 167
malware installation on, 27
management interfaces, 57–58
monitoring, 28
network interface virtualization, 58–59
performance monitoring, 241
protecting, 234, 239–40
snapshots of, 215
updates, managing, 240–41
virtual hardware, 57
virtualization technology, 58
in virtual network architecture, 30
See also VM security
Virtual memory managers (VMMs), 235–38
Virtual network architecture
about, 26
case study, 31–32
components of, 28–30

definition and understanding of, 28
essential components, 30
illustrated, 29
illustration of components, 31
network security relationship, 30–31, 32
Virtual network functions (VNFs), 30
Virtual networks
component configuration, 44–45
data encryption measures and, 41
firewall rules and, 40
identity and access control and, 40
regular software updates and, 39–40
securing, 39–41
spam filters and, 40
techniques to secure, 39
vulnerability audits and, 41
Virtual prevention systems (IPS), 170
Virtual private networks (VPNs), 61, 106
Virtual routers
case study, 38
in network security, 37
potential security risks with, 37–38
securing, 37–38
techniques for securing, 38
Virtual sprawl, 28
Virtual storage
active program operation under, 81
cases study, 81–82
introduction to, 80–81
techniques for securing, 82–83
Virtual storage architecture (VSA)
about, 79–80
applications, 79–80
benefits and efficiency of, 87–89
case study, 81–82, 99–100
challenges, 83–87
identifying performance constraints and, 84–85
infrastructure management/reporting and, 86
overview illustration, 80
scalability and, 86–87, 88
securing, 99–100
service-level agreement compliance and, 87
virtual storage techniques and, 82–83
Virtual switches
about, 30
case study, 34
network interface virtualization and, 58–59
in network security, 32–33
potential vulnerabilities in, 33–34
techniques for security, 34
VM encryption, 127–28
VM monitor (VMM), 4, 13, 120, 209
VM security
AI and ML for threat detection and response, 72–73
audits and compliance checks and, 72
best practices, 69–72
in cloud computing, 119–21
continuous monitoring and incident response and, 71
future trends, 72–73
guest OSs and, 59–62
hardening guest OSs and, 70
hypervisors and, 62–66
introduction to, 51–52
management servers and, 66–69
need for, 51
posture, managing, 241
risk assessment and, 69
securing hypervisor and management servers and, 70–71
securing virtual environment during deployment and, 69–70
summary, 73–75
user education and security awareness and, 71–72
ZTA and, 73, 74, 75
VM sprawl, 21, 119
VMware
about, 2
case study, 81–82
ESXiArgs case study, 182
Hypervisor Security Breach, 220–21
NSX solution, 12
ThinApp, 12
Update Manager, 209–10
vSphere, 8, 113
VMware NSX-T Distributed Firewall case study, 222
Vulnerability assessment tools, 43
Vulnerability audits, 41, 43, 47

W

Web analysis services, 144
Web Application Firewall (WAF), 17
Web servers
about, 136
activities, 136–37
application threats, 139–44
client-side technologies, 138
cloud environments and, 138
default procedures, 138–39
scenarios for securing, 137
securing, 136–45
security attack, 140
server side, 139

X

Xen Hypervisor Exploit, 15–16

Z

Zero trust architecture (ZTA), 72, 73, 74, 75, 251–52
Zero trust security model, 83, 176

Artech House
Information Security and Privacy Library

Rolf Oppliger, Series Editor

Attribute-Based Access Control, Vincent C. Hu, David F. Ferraiolo, Ramaswamy Chandramouli, and D. Richard Kuhn

Biometrics in Identity Management: Concepts to Applications, Shimon K. Modi

Bitcoin and Blockchain Security, Ghassan Karame and Elli Androulaki

Blockchain for Cyberphysical Systems, Ali Dorri, Salil Kanhere, and Raja Jurdak

Bluetooth Security, Christian Gehrmann, Joakim Persson, and Ben Smeets

Computer Forensics and Privacy, Michael A. Caloyannides

Computer and Intrusion Forensics, George Mohay, et al.

Contemporary Cryptography, Second Edition, Rolf Oppliger

Cryptography for Security and Privacy in Cloud Computing, Stefan Rass and Daniel Slamanig

Defense and Detection Strategies against Internet Worms, Jose Nazario

Demystifying the IPsec Puzzle, Sheila Frankel

Developing Secure Distributed Systems with CORBA, Ulrich Lang and Rudolf Schreiner

Electric Payment Systems for E-Commerce, Second Edition, Donal O'Mahony, Michael Peirce, and Hitesh Tewari

End-to-End Encrypted Messaging, Rolf Oppliger

Engineering Safe and Secure Software Systems, C. Warren Axelrod

Evaluating Agile Software Development: Methods for Your Organization, Alan S. Koch

Fuzzing for Software Security Testing and Quality Assurance, Second Edition, Ari Takanen, Jared DeMott, Charlie Miller, and Atte Kettunen

Homeland Security Threats, Countermeasures, and Privacy Issues, Giorgio Franceschetti and Marina Grossi, editors

Identity Management: Concepts, Technologies, and Systems, Elisa Bertino and Kenji Takahashi

Implementing Electronic Card Payment Systems, Cristian Radu

Implementing the ISO/IEC 27001 ISMS Standard, Third Edition, Edward Humphreys

Implementing Security for ATM Networks, Thomas Tarman and Edward Witzke

Information Hiding Techniques for Steganography and Digital Watermarking, Stefan Katzenbeisser and Fabien A. P. Petitcolas, editors

Introduction to Securing Virtual Environments, Rajkumar Singh Rathore, Liqaa Nawaf, and Shiv Prakash

Internet and Intranet Security, Second Edition, Rolf Oppliger

Introduction to Identity-Based Encryption, Luther Martin

Java Card for E-Payment Applications, Vesna Hassler, Martin Manninger, Mikail Gordeev, and Christoph Müller

Medical Device Cybersecurity for Engineers and Manufacturers, Axel Wirth, Christopher Gates, and Jason Smith

Multicast and Group Security, Thomas Hardjono and Lakshminath R. Dondeti

Non-Repudiation in Electronic Commerce, Jianying Zhou

Outsourcing Information Security, C. Warren Axelrod

The Penetration Tester's Guide to Web Applications, Serge Borso

A Practical Guide to Managing Information Security, Steve Purser

Privacy Protection and Computer Forensics, Second Edition, Michael A. Caloyannides

Role-Based Access Control, Second Edition, David F. Ferraiolo, D. Richard Kuhn, and Ramaswamy Chandramouli

Role Engineering for Enterprise Security Management, Edward J. Coyne and John M. Davis

Secure Messaging on the Internet, Rolf Oppliger

Secure Messaging with PGP and S/MIME, Rolf Oppliger

Securing Information and Communications Systems: Principles, Technologies, and Applications, Steven Furnell, Sokratis Katsitas, Javier Lopez, and Ahmed Patel

Security for Cloud Computing, Roberto Di Pietro and Flavio Lombardi

Security Fundamentals for E-Commerce, Vesna Hassler

Security in Wireless LANs and MANs, Lakshminath R. Dondeti and Thomas Hardjono

Security Technologies for the World Wide Web, Second Edition, Rolf Oppliger

Signal and Messaging Layer Security, Rolf Oppliger

SSL and TLS: Theory and Practice, Second Edition, Rolf Oppliger

Techniques and Applications of Digital Watermarking and Content Protection, Michael Arnold, Martin Schmucker, and Stephen D. Wolthusen

Understanding Voice over IP Security, Alan B. Johnston and David Piscitello

User's Guide to Cryptography and Standards, Alexander W. Dent and Chris J. Mitchell

For further information on these and other Artech House titles, including previously considered out-of-print books now available through our In-Print-Forever® (IPF®) program, contact:

Artech House
685 Canton Street
Norwood, MA 02062
Phone: 781-769-9750
Fax: 781-769-6334
e-mail: artech@artechhouse.com

Artech House
16 Sussex Street
London SW1V 4RW UK
Phone: +44 (0)20 7596-8750
Fax: +44 (0)20 7630-0166
e-mail: artech-uk@artechhouse.com

Find us on the World Wide Web at: www.artechhouse.com